Introduction to Human Development and Family Studies

Introduction to Human Development and Family Studies is the first text to introduce human development and family studies (HDFS) as inextricably linked areas of study, giving students a complex yet realistic view of individuals and families. Pioneers of research paradigms have acknowledged that the family is one setting in which human development occurs. Moreover, in many academic programs, the lines of these two disciplines blur and much work is inherently multidisciplinary and interdisciplinary. This book helps to fortify an understanding of HDFS and subareas within it.

Vignettes from current HDFS students as well as new professionals, an overview of the lifespan stage(s) within the family context, a wide description of research methods and applications, current policy issues relevant to the area, and discussions of practice/careers coupled with strategies for pursuing specializations or careers in the area are hallmarks of this textbook. *Introduction to Human Development and Family Studies* is essential reading for students new to the major and minor wanting to know:

- What is HDFS?
- Who are the people involved in HDFS?
- Why is HDFS important?
- How does theory and research inform work in HDFS?
- What does the pursuit of being an ethical professional require?
- What are the key areas in HDFS?

Incredibly user-friendly both on the page and online, the text also features the following resources:

- **Chapter Summaries** where the main points of each chapter are pinpointed at the end of every chapter for review and study.
- **Key Terms** listed and defined within the margins of every chapter, a complete **Glossary** at the end of the text, and **Flashcards** online for additional review and study.
- **Challenge: Integration** section at the end of each chapter that underscores concepts from the chapter and draws connections between content presented in other chapters.
- **Journal Questions** to encourage reflection about the content and encourage thinking about some of the content coupled with students' own experiences.
- **Suggested Resources** that lists relevant websites, books, articles, and video links ·for further study.
- **Closer Look at Applied Experiences Appendix** outlines the internship process and shows how the internship experience can be meaningful and useful, and a **Consuming Research Appendix** that focuses on what it means to be a consumer of research, the knowledge and skills consumers need, and considerations for transitioning from a consumer of research to a producer of research.

Bridget A. Walsh is Associate Professor of Human Development and Family Studies at the University of Nevada, Reno.

Lydia DeFlorio is Assistant Professor of Human Development and Family Studies and Early Childhood Education at the University of Nevada, Reno.

Melissa M. Burnham is Associate Dean for the College of Education and a Professor of Human Development and Family Studies and Early Childhood Education at the University of Nevada, Reno.

Dana A. Weiser is Assistant Professor of Human Development and Family Studies and a Women's Studies faculty affiliate at Texas Tech University.

Introduction to Human Development and Family Studies

Bridget A. Walsh, Lydia DeFlorio,
Melissa M. Burnham, and
Dana A. Weiser

Routledge
Taylor & Francis Group

NEW YORK AND LONDON

First published 2017
by Routledge
711 Third Avenue, New York, NY 10017

and by Routledge
2 Park Square, Milton Park, Abingdon, Oxon OX14 4RN

Routledge is an imprint of the Taylor & Francis Group, an informa business

© 2017 Taylor & Francis

Library of Congress Cataloging in Publication Data
A catalog record for this book has been requested

ISBN: 978-1-138-81531-5 (hbk)
ISBN: 978-1-138-81532-2 (pbk)
ISBN: 978-1-315-20800-8 (ebk)

Typeset in Bembo
by Wearset Ltd, Boldon, Tyne and Wear

This book is dedicated to Abbey and to Leah with love

Contents

Detailed Contents

Figures

Tables

About the Authors

Bridget A. Walsh is Associate Professor of HDFS at the University of Nevada, Reno. She received her Ph.D. from Texas Woman's University in Child Development, her master's in Psychology from Villanova University, and her bachelor's degree in Psychology with an emphasis in Early Childhood and Elementary Education from Albright College. Her research focuses on early childhood development and family engagement. She has also received two awards for teaching and mentoring.

Lydia DeFlorio is Assistant Professor of HDFS and Early Childhood Education at the University of Nevada, Reno. She received her Ph.D. from the University of California, Berkeley, and her master's in Early Childhood Education and bachelor's in Child Development from California State University, Sacramento. Prior to joining the faculty at the University of Nevada, Reno in 2012, she enjoyed a 20-year career as a professional in a variety of positions working with at-risk children, youth, and families.

Melissa M. Burnham is Associate Dean for the College of Education and a Professor of HDFS and Early Childhood Education at the University of Nevada, Reno. She obtained her Ph.D. in Human Development from the University of California, Davis in 2002, her master's degree in HDFS from the University of Nevada, Reno in 1996, and her bachelor's degree in HDFS from the University of Nevada, Reno in 1994. She has been a faculty member with the HDFS program since the fall of 2001.

Dana A. Weiser is Assistant Professor of HDFS and a Women's Studies faculty affiliate at Texas Tech University. She received her Ph.D. from the Interdisciplinary Social Psychology program at the University of Nevada, Reno, her master's degree in Psychology from California State University, Los Angeles, and her bachelor's degree in Psychology from Claremont McKenna College. Her work focuses on how earlier family experiences are associated with adults' romantic relationships and sexual behaviors.

Jencie Davies, M.S. is a graduate of the Human Development and Family Studies program at the University of Nevada, Reno and serves as the Northern Nevada TACSEI training coordinator.

Jenna Dewar, M.S., CFLE, is a graduate of the Human Development and Family Studies program at the University of Nevada, Reno and serves as a specialist in Advising and Internships at the University of Nevada, Reno.

Eva L. Essa is Professor Emerita and Foundation Professor of Human Development and Family Studies at the University of Nevada, Reno.

Jennifer A. Mortensen is Assistant Professor of Human Development and Family Studies at the University of Nevada, Reno

Abbreviations

AACM	American Academy of Case Management
AAMFT	American Association for Marriage and Family Therapy
ACEI	Association for Childhood Education International
ACF	Administration for Children and Families
ADHD	attention deficit/hyperactivity disorder
AERA	American Educational Research Association
AIHCP	American Institute of Health Care Professionals
APA	American Psychological Association
BMI	body mass index
CCLS	Certified Child Life Specialist
CDC	Centers for Disease Control and Prevention
CFLE	Certified Family Life Educator
CHIP	Children's Health Insurance Program
CLC	Child Life Council
CV	curriculum vitae
DAP	Developmentally Appropriate Practice
DELTA	Developing English Language Teaching Ability
DSM-5	Diagnostic and Statistical Manual of Mental Disorders
DST	Developmental Systems Theory
ELL	English Language Learner
ESL	English as a Second Language
ETV	Education Training Voucher
FCM	family case management
FLE	family life education/educator
FMLA	Family and Medical Leave Act of 1993
FPL	federal poverty level
FRC	Family Research Council
FSA	Family Science Association
GED	General Educational Development

GSA	Gerontological Society of America
HDFS	Human Development and Family Studies
IL	Independent Living
IRB	Institutional Review Board
LCDC	Licensed Chemical Dependency Counselor
LGBTQ	Lesbian, Gay, Bisexual, Transgender, Queer, and Questioning
MFT	Marriage and Family Therapist
NAEYC	National Association for the Education of Young Children
NCFR	National Council on Family Relations
NOHS	National Organization for Human Services
PFCE	Parent, Family, and Community Engagement
PPCT	Process-Person-Context-Time model
SGA	small-for-gestational age
SIECUS	Sexuality Information and Education Council of the United States
SNAP	Supplemental Nutrition Assistance Program
SRA	Society for Research on Adolescence
SRCD	Society for Research in Child Development
SSHD	Society for the Study of Human Development
STEM	Science, Technology, Engineering, and Mathematics
TBS	Therapeutic Behavioral Services
WHO	World Health Organization
WIC	Special Supplemental Nutrition Program for Women, Infants, and Children

PART I

What Is HDFS?

CHAPTER 1

HDFS

The professions and areas you are exploring through this text are within the area of **human development and family studies** (**HDFS**). Some programs are called HDFS, child and family studies, family studies, family and child studies, or other similar names. The varying names often create a fragmented identity; however, many courses in these programs are similar. HDFS is a relatively young field (Hamon & Smith, 2014) and the term HDFS will be used throughout this text to capture the variety of programs that prepare professionals and emerging professionals to work with individuals and families. The family can be thought of as one context or a setting that contributes to human development. Bronfenbrenner (1986) asserted that the family is the main context in which human development occurs. Traditionally, some academic programs have been organized around one area of focus, such as families, or the other: individuals. On one hand, human development is the study of how humans change and maintain some characteristics from conception to senescence, or aging. On the other hand, family studies is the study of a variety of family forms and how families function.

Strictly speaking, these definitions suggest that a developmentalist looks at individuals within families while a family scientist focuses on families that comprise individuals. In many programs, the lines of these two traditional disciplines blur (Blume & Benson, 1997) and many programs at the very least recognize the interaction of individual development in the context of the family (Adams, 1997; Boyd, 1997). The field of HDFS is inherently multidisciplinary, meaning that it often involves taking college courses from faculty and professionals with some training in psychology, education, and other fields in one program (O'Brien, 2005). Professional organizations, such as the Society for Research in Child Development (SRCD) and the National Council on Family Relations (NCFR), explicitly promote multidisciplinary (as well as interdisciplinary) research and practice and emphasize the advantages of it. However, when multidisciplinary and interdisciplinary training are involved, it is easy for students to feel like "jacks- and jills-of-all trades, but master/mistress of none" (Ganong, Coleman, & Demo, 1995, p. 506). As you

Image 1.1 Early Childhood Education Trains Emerging Professionals to Work with Children from Birth to 8 Years of Age (photo by Monkey Business/Depositphotos, Inc.).

explore HDFS, the acknowledgment of a complex view of both individuals within families and families comprising individuals will gain greater importance.

We next advocate for a small core-body of knowledge that is essential to know in an introduction to studying the area of HDFS. We suspect that, despite multidisciplinary perspectives, the following introductory information would be met with some degree of consensus as the core foundation for a student in HDFS to master.

WHAT IS THE CORE OF HUMAN DEVELOPMENT KNOWLEDGE?

The basic tenet of human development is that "people change and grow as long as they live" (Bredehoft, Eckhoff, & Gesme, 2003, p. 75). The average life expectancy, or the number of years the family of a newborn could expect him or her to live, is approximately 78 years (Administration on Aging, 2012). There are many ages and stages prior to the developmental period of late adulthood. The journey of development starts with conception, when the sperm and ovum unite. Approximately 9 months later, birth occurs and the **developmental stages** that follow are: infancy and toddlerhood (0 to 2 years), early childhood (2 to 6 years), middle childhood (6 to 11 years), adolescence (11 to 18 years), emerging adulthood (18 to 25 years), adulthood (25 to 65 years), and late adulthood (65 to death). There are many milestones or characteristics of each stage, some of which will be discussed in later chapters.

As shown in Figure 1.1, developmentalists study each age and stage with consideration given to three domains or the "PIE." The "P" is for the Physical domain, the "I" is for

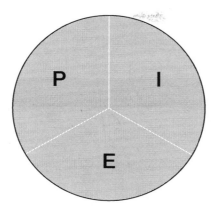

Figure 1.1 An Individual's Development Can Be Conceptualized as Three Separate but Interrelated Domains: Physical, Intellectual, and Emotional. Each Domain Is Equally Important throughout Development.

the Intellectual domain, and the "E" is for the Emotional domain. The physical domain includes biological aspects such as genes, brain and body development, and nutrition. The intellectual domain includes cognitive aspects such as language, cognition, and intelligences. The emotional domain includes socio–emotional aspects such as relationships, emotions, and motivations. It makes intuitive sense that the three domains are interrelated. Consider that if a person is hungry and did not get proper sleep (both examples of the physical domain), the person will most likely not be able to problem solve effectively during class (cognitive domain), and may be more easily upset or insensitive to the feelings of others (emotional domain).

WHAT IS THE CORE OF FAMILY STUDIES KNOWLEDGE?

Most professionals tend to value a framework that focuses on individual and family strengths rather than deficits in all families (Patterson, 2002). A family is a group of people that is united by marriage and/or adoption, blood, interpersonal relationships, or law. There is a widely accepted acknowledgment of families' importance on an individual child's domains of development, making it important for professionals to understand family forms and strategies to support them (Powell, 1989). Given the various possibilities of family ties, families are made up a multiplicity of forms.

Marriage is an important part of family studies (Seltzer, 2000). Dimensions of marriage behavior can include: (1) companionship, or the extent to which partners do things together; (2) the affective tone of the relationship, such as the extent of affection, quantity of conflict and negativity; and (3) involvement that spouses have with friends and the like (McHale & Huston, 1985). Marriage and the dimensions of it can be thought of as only one part of the core of family studies knowledge. The core of family studies can also include: family and relationships, a multidisciplinary/interdisciplinary approach to studying individuals and families, a focus on multiple perspectives, such as family systems, family strengths, life span, and ecosystem, an emphasis on prevention, and 10 content areas (e.g., human sexuality) of family life education (FLE) (Hamon & Smith, 2014).

Image 1.2 The Basic Tenet of Human Development Is that People Change and Grow as Long as They Live (photo by Michele Piacquadio/Depositphotos, Inc.).

Family forms can include a variety of forms and all are important. A nuclear family or conjugal family includes parents and their offspring. A single parent family includes a parent and one or more children. An extended family encompasses relatives (e.g., a grandmother, a mother, and her daughter or three generations) that live together in a household or in close proximity. A blended family results when a person remarries another person. Typically, one of the parties has a child or children and if either has children, it is classified as a step-family.

There are many other family forms, including: a cohabitating family (Seltzer, 2000), a foster family, such as kinship care (Berrick, 1997), a conditionally separated family, such as a military family (Drummet, Coleman, & Cable, 2003), a polygamous family (Al-Krenawi & Graham, 2006), and grandparents-as-parents (Hayslip & Kaminski, 2005). **Family function** is overall more important than family form. Family function is how a family operates to meet the needs of and care for each other (e.g., economic support or emotional security). Family processes matter more than structure for individual and family functioning (Walsh, 1996). Family processes, such as caring and problem solving, are essential to family functioning and wellbeing (Walsh, 2003).

FLE CONTENT AREAS

Up to this point, we have broadly described HDFS. We'll begin this section with a brief introduction of the NCFR content areas. This will help fortify our understanding of HDFS as we take a look at some of the subareas within it.

FLE has as its primary focus teaching individuals and families skills about healthy family functioning to strengthen individual and family development (Duncan & Goddard,

Image 1.3 An Extended Family Encompasses Relatives that Live Together in a Household or in Close Proximity (photo by Monkey Business/Depositphotos, Inc.).

Image 1.4 Marriage Is an Important Part of Family Studies (photo by Liudmyla Supynska/Depositphotos, Inc.).

2011; NCFR, 2013). NCFR provides certification for emerging professionals and professionals in FLE. As shown in Figure 1.2, there are essentially two pathways to become a **Certified Family Life Educator** (**CFLE**) with provisional status and, once work experience is documented, an individual is eligible to earn full status. One pathway is to get a passing score on the national exam that assesses the knowledge and application of the 10 family life content areas. The other approach is to complete coursework that meets the criteria for the 10 family life content areas.

CFLEs have knowledge and training in 10 content areas; these include: (1) families and individuals in society, (2) internal dynamics of families, (3) human growth and development, (4) human sexuality, (5) interpersonal relationships, (6) parent education and guidance, (7) family resource management, (8) family law and public policy, (9) professional ethics and practice, and (10) FLE methods (NCFR, 2009).

All of the 10 content areas were deemed by CFLEs and noncertified family practitioners as important to practice, with human growth and development ranked as the highest or most important (Darling, Fleming, & Cassidy, 2009). In the content area of human growth and development, the specific competencies that are important to FLE are the ability to:

(a) Identify developmental stages, transitions, tasks, and challenges throughout the life span, (b) Assist individuals and families in effective developmental transitions,

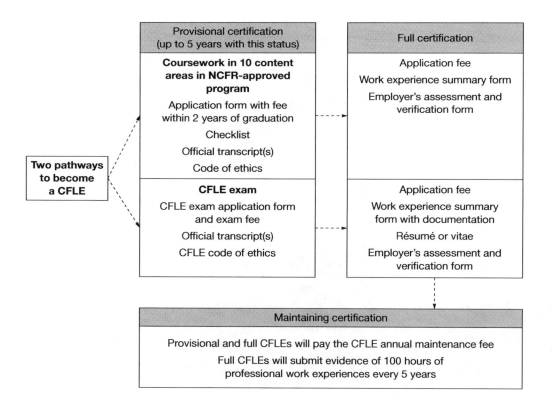

Figure 1.2 Suggested Overview of the Two Current Pathways with Application Requirements to Become a CFLE.

(c) Recognize reciprocal influences, (d) Recognize the impact of individual health and wellness on families (1. Family development on individuals 2. Individual development on families), and (e) Apply appropriate practices based on theories of human growth and development to individuals and families.

(Darling et al., 2009, p. 336)

The more individuals are informed about the specific competencies within the content areas of FLE, such as human growth and development, the closer the individual is to understanding the expectations related to being certified (Darling et al., 2009). Each content area has specific competencies and these will be discussed in a later chapter.

For now, keep in mind that FLE is a profession dedicated to promoting family well-being (Darling et al., 2009) and is germane to but distinct from family therapy (Myers-Walls, Ballard, Darling, & Myers-Bowman, 2011). We will next consider family therapy and other areas related to HDFS.

AREAS RELATED TO HDFS

Family Therapy

The field of **family therapy** views the family as a system while acknowledging individuals' influences (Piercy & Sprenkle, 1990). Family therapy typically helps families repair relationships and functioning (Myers-Walls et al., 2011). The American Association for Marriage and Family Therapy (AAMFT) is the main professional organization for Marriage and Family Therapists (MFTs). To become a licensed family therapist, one must earn a graduate degree—a master's or doctoral degree—as well as complete clinical training during and after graduate school, and finally earn a passing score on a licensing exam (AAMFT, 2011). State boards determine the length of the internship and administer the licensing exam. Alternatively, in some states it is possible to work as a non-licensed family therapist without clinical training or a graduate degree.

Child Life

The **child life profession** focuses on helping children and their families cope and adjust in medical settings or other potentially stressful contexts (American Academy of Pediatrics, CLC, and Committee on Hospital Care, 2006; Thompson, 1989). The professional organization of the child life profession is the Child Life Council (CLC). The CLC has established professional standards of practice, a code of ethical responsibility, and a mission, values, and vision for the child life profession (CLC, 2012). To become a Certified Child Life Specialist (CCLS), requirements include having a bachelor's degree in an area such as HDFS, taking a minimum of one child life course taught by a CCLS, having clinical child life work experience under the auspices of a CCLS, passing an exam, and paying certification fees (CLC, 2012). Central to the work of child life specialists is developmentally appropriate play, psychologically preparing children for procedures, and educating and advocating for families about what they are experiencing (American Academy of Pediatrics, CLC, and Committee on Hospital Care, 2006).

Early Childhood Education

The field of **early childhood education** trains professionals and emerging professionals for work with young children and their families. This field includes the education of children from birth to 8 years of age. Some students and professionals join the Association for Childhood Education International (ACEI), which covers early childhood but also considers the stages through early adolescence. One key area of early childhood education is the endorsement of developmentally appropriate approaches to teaching and learning by the professional organization of the National Association for the Education of Young Children (NAEYC). Developmentally Appropriate Practice, or DAP, aims to promote teaching and learning that takes into account knowledge of young children's learning and development (Copple & Bredekamp, 2009). For more information about DAP with infants and toddlers, preschoolers, kindergarteners, and in the early primary grades, the NAEYC website is a good starting point (www.naeyc.org/DAP). There are a variety of approaches within early childhood education that support different goals and methods (Roopnarine & Johnson, 2012; Walsh & Petty, 2007).

Human/Social Services

Human/social services can include professions within social work, health care, and **family case management (FCM)** with employment in such settings as private practice,

Image 1.5 The Primary Focus of FLE Is to Teach Individuals and Families Skills about Healthy Family Functioning (photo by Andres Rodriguez/Depositphotos, Inc.).

mental health centers, school systems, social service agencies, alcohol and drug treatment programs, and religious organizations. FCM involves work with families, particularly those who have entered the government child and family welfare system (Myers–Walls et al., 2011). FCM uses a strengths-based approach to working with families and guiding them to locate resources to help meet children's needs (Myers–Walls et al., 2011). The National Organization for Human Services (NOHS) focuses on prevention and remediation and serves students, educators, and other professionals (NOHS, n.d.). For case management in health-related areas, the American Academy of Case Management (AACM) within the American Institute of Health Care Professionals (AIHCP) is the main professional organization. The AACM offers certification for applicants, which involves criteria including being a health care professional with a certain quantity of hours of study as determined by the AACM, documenting appropriate work experiences, an examination of knowledge, and fees (AACM, AIHCP, 2011).

Summary

1   The area of HDFS values the interaction of individual development and the context of the family.

2   The foundation of human development includes the following:

   A   ages and stages of development from conception to senescence;

   B   the three interrelated domains of development.

3   The foundation of family studies includes the following:

   A   marriage and the complexity of the definition of family;

   B   family forms and family function.

4   FLE includes 10 content areas and these areas often are subareas with HDFS. These 10 family life content areas include:

   A   (1) families and individuals in society, (2) internal dynamics of families, (3) human growth and development, (4) human sexuality, (5) interpersonal relationships, (6) parent education and guidance, (7) family resource management, (8) family law and public policy, (9) professional ethics and practice, and (10) FLE methods.

   B   There are two pathways to become a CFLE.

5   Four areas related to HDFS include:

   A   Family therapy;

   B   Child life;

   C   Early childhood education;

   D   FCM.

Key Terms

Certified Family Life Educator
child life profession
developmental stages
early childhood education
family case management
family forms
family function
family therapy
human development and family studies

Challenge: Integration

In each chapter in this text, you will find a section called *Challenge: Integration*, which will underscore concepts from the chapter and promote thinking about them in complex ways. The purpose of integration is to make connections and meaning out of information that is known (Ganong et al., 1995).

It is important to use knowledge of HDFS to prevent problems from happening, slow them down, or prevent further harm. A *prevention model or systems of intervention* can take a three-tiered approach:

1 Primary prevention or intervention has the goal of not allowing an unwanted circumstance or event to occur;
2 Secondary prevention or intervention has the goal of slowing down or averting an unwanted circumstance or event;
3 Tertiary prevention or intervention has the goal of preventing further harm from developing.

Consider that a professional is thinking about aggression in a school setting and wants to create change to increase safety. Thinking about this topic using knowledge of HDFS will help the professional to consider points, such as why the aggression is occurring and what forces within the individual and family are contributing to the aggression. Primary prevention or intervention, such as skills training, would be targeted at the school students who do not have serious behavioral problems (Espelage et al., 2013). Secondary prevention or intervention, such as mentoring programs, would be aimed at the students who are starting to display behavioral problems (Espelage et al., 2013). Tertiary prevention or intervention, such as wraparound services, would be geared toward students with chronic behavioral problems (Espelage et al., 2013).

Do some professionals favor certain types of prevention or intervention over others? Let's consider FLE, family therapy, and FCM to explore the answer to this question. Myers-Walls et al. (2011) suggest that FLEs provide education and skills prior to problems arising or early in the process, meaning that primary and secondary levels are key ways for working with families and individuals. Family therapists focus on dealing with problems early in the process or after they have developed, meaning that secondary and tertiary prevention is used with families and individuals (Myers-Walls et al., 2011). Family case managers typically focus on rehabilitation or tertiary prevention.

Journal Questions

1   The fields of HDFS have been linked contemporarily. What are your views on studying individual development within families and studying the family, which is made up of individuals?

2   Would you like to become a CFLE? Why or why not? What would you need to do to become a CFLE?

3   Are you interested in any of the areas related to HDFS presented in this chapter? If so, should you consider talking to professionals with training and/ or experiences in family therapy, child life, early childhood education, or FCM? Find out what path they followed and what services they provide to individuals and families.

4   Imagine that you recently graduated with a degree in HDFS. You are on a job interview and a potential employer asks you to explain the field of HDFS. What would you say?

SUGGESTED RESOURCES

Some helpful websites for topics discussed in Chapter 1 include:

AACM, AIHCP: www.aihcp.org/cs~mgmnt.htm
AAMFT: www.aamft.org
ACEI: www.acei.org/
CLC: www.childlife.org/
Gerontological Society of America (GSA): www.geron.org
NAEYC: www.naeyc.org/
NCFR: www.ncfr.org/
NOHS: www.nationalhumanservices.org/
SRCD: www.srcd.org/

REFERENCES

Adams, G. R. (1997). On frameworks of science, the origins of programs, and the integration of family and developmental sciences curricula. *Family Science Review, 10,* 27–31.

Administration on Aging. (2012). *A profile of older Americans: 2011.* Retrieved from www.aoa.gov/aoaroot/aging_statistics/Profile/2011/docs/2011profile.pdf.

Al-Krenawi, A., & Graham, J. R. (2006). A comparison of family functioning, life and marital satisfaction, and mental health of women in polygamous and monogamous marriages. *International Journal of Social Psychiatry, 52,* 5–17.

AACM, AIHCP. (2011). *Fellowship program in case management.* Retrieved from www.aihcp.org/cs~mgmnt.htm.

American Academy of Pediatrics, CLC, and Committee on Hospital Care. (2006). Child Life Services. *Pediatrics, 118,* 1757–1763.

AAMFT. (2011). *Qualifications and FAQs.* Retrieved from www.aamft.org/imis15/Content/About_AAMFT/Qualifications.aspx.

Berrick, J. D. (1997). Assessing quality of care in kinship and foster family care. *Family Relations, 46,* 273–280.

Blume, L. B., & Benson, M. J. (1997). The deconstruction of curricula: Postmodern discourse on reconstructing human development and family studies programs. *Family Science Review, 10,* 4–9.

Boyd, B. J. (1997). Integrating human development and family studies curricula: Pitfalls and possibilities. *Family Science Review, 10,* 56–61.

Bredehoft, D. J., Eckhoff, D., & Gesme, C. (2003). Human growth and development. In D. J. Bredehoft & M. J. Walcheski (Eds.), *Family life education: Integrating theory and practice* (pp. 75–81). Minneapolis, MN: Author.

Bronfenbrenner, U. (1986). Ecology of the family as a context for human development: Research perspectives. *Developmental Psychology, 22,* 723–742.

CLC. (2012). *Child Life Council.* Retrieved from www.childlife.org/.

Copple, C., & Bredekamp, S. (2009). *Developmentally appropriate practice in early childhood programs serving children from birth through age 8* (3rd ed.). Washington, DC: NAEYC.

Darling, C. A., Fleming, W. M., & Cassidy, D. (2009). Professionalization of family life education: Defining the field. *Family Relations, 58,* 330–345.

Drummet, A. R., Coleman, M., & Cable, S. (2003). Military families under stress: Implications for family life education. *Family Relations, 52,* 279–287.

Duncan, S. F., & Goddard, H. W. (2011). *Family life education: Principles and practices for effective outreach* (2nd ed.). Thousand Oaks, CA: Sage Publications.

Espelage, D., Anderman, E. M., Brown, B. E., Jones, A., Lane, K. L., McMahon, S. D., ... Reynolds, C. R. (2013). Understanding and preventing violence directed against teachers: Recommendations for a national research, practice, and policy agenda. *American Psychologist, 68,* 75–87.

Ganong, L. H., Coleman, M., & Demo, D. H. (1995). Issues in training family scientists. *Family Relations, 44,* 501–507.

Hamon, R. R., & Smith, S. R. (2014). The discipline of Family Science and the continuing need for innovation. *Family Relations, 63,* 309–322.

Hayslip, B., Jr., & Kaminski, P. L. (2005). Grandparents raising their grandchildren: A review of the literature and suggestions for practice. *Gerontologist, 45,* 262–269.

McHale, S. M., & Huston, T. L. (1985). The effect of the transition to parenthood on the marriage relationship: A longitudinal study. *Journal of Family Issues, 6,* 409–433.

Myers-Walls, J. A., Ballard, S. M., Darling, C. A., & Myers-Bowman, K. S. (2011). Reconceptualizing the domain and boundaries of family life education. *Family Relations, 60,* 357–372.

NCFR. (2009). Certified family life educator (CFLE) exam content outline. In D. J. Bredehoft & M. J. Walcheski (Eds.), *Family life education: Integrating theory and practice* (2nd ed., pp. 261–263). Minneapolis, MN: Author.

NCFR. (2013). *CFLE Certification*. Retrieved from www.ncfr.org/cfle-certification.

NOHS. (n.d.). *About us*. Retrieved from www.nationalhumanservices.org/about-us-page.

O'Brien, M. (2005). Studying individual and family development: Linking theory and research. *Journal of Marriage and Family, 67*, 880–890.

Patterson, J. M. (2002). Understanding family resilience. *Journal of Clinical Psychology, 58*, 233–246.

Piercy, F. P., & Sprenkle, D. H. (1990). Marriage and family therapy: A decade review. *Journal of Marriage and the Family, 52*, 1116–1126.

Powell, D. R. (1989). *Families and early childhood programs*. Washington, DC: NAEYC.

Roopnarine, J., & Johnson, J. E. (2012). *Approaches to early childhood education* (6th ed.). Upper Saddle River, NJ: Pearson.

Seltzer, J. A. (2000). Families formed outside of marriage. *Journal of Marriage and the Family, 62*, 1247–1268.

Thompson, R. H. (1989). Child life programs in pediatric settings. *Infants and Young Children, 2*, 75–82.

Walsh, B. A., & Petty, K. (2007). Frequency of six early childhood education approaches: A 10-year content analysis of Early Childhood Education Journal. *Early Childhood Education Journal, 34*, 301–305.

Walsh, F. (1996). The concept of family resilience: Crisis and challenge. *Family Processes, 35*, 261–281.

Walsh, F. (2003). Family resilience: A framework for clinical practice. *Family Process, 42*, 1–18.

PART II

Who Are the People Involved in the Area of HDFS?

CHAPTER 2
Careers in HDFS

HDFS is an area of study and tends to be a "discovery major," meaning that students tend to learn about it after being enrolled in college for a semester or more (Hagenbuch & Hamon, 2011, p. 1). Some undergraduates tend to be attracted to HDFS programs more so than Psychology and Sociology due to their sense of job potential at the bachelor's level (Endsley, 1998). Students pursuing an HDFS degree have a plethora of career choices to consider, rather than a single clear-cut path. HDFS is different from Sociology and Psychology because it focuses on lifespan development, family and relationships, has a multi-disciplinary/interdisciplinary approach to studying families, and values the application of

Image 2.1 Students Pursuing an HDFS Degree Have a Plethora of Career Choices to Consider Rather than a Single, Clear-cut Path (photo by Hongqi Zhang/Depositphotos, Inc.).

content knowledge (Hamon & Smith, 2014). See Box 2.1 for survey research that hall-marks what makes HDFS different from other fields. Along this line, HDFS majors are more likely than non–HDFS majors to believe that their degree will prepare them for a variety of careers (Hagenbuch & Hamon, 2011). Although HDFS, Psychology, and Sociology are distinct areas of study, there is some overlap in the skills that bachelor's programs tend to cultivate and to desire in their students. Each area of study values specific skills (see American Sociological Association, n.d.; Hayes, 1997; NCFR, 2015). See Figure 2.1 for

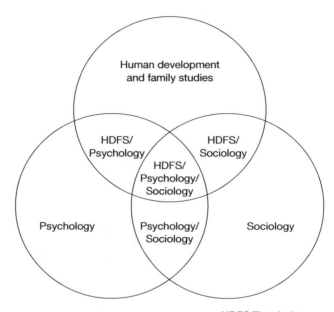

HDFS

- Learning skills
- Program development skills
- Program evaluation skills
- Grant writing skills
- Collaborative/teamwork skills
- Creative problem-solving skills
- Leadership skills

Psychology

- Highly literate
- Highly numerate
- Measurement skills
- Pragmatism

Sociology

- Gain a global perspective
- Prepare for graduate school

HDFS/Psychology

- Quantitative research

HDFS/Sociology

- Qualitative research

Psychology/Sociology

- Quantitative research and data analysis

HDFS/Psychology/Sociology

- Critical thinking skills
- Communication skills
- Research skills
- Ethical thinking

Figure 2.1 HDFS, Psychology, and Sociology.

BOX 2.1 THE STATE OF FAMILY SCIENCE

The development of family science could be likened to four stages: the discovery stage, the pioneering stage, the maturing stage, and the evaluation and innovation stage. Hamon and Smith's (2014) descriptive study is part of the evaluation and innovation stage because their work evaluated feedback about family science and suggests future areas for growth and innovation.

Hamon and Smith (2014) electronically surveyed 71 program representatives using a 28-item survey with mostly open-ended questions to assess what administrators in family science programs think about the field. Most of the respondents were from public universities in the United States. More than half of the programs represented had approved coursework to offer the provisional CFLE status through the coursework option in the last semester or after graduation. The survey assessed such topics as how participants define family science, resources used to educate students about family science, current challenges affecting family science, and potential solutions for addressing challenges. Response length varied from one sentence to multiple paragraphs. The responses were organized thematically and organized around the questions asked. Three individuals independently read the responses to determine the topical organization with disagreements being discussed until consensus was reached.

Participants suggested that family science is different from such fields as Sociology and Psychology because family science focuses on family and relationships, it takes a multidisciplinary/interdisciplinary approach to studying families, and it values application of content knowledge (Hamon & Smith, 2014). In addition, participants stated that family systems, family dynamics, and a family strength perspective are also hallmarks of family science (Hamon & Smith, 2014).

The 10 content areas also make family science a unique discipline. Most family science programs surveyed stated that human growth and development is required of all students in the program (Hamon & Smith, 2014).

Family science administrators were also asked what skills are important for undergraduates to possess. Most participants stated that critical thinking skills, written communication skills, oral communication skills, and interpersonal skills with diverse families and individuals were important, with the last skill identified as extremely important for family science majors (Hamon & Smith, 2014).

Challenges for the field of family science were germane to lack of identity and recognition as a field. Hamon and Smith (2014) found 43 different department or program names, such as HDFS, Child and Family Studies, Family Studies, and the like. Some solutions generated by participants include increasing the visibility of and value of family science on local and national levels, and perhaps finding a name (e.g., HDFS) that we all can agree with and identify with. Other suggestions to help alleviate challenges include empowering students to market themselves and improving our ability to educate students on career opportunities in our field.

1   According to Hamon and Smith's (2014) findings, how is family science different from other social sciences, such as Sociology and Psychology? Critical thinking skills, written communication skills, and oral communication skills may be important skills for all students in social sciences. Why might interpersonal skills with diverse families and individuals be an important skill for students learning about HDFS?

2   Take some time to think about questions from Hamon and Smith's (2014) study. For example, how would you respond to "What are the biggest challenges affecting the family science field right now?" and "What can be done to address these challenges?" To gather additional perspectives, you might want to ask these two questions of your instructor, other faculty in the program, and graduate students. Were any of the perspectives you informally collected similar to Hamon and Smith's (2014) findings?

Hamon, R. R., and Smith, S. R. (2014). The discipline of Family Science and the continuing need for innovation. *Family Relations, 63*, 309–322.

skills that are more distinct to an area of study and skills that HDFS, Psychology, and Sociology all value. Because of this overlap, students might graduate with a bachelor's degree in HDFS and then attend a graduate program in HDFS, Psychology, or Sociology. In addition, students with a bachelor's degree in HDFS may pursue a graduate degree in counseling, education, or social work.

For students in nursing programs the link between their training and career is often obvious to others and they tend to explore a specialty, such as pediatrics, within their undergraduate nursing program. In the area of HDFS, however, students have many career options that potentially run the gamut from preschool teaching to being a program coordinator of a child and family policy institute.

The unfamiliarity of HDFS for many students, and the variety of options, makes it essential for students to become informed about careers within HDFS and actively seek courses, out-of-class experiences, and experiential education to support their specialization. This is especially important given that graduating from college does not automatically equal finding a good job (Jacobson, Oravecz, Falk, & Osteen, 2011). Nonetheless, field experiences can provide opportunities for students to build connections with potential employers and develop skills that can help students make the transition from school to full-time employment (Jacobson et al., 2011). For example, an internship at the end of the senior year could lead to an offer of employment for some HDFS majors (Kopera-Frye, Hilton, Wilson, & Rice, 2006). For many students within the area of HDFS, however, there is an acknowledgment that flexibility and a willingness to explore multiple options are both important to a career search (Chuang, Walker, & Caine-Bish, 2009). Unfortunately, during hard economic times when employment possibilities are far and few, starting in a position that was not your original goal but then getting a more desirable job is common (Gonzalez, 2009).

The topics we will discuss in this chapter promote a better understanding of career options, training, and desired skills for professionals within the area of HDFS to possess. It is important to keep in mind that the information and shared wisdom presented in this chapter are not prescriptive, but rather we encourage you to consider the content in this chapter as you find your own approach to understanding the interrelationships between families and individual development. In this chapter, we will first consider career options.

CAREER OPTIONS IN HDFS

Once you have an understanding of what HDFS is, it is critical to become educated about career opportunities, and important to articulate what to do with an HDFS degree. We'd like to share some stories of HDFS program graduates and professionals. HDFS is largely a female-dominated major and field (Hagenbuch & Hamon, 2011), and in accord the below stories are mostly from female graduates of an HDFS program. These firsthand narratives may help you think of career options to explore and experience as you develop your own story.

The Field: Meet Angie McEvers, CCLS, CFLE, B.S. in HDFS

I currently am a Child Life Specialist at a children's hospital. I am responsible for helping our pediatric patients cope with the stress and uncertainty of illness, disability, and hospitalization. I promote effective coping through play, self-expression activities, and age-appropriate medical preparation and education.

Image 2.2 Becoming Educated about HDFS Career Opportunities Is Critical (photo by Paulus Rusyanto/Depositphotos, Inc.).

I focus on the psychosocial and developmental needs of the children and collaborate with their families and other health care providers to insure that a child's medical stay is less traumatizing.

I am a CFLE and not only do I use that for my work at the hospital, it is required for my contract work outside of the hospital.

I also contract with a non-profit group focused on tragedy assistance. I am a group leader for them and travel across the United States to provide bereavement camps for the families of the fallen. I also facilitate support groups for the families that are facing pediatric cancer. This group meets monthly and, after taking a two-year break, I am so excited to be providing this for our community again.

Every day I am thankful for my degree in HDFS. It has helped me professionally and personally. As a parent of two children, my studies have prepared me to be a better parent. The uniqueness of having certifications as a Child Life Specialist and a CFLE has opened many career opportunities for me.

This degree is a must for those who want to work with families or children. The multiple opportunities that this degree provides simply means you can find a job you love or even create a job that makes you happy.

The Field: Meet Eileen Schwartz, B.S. in HDFS

I am currently the Development and Communications Director of a non-profit organization serving individuals with Down syndrome. My job includes grant-writing, collecting data, supervising volunteers, supervising child care services at monthly support meetings, and serving as the accountant. I also care for our growing organization by working with families directly and indirectly as we currently serve 100 families a month. Within the organization, I initiated a new social group for young adults with Down syndrome.

A degree in HDFS has encouraged me to really know and understand what serving across the lifespan means. Also, I understand what developmentally appropriate means. Understanding context is really important. All of this knowledge helps me to better understand and to better relate to people.

It is important to listen to your gut when selecting a major. Ask yourself: Where do I want to see myself? With a major in HDFS, you acquire a core of knowledge and you get to make it into your own. I encourage you to have fun in your HDFS classes, put your all into it, evaluate your own interests, and think about how the knowledge and experiences apply to you and your goals. Evaluate your interests and passions early in your studies. This way you can keep the hunger alive so that when graduation comes around you have a passion and are ready to pursue it.

The Field: Meet Courtney Goodballet, B.S. in HDFS

I am currently working as a Graduate Assistant at a public university. My job includes teaching an undergraduate HDFS course in which I supervise students in their practicum placements at local child care settings. The main focus is to get the students to better understand how to work alongside children and families.

I also provide trainings at Head Start. The goal is to give the teachers the tools and knowledge they need in order to incorporate the various aspects of physical development into understanding human development.

Holding undergraduate degrees in Early Childhood Education and HDFS has done wonders for me as I pursue my master's in HDFS and a CFLE certification. I am able to guide my students who are seeking a bachelor's degree in HDFS by sharing my professional experiences. Similarly, as a mom and wife, my family has been able to benefit from the perks that having an HDFS degree offers. It is important to know how everyone inside and outside of our family contributes to our family's success.

The value of having an HDFS degree is knowing that you will have an everlasting effect on someone's life, no matter whether they already have a family or are planning to have a family. I find that those who are seeking an HDFS degree all have something in common: they have a burning desire to help others!

The Field: Meet Keith Olson, B.S. in HDFS

I am currently a drug and alcohol intern at a community counseling center. My job responsibilities include running daily groups, processing clients' intakes, developing personal treatment plans that best fit each individual, and assessing the progress of clients throughout the treatment program. While involved in the daily groups, I help clients learn effective coping skills, communication skills, and life skills training such as budgeting and daily planning.

My degree in HDFS has been valuable to my career because it has enabled me to be a more effective professional by increasing my understanding that while I am actually working with an individual, he or she is part of a family system. I have the knowledge to incorporate the family as a whole while treating one individual of that family. I have also been able to specifically apply the stages of life span development as that person has grown into an adult and use how their family and environment have impacted them. My degree has also provided me with unique qualifications that have aided me in obtaining employment as well as placement in a higher pay bracket.

People who are considering pursuing a degree in HDFS should first be informed that this field is open to so many different opportunities. I certainly was not aware of the vast possibilities that this degree would qualify me for. Not only is there the ability to work with either individuals or families, but also the complete age spectrum is available under this degree. A degree in HDFS also qualifies a person for immediate opportunities following graduation due to the many openings in the health or human services field. Since there are so many possibilities that this degree qualifies a person for, it is important to know and follow your true feelings regarding the areas that you want to be involved with. The satisfaction and internal happiness that are achieved by the professional in this field are very gratifying. The pleasure of being able to work with families and individuals to help them change their negative thinking or behaviors and to possibly make changes in their life and/or their children's lives through a change in the family system is immense. There has not been a nicer feeling than when I walk out of a session knowing that I was able to provide a client or family with the knowledge and techniques to improve their situation. Hearing them laugh and seeing them smile keeps me coming back to work every day with enthusiasm. My degree in HDFS has turned my dream of a satisfying career with strong financial benefits into a reality, as well as putting me in a position to pursue a master's degree that will allow me to continue achieving and assisting families at an even higher level.

The Field: Meet Brandon Morales, B.S. in HDFS

I am currently the Education Training Voucher (ETV) Coordinator and Independent Living (IL) Case Manager for a non-profit organization. The program I am a part of serves youth who age out of foster care. As the ETV Coordinator, I am responsible for overseeing the scholarship funds for any aged out youth who pursue any eligible postsecondary education paths as they develop from adolescence into adulthood. I also supervise the ETV Facilitator who allocates the funds to those youth, which includes providing support and guidance, reviewing monthly reports, and conducting quarterly audits of client charts. As an IL Case Manager, I work one-on-one with youth ages 15–21 who are either currently in foster care or who have aged out of foster care. These sessions involve helping the youth create and achieve goal plans that focus on managing their resources in order to successfully transition or develop from adolescence into adulthood. In addition, I also create and facilitate workshops for the youth geared toward educating them in areas that will support their transition.

A degree in HDFS has been invaluable to my career in that I have a better understanding of development and life stages, particularly the area of adolescence and young adulthood. Adolescence is a life stage full of physical and psychological changes. Coupled with the foster care system, this adds a whole other complex dynamic to the youth that I serve. The foster care system is a unique context. HDFS has helped me better understand people as individuals in their different life stages as well as part of bigger systems such as the family, the community, society at large, etc. HDFS has been a very useful degree for my career as my job is to help youth positively develop from adolescence into adulthood.

For anyone who is or will be pursuing a degree in HDFS, have fun with your classes and value what you learn in them. HDFS not only teaches you about how to work with people and help people when you reach your career, but also provides valuable knowledge that will give you a better understanding of yourself, your family, and your friends. In addition, HDFS opens up the doors to multiple different career paths to choose from. If you, like me, appreciate the option of taking different career paths, then HDFS could be the right major for you. Ultimately, go with what your heart is telling you.

The Field: Meet Carrie Aalberts, B.S. in HDFS

I am currently working on my HDFS graduate degree with an emphasis in gerontology, as well as a CFLE credential. Along with being a full-time student, I am an adult day care provider. I am responsible for assisting with the daytime care of senior clients. The majority of the older adults I care for have been diagnosed with Alzheimer's disease or other types of dementia. Working at the adult day care site also provides me the opportunity to spend a lot of time with children. The adult day center is known for its excellent on-site preschool. This unique intergenerational program brings together the children and older adults twice a day. With all generations involved, these visits benefit everyone in such a positive way. My knowledge in lifespan and overall human development has been so valuable while working with those across all stages of life.

I pursued an undergraduate degree and then a graduate degree in HDFS because I find this field of study to be imperative for anyone who will be working with individuals and families. My experience in the HDFS program has led me to my passion of helping families and individuals better themselves and their relationships as they age. With the skills that I have gained throughout the HDFS program and through the pursuit of a CFLE credential, I am able to connect with individuals and their families on a more personal level, which then helps me to effectively assist my clients and better understand their needs. Obtaining a degree in HDFS has not only benefited me professionally, but has been pertinent to my own life and family. Along with my HDFS degree, my emphasis in gerontology allowed me to focus exclusively on the aging population. With the growing need for caring professionals in the field of gerontology, I feel confident that my HDFS background will greatly aid me in my career.

I encourage all students considering HDFS to take the courses that interest you and find your passion within the lifespan or family studies. I never once had to take a course that was not intriguing or applicable to my own life. HDFS was my first and only choice because it opened the door to a plethora of career options, in which I could help others. The HDFS program has fueled my career goals and has gotten me ready for the successful career I have always wanted. HDFS is essential to each and every one of us.

EXPERIENCES AND SKILLS FOR A FUTURE MEMBER OF A PROFESSION

This next section will focus on you—as an individual and as a current or future member of a profession. Those who work with individuals and families need a clear concept of who they are and the importance of the work they do within the area of HDFS. One

Image 2.3 Attending a Conference as an Attendee or a Presenter Can Help Your Skills Grow (photo by Monkey Business/Depositphotos, Inc.).

important caveat is that other professionals and the public at large may have a lack of understanding of what the field is about and your current or future role in it. As a student thinking about or starting a journey in a career within HDFS, it is important to advocate for and to support the work done in this area. Some ways to advocate include: learn more about HDFS through every course you take, get experiences working with individuals and families, join a professional organization, and let your skills grow by attending a conference as an attendee or a presenter. You are in an important position and are the future of HDFS.

A typical HDFS **course** is 3 credit hours, or 3 hours of instructor contact per week with students engaging in learning or studying outside of class time each week. The credit hours will most likely differ for quarter schedules, online courses, mini-courses, and summer courses. Collectively, your HDFS courses may have the following student learning outcomes:

- Demonstrate knowledge of the three domains of development, with in-depth expertise in at least one domain (e.g., physical domain).
- Demonstrate knowledge and application of the interplay of issues and processes in diverse family systems.
- Demonstrate the ability to understand and to evaluate prominent theories, research, and practices relevant to HDFS.
- Demonstrate the ability to apply field-related knowledge, theory, and practices in a professional setting.

Field experiences may include field observations, practica, and internships that provide experiential education intended to support your growth within the area of HDFS in a professional setting. Many introductory level courses in HDFS require field observations of infants, toddlers, children, adolescents, adults, and/or families. The observations

Image 2.4 In an Internship, a Student Tends to Function Independently with the Guidance of the Site Supervisor and University Instructor (photo by Fabrice Michaudeau/Depositphotos, Inc.).

tend to require objectively observing individuals and families coupled with the observer's subjective interpretation of what was observed. See Table 2.1 for a sample observation.

The **practicum** is often the first hands-on field experience working with individuals and families in a professional setting (O'Malley & Wilson, 2003). The practicum often requires the student to attend supporting classes and work under the close guidance of site supervisors (O'Malley & Wilson, 2003). The **internship** requires more of a time commitment for students than the practicum and tends to be a capstone experience for advanced students with field experience, such as the practicum, already completed (O'Malley & Wilson, 2003). In an internship, the student tends to function independently with the guidance of the site supervisor and university instructor (O'Malley & Wilson, 2003). During field experiences, it is important to engage in **reflection**, for example in the form of journal entries, in order to integrate field experiences with content learned in courses (Jacobson et al., 2011).

It is important to consider joining a **professional organization**. Some colleges and universities have student chapters, and actively have regular meetings. Participation in student organizations can be an important factor of earning employment after students graduate from a college, particularly a college or school of education (Sagen, Dallam, & Laverty, 2000). Participation in student organizations during college may provide evidence to employers of potential employees' organizational and interpersonal abilities (Sagen et al., 2000). Student chapters of professional organizations, as well as instructors and those working in HDFS fields, will often readily have information about professional organizations. Joining a professional organization typically involves paying a membership fee, which is often discounted for students. Professional organizations allow you to receive cutting-edge information, to network with other members and/or professionals in the field, and to access opportunities to attend or present conferences and events at the

Table 2.1 Sample Observation Notes for Introducing the Box

Observation	Reflection notes
Teacher brings box into the classroom.	Did Addison hear the voices inside the box? Is that what prompted her to look through the hole?
Ryan and Nick crawl inside the box.	
Addison notices a handle hole punched in the side of the box, peeks through the hole, laughs.	The children enjoy playing peek-a-boo. Should we create windows/doors to open and close on the house first to encourage the continuation of peek-a-boo games?
Nick pokes his finger out of the handle hole that Addison is looking through.	
After watching Addison, Amy finds her own handle hole to look through.	Has Ryan seen his dad use tools on their house?
Ryan and Nick crawl outside of the box and take turns playing peek-a-boo with more children inside the box.	Do the other children agree it could be a house because it is a space big enough to crawl into?
Teachers ask the children, "What could we turn our box into? Could we build something with it using tools?"	Do the flaps and handle openings remind the children of doors and windows? Could this be why they call it a house?
Ryan says "House!"	
Amy and Nick start repeating "house, house!"	

local, state, or national level. We will briefly provide key information about professional organizations that are illustrative of groups within HDFS.

1   CLC is a non-profit organization that strives to help children and their families over-come challenging life events. This organization offers the CCLS credential. CLC holds an annual conference and a leadership development institute. The CLC Bulletin is a resource for the child life community (CLC, n.d.).

2   Family Science Association (FSA) is an independent organization focused on enhanc-ing the quality and dissemination of knowledge from researchers to practitioners within the field of family science. They sponsor an annual conference and publish the *Family Science Review* (FSA, 2011).

3   NAEYC serves children, families, and teachers with a focus on birth through third grade. NAEYC holds an annual conference and an annual institute for professional development. This early childhood organization has several publications, including *Young Children*, *Teaching Young Children*, and *Early Childhood Research Quarterly* (NAEYC, n.d.).

4   NCFR is a multidisciplinary association dedicated to strengthening families through research, education, and practice. The NCFR established the "Certified Family Life Educator" credential and offers the *CFLE Network Newsletter* (NCFR, 2013). This organization publishes the *Journal of Marriage and Family*, *Family Relations*, and the *Journal of Family Theory & Review* (NCFR, 2013).

5   SRCD is a not-for-profit association that works to advance the field of child devel-opment through research, the application of research findings, and a multidisciplinary exchange of information. The SRCD publishes *Child Development* and *Child Develop-ment Perspectives*, as well as an annual Social Policy Report (SRCD, 2013).

6   Society for Research on Adolescence (SRA) is an international organization whose goal is to promote the wellbeing of adolescents through research and scientific dis-course around parenting, policy, and schooling. The SRA serves members around the world and publishes the *Journal of Research on Adolescence* (SRA, 2010).

7   Society for the Study of Human Development (SSHD) seeks to advance scholarship on human development across all age groups rather than focusing on single ages/stages. This multidisciplinary society consists of members from diverse professional backgrounds sharing an interest in human development. The SSHD publishes the journal *Research in Human Development* (SSHD, 2013).

8   The GSA focuses on advancing research on and practice in the area of aging. GSA hosts an annual meeting. This interdisciplinary organization has several publications, including *Gerontologist*, *Gerontology & Geriatrics Education*, and *Gerontology News* (GSA, 2014).

There are other professional organizations that incorporate aspects of HDFS. For example, the American Educational Research Association (AERA) has special interest groups in early education and child development, adolescence and youth development, and family, school, and community partnerships.

Many professional organizations often have **conferences** at the local, state, or national level. Attending a conference provides opportunities for "making connections" or social-izing with other attendees or presenters (Cherrstrom, 2012, p. 148). The following prac-tices were identified by Cherrstrom (2012) to help attendees make connections and get the most out of attending a conference:

1   have a plan before arriving at the conference;
2   review the conference program or website to identify sessions of interest;
3   determine if there are any opportunities to volunteer at the conference;
4   be professional while attending the conference and conference-related events;
5   take time to reflect and talk with others;
6   take notes during sessions and apply the information to your own work.

Many organizations also allow presentations from undergraduate students at conferences. For example, SRCD encourages proposal submissions from undergraduate students. Typically, students conduct research or a project under the auspices of a faculty member. The guidelines for information about what type of proposals and what to include in the proposals are included on the organization website. Not everyone who submits a proposal will get their work accepted. For 2011, conference statistics showed that there was a 68.8% acceptance rate for student sessions at SRCD.

GRADUATE SCHOOL IN HDFS

Graduate programs in HDFS may emphasize specific areas of study, such as individual development and family development (Birkel, Lerner, & Smyer, 1989). The field of human development and the field of family studies have both acknowledged the importance of examining development within context (Parke & Buriel, 2008). HDFS graduate programs may explore the integration of these areas using a variety of approaches to teaching graduate students and preparing professionals.

Image 2.5 Graduate School Can Include Master's Level Work and Doctoral Level Work (photo by Hongqi Zhang/Depositphotos, Inc.).

MASTER'S PROGRAM

For instance, one graduate program in HDFS recreated their master's program based on employers' perspectives about the desirable experiences and skills for quality job applicants to possess (Benson et al., 2006). The following skills and experiences were identified as highly valued by employers of graduates of a master's degree in HDFS:

- application of theory and research;
- program planning and evaluation;
- research and analysis;
- grant writing;
- collaborative skills;
- and experiences in the field, such as an internship (Benson et al., 2006).

Dispositions or virtues that demonstrate good practice are important to nourish as a student and then as a professional in the area of HDFS. The following three virtues are important to practice:

1   Caring. This is "the disposition to support the wellbeing of family members as decision-makers in their own lives" (Palm, 2009, p. 194).
2   Practical Wisdom. This is "the ability to understand competing needs in complex situations and make decisions based on reflection and consultation with peers" (Palm, 2009, p. 194).
3   Hope/Optimism. This is "the disposition to focus on the strengths and positive potential of family members and other individuals and to maintain a positive attitude in the face of adversity" (Palm, 2009, p. 194).

Master's programs in the area of HDFS often prepare students for practitioner work, such as serving as an extension agent to develop educational programs and implement them in the community or state. A program typically ranges between 30 and 40 credits. A master's degree may also provide a basis for a research-type career or entry into a doctoral or Ph.D. program. A doctoral or Ph.D. program is more in-depth than a master's program and the credits vary by program and institution and can be double or triple the credits required for a master's degree. A master's degree will allow students to enter leadership roles in education, administration, or research. The capstone experience in a master's program may include three options: (a) the non-thesis option: professional experiences, such as writing a manuscript for a practitioner focused journal, putting together a portfolio, or taking a program exit exam or national exam, such as the CFLE exam; (b) the thesis option: proposing a research project and conducting it under the auspices of faculty; or (c) the comprehensive exam. Capstone experiences will vary by program and institution. The thesis option is often considered more desirable than the non-thesis option for students considering applying to doctoral programs in HDFS.

BOX 2.2 WHY ATTEND GRADUATE SCHOOL IN HDFS?

Meet Caitlynn Hansen, M.S. HDFS

As I was nearing the end of my time as an undergraduate student majoring in family studies, I thought to myself, "Wow. This subject is so awesome. I can't believe I'm almost graduating, because it feels like there is so much more to learn!" I started thinking about my options for **graduate school** and my ultimate career goal—teaching at the community college level. A graduate program in HDFS seemed like the natural next step.

Consider attending a graduate program in HDFS if you have a passion for the subject. Consider one if, like me, you are nearing the end of your undergraduate career and still feel like there is so much more to learn. Even if you are not sure of your future career goals, consider a graduate program to help you figure out those career goals, and most definitely consider one if you are interested in teaching HDFS at the college level. A graduate program in HDFS will help deepen your understanding of the subject and allow you to delve into specific topics of most interest to you. You will most likely have the opportunity to write a thesis, an at first seemingly impossible undertaking that will deepen your understanding of research, writing, and the field, and once completed, will be one of your greatest accomplishments. In an HDFS graduate program, you will have a real opportunity to shape the discipline through innovative research—an opportunity that does not exist in many other subjects.

At its core, HDFS is a field and subject that can help in so many ways because it is relevant to everyone, so learning about the subject will not only make your own life more fulfilling, but also have a positive ripple effect on the future families, communities, and children you will be working with. A graduate program in HDFS will not be easy, but it will be worth your effort and time because you will gain a tremendous amount of knowledge and experience. Hopefully, like me, this knowledge and experience will further deepen your passion for the subject and make you excited to be a part of such a relevant and innovative field.

BOX 2.3 PARTICIPATING IN UNDERGRADUATE COLLABORATIVE RESEARCH IN PREPARATION FOR GRADUATE SCHOOL

The undergraduate research team includes Dr. Walsh (Mentor), Joell M. Jex, Jennifer N. Churton, Shane R. Jones, and Jinan A. Barghouti.

This research team is conducting a study called "Motivational Factors after Viewing a Documentary Film on Drugs and Driving in Late Adolescence: An Experimental Study." This experimental work started as a class project in an introductory research course. In this class, the students worked collaboratively to create

a research proposal (see Walsh & Weiser, 2015). Their research proposal included an abstract, literature review, research questions, method, and references. At the end of the semester, the students were interested in pursuing the topic of drugged driving further and desired to collect data, analyze the data, and write-up the results and discussion. The associate professor (Walsh) was willing to mentor them and they started by having research team meetings to refine the proposal. Next, they presented their proposal to HDFS faculty, the Dean, and Social Psychology doctoral students. At the end of the proposal presentation, the students received praise and constructive feedback, which they addressed.

Under the auspices of their mentor, they submitted an application to the Institutional Review Board (IRB). After receiving IRB approval, they were ready to begin data collection. The research team will be presenting their study at a national conference and submitting for publication in a peer-reviewed journal.

This collaborative research project started as an undergraduate project but three of the four students have applied to graduate school and received acceptance. Meet two members from the research team and hear from them about participating in undergraduate research in preparation for graduate school.

Joell M. Jex, B.S. HDFS, attending M.S. HDFS program

Collaborative undergraduate research has prepared me for graduate school through a variety of ways. I have learned how to properly manage my time, work as a member of a team, and pay close attention to detail. The research process has taught me to be patient, as there is always something that needs to be completed or worked on in a timely manner. Specifically, I have played a major role in the idea phase of our undergraduate research, as well as addressing revisions, and making sure to stay consistent with APA. The idea phase of research can be tricky since you must formulate a topic that the team agrees to move forward with, along with an idea that may be a solid contribution to the world of research. I also fully understand that an experimental design includes independent variables, dependent variables, and random assignment. During my master's program in HDFS, I hope to pursue research relating to childhood cancer awareness as my thesis topic. I am still thinking about the research design for my thesis project. I am now aware of how extensive the research process can be and the many steps that must be taken to accomplish tasks. My undergraduate research experiences in the research course and implementing the project with a team of peers will help me feel more confident about approaching a thesis in graduate school.

The skills I learned during the research process as an undergraduate student will only be improved during the master's program, leading to more success with the research process. My involvement in undergraduate research has been an exciting process, and I look forward to transferring the skills I learned during this experience to my thesis work and other research projects in graduate school.

Shane R. Jones, B.S. HDFS, attending M.A. Counseling program

My experience conducting undergraduate research has helped me become more educated about adolescents, motivational factors, and the research process. I have been exposed to a variety of topics in HDFS and became open-minded about studying many topics within family science. Now that I am familiar with the research process, it has created many opportunities for me in my educational career.

For example, my experience on the research team makes me more responsible and reliable toward my colleagues. Each team member is assigned duties that we are held responsible for completing by the deadline. We are responsible to our mentor and to each other. My team plans to present our research at a national conference and perhaps even publish it.

My experience has allowed me to work closely with colleagues and people in our community. The most exciting thing about research to me is collecting data, which promotes discovery about our research topic by allowing the research questions or hypotheses to be tested.

I am now entering graduate school where I will continue to be a part of research. I feel like my foundation for understanding the research process is solid and will greatly help me in a graduate research course.

BOX 2.4 HDFS IS EXCELLENT PREPARATION FOR PURSUING GRADUATE DEGREES IN OTHER FIELDS

Alex Faught, B.S. in HDFS, currently pursuing a master's degree in Counseling and Educational Psychology

HDFS was a major that prepared me for pursuing a master's degree in Counseling and Educational Psychology with an emphasis in School Counseling. When applying to this graduate program, some of the requirements were to have a background in a semi-related field, para-counseling experience, and knowledge about children and families. Having my degree in HDFS was extremely helpful upon applying to this program. I was able to gain experience working with children within the practicum class, which is a requirement of the HDFS major. I also had the opportunity to do an internship with one of the region's major hospitals on the pediatric floor, which gave me experience working with families in a stressful environment. Both of these opportunities were extremely valuable in advancing my knowledge, but they also provided me with experiences that would be beneficial in my future, including applying to graduate school.

Once I was accepted into the graduate program and began taking classes, I started to notice a lot of similarities between the program I was in and the HDFS classes. Both of these programs talked in depth about family systems theory as well as evidence-based practice. I had been taught about family systems theory in the undergraduate HDFS coursework, so when I started learning about it within my counseling classes, it was more of a review and I was able to progress my understanding of the theory. Both HDFS and the graduate school counseling program strongly base their approaches and techniques on evidence-based practice. By completing the undergraduate research course, I was already well aware of evidence-based practice and how to write an appropriate research paper. In my graduate program, a lot of what I do consists of writing research papers and basing my counseling approaches on evidence-based practice. By having this knowledge and understanding instilled in me throughout my four years of undergraduate work, it made the transition to graduate school a lot easier, resulting in better quality work. By having the knowledge and experience that the HDFS program provides, I felt more competent and knowledgeable when taking the classes in my graduate program. I think that HDFS is an excellent major for anybody interested in pursuing a master's degree in any field relating to families or children. I can honestly say that HDFS was great preparation and has helped me continue to be successful in the counseling field.

Kashae Knox, B.S. in HDFS, currently pursuing a master's degree in Educational Leadership

I have had a wonderful experience pursuing a bachelor's degree in HDFS. HDFS has prepared me to pursue a Master of Art degree in Educational Leadership. Furthermore, my undergraduate experience has helped me to develop skills in family dynamics, development across the lifespan, and how to work respectively with individuals and families from diverse backgrounds. Thus, I have adopted multiple perspectives to work with individuals and families, which has equipped me to work in various environments.

In addition, being able to conduct research and examine society as a whole has been vital in the Educational Leadership program. HDFS sparked an interest for me to want to work with students because I now have background information pertaining to how culture, religion, and age influence one's decision-making processes, coupled with a foundation in research. HDFS has given me a strong foundation in diversity and I have been readily prepared to succeed. I look forward to applying these skills to an administrative position and to be influential in the community as well as advocate for those from culturally diverse backgrounds.

Kayla Valy, B.S. in HDFS, currently pursuing a master's degree in Social Work

My B.S. degree in HDFS equipped me with the knowledge to confidently enter a Master of Social Work (MSW) program. I was not limited in my options when it came to applying for graduate school programs. Since HDFS covers such a wide range of topics and theories I was able to get exposure to research, lifespan development, and much more which prepared me for a smooth transition into my current MSW program.

My HDFS background has provided me a unique perspective. While learning about micro, meso, and macro level social work I am able to tap into my understanding of people, what is typical for their stage of development, and what might be going on within a boarder context or contexts than what is present in one context. As an HDFS student I participated in an internship placement where I was able to work with pregnant and parenting adolescent mothers for the first time. My goal is to start my own non-profit organization that serves pregnant and parenting adolescent mothers and their children through direct service and by working toward social change. Without my degree in HDFS, I do not believe I would have started my first professional role as a case manager at an adolescent maternity group home only a few months after graduation and I certainly would not be as prepared for an MSW program. I have a comprehensive academic background that will allow me to fulfill my career goals.

Ashleigh Schulewitch, B.S. in HDFS, currently pursuing a master's degree in Special Education

Obtaining my B.S. in HDFS provided me with many opportunities after graduation. After contemplating if I wanted to enter the workforce or continue my education, I decided to pursue a master's degree in Special Education. At first, I was apprehensive to start a degree in a different field of study, but I quickly became aware of how much my HDFS background was applicable to my degree in education.

The field of HDFS provides students with an integrated curriculum that explores how individuals develop over their lifespan and how the family system operates.

> Each of these components is critical to my success in the field of education as understanding how to work with children and their families is at the heart of teaching. HDFS also fosters an understanding of theory and research findings. The field of education encompasses theory and research because that is how educators discover effective teaching and what makes children successful learners. Finally, and most importantly, earning a degree in Human Development and Family Studies helped me develop a passion for working with individuals and their families. I was inspired by cherished field experiences, diverse learning opportunities, and a comprehensive curriculum. I truly believe my bachelor's degree created the foundations for my degree in education, and also the foundations for my career as an educator.

DOCTORAL PROGRAM

The skills, particularly those related to research, and dispositions identified in the previous section are important to doctoral, or Ph.D., programs as well. Many graduate students know that faculty value research skills and an understanding of research methods in their graduate students as much as they value learning content about individuals and families (Ganong, Coleman, & Demo, 1995). In undergraduate programs in HDFS, students often read and evaluate research (Ganong & Coleman, 1993), create research proposals (Walsh & Weiser, 2015), or in some cases engage in the entire research process (Davis & Sandifer-Stech, 2006; Worthy, 2009). In graduate school, students will commonly experience the latter by not only creating research proposals but also collecting and analyzing data, writing up the results and discussion, and then preparing manuscripts and submitting them for publication in a journal (Ganong et al., 1995).

Doctoral programs in the area of HDFS often take a core set of courses in research design, methodology, statistics, and research practica (Birkel et al., 1989; Ganong et al., 1995). For example, students may takes classes that focus on research methods in developmental processes, measurement, and/or the multivariate study of change and development (Birkel et al., 1989). During doctoral training, the student has more independence in research and this is often demonstrated in the dissertation. We'll discuss research more in the next chapter.

In addition to mastering research methods, doctoral programs may emphasize other competencies. For instance, as identified by Ganong et al. (1995):

> Knowledge of interrelationships between family systems and lifespan human development; Ability to communicate to lay audiences; Ability to communicate to professional colleagues; Leadership/administrative skills; Ability to teach at the college level; Ability to teach in community settings (e.g., adult education workshops); Knowledge of ethical standards affecting their interactions with families, as well as ethics involved in research and publishing.

(p. 502)

The Ph.D. typically requires 4–5 years of study beyond the bachelor's degree to master competencies, develop expertise within HDFS, and complete the dissertation. Graduates of Ph.D. programs in HDFS typically enter careers as professors, researchers, or leaders in both public and private sectors.

Summary

1   Pursuing an HDFS degree leads to a variety of career choices to consider rather than a clear-cut path.
2   When thinking about or starting a journey in a career within HDFS, it is important to advocate or to support the work done in this area. This includes:

   A   Learn more about HDFS through every course you take.
   B   Get experiences working with individuals and families to support your career path:

      a   Experiences may be in the form of field observations, practica, internships, or others.
      b   Reflection that connects field experiences with content knowledge is important.

   C   Joining a professional organization is important to "making connections" and skill development.
   D   Let your skills grow by attending a conference as an attendee or a presenter.

3   Graduate work in HDFS emphasizes individual and family development across the lifespan.

   A   Master's programs in the area of HDFS often prepare students for practitioner work, but may also provide a foundation for a research-type career or further graduate study.
   B   Doctoral programs tend to emphasize research.

Key Terms

conferences
courses
field experiences
graduate school
internship
practicum
professional organization
reflection

Challenge: Integration

Sigmund Freud said that the secret to adult life is "to love and to work" (Erikson, 1950/1963). Undergraduates, graduate students, interns, and seasoned professionals all struggle from time-to-time with balancing career and family. The career/work and family/life balance "means different things to different people" but it is possible for these areas to be friends rather than enemies (Morris, 2009, p. 75).

Types of families have changed and make it difficult to emulate the type of family that you may have seen modeled by your parents and grandparents (Teachman, Tedrow, & Crowder, 2000). It may be beneficial to think about your expectations of family type as well as the balance of career and family, and the role your childhood experiences play in these views. Whether in your own family or not, it may be also helpful to think about models of different types of families that you know that demonstrate a balance between family and work. By exploring your career-family views at this age and stage, and in combination with training in the area of HDFS, you may make decisions about close relationships and find a suitable career path.

Journal Questions

1   What career options within the area of HDFS sound interesting to you? Why?
2   Do you consider yourself an advocate for the area of HDFS? Why or why not?
3   Write a brief educational autobiography describing your experiences up to where you are now. What are the major influences on your career trajectory?
4   Search the web for information on a graduate program in HDFS. Write the requirements, potential areas of study, and potential career directions after completing a graduate degree.

SUGGESTED RESOURCE

NCFR. (2015). *Careers in family science*. Minneapolis, MN: NCFR.

REFERENCES

American Sociological Association. (n.d.). *Sociology: A 21st century major.* Retrieved from http://asanet.org/students/majoring_sociology.cfm.

Benson, M. J., Allen, K. R., Few, A. L., Roberto, K. A., Blieszner, R., Meszaros, P. S., & Henderson, T. L. (2006). Transforming the master's degree in human development and family science. *Family Relations, 55,* 44–55.

Birkel, R. C., Lerner, R. M., & Smyer, M. A. (1989). Applied developmental psychology as an implementation of a life-span view of human development. *Journal of Applied Developmental Psychology, 10,* 425–445.

Cherrstrom, C. A. (2012). Making connections: Attending professional conferences. *Adult Learning, 23,* 148–152.

CLC. (n.d.). *Bulletin newsletter.* Retrieved from www.childlife.org/Bulletin%20Newsletter/.

Chuang, N. K., Walker, K., & Caine-Bish, N. (2009). Student perceptions of career choices: The impact of academic major. *Journal of Family & Consumer Sciences Education, 27,* 18–29.

Davis, J. C., & Sandifer-Stech, D. M. (2006). Wade into the water: Preparing students for successful quantitative research. *Family Relations, 55*(1), 56–66.

Endsley, R. C. (1998). Career development in human development and family science. *Family Science Review, 11,* 84–88.

Erikson, E. H. (1950/1963). *Childhood and society* (2nd ed.). New York: Norton.

FSA. (2011). Retrieved from http://familyscienceassociation.org.

Ganong, L. H., & Coleman, M. (1993). Teaching students how to evaluate family research. *Family Relations, 42,* 407–415.

Ganong, L. H., Coleman, M., & Demo, D. H. (1995). Issues in training family scientists. *Family Relations, 44,* 501–507.

GSA. (2014). *Publications.* Retrieved from www.geron.org/publications.

Gonzalez, N. (2009). Preparing for your profession. In D. J. Bredehoft & M. J. Walcheski (Eds.), *Family life education: Integrating theory and practice* (2nd ed., pp. 101–109). Minneapolis, MN: NCFR.

Hagenbuch, D. J., & Hamon, R. R. (2011). Understanding student attitudes toward majoring in human development and family science. *Family Science Review, 16,* 1–21.

Hamon, R. R., & Smith, S. R. (2014). The discipline of Family Science and the continuing need for innovation. *Family Relations, 63,* 309–322.

Hayes, N. (1997). The distinctive skills of a psychology graduate. *APA Monitor, 28,* 33.

Jacobson, J. M., Oravecz, L. M., Falk, A. F., & Osteen, P. (2011). Proximate outcomes of service-learning among family studies undergraduates. *Family Science Review, 16,* 22–33.

Kopera-Frye, K., Hilton, J., Wilson, S., & Rice, A. (2006). The evolution of a human development and family studies internship course: Challenges and recommendations. *Journal of Teaching in Marriage and Family, 6,* 140–159.

Morris, M. L. (2009). Promoting work/family balance through family life education. In D. J. Bredehoft & M. J. Walcheski (Eds.), *Family life education: Integrating theory and practice* (2nd ed., pp. 73–86). Minneapolis, MN: NCFR.

NAEYC. (n.d.). *Publications.* Retrieved from www.naeyc.org/publications.

NCFR. (2013). *Publications.* Retrieved from www.ncfr.org.

NCFR. (2015). *Careers in family science.* Minneapolis, MN: NCFR.

O'Malley, A. J., & Wilson, J. D. (Eds.). (2003). *Pathways to practice: A family life education internship/practicum handbook.* Minneapolis, MN: NCFR.

Palm, G. (2009). Professional ethics and practice. In D. J. Bredehoft & M. J. Walcheski (Eds.), *Family life education: Integrating theory and practice* (2nd ed., pp. 191–197). Minneapolis, MN: NCFR.

Parke, R. D., & Buriel, R. (2008). Socialization in the family: Ethnic and ecological perspectives. In W. Damon, R. M. Lerner, D. Kuhn, R. S. Siegler, & N. Eisenberg (Eds.), *Child and adolescent development: An advanced course* (pp. 95–138). Hoboken, NJ: Wiley.

Sagen, H. B., Dallam, J. W., & Laverty, J. R. (2000). Effects of career preparation experiences on the initial employment success of college graduates. *Research in Higher Education, 41*, 753–767.

SRCD. (2013). Retrieved from www.srcd.org.

SRA. (2010). Retrieved from www.s-r-a.org.

SSHD. (2013). Retrieved from www.sshdonline.org.

Teachman, J. D., Tedrow, L. M., & Crowder, K. D. (2000). The changing demography of America's families. *Journal of Marriage and the Family, 62*, 1234–1246.

Walsh, B. A., & Weiser, D. A. (2015). Teaching undergraduate research in human development and family studies: Piloting a collaborative method. *Family Science Review, 20*, 32–47.

Worthy, S. L. (2009). FCS undergrads at Mississippi State learn research process. *Journal of Family & Consumer Sciences, 101*(3), 47–48.

PART III

What Is the History and Future of the HDFS Field?

CHAPTER 3

History and Future of HDFS
With Eva L. Essa

As you have already learned, the field of HDFS merges the expertise of developmental scientists and family scholars to create departments and degree programs that prepare college students to understand and work with individuals and families across the lifespan. HDFS is a relatively new **social science**, with its interdisciplinary focus and unique emphasis on the contexts within which individuals and families live. HDFS has historical roots in a number of different fields, most notably Home Economics, although it has attracted faculty expertise from other social sciences such as Developmental Psychology and Sociology. In this chapter, we'll review the history of the field of HDFS, and then we will delve into the present and future of the field, as we see it.

HISTORY OF THE STUDY OF HDFS

HDFS has been part of college and university programs since the 1800s, but has undergone a number of significant changes that have resulted in its current form. Initially, HDFS was part of a larger program, known as Home Economics or Domestic Sciences (American Association of Family and Consumer Sciences, n.d.). In many ways, the rise of Home Economics paralleled the women's movement, particularly the increasing presence of women on college campuses across the country.

The most powerful promotion of Home Economics came through legislative channels, through the two **Morrill Acts** (the Morrill Acts of 1862 and 1890). The first, passed in 1862, established land grant colleges in every American state. A total of 30,000 acres of federal land was provided to each state to establish colleges that would "promote the liberal and practical education of the industrial classes in the several pursuits and professions in life" (Morrill Acts of 1862 and 1890). In effect, the initial Morrill Act expanded access to higher education to many more Americans than had previously had access to postsecondary education. The second law, passed in 1890, required that each land grant college establish an agricultural school to help farmers apply scientific methods to their production of farm goods. It also provided annual funding to each state for support of its land grant college and prohibited racial discrimination in admissions policies. At the same time, farmers' wives were provided equal access to information about the many aspects of home management. As a result, agricultural colleges generally included a Home Economics division.

Home Economics promoted the multidisciplinary and integrative study of all aspects of home and family management (Goldstein, 2012). It encompassed a number of areas of study which typically included consumer science, parenting, early childhood education, family studies, family economics, human development, nutrition, food preparation, textiles, and interior design. The focus in all of these areas was on application of scientific, research-based knowledge. Many Home Economics programs developed strong research programs that furthered understanding of these fields and promoted best practices. As a result, Home Economics began partnering with other areas of study, such as Chemistry, Physics, Biology, Art, Psychology, and Sociology, in their research programs.

Many campuses began to establish "living labs" so their Home Economics students could experience and apply the principles they learned in classes. The most prominent of such schools, which continues to exist on many campuses today, is the **Child Development Laboratory**. Such lab schools provide an opportunity for students to observe and interact with young children and families. In addition, many Home Economics programs included fully equipped kitchens where students were able to apply food and nutrition principles. Family living units were another type of experiential laboratory. A group of students would spend several days—and nights—in the **family living lab**, engaging in all aspects of home management and maintenance during their stay. In some of these labs, "practice babies" were included so that students had the opportunity to learn how to care for infants and young children (Dyas, 2014). Although sometimes these babies were orphans who were cared for full-time in the lab for the first year of life (Dyas, 2014), other programs temporarily borrowed children during the day for students to learn and practice child caregiving skills as well as to observe and learn about child development firsthand (S. K. Martin, personal communication, 9/10/16).

By the middle of the 20th century, however, the term Home Economics began to be viewed as a gender stereotype, something that many women had fervently fought to overcome. Although Home Economics was actually designed with the largely feminist principle of promoting women's education by increasing the efficiency of home management, it ultimately became viewed as anti-feminist (Dyas, 2014). During the latter part of the 1900s, the name, "Home Economics," was changed or eliminated on most American campuses. Many programs changed to alternative titles, such as Family and Consumer Sciences and Human Ecology (HEARTH Newsletter, 2005).

More relevant, however, was the change in the relationship among the sub-programs of Home Economics, as a discipline. Originally Home Economics encompassed a single integrated whole of subjects involved in family and home management. Over the years, however, these subjects became more complex as new knowledge was generated through research and through changes in society and technology. As Home Economics programs morphed into their new identities, many of them became self-contained rather than integrated disciplines. As a result, programs such as HDFS are often self-standing programs rather than ones associated with traditionally included fields, such as nutrition or fashion merchandising.

Image 3.1 Some Campuses Have Divided the Two Fields of HDFS into Discrete Programs or Offer One or the Other (photo by Monkey Business/Depositphotos, Inc.).

Similar to the splintering of Home Economics fields into more self-contained units, HDFS has also experienced some tension between the two elements of the field: human development and family studies. Some campuses have divided the two fields into discrete programs or offer one or the other. There are also a variety of department and program names within which "human development" and "family studies" majors are found, including "Family and Consumer Studies/Sciences," "Child and Family Studies," "Human Development and Family Science," and "Family, Youth, and Community," among many others (Hans, 2014). Most HDFS scholars, however, recognize that the two fields are indivisible and rely on each other for context and meaning.

Box 3.1 contains an interview of a faculty member who lived through this major transition from being a developmental scientist in an integrated unit of "Home Economics" to serving on the faculty of a separate department of HDFS. Her story illuminates the changes that occurred over her 40-year career in the field.

BOX 3.1 INTERVIEW WITH A RETIRED HDFS FACULTY MEMBER

Following is an interview with a professional who experienced the transition from Home Economics to HDFS. Her story sheds further light on how HDFS has become the program it is today.

Q1: *When did you become aware of the existence of "HDFS" programs and become interested in HDFS as a program of study and research?*

A: My undergraduate degree was in a totally different field. What precipitated the change was parenthood: In my mid-twenties, I had two children. My 3-year-old daughter was very anxious to go to school. We had recently moved to a new town and I asked people I knew what preschool they would recommend. Everyone I talked to said, the Child Development Lab at the University, although, they cautioned, it was very difficult to get your child in since they had a rigorous selection process. I made an appointment with the Lab School director and, to my delight, my daughter was accepted. I found that her classroom had an adjacent observation booth, and I spent time observing my child and the teachers' interactions with her and the other children. I fell in love! This was a field I wanted to learn more about.

After a couple of months I shared my interest with the Lab School director who encouraged me to talk about next steps with the faculty member in charge of the graduate program. That was when I found out that the child development/family studies program, which the Child Development Lab was part of, was in the School of Home Economics. I knew nothing about home economics but soon learned that it included a number of disciplines such as nutrition, family economics, housing, interior design, and clothing and textiles. I was required to take a class in each of the areas before applying to the graduate program. The classes were interesting, but my favorite was the introductory course in child development. When I had completed these classes, I started the graduate program and, 2 years later, had earned my M.S. degree.

By sheer coincidence, the director of the Lab School resigned and a faculty position in the School of Home Economics became available. I applied and was hired. This was in the early 1970s. Part of my load was to direct the Lab School (which at the time served 20 children in a program that was in session 2 hours, Mondays through Thursdays). The majority of my job was to teach child development courses and advise the students enrolled in the Pre-Kindergarten Education major. The classes I taught all had to do with early childhood education.

Q2: *What did the department and college look like when you started? How did it morph over time?*

A: The School of Home Economics was a division of the College of Agriculture, although, 2 years after I began taking classes, it became a self-standing school. The School of Home Economics had a faculty of 16 with one or more instructors in each of the subject areas I mentioned earlier.

The program did not experience smooth sailing, however. Over the years, faculty became increasingly discontent with the authoritarian, dictatorial style of the dean of the School of Home Economics. In fact, there was a succession of three deans, each with a similar dysfunctional leadership style. The president of the University twice replaced deans. The third time, however, he told the faculty that the School of Home Economics was to be disbanded and that we had 18 months to decide how we were to be organized.

I became acting dean during this transitional period and had the responsibility of overseeing the intense discussions and negotiations that took place. Eventually, faculty in the programs in our school made different decisions, which they felt would be most conducive to ensuring a successful future. One of the major decisions that we made involved programs outside our school as well. We formed a new college, the College of Human and Community Sciences, which included two former Home Economics units, Social Work, Criminal Justice, and Physical Education and Recreation. Here is what was decided: HDFS and Nutrition would each become stand-alone departments in the new college; the two faculty members in Clothing and Textiles chose to move to the College of Agriculture; and Housing and Interior Design became a program of one faculty member which was directly responsible to the Provost. The latter two programs disappeared when faculty left the university or retired.

Some years later, as part of broader campus changes, the new college was disbanded. Several HDFS faculty moved into the College of Education, although two moved into the School of Social Work and one to Sociology. Nutrition, which had gained some new faculty members from Biochemistry, joined the College of Agriculture as a department.

It took our HDFS program several years to find the right fit within the College of Education. That fit gradually emerged as HDFS was able to impact existing education programs with its somewhat different philosophy and approach, for example, in incorporating the importance of family and the use of more child-directed teaching methods.

Q3: *What do you recall about the early days of the "Lab School"? How does it compare now?*

A: I'm not sure how far back the Lab School existed, though some photographs that I saw in our library's Special Collections suggest that this school was there in the early years of the 20th century. A new building, with a separate wing that included two preschool classrooms, was constructed for the School of Home Economics in the 1950s. Having a facility that had space specifically dedicated for early childhood education was important in ensuring inclusion of the Lab School in Home Economics programs.

As I already mentioned, when I joined the faculty of Home Economics, the Lab School was a part-time preschool program. During the second year in my position, the Student Body President of our university approached me with a proposition. There were an increasing number of students on campus who were also parents of young children, she said. Since our facility was only in use 2 hours per day, 4 afternoons a week, would we be willing to open it to children of students in the mornings? On a trial basis, we agreed to operate a program three mornings per week, from 9:00 a.m. to noon, for the children of university students. The program was a great hit and we expanded it the next semester to five mornings a week, starting at 8:00 a.m. Within a few years, it became evident that our students learned just as much in working with the children of students as they did with the carefully selected children in the Child Development Lab. The Lab was eventually discontinued and full-day child care became available. Over those initial years, there was also interest from faculty and staff parents and, eventually, our program served all campus families. In addition, through a grant from the State Department of Education, we included children with special needs in the program.

In the mid–1980s, an increasing need for infant and toddler care on campus emerged. A new director of our children's program spearheaded development of three new classrooms—one for infants, one for 1–year–olds, and one for 2–year–olds. A couple of years later, the university allocated a nearby building, which had formerly been a privately owned preschool, to our Center. This facility housed a mixed-age classroom and a kindergarten. Thus, within a few years, our Center went from serving 40 campus children and families to serving about 100. As the campus grows, so does the need for child care. This need will shape what the future holds for the Center.

Q4: *When thinking about HDFS "back then" to HDFS "now," what are your impressions? Do you think it's headed in the right direction? What are the prospects for the future?*

A: HDFS, in the early years of my career, was one part of a larger whole. The importance of maintaining an integrated program was often emphasized. I think there has been a proliferation of research which has contributed to HDFS growing into a strong presence of its own. The issues for earlier Home Economics programs had much to do with the promotion of successful home management. Now the field is both broader and narrower. It is broader in the sense that there is a huge range of research areas that continue to define and refine HDFS. It is narrower in that it is more focused than it had been in the past. Home Economics depended on the interaction and connection among specified areas important to families; HDFS today contributes a wide range of relevant research in the areas of HDFS. I think the future of HDFS is promising. HDFS programs today are rarely in Home Economics units; rather they can be found joined with a variety of other academic disciplines, such as education, health sciences, or social justice. As such, they are able to enrich and add their unique contributions to those fields.

THE FUTURE OF HDFS

The future is bright for HDFS programs. Higher education institutions across the United States are experiencing exponential growth in HDFS majors, as the demand for positions that benefit from knowledge of human development and working with families increases. We have experienced this growth firsthand at our institution. Just 4 years ago, our HDFS program had 183 students enrolled. This year, we had close to 400. HDFS has grown to be one of the largest programs in our college. Because it does not prepare students for just one career track like nursing or teaching programs, HDFS is sometimes overlooked when students initially declare their major as freshmen. Indeed, HDFS has been called a "discovery major" (Hagenbuch & Hamon, 2011) rather than a "destination degree" (Hamon & Smith, 2014). However, students find HDFS once they understand that this major serves as excellent preparation for work in the community involving children, adults, and families. Many HDFS programs also offer coursework related to early childhood education, thus entering the realm of educator preparation as well as the preparation of students for work in community agencies.

Image 3.2 Higher Education Institutions across the United States Are Experiencing Exponential Growth in HDFS Majors (photo by Robert Churchill/Depositphotos, Inc.).

We have not yet mentioned one of the directions that many HDFS programs are pursuing: CFLE certification. The NCFR, a national organization that promotes understanding of healthy family development and functioning, sponsors this internationally recognized certification for family life educators (FLEs) (NCFR, 2016a). A later chapter in this book will discuss the CFLE in more depth, but we want to introduce this certification to you here because it is relevant to our discussion of the future of HDFS.

HDFS programs that offer students a path toward earning the CFLE give them specific knowledge and experience in relevant areas related to working with families. Students are thus equipped with the skills to work in a variety of professional settings, for instance, social services, health services, education, government agencies, private or corporate organizations, and the military (NCFR, 2016b). Often job descriptions specify a degree or certification which is required or preferred for that job. As more agencies and organizations recognize the value of employees who are CFLEs, HDFS graduates will gain expanded access to a range of jobs for which they are qualified.

Image 3.3 Flipped Classrooms Dedicate More Class Time to Hands-on Learning (photo by Andriy Popov/Depositphotos, Inc.).

HDFS faculty are involved in many exciting areas of research, teaching, and community involvement, maintaining a rich connection to the three-part mission of land grant institutions (teaching, research, and service). Many of these existing and future areas of research and community involvement will be discussed in later chapters. Mirroring the national trends toward more innovative, experiential, and online approaches to teaching courses in institutions of higher education, teaching in HDFS programs also has changed. Although some HDFS courses may still be lecture-based, there is a growing trend toward more student involvement in the learning process, whether that be in the traditional college classroom, in the online course environment, or in hybrid courses that combine elements of the two. One innovative approach to teaching that has been used in HDFS programs is the "**flipped classroom**" model, which "dedicates more class time to hands-on learning, replacing lectures with supplemental materials, such as screencasts and videos, that students can view outside of class" (Bull, Ferster, & Kjellstrom, 2012, p. 10). One faculty member's experience using a flipped classroom is discussed in Box 3.2.

BOX 3.2 A FLIPPED FLE COURSE

Bridget A. Walsh

The flipped classroom model is gaining ground in family science programs (Greaves, 2015; Roehl, Reddy, & Shannon, 2013). In a flipped classroom, it is common to have students view the lecture online as part of homework or class preparation. Quizzes, discussion boards, and in-class activities all help to make sure that the flip is successful and that students benefit from viewing the lectures online (Greaves, 2015). One argument for flipping the classroom in family science programs is that it allows students to use class time to work with concepts in greater depth, advance their understanding, engage in collaborative learning, and it promotes students becoming more aware of their own learning processes compared to students in traditional classrooms (Roehl et al., 2013). FLE courses offered through family science programs may be candidates for flipped classrooms that blend in-person and online training to promote exposure to multiple modes of learning. The Birds and the Bees is an example of an FLE program that blends in-person and online training (see Hughes, Ebata, Bowers, Mitchell, & Curtiss, 2015).

Reflection on Flipped Course Successes and Future Improvements

In February 2016, the first author of this textbook and two students from the flipped FLE course met to reflect on the course. One student is an undergraduate HDFS student. The second student is a graduate student in Educational Leadership and works at a community college as the adult (non-traditional student) success coordinator.

Strengths of the flipped course included:

• serving as a catalyst to flip new-student orientations at the community college to allow for better engagement with content;

- allowing Millennials to better engage with the course due to the use of such technology as online lecture videos, discussion boards, online databases, and programs to create a poster for the FLE program;
- simplified workload for the instructor during the actual course;
- better overall engagement of students who applied concepts from the online lectures to create their FLE proposals;
- enabling students to learn at their own pace by repeating or pausing lectures to look up abbreviations or reread content in the text.

Possible future improvements for the course included:

- investing time at the beginning of the semester to discuss what a flipped classroom is and its benefits;
- requiring students to submit and reflect on progress reports on their engagement with online components;
- asking students to journal (e.g., questions or insights about any of the online content) after watching the lecture to facilitate in-class discussion, or asking students to write summaries of key points from the lectures;
- assigning grades to journaling and reflection activities, or to explicitly require students to use their insights during small- and large-group discussions.

Technology continues to proliferate in higher education and a flipped FLE class can have benefits for both the professor and the learners. This flipped FLE course could be used as a template for other FLE courses (Steffen, Aragona, & Walsh, 2016). At minimum, the successes and lessons learned from this flipped FLE course can provide the foundation for a good discussion with interested CFLEs, faculty, graduate students, and undergraduates.

Summary

1   History of the Study of HDFS:

   A   HDFS has been a field of study since the 1800s as part of larger programs of Home Economics.

   B   Home Economics began in Colleges of Agriculture with the passage of the Morrill Acts of 1862 and 1890.

   C   Many Home Economics programs had family living labs and child development labs to promote the practical application of what students were learning.

   D   HDFS was integrated into the study of Home Economics, but was separated out when Home Economics became viewed as anti-feminist and colleges were restructured.

2   Future of HDFS:

A   HDFS programs have flourished in the 21st century.

B   Today, HDFS programs are vibrant and dynamic, often including the option for students to gain certification as an FLE.

C   In keeping with the tradition of land grant institutions, HDFS faculty members are involved in innovative research, teaching, and service to the profession and the community.

D   One example of an innovation in teaching is the "flipped classroom."

Key Terms

child development laboratory
family living lab
flipped classroom
Morrill Acts
social science

Challenge: Integration

Interview the department chair or a faculty member in your HDFS program about the history, present, and future of your program. Below are some suggested interview questions. Think about these carefully and add to them where you see fit.

When conducting an interview, consider the following guidelines:

- It is helpful to send an interview request well in advance of your deadline to the faculty member or to the faculty member's administrative assistant.
- Include a list of prepared questions in your request so the faculty member can judge whether s/he would be an appropriate source or not, and can be prepared for your interview.
- Arrive on time for your interview, and conduct yourself professionally.
- It is a nice touch—although certainly not required—to send a thank you note to the faculty member to let him/her know that you appreciate the time spent with you.

Suggested Interview Questions

1   Can you spend some time briefly describing the history of our department/
    program? (When was it first developed? In what year did the first students
    graduate?)
2   What changes has the department/program undergone since the beginning
    years?
3   What is the history of the name of our department/program? Has it changed
    over time? Why/why not?
4   Is the department/program growing or shrinking in size? (Number of faculty?
    Number of students/majors?) Why?
5   Does our program offer FLE coursework?
6   Where do you see the department/program in 10 years? What are your
    goals?

Journal Questions

1   Find out if your institution of higher education is the "land grant" institution for
    your state. What does this mean?
2   How do you feel about the use of orphaned children as "practice babies" in
    the mid-20th century?
3   Does your program have a child development lab school? What is its mission?

SUGGESTED RESOURCES

American Association of Family and Consumer Sciences: www.aafcs.org.
Cornell's online exhibition on Home Economics: http://rmc.library.cornell.edu/homeEc/master-
    label.html.
The Irresistible Henry House (Lisa Grunwald's novel about a fictional "practice baby").

REFERENCES

American Association of Family and Consumer Sciences. (n.d.). *AAFCS Brand Story*. Retrieved
    from www.aafcs.org/res/branding/AAFCS_Brand_Story.pdf.
Bull, G., Ferster, B., & Kjellstrom, W. (2012). Inventing the flipped classroom. *Learning & Leading
    with Technology, 40*(1), 10–11.
Dyas, B. (2014, September 30). Who killed home ec? Here's the real story behind its demise.
    Huffington Post. Retrieved from www.huffingtonpost.com.

Goldstein, C. M. (2012). *Creating consumers: Home economists in twentieth-century America*. Chapel Hill: The University of North Carolina Press.

Greaves, K. (2015). The flipped classroom: A hybrid success story with a family survey course. A roundtable presentation at the NCFR conference, Vancouver, Canada.

Hagenbuch, D. J., & Hamon, R. R. (2011). Understanding student attitudes toward majoring in human development and family science. *Family Science Review, 16*, 1–21.

Hamon, R. R., & Smith, S. R. (2014). The discipline of family science and the continuing need for innovation. *Family Relations, 63*, 309–322.

Hans, J. D. (2014). Whither famology? Department name trends across four decades. *Family Relations, 63*, 323–332.

HEARTH. (2005). *Home economics archive: Research, tradition and history (HEARTH)*. Ithaca, NY: Albert R. Mann Library, Cornell University. Retrieved from http://hearth.library.cornell.edu.

Hughes, R., Ebata, A. T., Bowers, J., Mitchell, E. T., & Curtiss, S. L. (2015). Strategies for designing online family life education programs. In M. J. Walcheski & J. S. Reinke (Eds.), *Family life education: The practice of family science* (pp. 131–140). Minneapolis, MN: NCFR.

Morrill Acts of 1862 and 1890. Retrieved from www.1890universities.org/history.

NCFR. (2016a). CFLE certification.

NCFR. (2016b). Where are family life educators employed?

Roehl, A., Reddy, S. L., & Shannon, G. J. (2013). The flipped classroom: An opportunity to engage millennial students through active learning strategies. *Journal of Family & Consumer Sciences, 105*, 44–49.

Steffen, R., Aragona, P., & Walsh, B. A. (2016). Lessons and successes from piloting a flipped family life education course. A roundtable presentation at the National Council of Family Relations conference, Minneapolis, MN.

PART IV

Why Is HDFS Important?

How Does Theory and Research Inform Work in HDFS?

CHAPTER 4

Introduction to Research in HDFS

As a student in HDFS, it is likely that at some point you will begrudgingly (or perhaps happily) take a course on research methods. The reason why students face the topic of research methods with such apprehension is that they do not believe they will ever *conduct* research. It is true that some HDFS students will not conduct research beyond, perhaps, class projects. However, regardless of your career plans, a comprehensive understanding of research methods will enhance your education and better prepare you for your future career in HDFS.

First and foremost, as a student you will read a number of original journal articles as well as summaries of research in your textbook. Understanding research methods will allow you to better comprehend and critically examine the information presented in your other courses. For example, in a class on early childhood education you will likely read about multiple pedagogical approaches. If you read several journal articles that advocate for different and perhaps conflicting approaches to early childhood education, how might you reconcile this information? With a firm understanding of research methods, and the advantages and disadvantages of various methodologies, you will be able to form a comprehensive view of the HDFS literature. As one student articulates, being able to consume research enhances your overall education:

> Exploring others' research has kept me up-to-date on how children learn and develop and has provided me with knowledge to incorporate in my own interactions with children and families.
>
> (Heidi Cromer, Human Development and Family Studies)

Second, many undergraduate students wanting to work with individuals and families will become consumers of research in their professional careers (Ganong & Coleman, 1993). As more information is accumulated in a particular research area, recommended practices may change as well. As such it is likely that throughout your career you will need to stay up-to-date with the research literature in order to perform your duties adequately. For example:

> I read research articles on a regular basis from the fields of education, social work, and psychology. Keeping current on research is imperative for me to work effectively with children, families, and staff. I regularly incorporate research into my teacher meetings, reflective supervision, and home visitor meetings. Additionally, I supervise interns from Social Work and Human Development and Family Studies and incorporate research information into their internships so they are aware of the latest developments.
>
> (Becky Carter-Steele, Family and Community Partnership Coordinator)

Third, for many of you, consuming (and perhaps even conducting!) research may surprisingly be a part of your future career. Therapists, FLEs, early childhood professionals, and community organizers may all find themselves needing to evaluate the effectiveness of certain techniques, interventions, or programs. For example, Dr. Weiser was involved in a research project that evaluated an after-school program aimed at increasing junior high school girls' interest in science. In order for the program to receive the money needed to fund it, the program was required to be evaluated in order to gauge its effectiveness. The individual who developed and ran the program then unexpectedly found herself as a member on a research team studying adolescent girls' attitudes toward science! Therefore, even if you plan to enter a career that is not research based, it is still always possible that you will find yourself engaged in research.

Finally, although it seems far away, a number of you likely will attend graduate school. There is a wide variety of graduate degrees open to individuals who major in HDFS. As a graduate student in the social sciences, you will likely be expected to take advanced statistics and research methods courses, as well as conduct your own original research. A working knowledge of research methods will not only prepare you for graduate school, but a strong research background will likely make your applications to graduate programs more competitive.

For these reasons, we think students studying HDFS should learn as much as possible about research. Many colleges and universities support increasing undergraduate exposure to research experiences (Behar-Horenstein & Johnson, 2010; Taraban & Logue, 2012). Such undergraduate research experiences can contribute to students' problem solving, communication, intellectual curiosity, future confidence, and even positively influence how they contribute later to their disciplines and society (Taraban & Logue, 2012). The nature of undergraduate research varies across and within disciplines (Halstead, 1997), and ranges from understanding and evaluating research results to conducting and presenting novel research.

> Successfully reading and interpreting a research article requires a basic understanding of research methods. Being required to create a research proposal at the undergraduate level has made reading articles less intimidating in graduate schoo.
>
> (Katrina Lawson, 1st Year Graduate Student in Masters of Arts in Counseling with emphasis in School Counseling)

The purpose of the current chapter is to begin introducing you to some important research concepts in HDFS. First, we will explain what we mean by research. We will then briefly discuss issues surrounding participant selection and research ethics. Next, we will go into more detail about particular methods you are likely to encounter as a student in HDFS. Finally, we will discuss how researchers, as well as students, present and analyze research in a comprehensive manner.

WHAT IS RESEARCH?

Research in general may be considered the process of asking questions and discovering answers (Keyton, 2011). When scholars discuss research, we are typically referring to **empirical research**. Empirical research is when individuals use systematic observations to test hypotheses, or predictions that can be tested, and answer research questions. Thus, empirical research relies on data that are collected in an organized manner to uncover a specific set of questions.

One type of empirical research is **basic research**. Basic research is conducted to test and build theories. A **theory** is a set of interconnected ideas that logically explain a particular pattern of behaviors and events (Doherty, Boss, LaRossa, Schumm, & Steinmetz, 1993). Throughout this textbook, you will be introduced to a number of theories within the field of HDFS. The main purpose of basic research is to develop theories and generate general information, with little emphasis placed on real-world applications (Bordens & Abbott, 2014). Rather than focusing on real-world applications, individuals interested in basic research instead play around with ideas in order to develop theoretical models that explain human behavior.

The other type of empirical research is **applied research**. Applied research continuously informs the work we do with individuals and families. Applied research is aimed at solving day-to-day problems within the area of HDFS. The development of an intervention designed to promote parents' involvement in their child's learning is an example of applied research.

Much of the research done in HDFS has an applied focus and professionals are in a position to make connections between research and practice. For example, professionals working with young children are susceptible to hearing such expressions as "all you do is play all day" (Baum & McMurray-Schwarz, 2007). Many studies have been conducted that explain why play is beneficial. For example, play is related to a healthy self-concept (Nelson, Hart, & Evans, 2008). Developmentally appropriate practice, which is based on research, suggests that play is important for developing self-regulation and promoting language (Copple & Bredekamp, 2009). Findings from two survey studies published in one empirical article revealed that mothers and child development professionals have different beliefs about play but one common finding is that these two groups believe that children's play is a foundation for future academic learning (Fisher, Hirsh-Pasek, Golinkoff, & Gryfe, 2008). Because of applied research we know that play promotes children's healthy development and should be a central component of early childhood education.

It is often simplistic to define research as either basic or applied because many research areas have both basic and applied components (Bordens & Abbott, 2014). Applied research may have implications for theory, and basic research may also be used to inform practices in the real world. Bandura (1992) proposed that social cognitive theory be used in interventions aimed at preventing AIDS. Programs could be developed based on the principles of social cognitive theory (e.g., building self-efficacy enhances the likelihood of safer sex practices). Research could then be conducted to test the effectiveness of such intervention programs. The findings of the research would then have an applied outcome (Are the programs effective?) as well as a basic outcome (Are the ideas of social cognitive theory supported?). An important point here is that the best research, even if the major focus is applied work, should be grounded in theory.

WHO PARTICIPATES IN RESEARCH STUDIES?

One of the most important choices researchers must make when conducting research is selecting who will be asked to participate in their research. Depending on the purpose of the study and the intended methodology, researchers may choose from an array of **sampling techniques**. Sampling technique refers to the strategy researchers use to recruit participants. Typically, researchers conducting **quantitative research** will utilize different sampling techniques from researchers conducting **qualitative research** because each research type has different goals. We will discuss additional distinctions between quantitative and qualitative research in the next section, but briefly introduce these research types here in order to explain the strengths and limitations of different sampling techniques.

Quantitative research generates numerical data and uses statistical analyses to answer research questions. A goal of quantitative research is to generate conclusions that may describe the variables of interest in general. Quantitative researchers are therefore interested in selecting participants who are representative of the general population, and typically gather data from lots of participants. Quantitative researchers will use a variety of **probability** and **nonprobability sampling** techniques. Probability sampling (or **random sampling**) means that every person from a known group has an equal opportunity to be selected to participate in the study. We can then assume to a certain degree that the individuals who take part in the study are representative of the larger group. For example, if a researcher was interested in conducting a study on the relationship satisfaction of newlyweds in a large metropolitan area, he may acquire a list from the appropriate government office of all individuals who had applied for a marriage license in the last year. He could then randomly select individuals from the list and these selected individuals will be asked to participate in the study. Because selection was random (i.e., every person had equal odds of being selected), we can assume that the individuals selected to participate in the study look like the population in general. That is, we expect from random sampling individuals of varying ages, ethnicities, relationship lengths, relationship satisfaction, family histories, etc. to be recruited for the study. Essentially, there is no distinct reason that one individual is included in the study while another from the same group is not, thus we expect that our sample will be able to represent or be generalized to the larger population. Because of that assumption, the findings of the researcher may be generalized to a greater degree than those of a researcher using nonprobability sampling.

Nonprobability sampling means that not every individual of a larger group has a known and equal chance of participating in research. Typically, quantitative researchers using nonprobability sampling rely on large numbers of individuals who are easily and

Image 4.1 Probability Sampling (or Random Sampling) Means that Every Person from a Known Group Has an Equal Chance of Being Selected for a Study (photo by Robert Churchill/Depositphotos, Inc.).

readily available to participate in the research. For example, the same researcher who wished to study relationship satisfaction among newlyweds could have asked local places of worship to advertise his study and request volunteers. However, we cannot assume that the resulting sample will be representative of the greater population. Instead, it is likely that individuals recruited from places of worship will be much higher in religiosity, and may report different relationship qualities and family histories compared to the general population. Essentially, by using nonprobability sampling the results of the study may be generalized to a lesser degree.

You can see the difference between probability and nonprobability sampling illustrated in Figure 4.1. By using probability sampling, the researcher is able to recruit participants who are representative of each group in the population. The conclusions of the study then are much broader. However, the researcher using nonprobability sampling does not gather as representative of a group and therefore their conclusions are a bit more limited. The results of a study are still certainly meaningful but it is important to keep this limitation in mind.

As you read about research studies, it is important to keep in mind how researchers recruited participants for a study. Using probability sampling certainly strengthens the findings of a quantitative research study. However, nonprobability sampling techniques typically result in an adequate sample, although the conclusions of the study may not be as easily generalized as those obtained from studies using probability sampling (Keyton, 2011). Researchers often use nonprobability sampling techniques because such a strategy is easier to undertake and often less costly. If probability sampling is not possible for researchers to conduct, nonprobability sampling offers a good alternative in order to ensure that an important research study is conducted. This is why the vast majority of social science research utilizes a sample convenient to researchers: college students!

In contrast to quantitative researchers, qualitative researchers use verbal and textual data, and analyze the participants' actual words. Qualitative researchers are interested in gathering highly detailed, contextual information about their participants. Qualitative

Probability sampling

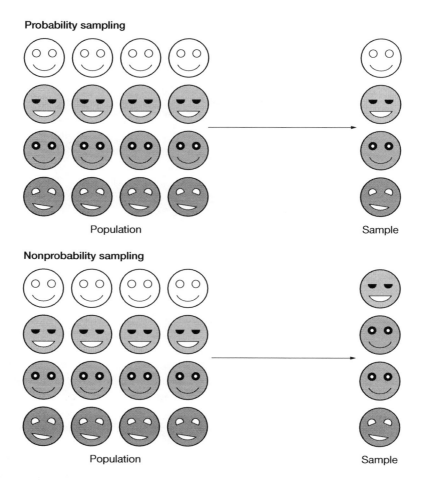

Population   Sample

Nonprobability sampling

Population   Sample

Figure 4.1 Sampling.

researchers tend to select participants or data sources (e.g., obituaries, television commercials) based on their information value (Acock, van Dulmen, Allen, & Piercy, 2005). Simply put, this means that qualitative researchers are interested in gathering data from smaller groups of participants and focusing in depth about particular participants' experiences. In qualitative research, nonprobability sampling techniques are used almost exclusively because researchers are interested in getting information from a smaller number of data sources and generalization is not a major goal. Therefore, in qualitative research, such sampling techniques should not be viewed as a limitation. Rather, qualitative researchers seek out particular individuals in order to gain insight into those individuals' experiences.

Image 4.2 Qualitative Researchers Use Verbal and Textual Data, and Analyze the Participants' Actual Words (photo by Sean Prior/Depositphotos, Inc.).

HOW DO WE PROTECT PARTICIPANTS?

Regardless of how participants, or people, are selected, it is vitally important for researchers to follow ethical guidelines that protect participants and subjects (animals and/or people). Ethics are important for working with and studying individuals, couples, or families in the context of practice and research. As such, a number of ethical guidelines have been developed over the years and all researchers are expected to follow these rules. Prior to conducting research with participants, the study procedures will need to be approved by an Institutional Review Board (IRB). An IRB is a group that reviews the research protocol to make sure that participants will be honored in an ethical manner. Overall, researchers must comply with three general ethical principles: Beneficence, Respect for Persons, and Justice (Belmont Report, 1978).

Beneficence means that the wellbeing of participants is ensured and that any possible risks associated with participating in the research are minimized. Central to the idea of beneficence is that the benefits of the study must outweigh any potential risks for participants. **Respect for persons** means that researchers provide potential participants with detailed information about the procedures of a study prior to participation, which allows individuals to make an informed decision as to whether they want to participate. Respect for persons also means that researchers protect those individuals who are not able to give consent to participate themselves. In HDFS, this issue is of the upmost importance as researchers who study children and adolescents will also need permission from parents or legal guardians for minors to participate. In order to ensure respect for persons, researchers will also inform participants that their participation is completely voluntary and that they may stop participation at any point in time without a penalty. **Justice** deals with the idea that all participants should be dealt with fairly and equally. Justice also entails that researchers carefully select their participants so that no one group is unfairly targeted for participation because of the group's easy availability or manipulability (i.e., with prisoners, individuals of low socioeconomic status, etc.) (Belmont Report, 1978).

Researchers, practitioners, and other professionals must also be concerned with keeping all information provided by participants and clients private. NCFR provides a code of ethics intended to guide professional and research decisions. For example, one statement is "I will create data privacy and confidentiality guidelines respectful of family members and protective of their legal rights" (NCFR, 2012). Essentially, this means that no individuals besides the researchers or practitioners will have access to any form of data. Ethical principles inform many of the decisions researchers make about how to conduct research, including the selection of the method. As you will see in the following section, researchers have many options available for how to gather data and test their research questions, each with limitations and strengths.

POPULAR METHODS

There are a plethora of research methods, and it is tempting to feel overwhelmed by the variety of methods, such as experiments, surveys, ethnographic studies, and action research (Ganong & Coleman, 1993). Ideally, understanding a variety of methods will help form the foundation for consuming reports of research about individuals and families (Acock et al., 2005). We already introduced the differences between quantitative and qualitative research, although both approaches have many features in common (Acock et al., 2005). For example, quantitative and qualitative research methods both use systematic observations to describe and explain a phenomenon of interest, and should be considered equally empirical.

The major distinction between quantitative and qualitative methods is the type of data researchers collect. Quantitative researchers collect numerical and categorical data with the goal of using statistical analyses to test research questions. Quantitative researchers assume they are able to accurately measure theoretical constructs in a numerical manner (Wampler & Halverson, 1993). For example, in order for a quantitative researcher to do work studying self-esteem, a valid and a reliable measure of self-esteem must be administered to participants. **Validity** refers to the idea that the measure successfully captures the theoretical construct (e.g., self-esteem), and **reliability** refers to the idea that the construct is measured in a consistent manner. The quantitative researcher may accomplish this by having participants complete a self-esteem questionnaire that will give each participant a numerical value that represents their level of "self-esteem." The quantitative researcher may then explore differences between individuals on self-esteem scores or whether self-esteem relates to other constructs, such as agreeableness.

In qualitative studies, researchers interpret participants' own words in order to capture the complexity of individuals' experiences (Rosenblatt & Fischer, 1993), and little to no focus is given to numerical values and statistical analyses. Qualitative research is most appropriate when researchers want to understand participants' unique viewpoints and how they create meaning (Rosenblatt & Fischer, 1993). Instead of focusing on how participants may compare to one another with regards to self-esteem, qualitative researchers focus on how each individual participant views their self-esteem and how they believe the construct is a part of their lives. The qualitative researchers will then explore how patterns and themes emerge from participants' narratives. Qualitative researchers analyze the data by becoming familiar with the participants' words and extracting meaning from the information shared with researchers.

Another distinction between quantitative and qualitative research is the role of the researcher while conducting a project. Quantitative researchers assume a certain level of objectivity since conclusions are interpreted through statistics. Certainly, quantitative researchers make a number of decisions during the research process but the data is not interpreted solely through the eyes of the researcher. In contrast, qualitative researchers explicitly acknowledge that their research is somewhat subjective, as all data are collected and interpreted through the lens of the researcher. Some researchers use reliability procedures to promote the trustworthiness of their findings. Because of this analytical process, multiple interpretations are always possible in qualitative research and it is vital that researchers determine the most credible explanation (Acock et al., 2005).

There tends to be a gross underrepresentation of qualitative articles in flagship development journals like *Developmental Psychology* and *Child Development*. Specifically, from 2000 to 2010 only 0.3% of articles from *Child Development* and 0.2% of articles from *Developmental Psychology* were categorized as qualitative (Walsh, Burnham, Pasley, & Maitoza, 2014). In a similar vein, Taylor and Bagd's (2005) analysis of *Journal of Marriage and the Family* revealed that quantitative articles (94%) were more common than qualitative articles (2.6%). We are unsure why this low representation of qualitative work exists in flagship journals in the field of development and the field of family. Nonetheless, we agree with Ganong, Coleman, and Demo (1995) that students should learn as much as possible about qualitative and quantitative approaches.

Because HDFS is multidisciplinary, studies may be qualitative, quantitative, or mixed. Mixed-methods research includes components of both quantitative and qualitative studies. In fact, to only focus on quantitative *or* qualitative methods should be considered a limitation within the field (Creswell, 2003). Studies that use both quantitative and qualitative methods could be used to approach research questions about individuals and families from more than one angle. Thus, as a field we are increasingly focusing on how methodologies may complement one another in order to answer research questions from multiple perspectives.

Experiments and Quasi-Experiments

Two types of quantitative research methodologies are experiments and quasi-experiments. Likely, what you think of as scientific research is an **experiment**. In an experiment, the researcher seeks to understand the effects of the independent variable (or causal variable) on the dependent variable (or outcome variable). The independent variable is what the researcher manipulates and then determines whether it had an impact on the dependent variable. Typically, in an experiment researchers will compare two or more groups in which participants receive different values of the independent variable. The researcher will subsequently compare values of the dependent variable based on the value of the independent variables participants received.

A major component of experimental research is **random assignment**. Random assignment means that researchers will sort participants into groups (typically known as a control condition and an experimental condition) in a random manner. The researcher is then able to assume that all groups start off approximately equal and that any changes in the dependent variable are due to the manipulation of the independent variable. Because of random assignment and the manipulation of the independent variable, researchers who conduct experiments are able to make some assumptions about causality. No other research method allows researchers to begin to say that variables have a causal relationship.

For example, the researchers may examine the effects of different types of adult questioning styles during storybook reading on young children's vocabulary skills (see Walsh & Rose, 2013). The researchers purposely manipulate the questioning styles (independent variable) to measure the impact of this on how many new words are learned (dependent variable) during the storybook reading. In an experiment, the researcher randomly assigns participants to the experimental condition or the control condition, meaning that each participant has an equal chance of being in the experimental or control conditions.

The researchers may administer a pretest to examine the dependent variable prior to the intervention. Walsh and Rose (2013) used matched random assignment to ensure that in the three conditions, the groups were not significantly different in terms of vocabulary knowledge. In one experimental condition, storybooks were read to young children with adults asking questions that include the novel words (e.g., What color are the *snowcaps*?) during the storybook readings (Walsh & Rose, 2013). In the other experimental condition, the storybook was read with the adults asking questions that did not include the novel words (e.g., What is on top of the mountain?) (Walsh & Rose, 2013). In the control condition, the reader received storybook readings without any questions to be asked by the adult reader (Walsh & Rose, 2013). All the groups were compared on their scores on vocabulary tests, which are the dependent variable, after the intervention or at posttest. It can then be assumed that any differences between groups on the vocabulary tests are due to the intervention.

Sometimes researchers are not able to randomly assign participants to conditions. This may be because of ethical reasons or because random assignment is not possible. In these cases, researchers may instead conduct what is known as a **quasi-experiment**. There are multiple types of quasi-experiments including time series designs, equivalent time samples designs, and nonequivalent control group designs (Bordens & Abbott, 2011). These designs are popular because researchers are often unable to randomly assign participants, particularly when researchers are studying real-world issues. For example, if researchers are interested in studying the impact of different teaching philosophies on student outcomes, it is unlikely that researchers will be able to randomly assign students to real-world classrooms. Instead, the researcher may assign each teacher to a condition; however, we cannot assume that the students in each classroom start off the same. Because of this, researchers are unable to make strong causal statements when conducting quasi-experiments. Quasi-experimental designs are important because they allow researchers to explore a number of very important issues in a scientific manner when conducting a true experiment is not possible.

Observational Research

Observational research may take the form of either quantitative or qualitative research. The central feature of observational research is what the name implies; researchers gather data by observing individuals' behaviors. In observational studies, researchers code and record what participants say and do. Researchers may take detailed notes about participants' behaviors or actually record these behaviors with video or audio recordings. The method gives little insight into individuals' beliefs, attitudes, or intentions but a great deal

Image 4.3 The Central Feature of Observational Research Is to Gather Data by Observing Individuals' Behaviors (photo by IOFOTO Images/Depositphotos, Inc.).

of information is garnered by focusing on individuals' words and behaviors. Quantitative researchers who collect data via observation often do so with well-developed categories in mind prior to data collection. For example, Madhyastha, Hamaker, and Gottman (2011) had couples engage in a conflict discussion and coded their discussions for positive and negative affect using an existing coding system (the Specific Affect Coding System). This allowed the researchers to systematically categorize participants' behaviors as either possessing positive or negative affect qualities, and the researchers then used the coded behaviors in statistical analyses.

In contrast, qualitative researchers typically record observations in a manner that describes both the environment as well as participants' actions in a holistic manner. Qualitative researchers capture as much information as possible about the context during observations. It is during and after data collection that researchers begin categorizing and coding data as themes and patterns emerge. Therefore, qualitative researchers allow the observations to guide data analysis whereas quantitative researchers begin with a much more detailed analysis plan in mind prior to data collection. Qualitative researchers using observational data analyze their data by exploring participants' words and actions, but, again, do not use statistical analyses.

The quality of both quantitative and qualitative research designs is dependent on the quality of the data collection. Researchers must follow their data collection plan and pay close attention in order to ensure that they are capturing all information relevant to the study. If a certain behavior is missed by the researcher, then valuable data may be left out of the study. Therefore, in observational research it is particularly important to have well-trained and motivated individuals doing the data collection and coding. Additionally, it is important to note that observational research is typically descriptive in nature and because of that researchers may make no conclusions about causality. Researchers are able to describe in depth what behaviors occur and who is more likely to engage in certain actions, but should be careful to avoid statements which imply that one variable causes a certain behavior to occur.

Surveys

The **survey** is a quantitative methodology that is very popular among researchers. In direct contrast to observational research, surveys allow researchers to gather information about participants' beliefs, attitudes, thoughts, feelings, and private (non-observable) behaviors. However, surveys provide little information about what participants actually say and do. Essentially, the strength of survey methodology is that it allows researchers to gather information from participants that may not be easily observed (Groves et al., 2009). Researchers utilizing the survey methodology typically have participants fill out multiple questionnaires. These questionnaires may ask participants about their demographics (i.e., age, gender, relationship status) and behaviors (i.e., how many cigarettes they smoked in the last month), as well as more theoretical constructs (e.g., attachment style, attitudes toward jaywalking, etc.).

Researchers must be careful in how they phrase questions for surveys so they can ensure that participants are able to understand the questions, and that all participants interpret the question in the same way (Groves et al., 2009). Good survey questions are clear and concise, simple and straightforward, and allow for little ambiguity in how a participant should respond (Dillman, Smyth, & Christian, 2009). Survey questions may be classified as either closed-ended or open-ended. Closed-ended questions give the participants a set of responses from which to respond (like a multiple choice test) while open-ended questions allow participants to respond in their own words and they are not limited to pre-selected responses. Many of you are likely familiar with a Likert-scale, which is a commonly used type of closed-ended question. A Likert-scale provides participants with a series of statements, which they are asked to rate in some manner, typically how much they agree or disagree with a statement. Below is an example of a Likert-scale item taken from the Adult Attachment Questionnaire (Simpson, Rholes, & Phillips, 1996):

I find it relatively easy to get close to others.

1	2	3	4	5	6	7
Strongly disagree						Strongly agree

One of the goals of survey research is to describe participants' self-reported attitudes, beliefs, and behaviors in general. Researchers who conduct surveys are interested in gathering data from a large number of people who will provide a wide variety of opinions that may represent the greater population. Therefore, researchers utilizing survey methods are very conscious of how participants are selected. Researchers utilizing probability sampling are able to make stronger conclusions about their findings because they have gathered data from a wide variety of individuals who should represent the general population. How a survey is conducted also has implications for the conclusions researchers may draw. Researchers may gather survey data in-person, online, through the mail, or over the telephone and there are advantages and disadvantages to each approach (Dillman et al., 2009). Researchers who collect data online may get lots of data from younger people who frequently access the internet and feel comfortable responding to questionnaires online. Thus, the researchers' conclusions may be a bit biased because more data were gathered from younger individuals than older individuals who are less likely to interact online. In contrast, if researchers collected data over the phone, they may oversample older individuals because, typically, researchers only have access to landline phone numbers, rather than cellular phone numbers. Finally, survey research is a descriptive method, meaning that because no independent variables are manipulated and participants are not randomly assigned, it is therefore impossible to make causal conclusions.

Developmental Designs

Because human development is about growth, stability, and change across the lifespan, the three developmental designs included in this section support the study of age effects. These designs allow researchers to study how variables of interest are related to individuals' ages. It is impossible to conclude that age causes changes in individuals' behaviors or beliefs, but researchers may use the data to examine how these variables are related. The three designs are longitudinal, cross-sectional, and cross-sequential.

Longitudinal studies examine the same group of participants, about the same age, across time. For example, the Early Childhood Longitudinal Study-Kindergarten Class followed children in kindergarten in 1998–1999 to middle school in the United States. Using data from this analysis, Bratter and Kimbro (2013) have examined the poverty profile of multiracial (e.g., the mother of child identified as White and the father of the child identified as Black) kindergarteners. In longitudinal studies, researchers are able to assess how individuals change and mature over time. One limitation of the methodology though is that there are possible cross-generational effects (Bordens & Abbott, 2011). In other words, longitudinal designs allow researchers to see how one generation matures but we may not find the same patterns with subsequent generations who are exposed to other cultural and historical circumstances. Longitudinal studies may also be difficult to conduct as many participants may choose to not continue to participate or researchers may have difficulty reaching individuals over the years.

Cross-sectional studies allow researchers to study different ages of participants at approximately the same time. Each participant's *chronological age* is then the major variable of interest. A recent cross-sectional study investigated age differences in motivational processes by administering assessments of the Big Five in a sample of participants spanning from ages 16 to 60 (Lehmann, Denissen, Allemand, & Penke, 2013). The main limitation of cross-sectional studies is that they do not take into account generational effects (Bordens & Abbott, 2011). In a cross-sectional study, it is then difficult to tell whether differences are due specifically to age, or because of cultural and historical changes. In a hypothetical cross-sectional study on comfort using cell phones, younger people likely will report greater comfort using cell phones. However, it would be unclear as to whether this is due to age or because the younger individuals were born into a society with cellular technology.

Cross-sequential studies allow researchers to get the best of both worlds. That is, they combine the hallmarks of longitudinal and cross-sectional studies. Schaie and Strother (1968) investigated age and generation differences in cognitive behavior. Participants ranging in age from 20 to 70 years were administered cognitive behavior assessments and then assessed again 7 years later. Such a design allows researchers to explore both age effects as well as generational effects. Once again though, it may be difficult to conduct such a study because researchers must be in consistent contact with participants.

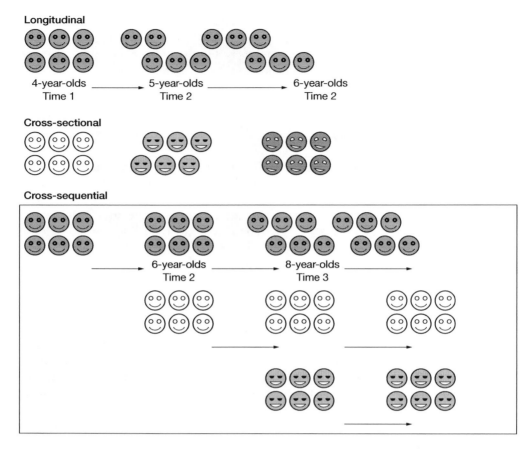

Longitudinal

4-year-olds ⟶ 5-year-olds ⟶ 6-year-olds
Time 1   Time 2   Time 2

Cross-sectional

Cross-sequential

⟶ 6-year-olds ⟶ 8-year-olds ⟶
    Time 2   Time 3

Figure 4.2 Developmental Designs.

Qualitative Interviews

In-depth **qualitative interviews** are the most common qualitative research method (Rosenblatt & Fischer, 1993). Researchers who conduct qualitative interviews are primarily interested in participants' viewpoints. Qualitative interviews usually follow a rather flexible outline in which the researcher has a broad plan about which topics should be discussed, but allows the conversation to unfold naturally. Instead of the researcher determining what topics are to be discussed, often it is the participant who guides the interview as they discuss how they create meaning and experienced a particular life event. Again, no statistical analyses are used. Instead, the researcher focuses on participants' words and extracts meaning from the patterns they observe. This methodology gives great detailed insight into how a few particular individuals experience their social world.

Exploring Culture and Ethnographies

Culture is an example of context. In the next chapter, you'll learn about theories that emphasize context, such as Bronfenbrenner's bioecological systems theory (Bronfenbrenner

Image 4.4 Researchers Will Typically Immerse Themselves in a Culture for Weeks, Months, or Even Years during the Process of Ethnography (photo by Dorine Voorhout/Deposit-photos, Inc.).

& Morris, 2006). Culture in a general sense is part of the outermost system of the bio-ecological model. Cross-cultural research examines human development by exploring a variety of the world's cultures (Miller, 2013). For example, Hoxha and Hatala (2012) found differences between Albanian and American college students' romantic attitudes. Albanians tended to agree with traditional statements such as men paying on the first date whereas Americans agreed with more non-traditional statements, such as acceptance of women asking men on a date.

Ethnographies are one popular qualitative method used to study cultures in-depth. Ethnographies typically are conducted by researchers to gather a very detailed and holistic description of groups of individuals within a culture (Keyton, 2011). Typically, researchers will immerse themselves in a culture in order to understand how individuals create and experience their everyday lives within that culture. Researchers will typically immerse themselves in a culture for weeks, months, or even years. Usually, a tremendous amount of data is collected during the process of ethnography. It is likely that researchers will observe, conduct interviews, and take volumes of notes in order to comprehend how a cultural group functions.

Program Evaluation, Action Research, and Design-Based Research

Program evaluation, action research, and design-based research represent very broad research approaches that are commonly used by individuals within the field of HDFS. All three methodologies are utilized to conduct applied research. Researchers may use a number of specific methodological designs (experiments, surveys, qualitative interviews, etc.) to accomplish the main goal of designing and evaluating real-world programs to help improve the quality of life for a community. Thus, a variety of both quantitative and qualitative methods may be used in program evaluation, action research, and design-based research to develop interventions, trainings, teaching techniques, or community programs.

The goal of **program evaluation** is essentially what the name suggests: researchers evaluate the effectiveness of a specific program. Program evaluation involves a research team identifying a need within a community, developing a program that addresses the need, identifying the desired outcomes for this program, and then testing to see whether the program does indeed create these desired outcomes (Isaac & Michael, 1995). Program evaluations may therefore check for accountability (the program accomplishes what it is intended to) as well as provide feedback (based on data, the program may be improved). The overall research goal of program evaluation then is to test whether an established program is effective.

In contrast to program evaluation, **action research** is more dynamic and there is a cyclical process of program development and evaluation. Action research is often characterized by active participation of the individuals for whom a program is intended to serve. Participants who are able to help generate and develop action research programs often feel very committed to these projects and the programs typically better accommodate the intended recipients (Acock et al., 2005). In action research, individuals take on multiple roles in order to understand an issue and create positive change to address this issue (Kemmis, 2009). Action research is also very process oriented, in that the focus is on long-term program development, community involvement, and continual improvement.

Design–based research is conducted more specifically in the context of educational research and the main goal of such research is to evaluate a learning-based intervention. Design-based research is also characterized by collaboration between researchers, practitioners, and teachers (Anderson & Shattuck, 2012) but there is more emphasis on theory development in comparison to action research. In particular, individuals who conduct design-based research are not just interested in developing a program at a local level but also using program development to further inform educational research at a grander level. Design-based research is therefore considered a blend of both basic and applied research although researchers typically do focus more on the outcomes of the designed interventions (McKenney & Reeves, 2013). For example, Hung (2011) utilized a design-based research paradigm in order to test the effectiveness of a multimedia intervention for Taiwanese students learning English. In the study, the researcher not only evaluated whether the learning intervention was successful, but also explicitly tested contemporary theories about language learning and multimedia activities as an educational vehicle (Hung, 2011).

One of the major limitations of program evaluation, action research, and design-based research is that because the researchers often developed the program, their evaluation of the programs may be somewhat biased (Anderson & Shattuck, 2012). Therefore, often these methodologies may be considered to be a "double-edged sword," as interventions are designed by the individuals who are most knowledgeable about a community's need. It is then much harder for the researchers to objectively evaluate these programs.

WRITING ABOUT RESEARCH AND THE RESEARCH CYCLE

Many of you are probably already familiar with the scientific method shown in Figure 4.3. We present it here again to remind you of a few important points. The first point being that there is no such thing as a perfect research study. We have highlighted some

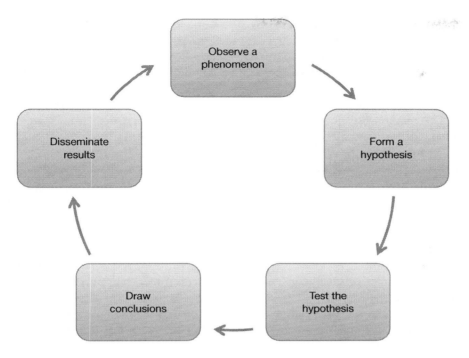

Figure 4.3 Scientific Method.

Note
This traditional depiction of the scientific method does not reflect the richness of scientific research. It does demonstrate that once researchers progress through the steps, they go back to the start and start again.

of the limitations of certain research methodologies, but it is important to remember that valuable information is gained even from imperfect studies. It is because of these limitations that new study ideas and techniques should develop from completed studies. This is why the scientific method is a circular process.

Another point to be made is that the sharing of scientific findings is a vital step in the research process so that new research questions may be formed. Throughout your educational career, it is likely that you will not only read summaries of research in your textbooks but you will also read original research articles. You, as a consumer of research, will be able to understand what researchers have done and why. The main components of a research article include:

The **abstract** or brief summary of what the research is about and appears first in the article (Gall, Gall, & Borg, 2010). The typical length of an abstract is 150 to 250 words (American Psychological Association (APA), 2010). As a consumer of research in HDFS, the abstract will help you decide whether you should invest in reading the entire article.

The **literature review** or **introduction** provides information about the need or rationale for the current study. This part of the research study often starts with an introduction to the problem area and an establishment of its relevance. The literature includes a synthesis of the extant quantitative and qualitative literature to help the reader understand the research and perspectives that already exist. The literature review is far more than summarizing past work, but explaining how all this information fits together and identifies the need for exploring a given topic.

Hypotheses and **research questions** are identified in the literature review and serve as a bridge to the method. Typically, a researcher furthering the investigation of a topic in a well-defined area will state hypotheses, which are typically a key part in the scientific method. See Figure 4.3. When there is not enough information in the existing literature to compose hypotheses, research questions or objectives will be stated.

The **method** is the recipe for how to study the research purpose or research questions. The method usually includes information about the participants, how they were recruited, what materials were used in the study, and the procedure.

The **results** section explains the procedure the researcher used to analyze data. If the research was quantitative in nature, then there will likely be a number of statistics presented. Do not be overwhelmed with the numbers and symbols you see. Rather, try to focus on the researcher's words. For a qualitative project, the results section will likely have a number of participants' quotes so that you as a reader can understand the themes and points the researcher is making.

The **discussion** section is perhaps the most important part of the research article. In the discussion, researchers summarize the results and also reflect on what their findings mean. Here, the researchers discuss how their particular project fits into a broader area of research. Upon reading a discussion section, you should understand what the researchers' conclusions are, and what they mean for the area of study. Researchers will also discuss the limitations and implications for their project. The results may matter for practice, policy, or future research with individuals and families.

The **references** include important information, such as the name of the author or authors, the date of publication, the title of the work, and the title of the journal (APA, 2010). References may be primary and secondary sources related to HDFS. A primary source is the firsthand account of research (Whitson & Phillips, 2009) and is typically a complete research report including information about the rationale for the study, the method, and results (Bordens & Abbott, 2011). A secondary source interprets a primary source (Whitson & Phillips, 2009), such as a published literature review or book (Bordens & Abbott, 2011). For examples of primary and secondary sources related to HDFS, see Table 4.1. Primary sources are typically preferred because then the reader is reading the original source for themselves, rather than how another individual has interpreted the study.

Table 4.1 Examples of Primary and Secondary Sources

Journal	Primary source	Secondary source	Primary and secondary source
American Educational Research Journal	X	–	–
American Psychologist	–	X	–
Child Development	X	–	–
Child Development Perspectives	–	X	–
Developmental Psychology	X	–	–
Educational Researcher	–	–	X
Family Relations: Interdisciplinary Journal of Applied Family Studies	–	–	X
Journal of Early Intervention	–	–	X
Young Children	–	X	–

As you read through the rest of the textbook, as well as in your future courses, we hope you keep in mind why an understanding of research methods is important. The information we have provided you should constitute a strong foundation with which you can begin your educational career in HDFS.

Summary

1   It is important to learn about research methods as such information will help you understand concepts introduced in class, as well as guide you throughout a career in HDFS.

2   Empirical research is when individuals make systematic observations in order to answer questions:

    A   Research may be basic, in which researchers develop theoretical models.

    B   Research may be applied, in which researchers are motivated to answer questions that help solve real-world problems.

3   Researchers choose from a number of sampling methods:

    A   Quantitative researchers may use both probability and nonprobability sampling techniques, although conclusions may be generalized to a greater degree when they use probability sampling.

    B   Qualitative researchers typically rely on nonprobability sampling techniques.

4   Researchers are always concerned about ethics and how participants, whether human or an animal, are treated:

    A   All research projects are reviewed by the IRB.

    B   Researchers are concerned with beneficence, respect for persons, justice, and keeping information private.

5   There are a number of research methodologies to choose from when conducting a study:

    A   Quantitative research relies on numerical data and researchers use statistical analyses to test questions, whereas qualitative researchers collect textual data and analyze their data by looking for themes and patterns.

    B   Experiments allow researchers to test causal relationships because they manipulate independent variables and utilize random assignment. If random assignment is not possible, researchers may conduct a quasi-experiment.

    C   Observational research allows researchers to gather data about individuals' actual behaviors.

Image 4.5 Researchers Who Collect Data Online May Gather More Data from Younger
People (photo by Alexander Raths/Depositphotos, Inc.).

D   Survey research allows researchers to gather data about beliefs, atti-
    tudes, and behaviors that are not easily observed.
E   Developmental designs study age effects and may include longitudinal,
    cross-sectional, or cross-sequential designs.
F   Qualitative interviews allow researchers to gather a great deal of informa-
    tion about participants' views and experiences.
G   Ethnographies facilitate the study of culture and are a very time-
    consuming research methodology.
H   Program evaluation, action research, and design-based research all allow
    researchers to explore the effectiveness of particular applied programs.

6   As you read research articles, it is important not only to understand the
    content but also to critically examine the researchers' findings and pose new
    ideas:

A   The major parts of a research article are the abstract, literature review/
    introduction, method, results, discussion and references.
B   A primary source is typically preferred over a secondary source.

Key Terms

abstract
action research
applied research
basic research
beneficence
cross-sectional studies
cross-sequential studies
design-based research
discussion
empirical research
ethics
ethnographies
experiment
hypotheses
justice
literature review
longitudinal studies
method
nonprobability sampling
observational research
probability sampling
program evaluation
reliability
results
qualitative interview
qualitative research
quantitative research
quasi-experiment
random assignment
references
research questions
respect for persons
sampling technique
surveys
theory
validity

Challenge: Integration

The purpose of this section is to locate a journal article that is of interest or meaning to you.

Think about a broad topic or question within HDFS that is interesting to you. If a topic does not readily come to mind, you might want to explore other chapters in this book to get some ideas or think about personal or professional experiences that are meaningful to you.

Once you have a broad topic or question in mind, think of synonyms for the keywords within the topic or question. For instance, let's pretend that you are interested in the question of "How do preschoolers learn new words?" Synonyms for "preschoolers" include young children and early childhood, and synonyms for "new words" include vocabulary and novel words.

Next, it is essential to use a computer or electronic database (e.g., OneSearch or PsycINFO) to search for a primary source or journal article. By entering keywords or synonyms into search fields, you will have access to bibliographic information, abstracts, and full-text articles published in journals. Once you select an article that addresses the broad question or topic, review the article and determine whether the keywords or search terms that you used were effective to getting you to an article of interest.

You learned in this chapter that the main components of a research article include the following: abstract, literature review or introduction, hypotheses and/or research questions, method, results or findings, discussion, and references. For each component, use the information that you learned in this chapter to make observations about the journal article you selected. For the method, you might observe how participants were recruited, what type of research design was used, what materials were needed, and how data was collected.

Journal Questions

1   How might you use an understanding of research methods in your future career?

2   Which method do you believe would be the most interesting to conduct and why?

3   If you were to conduct a research study, what question would you want to answer? What do you think would be the best method to test that question?

SUGGESTED RESOURCES

Babbie, E. R. (2013). *The practice of social research* (13th ed.). Belmont, CA: Cengage Learning.

Daly, K. J. (2007). *Qualitative methods for family studies and human development*. Thousand Oaks, CA: Sage.

Wysock, D. K. (2007). *Readings in social research methods* (3rd ed.). Belmont, CA: Thomson Wadsworth.

REFERENCES

Acock, A. C., van Dulmen, M. M. H., Allen, K. R., & Piercy, F. P. (2005). Contemporary and emerging research methods in studying families. In V. L. Bengston, A. C. Acock, K. R. Allen, P. Dilworth-Anderson, & D. M. Klein (Eds.), *Sourcebook of family theory & research* (pp. 22–25). Thousand Oaks, CA: Sage.

APA. (2010). *Publication manual of the American Psychological Association* (6th ed.). Washington, DC: APA.

Anderson, T., & Shattuck, J. (2012). Design-based research: A decade of progress in education research? *Educational Researcher, 41*, 16–25.

Bandura, A. (1992). A social cognitive approach to the exercise of control over AIDS infection. In R. J. DiClemente (Ed.), *Adolescents and AIDS: A generation in jeopardy* (pp. 89–116). Newbury Park, CA: Sage.

Baum, A. C., & McMurray-Schwarz, P. (2007). Research 101: Tools for reading and interpreting early childhood research. *Early Childhood Education Journal, 34*, 367–370.

Behar-Horenstein, L. S., & Johnson, M. L. (2010). Enticing students to enter into undergraduate research: The instrumentality of an undergraduate course. *Journal of College Science Teaching, 39*, 62–70.

Belmont Report. (1978). *The Belmont Report: Ethical principles and guidelines for the protection of human subjects of research*. Retrieved from http://videocast.nih.gov/pdf/ohrp_belmont_ report. pdf.

Bordens, K. S., & Abbott, B. B. (2011). *Research design and methods: A process approach* (8th ed.). New York: McGraw-Hill.

Bordens, K. S., & Abbott, B. B. (2014). *Research design and methods: A process approach* (9th ed.). New York: McGraw-Hill.

Bratter, J., & Kimbro, R. T. (2013). Multiracial children and poverty: Evidence from the Early Childhood Longitudinal Study of Kindergarteners. *Family Relations, 62*, 175–189.

Bronfenbrenner, U., & Morris, P. A. (2006). The bioecological model of human development. In W. Damon & R. M. Lerner (Eds.), *Handbook of child psychology: Vol. 1. Theoretical models of human development* (6th ed., pp. 793–828). Hoboken, NJ: Wiley.

Copple, C., & Bredekamp, S. (2009). *Developmentally appropriate practice in early childhood programs serving children from birth through age 8* (3rd ed.). Washington, DC: NAEYC.

Creswell, J. W. (2003). *Research design: Qualitative, quantitative, and mixed method approaches* (2nd ed.). Thousand Oaks, CA: Sage.

Dillman, D. A., Smyth, J. D., & Christian, L. M. (2009). *Internet, mail, and mixed-mode surveys: The tailored design method* (3rd ed.). Hoboken, NJ: Wiley.

Doherty, W. J., Boss, P. G., LaRossa, R., Schumm, W. R., & Steinmetz, S. K. (1993). Family theories and methods: A contextual approach. In P. G. Boss, W. J. Doherty, R. LaRossa, W. R. Schumm, & S. K. Steinmetz (Eds.), *Sourcebook of family theories and methods: A conceptual approach* (pp. 3–30). New York: Springer.

Fisher, K. R., Hirsh-Pasek, K., Golinkoff, R. M., & Gryfe, S. G. (2008). Conceptual split? Parents' and experts' perceptions of play in the 21st century. *Journal of Applied Developmental Psychology, 29*, 305–316.

Gall, M. D., Gall, J. P., & Borg, W. R. (2010). *Applying educational research* (6th ed.). Boston: Pearson.

Ganong, L. H., & Coleman, M. (1993). Teaching students how to evaluate family research. *Family Relations, 42*, 407–415.

Ganong, L. H., Coleman, M., & Demo, D. H. (1995). Issues in training family scientists. *Family Relations, 44*, 501–507.

Groves, R. M., Fowler, F. J., Jr., Couper, M. P., Lepkowski, J. M., Singer, E., & Tourangeau, R. (2009). *Survey methodology* (2nd ed.). Hoboken, NJ: Wiley.

Halstead, J. A. (1997). What is undergraduate research? *Journal of Chemical Education, 74*, 1390–1391.

Hoxha, E., & Hatala, M. N. (2012). A cross-cultural study of differences in romantic attitudes between American and Albanian college students. *College Student Journal, 46*, 467–469.

Hung, H. (2011). Design-based research: Designing a multimedia environment to support language learning. *Innovations in Education and Teaching International, 48*, 159–169.

Isaac, S., & Michael, W. B. (1995). *Handbook in research and evaluation: For education and the behavioral sciences* (3rd ed.). San Diego, CA: EdITS.

Kemmis, S. (2009). Action research as a practice-based practice. *Educational Action Research, 17*, 463–474.

Keyton, J. (2011). *Communication research: Asking questions, finding answers* (3rd ed.). New York: McGraw-Hill.

Lehmann, R., Denissen, J. J. A., Allemand, M., & Penke, L. (2013). Age and gender differences in motivational manifestations of the Big Five from age 16 to 60. *Developmental Psychology, 49*, 365–383.

Madhyastha, T. M., Hamaker, E. L., & Gottman, J. M. (2011). Investigating spousal influence using moment-to-moment affect from marital conflict. *Journal of Family Psychology, 25*, 292–300.

McKenney, S., & Reeves, T. C. (2013). Systematic review of design-based research progress: Is a little knowledge a dangerous thing? *Educational Researcher, 42*, 97–100.

Miller, S. A. (2013). *Developmental research methods* (4th ed.). Thousand Oaks, CA: Sage.

NCFR. (2012). *Family life educators code of ethics.* Retrieved from www.ncfr.org/sites/default/files/downloads/news/cfle_code__of_ethics_2012.pdf.

Nelson, L. J., Hart, C. H., & Evans, C. A. (2008). Solitary-functional play and solitary-pretend play: Another look at the construct of solitary-active behavior using playground observations. *Social Development, 17*, 812–831.

Rosenblatt, P. C., & Fischer, L. R. (1993). Qualitative family research. In P. G. Boss, W. J. Doherty, R. LaRossa, W. R. Schumm, & S. K. Steinmetz (Eds.), *Sourcebook of family theories and methods: A conceptual approach* (pp. 167–177). New York: Springer.

Schaie, K. W., & Strother, C. R. (1968). A cross-sequential study of age changes in cognitive behavior. *Psychological Bulletin, 70*, 671–680.

Simpson, J. A., Rholes, W. S., & Phillips, D. (1996). Conflict in close relationships: An attachment perspective. *Journal of Personality and Social Psychology, 71*, 899–914.

Taraban, R., & Logue, E. (2012). Academic factors that affect undergraduate research experiences. *Journal of Educational Psychology, 104*, 499–514.

Taylor, A. C., & Bagd, A. (2005). The lack of explicit theory in family research. In V. L. Bengston, A. C. Acock, K. R. Allen, P. Dilworth-Anderson, & D. M. Klein (Eds.), *Sourcebook of family theory & research* (pp. 22–25). Thousand Oaks, CA: Sage.

Walsh, B. A., Burnham, M. M., Pasley, C., & Maitoza, R. B. (2014). Explicit reference to theory: A content analysis of two prominent human development journals. *Family Science Review, 19*, 105–119.

Walsh, B. A., & Rose, K. K. (2013). Impact of adult vocabulary noneliciting and eliciting questions on the novel vocabulary acquisition of preschoolers enrolled in Head Start. *Journal of Research in Childhood Education, 27*, 31–45.

Wampler, K. S., & Halverson, C. F., Jr. (1993). Quantitative measurement in family research. In P. G. Boss, W. J. Doherty, R. LaRossa, W. R. Schumm, & S. K. Steinmetz (Eds.), *Sourcebook of family theories and methods: A conceptual approach* (pp. 181–194). New York: Springer.

Whitson, B., & Phillips, M. (2009). *Library research using primary sources.* Retrieved from www.lib.berkeley.edu/TeachingLib/Guides/Primary Sources.html.

CHAPTER 5

Introduction to Theories in HDFS

As you read throughout your academic and professional career, you will find there are a variety of theories and perspectives to inform our work in HDFS. Theory is an essential component to understanding our field and the foundation for all science. In fact, you can think of theory like the foundation of a building. The foundation is the bedrock which allows the building to rise soundly off the ground and provides long-term stability for the structure. Our HDFS theories are similarly a bedrock which allows research and practice to move forward in a logical manner, connects ideas and concepts, and provides stability and cohesion to the field.

WHAT IS A THEORY?

A **theory** is a set of interconnected ideas that logically explain a particular pattern of behaviors and events (Doherty, Boss, LaRossa, Schumm, & Steinmetz, 1993). More simply, theories are explanations constructed by scientists to explain why people behave and develop as they do (Bengston, Acock, Allen, Dilworth-Anderson, & Klein, 2005; Fine & Fincham, 2013). Theory may also be considered a *process* of developing ideas in order to reach these explanations (Bengston et al., 2005). Theories are developed and continuously refined over time and are based on observable evidence which may either support or fail to support the explanations offered by theory (White & Klein, 2008). In other words, theories are not just hunches or feelings that we have about the way the world works but are organized, evidence-based explanations. Theories are also a lens for practice. For example, a teacher that identifies with behaviorism may reinforce positive behaviors (e.g., providing a child with a gold star after good class participation).

All theories have certain core components. According to White and Klein (2008) all theories contain concepts, relations, and propositions. A **concept** (also called a construct) is an abstract, intangible idea or thing. Since they are abstract, concepts are not necessarily observable so we have to identify features which help us to more concretely define a concept. For example, the concept *aggression* cannot be directly measured because it is an abstract idea but we can measure observable behaviors like yelling, punching, or kicking (Fine & Fincham, 2013). **Relations** are the associations or links between concepts. So we could specify a relation that aggression in young children is associated with parental affection (another concept). A **proposition** is when concepts are related to one another in a meaningful and specific way (White & Klein, 2008). For example, a theoretical proposition would state that higher levels of aggression are observed in young children who receive lower levels of parental affection. Theories contain multiple propositions which systematically predict how individuals and families develop and behave.

Theories have numerous functions including helping scientists design studies, organize their findings, and make predictions. Theories are especially useful in HDFS because theories help us understand why researchers explored certain ideas and why individuals or programs used a particular educational or clinical approach. In the current chapter we will discuss some of the most popular theories in use today. However, this is not an exhaustive list of theories which you may encounter. Whenever you come across a new theory, we recommend that you investigate this new theory (e.g., do library research to find out more). This will help you understand the assumptions researchers, clinicians, educators, and practitioners are making and clarify new concepts and ideas to which you may be introduced. Finally, since theorizing is a process, new theories emerge and established theories continue to evolve so it is important to not think of theory as static (Dilworth-Anderson, Burton, & Klein, 2005).

BOX 5.1 RESEARCHERS' USE OF THEORY

As researchers in HDFS, we use a variety of theories to frame our own programs of research. Which theories we use are based on the topics and age groups we study as well as our personal philosophical approaches to these topics. Theory helps guide us to formulate hypotheses and develop ways to test our hypotheses. As you can see, theory guides research and research guides theory in a reciprocal relationship. Here you can read a couple of the ways your textbook authors have used theory in our own work.

According to Dr. Walsh:

In my applied research studies, I use theory to frame the study and to interpret the findings. For example, in a qualitative study on parental involvement (Walsh, Cromer, & Weigel, 2014) we used Bronfenbrenner's bioecological systems theory to frame an intervention that focused on the importance of strong home–school connections. The supportive links between the home and school promote child development and continuity between two microsystems (home and school). Bioecological systems theory highlights why it is beneficial to look at multiple contexts simultaneously in order to best understand human development.

According to Dr. Weiser:

> In my studies of family infidelity patterns, I typically use social learning theory to frame my work (Weiser, Weigel, Lalasz, & Evans, 2015). I study how the experience of parental infidelity is associated with young adults' likelihood of engaging in infidelity themselves. Social learning theory is a theoretical perspective which is often used to explore how behavioral patterns are replicated across generations. In my work, I find adults whose parents engaged in infidelity are more likely to have engaged in infidelity compared to adults whose parents did not engage in infidelity. I argue that the adult children whose parents cheated gained messages that infidelity was acceptable through modeling and direct communications. These experiences shape individuals' beliefs about infidelity, and help explain why we see these family infidelity patterns.

According to Dr. Burnham:

> In my studies of sleep development in childhood, we have used Developmental Systems Theory as a frame (Burnham & Gaylor, 2011; Ford & Lerner, 1992). Developmental Systems Theory (DST) recognizes the transactional nature of human development; a central proposition of the theory is that the person and his/her cultural, societal, and community context "dynamically interact" (Ford & Lerner, 1992, p. 11). DST is relevant for my work related to child sleep because I'm particularly interested in how sleep patterns develop across different contexts and how these contexts may drive variability in sleep patterns. For example, the decision of parents regarding where a new baby sleeps is influenced by individual characteristics of the child in transaction with family circumstances, beliefs and values of the family, where the family lives, the broader social context, and cultural values. At first glance, sleep is sleep. However, it's clear in the complex reality of families and framed using DST that sleep is sleep, in context.

BROAD THEORIES AND PERSPECTIVES

There are different levels of theories based on the scope and abstractness of ideas and propositions proposed by a particular theory (Dilworth-Anderson et al., 2005; Doherty et al., 1993). In this section, we will discuss some of the most popular expansive and abstract theories and perspectives used in HDFS. In other words, in this section we look at theories which may be considered general frameworks with which to view individuals and families. A framework consists of a number of concepts and some general assumptions about how these concepts are related (Dilworth-Anderson et al., 2005). A perspective is even broader than a theory and provides a wide lens through which to examine human development and families (Fine & Fincham, 2013). Typically, perspectives do not make specific predictions about how constructs are related but instead highlight important constructs to consider when explaining behavior.

Lifespan and Life Course Perspectives

A **lifespan perspective** is one of the most popular and widely used theoretical perspectives in HDFS. A lifespan perspective involves the study of development throughout the entire lifetime (Baltes, 1987). Too often individuals think of development as only occurring in the early years of life when in fact development occurs from before birth to death (i.e., womb to tomb). The lifespan perspective is concerned with understanding normative biological development (ontogenetic growth) as well as highlighting the tremendous amount of variability possible due to environmental context and within person traits (Baltes, 1987). The lifespan perspective also recognizes that development is not a simple linear process but rather forces of gain (growth) and loss (decline) are present at all ages (Baltes, 1987). For example, as an individual ages they acquire more knowledge and factual information but they may also experience a decline in memory functions. The primary focus of lifespan theory is individual growth but with an understanding that development occurs within a given sociocultural period and context (White & Klein, 2008).

Although some theorists view lifespan and life course perspectives as nearly the same (White & Klein, 2008), the **life course perspective** includes a few additional concepts. The life course perspective focuses on the timing and ordering of events that shape development (Bengston & Allen, 1993; Longmore, Manning, & Giordano, 2013). The life course perspective considers not only ontogenetic growth, but also events and family transitions which shape our life and how different generations may have different expectations for the life course. A life course perspective recognizes that our social environments are continuously changing and this impacts how we time life events (Bengston & Allen, 1993). Using a life course perspective, scholars in HDFS are often concerned if an event occurs on-time or off-time but the definition of what is on-time is evolving based on individuals' sociocultural context (Bengston & Allen, 1993). For example, the birth of a first child may be considered a developmental milestone but we would expect different life experiences for an individual who first becomes a parent at age 15, age 25, or age 45.

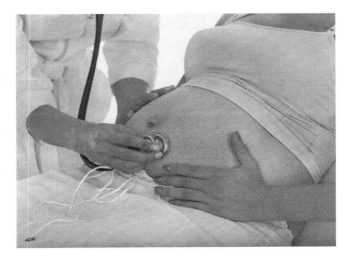

Image 5.1 Development Occurs from Before Birth (photo by Gennadiy Poznyakov/Depositphotos, Inc.).

In our current sociocultural period, we likely would consider both age 15 and age 45 to be off-time whereas 200 years ago, becoming a parent for the first time at 15 would have been on-time. Unquestionably, at any age becoming a parent is a milestone life event. Both lifespan and life course perspectives highlight the importance of lifetime growth and development and how a given context may impact or define development.

Bioecological Systems Theory

Bioecological systems theory is a broad theoretical perspective which has gone through many iterations since the theory was first developed (Rosa & Tudge, 2013). Urie Bronfenbrenner is the scholar associated with the development and conceptualization of the theory. Bioecological systems theory proposes that development occurs within a number of nested and interactive environmental systems (Bubolz & Sontag, 1993). Bioecological systems theory proposes that an individual is embedded within a number of interactive systems known as the microsystem, mesosystem, exosystem, and macrosystem (Rosa & Tudge, 2013). These systems are often thought of as layers with the microsystem closest to the individual and the macrosystem the most distal. The microsystem is the most proximal environment an individual is situated within and the individual directly interacts within the microsystem. Families, schools, and places of work are common

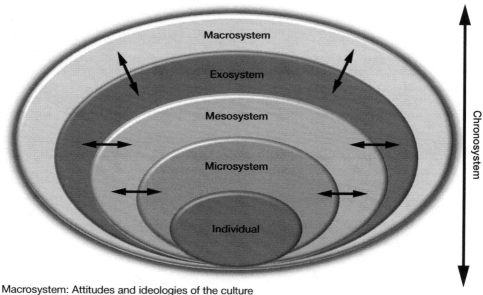

Macrosystem: Attitudes and ideologies of the culture
Exosystem: Mass media, neighbors, social welfare services
Mesosystem: Interactions among microsystems
Microsystem: Family, church, school
Individual: Sex, age, personality
Chronosystem: Time, sociohistorical events, life course transitions

Source: *Adapted from Bronfenbrenner & Morris, 1998.*

Figure 5.1 Bioecological Systems Theory Model.

microsystems and an individual directly participates in these environments. The mesosystem is the relationship between two or more microsystems. An exosystem is then a context which impacts the individual but they do not directly participate in the system. For example, a parent's workplace would be an exosystem for a developing child. They do not actively participate in this environment but a child is certainly affected by a parent's workplace. The macrosystem then encompasses all the broader social and cultural institutions in which an individual is embedded. Later Bronfenbrenner added another system known as the chronosystem which highlights how time is also an essential component to human development (Rosa & Tudge, 2013).

Proximal processes are a central concept within bioecological systems theory (Rosa & Tudge, 2013). According to bioecological systems theory, proximal processes are the reciprocal interactions between a person and his or her environment. Proximal processes are key to understanding individuals' developmental pathways (Bronfenbrenner & Ceci, 1994). The Process–Person–Context–Time model (PPCT model) is a core proposition of the theory and highlights the importance of proximal processes. The PPCT model proposes that an individual's disposition (genetic qualities, personality traits) interacts with their context over time and it is these simultaneous, reciprocal forces explain how an individual develops over their lifetime (Rosa & Tudge, 2013).

Symbolic Interaction Theory

Symbolic interaction theory focuses on how our social rules are created through human interactions (White & Klein, 2008). Symbolic interaction theorists focus on the connection between symbols (shared meanings) and interactions (including nonverbal communications and language) (LaRossa & Reitzes, 1993). A core proposition of symbolic interaction theory is that shared meanings result through our interactions with others and our understanding of social rules are learned and continuously shaped through our interactions with others. Symbolic interaction theory assumes that our interactions also work to create, reproduce, and shift our shared meanings and social rules (LaRossa & Reitzes, 1993). In other words, broader societal norms and expectations shape our interactions and our interactions shape broader societal norms and expectations. It is a continuous process in which both our meanings and culture are replicated and evolve.

Symbolic interaction theory is also concerned with how we develop our self-concept and identity. Theorists assumed that we are not born with an innate sense of self but rather it is through the interactions with close others we learn about ourselves and expectations for how we should behave (LaRossa & Reitzes, 1993). George Herbert Mead, a symbolic interaction theorist, argued that the self emerges through interactions with significant others, particularly parents (LaRossa & Reitzes, 1993). Charles Cooley, another symbolic interaction theorist, developed the concept of the looking glass self. According to Cooley, our sense of self grows through our interactions with others and we view ourselves based on others' perceptions (White & Klein, 2008). Essentially, how we view ourselves is based on how we think others view us. Because of this interactive nature of self, how we view ourselves can change based on who we are interacting with and the situation (LaRossa & Reitzes, 1993).

Social Exchange Theory

Social exchange theory argues individuals behave based on perceptions of rewards and costs with a goal of maximizing our rewards while minimizing costs. Social exchange theorists argue that individuals are rational beings able to freely choose and accurately assess the rewards and costs they may experience if they choose to act in a certain way (White & Klein, 2008). According to the theory, social relationships are exchanges in which we may reap a variety of rewards including affection, money, services, approval, and also incur a variety of costs including embarrassment, hurt, time, effort (Sabatelli & Shehan, 1993). Social exchange theorists assume we always have alternative options to actions and relationships, and so we are able to actively choose our optimal relationships and behavioral patterns (White & Klein, 2008).

Exchange theorists argue that relationships develop, are maintained, or come apart based on our expectations for the rewards reaped and costs incurred (Sabatelli & Shehan, 1993). According to exchange theory, we are interdependent with our friends, family members, and romantic partners, meaning that our actions reciprocally impact one another. Personal experiences tell us the rewards and costs we may expect from a relationship and our relationships remain stable when we anticipate similar levels of rewards and costs in the future. However, if a relationship begins to incur costs which outweigh the rewards, then the relationship might end or we see conflict as individuals consider their alternative options. Social exchange theory is sometimes critiqued because we are not always successful at weighing the costs and benefits of our relationships (Sabatelli & Shehan, 1993). The theory is also critiqued because it does not acknowledge that some individuals have more or less power in relationships, so not everyone has the same ability to navigate an optimal award and avoid costs.

Sociobiology/Evolutionary Psychology

Sociobiology explores how biological needs and human nature influence our social behaviors (Hyde & DeLamater, 2017). This perspective argues that our behaviors have evolved through the process of natural selection. Natural selection is the process by which animals, including humans, who are best suited to their environment are more likely to survive, reproduce, and pass their genes on to offspring and subsequent generations (Hyde & DeLamater, 2017). From the **sociobiological perspective**, the human behavioral patterns we see today are due to natural selection and a drive to create healthy offspring. **Evolutionary psychology** specifically focuses on how psychological mechanisms explain our behavior and argues that our psychology is based on forces shaped by natural selection.

Sociobiologists argue that sexual selection also plays a role in explaining contemporary human behavior. Sexual selection is a process that explains differences among males and females as one sex (usually males) competes to mate with another sex (usually females). Females tend to have higher levels of parental investment since they are the sex which goes through the process of pregnancy and labor and, as such, are motivated to be quite choosy about partners. Sexual strategies theory is a more specific theory which emerged from the sociobiological/evolutionary psychology perspective. Sexual strategies theory argues that males and females have different challenges when selecting sexual partners,

Image 5.2 Natural Selection Is the Process by Which Animals, Including Humans, Who Are Best Suited to Their Environment, Are More Likely to Survive, Reproduce, and Pass Their Genes on to Offspring (photo by Anna Kucherova/Depositphotos, Inc.).

particularly when considering long-term vs. short-term partners (Buss & Schmitt, 1993). This theory has been used to explain some of the gender differences we observe with regards to partner selection. For example, sexual strategies theory argues that men looking for a short-term partner may value a partner who is very open sexually but when looking for a long-term partner may value a partner who is more sexually conservative. There are many criticisms of the sociobiological perspective. Many of the tenets are not fully testable and ignore the tremendous amount of influence culture and learning have on our development. Feminist scholars in particular have been critical of the sociobiological perspective because it often treats gender differences as biologically determined. We discuss feminist theory in the next section.

Feminist Theory

At its core, **feminist theory** requires HDFS scholars to challenge the status quo and think critically about how gender, power, privilege, context, and diversity are relevant to the study of families and development (Allen, 2016; Allen, Lloyd, & Few, 2009). Feminist theory focuses on "gender as a key axis on which power is distributed, deployed, and misused in families" (Allen et al., 2009, p. 4). Essentially, women's and men's experiences throughout the lifespan are different based on the numerous ways men are privileged in a patriarchal system. Feminists highlight and problematize how our societal expectations for all genders can have negative consequences including unequal divisions of household labor, sexual violence, and poverty of women and children worldwide (Allen, 2016; Osmond & Thorne, 1993). Feminist theorists are concerned with the numerous systematic inequalities observed in broader social, educational, legal, economic, and political domains. In addition to drawing attention to these issues, feminist theory also calls for us to engage in praxis. Praxis is generally referred to as putting theory into practice and is a call for social activism (Allen et al., 2009).

There are multiple types of feminist thought and the theory is consistently evolving as new social issues arise and our social justice consciousness evolves (Allen, 2016; Osmond & Thorne, 1993). Related to and intimately linked to feminist theory are **queer theory** and **intersectionality theory**. Queer theory highlights both gender and sexual diversity and acknowledges that there is fluidity in our identities and behaviors across the lifespan (Few-Demo, Humble, Curran, & Lloyd, 2016). Queer theory also challenges binaries (the idea that people can only fall into one of two oppositional categories, such as gay or heterosexual, male or female). Intersectionality theory explores how multiple, simultaneously existing identities (gender, race, class, sexual orientation) influence individuals' development and experiences. Intersectionality is currently a central concept of feminist thought (Allen, 2016; Allen et al., 2009; Few-Demo et al., 2016) and as an HDFS student it is important to consider how these layers of identity are impactful. Together, these theories highlight the diversity of human experiences and bring attention to the numerous inequalities many of us face.

THEORIES OF LEARNING AND CHILD DEVELOPMENT

In this section we discuss more specific, but equally important, theories which help explain how individuals learn and develop. You will notice that the theories in this section offer some more precise propositions and are focused on more specific behavioral patterns. All of the theories discussed in this section are still popular with HDFS scholars, educators, and clinicians.

Behaviorism

Early developmental psychologists were extremely interested in how individuals learned. John Watson was one of the founding scholars of **behaviorism**. Watson believed that psychologists should be concerned with studying observable behaviors, rather than internal mental processes, which is why the theory is named behaviorism (Bretherton, 1993; Crosbie-Burnett & Lewis, 1993). Watson argued that all behavior was learned and that children learn to behave, or not behave, in a certain manner through conditioning processes. According to Watson, parents were responsible for reinforcing desirable behaviors and punishing undesirable behaviors and that any parent is capable of raising well-developed intelligent children (Bretherton, 1993). Watson also argued that children had no active role in their development and that their development was completely contingent on outside processes (Bretherton, 1993).

The two most commonly studied conditioning processes are classical conditioning and operant conditioning. Classical conditioning is a concept commonly associated with Ivan Pavlov (you may already know about Pavlov and his dog!). As animals, humans included, we have a number of unconditioned responses. In Pavlov's case, he found that his dog began to salivate (an unconditioned response) when he presented food (an unconditioned stimulus). Pavlov then introduced a new stimulus of ringing a bell (a conditioned stimulus) when presenting the food. After repeatedly exposing the dog to this scenario (ringing

Image 5.3 If a Person Is Rewarded for Performing a Behavior, then the Person Is More Likely to Repeat the Behavior According to Operant Conditioning (photo by Paulus Rusyanto/ Depositphotos, Inc.).

the bell when he presented food to his dog), the dog learned to associate the bell with the food and began salivating at the sound of the bell, even when food was not present. This learned response was classically conditioned. Operant conditioning is a concept commonly associated with B. F. Skinner. According to operant conditioning, a person performs a behavior (the operant) and if the behavior is rewarded (the reward could be food, praise, a nod of approval), the person is more likely to repeat the behavior. If the behavior is punished, the person is less likely to repeat the behavior. Many of the principles of behaviorism are used today in clinical settings, and the cognitive–behavioral therapy approach is extremely popular.

Cognitive Developmental Theory

In contrast to behaviorism, **cognitive developmental theory** is very much focused on children's internal processes and thoughts. Cognitive developmental theory is concerned with how children learn and develop an identity, acquire new skills, and think abstractly. Cognitive developmental theory recognizes the role social interactions play although the major focus of the theory is on developmental stages which result from maturation (Wood, 2013). A number of theorists have generated models using cognitive developmental theory, notably Jean Piaget, Carol Gilligan, and Lawrence Kohlberg. Both Gilligan and Kohlberg are known for cognitive developmental models of moral development whereas Piaget is famous for his broad theory of cognitive development. Piaget argued children pass through four stages of cognitive development (sensorimotor, preoperational, concrete operational, and formal operational). The sensorimotor stage is quite intense with six sub-stages, ranging from reflexes to mental combinations. Individuals pass along each of the four major stages and around adolescence enter the formal operational stage in which they have matured to the point that they are capable of abstract thought and complex problem solving. Some theorists argue that some adolescents and adults never reach the formal operational stage!

Cognitive development theory has also been used to understand how children learn gendered behaviors and develop a gender identity. Kohlberg first developed the concept of gender constancy. Kohlberg argued that while children as young as 7 months can distinguish males and females, they do not understand that one's gender is stable until much later, about 3 years old (Wood, 2013). According to cognitive developmental theory, once children understand that their gender is a stable trait they are motivated to learn how to behave in accordance with gender norms and enact the behaviors expected of their gender (Martin, Ruble, & Szkrybalo, 2002). In particular, children pay great attention to how their parents model masculinity and femininity.

Sociocultural Theory

Sociocultural theory is another important theory which helps explain how children learn and develop. Lev Vygotsky is the founder of sociocultural theory and key to the theory is an emphasis on *cultural* development rather than development in general (Miller, 2011). Sociocultural theory focuses on how social interactions as well as internal psychological processes interact so children can learn how to behave and respond in their cultural environment (Smith Leavell & Tamis-LeMonda, 2013). Children and parents co–construct knowledge together through shared communications and children internalize the content of these messages (John–Steiner & Mahn, 1996). In contrast to cognitive developmental theory, sociocultural theory assumes that development is a complex, interactive process with ongoing tensions and unevenness in the acquisition of new skills and knowledge (John–Steiner & Mahn, 1996). There are no distinct developmental stages but rather recognition that development is a dynamic, continuous process with both internal forces (within person) and external forces (social interactions). Unlike cognitive developmental theory, maturation and growth are both a precondition for and a product of learning (John–Steiner & Mahn, 1996).

Sociocultural theorists argue that we learn through direct interactions with parents, teachers, and peers although the greatest focus is given to interactions between parents and children (Smith Leavell & Tamis–LeMonda, 2013). Sociocultural theory emphasizes that language is an essential tool for how we learn (John–Steiner & Mahn, 1996; Miller, 2011). Vygotsky also introduced the concept of the zone of proximal development which is defined as the gap between actual development level (what an individual can currently do) and the level of potential development an individual displays (what an individual could do with help and instruction) (John–Steiner & Mahn, 1996). Through social interactions, individuals are able to close this gap and begin to accomplish tasks independently.

Social Learning Theory/Social Cognitive Theory

Similar to sociocultural theory, **social learning theory** (social cognitive theory) stresses how social interactions influence our development. Social learning theory argues individuals learn through personal experience, direct communication, and modeling (also known as observational learning or vicarious learning) (Bandura, 1977, 1986). According to social learning theory, individuals internalize information about whether certain behaviors are desirable based on their own experiences, observations of others, and direct

Image 5.4 According to Social Learning Theory, Individuals Learn through Personal Experience, Direct Communication, and Modeling (photo by Stefan Dahl Langstrup/
Depositphotos, Inc.).

instruction from others. Individuals who learn that a certain behavior is appropriate and
rewarding are then more likely to engage in that behavior themselves (Bandura, 1986).
Individuals who learn that a certain behavior is not appropriate are also less likely to
engage in that behavior. One famous experiment of social learning theory is called the
Bobo doll study (Bandura, Ross, & Ross, 1961). In this study, children were randomly
assigned into one of three conditions: a condition in which children observed an adult be
aggressive to a Bobo doll, a condition in which children observed an adult being non-
aggressive toward a Bobo doll, or a condition in which children did not observe an adult
interact with the doll. Following this exposure, the researchers found children who
viewed the aggressive model were more likely to engage in aggressive play compared to
children who witnessed the non-aggressive model or were in the control condition.
These results indicate that observing the aggressive adult model taught the children that
such aggression was appropriate and they were more likely to behave accordingly.
Modeling is a powerful way to communicate values, attitudes, thoughts, and behaviors to
individuals and Bandura (1986) stressed that "virtually all learning phenomena ... can occur
vicariously by observing other people's behavior and its consequences for them" (p. 19).

Social learning theory is unique in its emphasis on modeling and observational learning. Social learning theory also stresses that individuals actively construct their own belief
systems, rather than mindlessly mimicking models or anticipating rewards. Cognition and
decision-making are therefore essential concepts for the theory. In fact, Bandura eventually renamed the theory social cognitive theory in order to reflect the active role cognition plays in explaining why individuals are more or less likely to engage in certain
behaviors (Crosbie-Burnett & Lewis, 1993). Individuals still often use the label social
learning theory, so you may see either name for the same theory.

FAMILY THEORIES

The theories described in this section focus on how family and interpersonal dynamics
specifically shape our experiences. Although these theories may be used in other domains

besides family science, all the theories in this section explore how different family members interact and influence one another.

Attachment Theory

Attachment theory is a theory which also explores how individuals develop but specifically within the context of family and intimate relationships. Attachment theory was first developed by John Bowlby who argued that humans have an innate need for protection, affection, and security, which should be offered by responsive caregivers in early life (Mikulincer & Shaver, 2012). Infants remember interactions with caregivers and over time form cognitive models which influence their behavior and expectations (Bowlby, 1982). Children with consistent and responsive caregiving develop a "secure base" in which children will seek comfort from their caregiver when distressed (crying, crawling toward caregiver) but also feel free to explore their environment. Mary Ainsworth developed the "Strange Situation" paradigm to assess children's attachment style (Ainsworth, Blehar, Waters, & Wall, 1978). In the Strange Situation, infants and their caregiver are placed in an experimental room, a stranger enters the room and interacts with the infant, the parent then leaves for a short period of time and returns, the child is then left alone, the stranger again enters the room and interacts with the infant, and, finally, the parent again enters the room and greets the infant while the stranger leaves. An infant who is securely attached will freely explore the room, engage with the stranger, and while the infant is upset when the caregiver leaves, he or she is happy to see the caregiver upon their return.

One of the major principles of attachment theory is that individuals use their personal experiences to construct models of "the self" and "others" which continue to influence our behaviors as adults and impacts our later relationships (Mikulincer & Shaver, 2012). Individuals who experienced warm and supportive caregiving develop positive models of themselves and others, and are considered to be securely attached. Individuals classified as having a secure attachment style are better equipped to develop an adequate sense of trust and autonomy, characteristics which facilitate individual growth and the development of high quality personal relationships (Simpson, 2007). In contrast, avoidant individuals (who have limited experience with adequate caregiving) find it difficult to trust others and are less willing to provide care to their partners. Anxious individuals (who have a history of inconsistent caregiving) are likely to need very high levels of care from their partners but are willing to give extremely high levels of care to others. Therefore, we can see attachment plays a role throughout our lifespan, and influences our romantic relationships as adults (Mikulincer & Shaver, 2012).

Family Systems Theory

Family systems theory focuses on the family as a whole unit, rather than individual family members (White & Klein, 2008). The theory assumes that all parts of the system (family members) are interconnected and interdependent, and it is essential to consider the whole system (the entire family) when attempting to understand family dynamics. In other words, family systems theory argues that family members mutually influence one another and in order to understand family patterns and conflicts, it is necessary to look at

Image 5.5 Family Systems Theory Focuses on the Family as a Whole Unit and Assumes that All Parts of the System (Family Members) are Interconnected and Interdependent (photo by Elizabeth J. Christensen).

the entire family rather than just one or two individuals (White & Klein, 2008). Families are organized into subsystems of dyads, and triads, or larger groups (Whitchurch & Constantine, 1993) which influence broader family dynamics. Families also exist within suprasystems including extended family networks, ethnic subcultures, and communities. An important concept in family systems theories is boundaries (Whitchurch & Constantine, 1993). A boundary is a border between the system and its environment that influences how information enters and exits the system (White & Klein, 2008). Families are typically open systems since information from school, work, and other families are transmitted to and from the family system, although the degree of openness varies from family to family. Therefore, family systems are influenced by external as well as internal forces.

A feedback loop is another core concept of family systems theory. Feedback is information which comes from one point in the system and is transmitted to another part or parts of the system (Whitchurch & Constantine, 1993). More simply, feedback loops are interactions among family members which promote stability or change. There are negative feedback loops which help to maintain the status quo. For example, if one family member wished to lose weight but all other members do not change unhealthy eating habits or support the family member, it is likely that the family member will not actually lose weight because the feedback from the system is not change promoting. Positive feedback loops instead promote change and encourage the system to deviate from the typical pattern. So in our example, a positive feedback loop would occur if all family members encouraged the family member on their weight loss journey and agreed to not bring junk food into the house. It is important to understand that in feedback loops, the positive and negative refer to whether a loop is change promoting or constancy promoting, not whether a behavior is good or bad (Whitchurch & Constanine, 1993). Family system theory is commonly used in psychotherapy (Grych, Oxtoby, & Lynn, 2013) and illuminates that dealing with a problem (e.g., problems in school, alcohol abuse) is typically not an individual issue but rather an issue for the entire family system to work through. From a family systems perspective, a family can only be understood as a holistic unit and any substantive changes must include all family members.

Conflict Theory

Conflict theory also theorizes about the interdependent nature of families. Conflict theory recognizes that tensions, stressors, and divergent interests are an integral and normal part of family life (Farrington & Chertok, 1993). In fact, conflict theory is rooted in the assumption that conflict is an integral component of human nature (White & Klein, 2008). Because humans often have divergent interests and a set amount of resources (time, food, energy), competition for resources and disagreement is natural. Similar to social exchange theory, conflict theory argues that humans are in consistent negotiations in order to optimize their wellbeing. Unique to conflict theory is the proposition that such conflict is beneficial. You should not confuse conflict with fighting, as fighting is an unhealthy behavioral pattern in which negotiation is unlikely to occur.

Jetse Sprey is considered to be the first family scientist who specifically applied conflict theory to the study of families. Sprey (1979) argued that families should not seek to abolish conflict but conflict was actually a vital and healthy experience within families. This assumption was a departure from most family scholars who valued cohesion and harmony, and viewed the family as a site for all family members to find equal fulfillment (Farrington & Chertok, 1993). This harmonious view of families is not always reflected in the reality of families. For example, we know that in many families, household responsibilities and child care are inequitably divided among members. From a conflict theory perspective, raising dissatisfaction with this set of circumstances is beneficial to the family in the long run and avoidance or suppression of conflict is problematic (Farrington & Chertok, 1993). Families which are able to negotiate and find agreement are families with optimal outcomes (White & Klein, 2008). Power is another central concept to conflict theory and conflict theorists stress that it is important to consider power differentials in order to understand how family members can negotiate conflict (Farrington & Chertok, 1993). Age and gender are two extremely important features to consider when we look at who has more power in conflicts within families. For example, parents will typically have more power during conflict and it is much more likely the outcome of conflict negotiations will benefit the parents because of that power.

WEAVING THEORY TOGETHER

In this chapter you were introduced to a number of theories, many of which likely resonated with your own understanding of how humans develop and families are experienced. The good news is that you do not need to pick just one theory to appreciate and use! Many of these theories are quite complementary and work together to explain more about human behavior, thoughts, and feelings than a singular theory alone. For example, researchers consistently find that children who grow up in homes characterized with intimate partner violence are more likely to engage in violence themselves as they grow older, a pattern known as the intergenerational transmission of violence. Social learning theory can explain these patterns by outlining how observing, and possibly experiencing, violence can shape children's beliefs about the appropriateness of violence (Heyman, Foran, & Wilkinson, 2013; Rivera & Fincham, 2015). By modeling violence in relationships, children can learn that violence is acceptable in romantic relationships.

To complement the social learning theory perspective, feminist theory would highlight how gender also influences the likelihood of engaging in violence with romantic partners (Heyman et al., 2013). Researchers have found that children are more likely to model their same-sex parent (Milletich, Kelley, Doane, & Pearson, 2010) and we can see that there are distinct gendered patterns with regards to violence (Johnson, 2011). Johnson (2011) outlines how there are actually different types of intimate partner violence and that the most serious and continuous form of violence, intimate terrorism, is most often committed by men. Intimate terrorism is characterized by psychological control, manipulation, and severe and frequent physical violence. Feminist theory argues that coercive control and physical violence is a way for men to exert power over women in relationships (Heyman et al., 2013).

Therefore, when we bring these two theories together we can see how both social forces and interpersonal interactions help to explain the intergenerational transmission of violence. Feminist theories highlight how gendered institutions often contribute to patterns of violence in a given society, whereas social learning theory discusses how particular personal experiences also shape individuals' views of violence. Our understanding of this topic is better and more thorough because we are using multiple theoretical lenses to explain this phenomenon.

Summary

1   Theories are explanations constructed by scientists to explain why people behave and develop:

   A   Theories inform both research and practice.

   B   Theories contain concepts, relationships, and propositions.

2   Broad theories and perspectives look at abstract ideas and highlight important concepts:

   A   Lifespan and life course perspectives highlight how individuals develop in a particular sociohistorical context. Both perspectives discuss how development is a lifelong process.

   B   Bioecological systems theory explores how individuals develop within a context of varying layers. Proximal processes are instrumental to understanding how individuals develop within his or her environment.

C   Symbolic interaction theory argues through interactions we create shared meanings. These shared meanings allow us to develop a self-concept and understand the rules of society. Our interactions shape social norms and social norms simultaneously shape our interactions.

D   Social exchange theory assumes individuals are motivated to behave in ways which maximize rewards and minimize costs. Individuals must weigh alternative paths and decide an optimal course of behavior.

E   Sociobiological perspective explores how human nature is associated with our social behaviors. The perspective assumes that our current behavioral patterns persist because of natural selection.

   a   Evolutionary psychology explores how psychological mechanisms have evolved.

F   Feminist theory is a theoretical perspective which challenges us to think critically about gender, power, and privilege and challenge where inequalities exist. Social activism is a central tenet of the theory.

   a   Queer theory acknowledges the great amount of diversity we observe with regards to gender and sexuality.

   b   Intersectionality theory explores how individuals have multiple, existing identities which all need to be considered when exploring the roles of power and privilege.

3   There are multiple theories which explore how individuals develop and learn:

A   Behaviorism explores how individuals learn through direct experiences, rewards, and punishments. The theory does not acknowledge the role of internal mental processes.

B   Cognitive developmental theory studies the role of individuals' cognitive development through maturation.

   a   Once children have a sense of gender constancy they are motivated to learn how to behave in accordance with their gender.

C   Sociocultural theory is a theory which explains how social interactions shape children's cultural and language development.

D   Social learning theory argues learning occurs through direct experiences, verbal communication, and modelling.

4   There are multiple theories which highlight family dynamics and the importance of interpersonal relationships:

A   Attachment theory studies how early caregiving experiences shape future behaviors and expectations from caregivers and significant others.

B   Family systems theory focuses on the family as an interdependent, holistic unit. The theory argues that we can only understand individual behavior within the context of the family system.

C   Conflict theory assumes conflict is a normal and beneficial component of family life. Conflict allows family members to negotiate their differences and avoiding conflict can be detrimental.

5   Many theories are complementary and we are best able to explain human development and family dynamics by weaving multiple theoretical perspectives together.

Key Terms

attachment theory
behaviorism
bioecological systems theory
cognitive developmental theory
concept
conflict theory
evolutionary psychology
family systems theory
feminist theory
intersectionality theory
life course perspective
lifespan perspective
propositions
queer theory
relations
social cognitive theory
social exchange theory
social learning theory
sociobiological perspective
sociocultural theory
symbolic interaction theory
theory

Challenge: Integration

Many of the theories discussed in this chapter discuss how individual growth, families, context, and societal factors all influence our development. Think back to your childhood and consider your current life stage:

1   How has your own biological growth and personality impacted your development?
2   How have your family interactions helped or hindered your development?
3   How have your neighborhood, school, and geographical region influenced your development?
4   How has your cultural/ethnic background influenced your development?
5   How have broader social forces (e.g., public policy, gender norms) contributed to your own beliefs and behaviors?
6   How do you think *you* have influenced your family and broader social environment?

Journal Questions

1   Which of the theories is most interesting to you? Why?
2   Is there any theory that you disagree with or have your own critique? Why?
3   Which two theories do you think have the most in common? Which two theories do you think are the most different?

SUGGESTED RESOURCES

Bengston, V. L., Acock, A. C., Allen, K. R., Dilworth-Anderson, P., & Klein, D. M. *Sourcebook of family theory and research*. Thousand Oaks, CA: Sage.
NCFR. *Journal of family theory and review blog*. Retrieved from www.ncfr.org/jftr/blog.

REFERENCES

Ainsworth, M. D. S., Blehar, M. C., Waters, E., & Wall, S. (1978). *Patterns of attachment: Assessed in the strange situation and at home*. Hillsdale, NJ: Erlbaum.
Allen, K. R. (2016). Feminist theory in family studies: History, reflection, and critique. *Journal of Family Theory & Review, 8*, 207–224.
Allen, K. R., Lloyd, S. A., & Few, A. L. (2009). Reclaiming feminist theory, method, and praxis for family studies. In S. A. Lloyd, A. L. Few, & K. R. Allen (Eds.), *Handbook of feminist family studies* (pp. 3–17). Thousand Oaks, CA: Sage.

Baltes, P. B. (1987). Theoretical propositions of life-span developmental psychology: On the dynamics between growth and decline. *Developmental Psychology, 23*, 611–626.

Bandura, A. (1977). *Social learning theory.* Upper Saddle, NJ: Prentice Hall.

Bandura, A. (1986). *Social foundations of thought and action: A social cognitive theory.* Englewood Cliffs, NJ: Prentice Hall.

Bandura, A., Ross, D., & Ross, S. A. (1961). Transmission of aggression through imitation of aggressive models. *Journal of Abnormal and Social Psychology, 63*, 575–582.

Bengston, V. L., & Allen, K. R. (1993). The life course perspective applied to families over time. In P. G. Boss, W. J. Doherty, R. LaRossa, W. R. Schumm, & S. K. Steinmetz (Eds.), *Sourcebook of family theories and methods: A conceptual approach* (pp. 469–498). New York: Springer.

Bengston, V. L., Acock, A. C., Allen, K. R., Dilworth-Anderson, P., & Klein, D. M. (2005). Theory and theorizing in family research. In V. L. Bengston, A. C. Acock, K. R. Allen, P. Dilworth-Anderson, & D. M. Klein (Eds.), *Sourcebook of family theory and research* (pp. 3–33). Thousand Oaks, CA: Sage.

Bowlby, J. (1982). *Attachment and loss: Vol. 1. Attachment* (2nd ed.). New York. Basic Books.

Bretherton, I. (1993). Theoretical contributions from development psychology. In P. G. Boss, W. J. Doherty, R. LaRossa, W. R. Schumm, & S. K. Steinmetz (Eds.), *Sourcebook of family theories and methods: A conceptual approach* (pp. 275–297). New York: Springer.

Bronfenbrenner, U., & Ceci, S. J. (1994). Nature–nurture reconceptualized: A bioecological model. *Psychological Review, 101*, 568–586.

Bronfenbrenner, U., & Morris, P. A. (1998). The ecology of developmental processes. In W. Damon, & R. M. Lerner (Eds.), *Handbook of child psychology: Theoretical models of human development* (5th ed., Volume 1, pp. 993–1028). Hoboken, NJ: John Wiley & Sons.

Bubolz, M. M., & Sontag, M. S. (1993). Human ecology theory. In P. G. Boss, W. J. Doherty, R. LaRossa, W. R. Schumm, & S. K. Steinmetz (Eds.), *Sourcebook of family theories and methods: A conceptual approach* (pp. 419–447). New York: Springer.

Burnham, M. M., & Gaylor, E. E. (2011). Sleep environments of young children in post-industrial societies. In M. El-Sheikh (Ed.), *Sleep and development: Familial and socio-cultural considerations* (pp. 195–217). New York: Oxford.

Buss, D. M., & Schmitt, D. P. (1993). Sexual strategies theory: An evolutionary perspective on human mating. *Psychological Review, 100*, 204–232.

Crosbie-Burnett, M., & Lewis, E. A. (1993). Theoretical contributions from social and cognitive-behavioral psychology. In P. G. Boss, W. J. Doherty, R. LaRossa, W. R. Schumm, & S. K. Steinmetz (Eds.), *Sourcebook of family theories and methods: A conceptual approach* (pp. 531–561). New York: Springer.

Dilworth-Anderson, P., Burton, L. M., & Klein, D. M. (2005). Contemporary and emerging theories in studying families. In V. L. Bengston, A. C. Acock, K. R. Allen, P. Dilworth-Anderson, & D. M. Klein (Eds.), *Sourcebook of family theory and research* (pp. 35–58). Thousand Oaks, CA: Sage.

Doherty, W. J., Boss, P. G., LaRossa, R., Schumm, W. R., & Steinmetz, S. K. (1993). Family theories and methods: A contextual approach. In P. G. Boss, W. J. Doherty, R. LaRossa, W. R. Schumm, & S. K. Steinmetz (Eds.), *Sourcebook of family theories and methods: A conceptual approach* (pp. 3–30). New York: Springer.

Farrington, K., & Chertok, E. (1993). Social conflict theories of the family. In P. G. Boss, W. J. Doherty, R. LaRossa, W. R. Schumm, & S. K. Steinmetz (Eds.), *Sourcebook of family theories and methods: A conceptual approach* (pp. 357–381). New York: Springer.

Few-Demo, A. L., Humble, Á. M., Curran, M. A., & Lloyd, S. A. (2016). Queer theory, intersectionality, and LGBT-parent families: Transformative critical pedagogy in family theory. *Journal of Family Theory & Review, 8*, 74–94.

Fine, M. A., & Fincham, F. D. (2013). Introduction: The role of theory in family science. In M. A. Fine & F. D. Fincham (Eds.), *Handbook of family theories: A content-based approach* (pp. 1–7). New York: Routledge.

Ford, D. H., & Lerner, R. M. (1992). *Developmental systems theory: An integrative approach.* Newbury Park, CA: Sage.

Grych, J., Oxtoby, C., & Lynn, M. (2013). The effects of interparental conflict on children. In M. A. Fine & F. D. Fincham (Eds.), *Handbook of family theories: A content-based approach* (pp. 228–245). New York: Routledge.

Heyman, R. E., Foran, H. M., & Wilkinson, J. L. (2013). Theories of intimate partner violence. In M. A. Fine & F. D. Fincham (Eds.), *Handbook of family theories: A content-based approach* (pp. 190–207). New York: Routledge.

Hyde, J. S., & DeLamater, J. D. (2017). *Understanding human sexuality.* New York: McGraw Hill.

John-Steiner, V., & Mahn, H. (1996). Sociocultural approaches to learning and development: A Vygotskian framework. *Educational psychologist, 31,* 191–206.

Johnson, M. P. (2011). Gender and types of intimate partner violence: A response to an anti-feminist literature review. *Aggression and Violent Behavior, 16,* 289–296.

LaRossa, R., & Reitzes, D. C. (1993). Symbolic interactionism and family studies. In P. G. Boss, W. J. Doherty, R. LaRossa, W. R. Schumm, & S. K. Steinmetz (Eds.), *Sourcebook of family theories and methods: A conceptual approach* (pp. 135–162). New York: Springer.

Longmore, M. A., Manning, W. D., & Giordano, P. C. (2013). Parent–child relationships in adolescence. In M. A. Fine & F. D. Fincham (Eds.), *Handbook of family theories: A content-based approach* (pp. 28–50). New York: Routledge.

Martin, C. L., Ruble, D. N., & Szkrybalo, J. (2002). Cognitive theories of early gender development. *Psychological Bulletin, 128,* 903–933.

Mikulincer, M., & Shaver, P. R. (2012). Adult attachment orientations and relationship processes. *Journal of Family Theory & Review, 4,* 259–274.

Miller, R. (2011). *Vygotsky in perspective.* Cambridge, UK: Cambridge University Press.

Milletich, R., Kelley, M., Doane, A., & Pearson, M. (2010). Exposure to interparental violence and childhood physical and emotional abuse as related to physical aggression in undergraduate dating relationships. *Journal of Family Violence, 25,* 627–637.

Osmond, M. W., & Thorne, B. (1993). Feminist theories: The social construction of gender in families and society. In P. G. Boss, W. J. Doherty, R. LaRossa, W. R. Schumm, & S. K. Steinmetz (Eds.), *Sourcebook of family theories and methods: A conceptual approach* (pp. 591–623). New York: Springer.

Rivera, P. M., & Fincham, F. (2015). Forgiveness as a mediator of the intergenerational transmission of violence. *Journal of Interpersonal Violence, 30,* 895–910.

Rosa, E. M., & Tudge, J. (2013). Urie Bronfenbrenner's theory of human development: Its evolution from ecology to bioecology. *Journal of Family Theory & Review, 5*(4), 243–258.

Sabatelli, R. M., & Shehan, C. L. (1993). Exchange and resource theories. In P. G. Boss, W. J. Doherty, R. LaRossa, W. R. Schumm, & S. K. Steinmetz (Eds.), *Sourcebook of family theories and methods: A conceptual approach* (pp. 385–411). New York: Springer.

Simpson, J. A. (2007). Foundations of interpersonal trust. In A. W. Kruglanski & E. T. Higgins (Eds.), *Social psychology: Handbook of basic principles* (2nd ed., pp. 587–607). New York: Guilford Press.

Smith Leavell, A., & Tamis-LeMonda, C. S. (2013). Parenting in infancy and early childhood: A focus on gender socialization. In M. A. Fine & F. D. Fincham (Eds.), *Handbook of family theories: A content-based approach* (pp. 11–27). New York: Routledge.

Sprey, J. (1979). Conflict theory and the study of marriage and the family. In W. R. Burr, R. Hill, F. I. Nye, & I. Reiss (Eds.), *Contemporary theories about the family* (Vol. 2, pp. 130–159). New York: Free Press.

Walsh, B. A., Cromer, H., & Weigel, D. J. (2014). Classroom-to-home connections: Young children's experiences with a technology-based parent involvement tool. *Early Education and Development, 25,* 1142–1161.

Weiser, D. A., Weigel, D. J., Lalasz, C. B., & Evans, W. P. (2015). Family background and propensity to engage in infidelity. *Journal of Family Issues*, online first. doi: 10.1177/0192513 X15581660.

Whitchurch, G. G., & Constantine, L. L. (1993). Systems theory. In P. G. Boss, W. J. Doherty, R. LaRossa, W. R. Schumm, & S. K. Steinmetz (Eds.), *Sourcebook of family theories and methods: A conceptual approach* (pp. 325–352). New York: Springer.

White, J. M., & Klein, D. M. (2008). *Family theories* (3rd ed.). Thousand Oaks, CA: Sage.

Wood, J. T. (2013). Becoming gendered: Theories of gendering processes in early life. In M. A. Fine & F. D. Fincham (Eds.), *Handbook of family theories: A content-based approach* (pp. 301–315). New York: Routledge.

PART V

Professionals and Ethical Thinking and Growth

CHAPTER 6

Introduction to FLE and Its Applications

Intellectuals solve problems; geniuses prevent them.

(Albert Einstein)

PERSPECTIVES ON FLE AND OTHER FAMILY PROFESSIONS

Recall from the first chapter that FLE emphasizes teaching individuals and families skills to promote strong and healthy families (Duncan & Goddard, 2011; Myers–Walls, Ballard, Darling, and Myers–Bowman, 2011). In a recent interactive guest lecture on FLE, Walsh highlighted some of the main ideas from Myers–Walls et al.'s (2011) article on the domains of family practice as well as the NCFR webinar, "The Domains of Family Practice Model: Differentiating the Roles of Family Professionals" which complements Myers–Walls et al.'s (2011) publication. The domains of family practice model is discussed later in this chapter and essentially describes similarities and differences between FLE, family therapy, and FCM. In the NCFR webinar, one suggested classroom activity was to have students write down hallmarks of FLE, family therapy, or FCM on post-its. The first author of this text did this activity in her interactive guest lecture and asked students to select one of the three aforementioned areas.

Table 6.1 captures what the undergraduate students wrote on a post-it to define these three family areas. How do you define FLE, family therapy, and FCM? Do you agree with the definitions that the students wrote? Would you make any additions or changes? You can revisit Chapter 1 for more formal definitions.

In another presentation on FLE by the first author (Walsh), students looked at job advertisements in the family field. Students asserted that the job advertisements were not always clear-cut and they felt that many of the mock advertisements desired applicants with skills that sounded like FLE, family therapy, and FCM. Next, the class discussed the domains of family practice model and the uniqueness and overlap between FLE, family

Image 6.1 The Domains of Family Practice Model States that Hallmarks of FLE, Family Therapy, and FCM Have Similarities and Differences (photo by Lydia DeFlorio and Bridget Walsh).

Table 6.1 Undergraduate Students' Main Points for Three Domains of Family Practice

Family life education	Family therapy	Family case management
"Proactive in prevention and teaching families"	"Helping others with their problems"	"Learning about available resources in the community and helping people access them"
"Educating and preventing"	"Healing"	–
"Defusing the bomb before it goes off"	"Repairing relationships in the family"	"Management and prevention of further family problems; helping families navigate legal stuff"
"Prevention through education; Help individuals and families; Connect with community resources"	"Help families/individuals solve problems"	"Problem solving and assessing a situation for a solution"
"Promote healthy family interaction"	"Helping people and families heal from stress and problems"	–
"Helping people before major problems occur"	"Psychology or counseling background are required by the therapist"	–
"Teaching families certain skills"	"Helping people deal with the worries and problems in their family"	–
"Preventative. Education-based. Broad."	–	–
"Provides knowledge to people about family and life-related topics"	–	–

Figure 6.1 Keywords of FLE.

therapy, and FCM. Because students were required to read Myers–Walls et al.'s (2011) article on the **domains of family practice** model before their lecture, it was not surprising that their responses on what components these three professions share included:

- ethics;
- values;
- ecological model;
- using research to inform practice;
- valuing and respecting diverse families;
- family systems theory;
- shared goal of strong healthy families (Myers–Walls et al., 2011).

Several students in the class stated that they desire to attend graduate school in Marriage and Family Therapy. In a large-group setting, they discussed the role of a therapist as a healer and the role of an FLE as an educator. Some students were interested in pursuing the CFLE certification in their last semester or immediately after graduation, and then attending graduate school to be prepared to gain licensure in Marriage and Family Therapy. There were many students interested in pursuing only the CFLE certification. Asking students to identify with one or more of the three professions led to further discussion about differences between these three professions.

For example, one student stated that she desires to become a CFLE because prevention and education really resonate with her and her career aspirations (see Box 6.1 to explore perspectives about CFLE from CFLEs). She asked, "What if someone attended FLE sessions and started to talk about that as of lately they don't experience much pleasure in life's activities and are feeling depressed?" She said that as a CFLE with a B.S. in HDFS, she would not have training with the Diagnostic and Statistical Manual of Mental

BOX 6.1 PERSPECTIVES ABOUT CFLE FROM CFLES

As you learned in Chapter 1, NCFR has a certification program for emerging and current professionals to gain the FLE credential known as CFLE. This next section provides perspectives on FLE from CFLEs themselves.

Karen Mowry, B.S., CFLE–Provisional

Q1: *In your own words, how do you understand FLE?*

A: FLE means having knowledge about the human lifespan across all stages and aspects of family life in society. Each and every one of us is part of a family. FLE also means providing information through a variety of ways to individuals about life as part of a family. It is proactive education with the purpose of strengthening families, relationships, and preventing problems.

Q2: *What does being a CFLE mean to you? What is your status?*

A: I am currently a CFLE-Provisional as of January 2014. Relying on research and best practices, being a CFLE means I can work with individuals to educate them by presenting workshops, classes, or programs that provide information, skills, and resources in a specific area of the human lifespan. Education is a major key to better understanding which in turn leads to healthier, stronger, and well-balanced relationships. This can be done either through paid employment or on a volunteer basis. All work performed is on an ethical, professional level. My goal is to become a full CFLE in order to help enrich families so lives can be changed to prevent problems in the future.

Q3: *Why do you think the CFLE certification is meaningful to your HDFS background?*

A: I believe that because HDFS is a non-licensure degree within the Department of Education at UNR the CFLE certification gives it more substance, understanding, and direction of its usefulness. Both acronyms are a mouthful, but the word "certified" carries a little more weight. The knowledge demonstrated to have this designation is quite extensive as it covers 10 family science areas and the subsequent required hours of experience in FLE to be fully certified within 5 years of application demonstrates a serious commitment. As with a licensed profession, this credential mandates required continuing education. All this combined is important as I advocate for myself as a CFLE.

Q4: *What is something you would like the reader to know about you?*

A: I would like the reader to know that I earned my bachelor's degree in HDFS following the CFLE course work at the ripe age of 57. Currently, I am volunteering at a home for pregnant young women in need by providing a life skills class. Because I have had the experience of raising three children of my own, I desire to work with young parents. Also, I have a passion for literacy, in particular early literacy development. Being a CFLE-Provisional has given me the knowledge and tools to work toward being fully certified. I would like at some point to advocate for the importance of CFLE so it is more recognizable and visible in the State of Nevada for future FLEs.

Julie Leventhal, M.S., CFLE

Q1: *What does being a CFLE mean to you?*

A: It means having the support of a national organization; not only do I know the content needed to assist children and families but I also have a major group of professionals that provides guidance and continued education regarding that content. I have had full status since last year.

Q2: *What type of work do you do in FLE?*

A: I mostly teach as a lecturer but I do also work a bit internationally, like helping with parent education or life skills workshops in Romania.

Q3: *Why do you think CFLE is a meaningful certification for someone in the HDFS (or related) field?*

A: I think it's a meaningful certification because it indicates that you've had specialized or more focused training on growth and change within the family. Again, it also provides that additional support and more resources for the work with families.

Disorders (DSM–5; American Psychiatric Association, 2013) and in psychotherapy. In other words, she did not think that the individual would be a good fit for her FLE program. This student was correct in her ethical and professional thinking. Therapy is designed to treat serious psychological and family problems (Doherty, 2009). After the instructor validated the student's thinking, they concluded that it would be best to connect the participant with a therapist and respectfully ask the participant to leave the session. One take-home message from the student's example is that a CFLE should be connected to a therapist in order to ethically handle situations like this one. Family therapists should be connected to psychiatrists or clinical psychologists in case more help is needed. Helping professionals often share the goal of strong and healthy individuals and families (Myers-Walls et al., 2011) and in some cases more than one professional is needed to reach this goal.

In order to encourage CFLEs to demonstrate ethical and professional thinking and behavior, NCFR has established the **Family Life Educators code of ethics** (NCFR, 2012). The Family Life Educators code of ethics includes 36 ethical principles across four areas: relationships with parents and families, relationships with children and youth, relationships with colleagues and the profession, and relationships with community/society (NCFR, 2012). This document is read and signed by CFLE applicants and used to promote ethical thinking and practice in the work of CFLEs. Ethics are discussed more in Chapter 7.

Finally, the students concluded that the domains of family practice model illustrates that there are similarities and differences between FLE, family therapy, and FCM (see Myers-Walls et al., 2011). One major difference is that the method of each profession is different. Next, this chapter will explore key methodological frameworks of FLE programs.

COMPONENTS OF FLE PROGRAMS

FLE programs may take a variety of forms but there are often common elements of design and practice. In this section, these elements will be covered and include: (1) staying current and preparing for the program, (2) indirect and direct assessments, (3) creating a vision, goals, objectives, outcomes, and impacts, (4) planning and implementing a welcome session, three core sessions, and a goodbye session, and (5) processing and evaluation questions. For each of these components, an example of an FLE program that the first author (Walsh) is developing will be used to further illustrate components of FLE programs. Specifically, one situation is there are cases of poor academic performance of English Language Learner (ELL) Latinos, particularly in Science, Technology, Engineering, and Mathematics (STEM) content areas coupled with poor praxis scores of ELL Latino pre-service teachers. The umbrella term that captures multiple programs designed to address this need is called Developing English Language Teaching Ability (DELTA) and it was initiated by Sandra J. Prytherch at the University of Nevada, Reno. Within DELTA, there is a program that is being developed called Strengthening Latino/Hispanic English Language Learners and Their Families. You will learn more about this program throughout the chapter.

A major component of FLE programs assumes that FLEs will want to stay current on the research base relevant to the program. **Staying current and preparing** can include reviewing research on the topic, reviewing existing programs, if any, on the topic, thinking about theory in the design of the program (see Box 6.2), finding demographic information, collecting a list of community resources, updating a personal philosophy statement, and acknowledging any biases that you may have as a facilitator about the target group.

BOX 6.2 USING FAMILY THEORIES FOR THE DESIGN OF FLE PROGRAMS

When applied researchers situate research questions in a theoretical and empirical context, the work is more likely to be stronger than research questions without this context. Similarly, it is important for FLEs to understand research and theories in order to apply them to program design and implementation. Many theories are essential for effective work with families and it is common for FLEs to value many theories compared to operating from one theoretical position.

Table 6.2 Using Family Theories for the Design of Family Life Education Programs

Theory	Key principles	Application to FLE
Family systems theory	Family members interact with one another in an interdependent, coherently characteristic way. Family systems have a powerful effect on individual family member behavior. Family systems reflect input received by family members synergistically interacting together. Inputs (such as educational information) have predictable outputs (such as relationship outcomes). A system may embrace change (morphogenesis) or resist it (morphostasis). Family systems are nested within and are influenced by larger social systems (community, culture).	Try to teach all members of a target audience system (couples rather than one partner, both parents rather than one parent, parents and children rather than just parents, and children and parents rather than parents alone) because a change in one member may be sabotaged by other family members. One family member can trigger change in a relationship system. Positive change potential is enhanced at timely transitions (during developmental change).
Social exchange theory	Relationship stability and quality predicted by rewards minus costs in interaction.	Programs attempt to build relationship assets (e.g., enhance positivity in marriage) and reduce relationship liabilities (e.g., reduce negativity in marriage).
Family development theory	Families grow and change over developmental time.	Programs targeted in different ways dependent on persons dependent on their family developmental course (Becoming a Couple; Parenting Teens and Handling Your Midlife Challenges; Getting Ready for Retirement).

continued

Table 6.2 Continued

Theory	Key principles	Application to FLE
Human ecology theory	Development occurs through the interaction of a mosaic of factors; family microsystems influence and are influenced by transactions with other systems (e.g., neighborhood, peer group, school, workplace).	"Silver bullet" programs addressing only one aspect of the ecological system typically are insufficient; must address several areas of the social ecology simultaneously. A balancing work and family program teaching parents balance skills should also teach businesses how to establish family-friendly policies.
Symbolic interaction	Families make meaning and interpret events based on norms, values, expectations, patterns of behavior, and interaction.	Allow opportunities for families to construct their own meanings of events and ideas. Ask questions such as, "What meaning does this have for you?"

Source: Duncan and Goddard (2011, p. 35, Table 2.1).

The following section illustrates how Walsh thinks through and plans each element of the key FLE program components. Walsh has applied the FLE component *staying current and preparing* to the DELTA program and developed statements and questions to guide her preparations:

- I am reviewing research on the power of academic support on Latinos' academic motivation (e.g., Alfaro, Umaña-Taylor, & Bámaca, 2006).
- I am reflecting on my applied research (see Chapter 3) experiences on Latino/Hispanic samples (e.g., Walsh, Cromer, & Weigel, 2014; Walsh, Sánchez, & Burnham, 2016). What information or lessons were gleaned from my experiences that may be useful in designing and implementing an FLE program?
- I am thinking about theory in the design of the program. For example, Bronfenbrenner (1989) asserted that family and school have important bidirectional relationships on developmental outcomes of the individual and thus these microsystems will influence the college student and vice versa. Also, in light of human ecology theory it is important to teach college students and their families skills; however, it is also important to change the university setting to establish long-term support and resources to improve academic performance of ELL Latinos, particularly in STEM content areas and to improve praxis scores of ELL Latino pre-service teachers.
- As a developmental scientist, and an instructor of a lifespan development course for 10 years, I have a solid understanding of all ages and stages throughout the lifespan. This will help me understand some of the strengths of the participants and some of their needs.
- I am part of a group on campus that is collecting demographic information about all students enrolled in teacher education programs. This will help me understand the audience. For example, most students currently enrolled in teacher education programs identify as White females.

- A list of all services at the University (e.g., counseling, academic services) is provided in a brochure. I am also updating a list of possible applicable resources in the community in case college students or family members might be interested or in need of these. These will be housed on a table during each FLE session and they will be available on campus.
- My personal philosophy statement is always evolving. I will share this with participants prior to when the FLE program begins. I will invite them to ask questions, if any.
- I am not fluent in Spanish. As a result, a native Spanish speaker will help facilitate the program. We will discuss any biases, attitudes, and beliefs about the target group that each of us may possess. We are not directly involved in teacher education courses and this means that we will not have **dual relationships** with the target audience.

Indirectly (i.e. **indirect assessment**) identifying the needs, cultural values, interests, goals, and future needs of target groups can be helpful when planning a program. Information gleaned from the literature review and demographic information can be helpful. In addition, discussions with an advisory board can also serve as indirect assessments.

- I am reviewing literature on this topic and analyzing demographic information.
- I will gather perspectives from faculty, advisors, and school district personnel directly involved in teacher education programs.
- These efforts have helped me to understand more about the target audience; however, getting information from the target audience themselves will help me understand their felt needs.

Directly (i.e. **direct assessment**) identifying needs, cultural values, interests, goals, and future needs of the target group is also an important part of the process and helps the FLE designer understand what they are identifying or feel is important to reaching their goals. FLEs may approach direct assessments as researchers. In other words, the FLE program designer will need to decide whether qualitative, quantitative, or both techniques are needed. Furthermore, the FLE program designer will need to decide whether surveys, qualitative interviews, or other methods of data collection are best. IRB approval may be needed. (Please consult with Chapter 4 for a review of any research term mentioned in this paragraph.)

- I am currently working on an IRB application.
- I plan to use an online survey platform to administer a mixed-method survey to college students in the sampling pool for the FLE program. In addition to assessing needs, cultural values, interests, and goals, the survey will ask the best location on campus, time, and modes for the class. Finally, college students will be asked to provide a phone number or email address of a family member who is most supportive of their educational goals. The family member will be contacted to determine three hopes that they have for their family member as he or she achieves his or her dream of becoming an educator. The survey, email script, and phone script will be available in English and Spanish.

It is important to establish an FLE program **vision**, **goals**, **objectives**, **outcomes**, and **impacts**. A vision statement can convey what the dreams and desires for the program include (Duncan & Goddard, 2011). FLE program staff often assert different perspectives about the vision for a program. These diverse perspectives can make the process of creating a vision statement tedious yet rich in breadth and depth.

- After much discussion among stakeholders, the shared vision for the DELTA program is to "empower English language learning paraprofessionals and college students to develop and to nourish skills, competencies, and family support necessary to reach their goal of becoming a teacher."

The goals of a program are more specific than a vision and convey a general purpose (Duncan & Goddard, 2011).

- There are several goals of the DELTA program.
    - "To teach concepts relevant to the basics of second language acquisition theory and applications of this to their own professional goals and growth."
    - "To analyze what it takes to become a teacher and how to become a better student to reach this goal."
    - "To connect college students and paraprofessionals to support systems that value the goal of becoming a teacher."
    - "To demonstrate inquiry about STEM content areas and/or Praxis exam preparation and resources."

Goals cannot fully function alone and need to be coupled with objectives. In other words, good objectives are clearly related to program goals (Duncan & Goddard, 2011). Objectives are more specific than goals and objectives are often written in measurable terms (Darling & Cassidy, 2014; Duncan & Goddard, 2011).

- Participants will explain in writing or in a large group discussion second language acquisition theory and give examples of this in their own learning and teaching experiences.
- Participants will share with the facilitator and other participants their written reflection on what it takes to become a teacher and will build an action plan to reach this goal.
- Participants will report involvement with family member(s) through technology or face-to-face interactions that show support about the goal of becoming a teacher. Participants will join a private social media site and post at least twice to share strengths, needs, and parts of their action plan to become a teacher. (Please note that this objective is optional.) Participants will meet two times with a mentor (i.e., veteran teacher, graduate student, faculty) to discuss their goal of becoming a teacher.
- Participants will generate five questions and answers about STEM content areas and/ or the Praxis exam.

Outcomes are the benefits or changes in participants during or after participation in an FLE program (Darling & Cassidy, 2014). It is sometimes helpful to think about initial outcomes, intermediate outcomes, or longer-term outcomes (i.e., impacts).

- Initial outcomes. At 1 month into the FLE program, students will have identified their needs and strengths and set goals for courses in STEM content areas and/or passing the teaching licensing exam. Student participants will feel connected and supported in their goal of becoming a teacher.
- Intermediate outcomes. After a few months of the FLE program, students and families will have participated in 80% of the program sessions and activities. Student participants will feel connected and supported in their goal of becoming a teacher.
- Longer-term outcomes or impacts. Student participants will report feeling closer to reaching their goal of becoming a teacher or will have met that goal. In other words, Latino English Language Learning pre-service teacher students will have passed their STEM courses and been placed in internship/student teaching sites and/or will have passed the teaching licensing exam.

Once the planning and assessments for the program are done, it is probably time to implement the program. The **welcome session** is a time that allows the participants of the FLE program to get familiar with it (Crosswhite, n.d.). During the welcome session it is important to do icebreaker activities and to build rapport with participants and help them build rapport with each other. Participants should be introduced to the FLE program vision, goals, objectives, and activities (Crosswhite, n.d.). The FLE taking a facilitator approach will want to be open to participant feedback on program goals and objectives and be open to modifying them or changing them based on participant feedback.

- The welcome session, like all the sessions, will provide food to participants and free child care. Some highlights of the welcome session will include the following activities. To break the ice, each person will be given a colored dot sticker. Then, the meaning of the color will be shared with participants. For example, a blue sticker means that participants will be invited to share their favorite food and so on. The CFLE facilitator will integrate humor into her sessions, with a particular emphasis on self-deprecating humor. The bilingual facilitator has a positive and upbeat attitude, which often makes students feel cared for and eager to learn. The strengths of the facilitators should help the rapport building process. Very importantly, during the welcome session, the facilitators will share the program, vision, goals, objectives, and activities of the FLE program and give participants ample opportunities to provide feedback and ask questions. They will make any changes to these, if necessary.

The **objective sessions and activities** are the heart of the FLE program. For each session, the FLE facilitator will want to have objectives, teaching-learning activities to meet the objectives, assessment questions, and necessary materials or resources (Crosswhite, n.d.; Darling & Cassidy, 2014).

- For one session that is approximately 1 hour and 15 minutes long, one objective will be met. Specifically, the objective is that participants will explain in writing or in a large group discussion second language acquisition theory and give examples of this in their own learning and teaching experiences. The teaching-learning activities to meet this objective include a symposium of four faculty presenting for 5 minutes each on concepts germane to second language acquisition theory. Next, there will be a 15-minute question period that will allow participants to ask the speakers questions. Then, the speakers, facilitators, and participants will form small groups to discuss examples of these concepts in their own teaching and learning experiences (about 10 minutes). Finally, to partially assess participants' learning in this session, they will be asked to work independently for about 3 minutes to write down the most important points from today's session. Participants will have the option to share part of what they wrote with the large group (approximately 10 minutes). Participants will be given five simple questions to help evaluate their learning in the session (about 10 minutes). For instance:

> Compared to before the session, how good are you at stating main concepts of second language acquisition and applying these to your own experiences?

- Much worse
- Worse
- About the same
- Better
- Much better

The **goodbye session** is when participants further process and reflect upon what they learned from the program. The bottom line is that this is the time to further process what was learned, to evaluate the entire program, and it is an opportunity for participants to close their face-to-face participation with the group and the facilitator (Crosswhite, n.d.). The **processing and evaluation questions** will help participants understand what they learned in the FLE program and evaluate the program.

- In the goodbye session for DELTA, each participant will be asked program processing questions or to write what they learned by participating in the program and to write three insights that they learned about themselves, their families, or their goal of becoming a teacher. To help evaluate the program, participants will be invited to complete a quantitative survey that determines whether the participants felt the FLE program met their needs and how it might improve in the future. Specifically, a Likert scale will be used to assess if participants felt the program objectives were met in a satisfactory manner. Finally, participants, facilitators, and mentors will do a goodbye activity by writing a short anonymous goodbye message and then storing it in a bottle. Participants will be aware that future participants will be invited to read the messages. The bottle will be kept in an office on campus. Participants will be invited to visit the office to use resources within it, to keep connected to the group and the facilitators on the private social media page, and they will be invited to take an electronic survey approximately 1 year after the program ends to assess if they have met or are getting closer to their goal of becoming a teacher.

CONTENT AREA CONSIDERATIONS IN FLE PLANNING

It is important to think about which of the 10 **NCFR content areas** are most germane to the FLE program. As mentioned in Chapter 1, the 10 content areas are: (1) families and individuals in society, (2) internal dynamics of families, (3) human growth and development, (4) human sexuality, (5) interpersonal relationships, (6) parent education and guidance, (7) family resource management, (8) family law and public policy, (9) professional ethics and practice, and (10) FLE methods (NCFR, 2009). In addition to knowing the subject matter of each content area, there is another step. Specifically, each content area has "Practice" which includes the skill sets of CFLEs (Darling & Cassidy, 2014; Darling, Fleming, & Cassidy, 2009; Duncan & Goddard, 2011; NCFR, 2014). See Box 6.3 for the practice guidelines for Human Growth and Development across the Lifespan. The NCFR website includes the content and practice guidelines for each of the 10 content areas. It is important to note, as does NCFR (2014), that the "Practice" sections are what the CFLE exam assesses. (See Figure 1.2 in Chapter 1 for the two pathways to become a CFLE.)

- In my professional opinion, the content areas that are most relevant to the FLE program called DELTA are: Families and Individuals in Societal Contexts (Content Area 1), Internal Dynamics of Families (Content Area 2), Human Growth and Development across the Lifespan (Content Area 3), and Family Resource Management (Content Area 6).

Miguel Brambila is a CFLE and likes that he can focus on several CFLE content areas in his work. He currently manages a family enhancement program and teaches FLE workshops and supervises or often develops various components of FLE programs.

BOX 6.3 PRACTICE GUIDELINES

The "Practice" of the third content area of Human Growth and Development across the Lifespan includes:

a. Identify developmental stages, transitions, elements and challenges throughout the lifespan
b. Recognize reciprocal influences:

   1. Individual development on families
   2. Family development on individuals

c. Recognize the impact of individual health and wellness on families
d. Assist individuals and families in effective developmental transitions
e. Apply appropriate practices based on theories of human growth and development to individuals and families
f. Recognize socio-ecological influences on human development across the lifespan (e.g. sexual/gender identity, trauma, etc.)

(NCFR, 2014)

THE BEAUTIFUL WORK WE DO: A STORY FROM THE FIELD BY MIGUEL BRAMBILA, M.S., CFLE

Someone once told me, "Learning is beautiful" and I couldn't agree more with that truth. Learning and education lifts up our spirit because it expands our possibilities and view of the world. The very essence of education is empowerment, from a 5-year-old boy who realizes he has learned to read, to a surgeon who successfully frees a cancer patient from a brain tumor. The beauty of education is that it extends beyond the kindergarten classroom or the surgeon's OR. We can spend thousands of dollars and countless hours of study to become a doctor or any other profession, and yet assume that having a child will automatically teach us how to parent, or that getting married will guarantee a successful marriage, or earning our first paycheck will make us financial experts. There are skills that are as important as reading or performing brain surgery. Those skills are what we, FLEs, so passionately teach. Our family life is the school we all go to, every day is a test, and it is our choice if we get prepared or not. I often ask participants in my relationship skills class to find the solution to a complex algebra problem. I will always have one person that takes the challenge and gives it a shot. After a couple of tries, I tell them that although algebra is an important subject during our high school years, the truth is that most of us rarely use it; however, on the other hand, learning about relationships, conflict resolution, human development, and financial management develops skills that we will always use regardless of our career choice. CFLEs teach individuals and families throughout the lifespan numerous skills such as conflict resolution, financial management, parenting, family resiliency, goal-setting, and co-parenting, to name a few. FLE gives helping professionals the framework to help families along the way. What I love about FLE as a helping and educational profession is that its focus is prevention and education. FLE is also a very versatile profession because CFLEs can focus on one or more content areas—such as human development, family resource management, interpersonal relationships, parenting education, human sexuality, etc.—and then decide who is going to be their target population: adults or children, elderly, married, single, stepfamilies, formerly incarcerated, teenagers, you name it. Finally, CFLEs can concentrate on teaching, program development, research, consulting, etc. Becoming a CFLE has certainly given me a lot of great opportunities: after getting my master's in Family Studies and becoming a CFLE with full status, I was promoted and now manage the Family Enhancement program at the Wilkinson Center in Dallas, TX. In addition, I've had the opportunity to teach marriage and relationship education for adults and teenagers and, most recently, court-ordered anger management and co-parenting classes. Often in my court-ordered classes, participants feel broken and angry but that is where I see once again that "learning is beautiful." Soon after we start the class, there is a new hope, we can see positive changes in attitudes, and they feel empowered. My recent involvement teaching co-parenting education and anger management in English and Spanish came to fruition as a result of being a CFLE and member of the NCFR. The CFLE designation can really give us many opportunities, if we look for them. For those that already know about CFLE it certainly is a plus, and for those that do not know much about it, it is a great opportunity for us to start something new. That's what I have done.

It all started while I was about to finish my master's in Family Studies. At the time I was working as a case manager for the adult education program. I began to realize that a lot of the barriers that adult students face were related to their family life. Some students would drop out because they had problems with their spouse. Others dropped out because their teenage daughter became pregnant; others wouldn't continue because of financial stress. I knew that the solution was not just to bring them back but to prevent those situations from happening again to them or other families. So, I was facing an opportunity much bigger than the English as a Second Language (ESL) or General Educational Development (GED) certificate those adult students would receive at the end of the semester. I had an opportunity to help individuals enhance their family life. I decided to write a proposal to my supervisor about how FLE could improve the lives of our adult students. My goal was to integrate adult education classes (i.e., ESL, GED, Computer Literacy) with FLE. Today, ESL students learn more than vocabulary and grammar, they learn about child development, they learn how to effectively parent and communicate with their spouse, to resolve conflict, budget, start a savings account ... they learn to be a stronger healthier family! Today, I manage the Family Enhancement program at the Wilkinson Center; I may be teaching some of the FLE workshops and supervising or developing different components of the program. On the weekends and evenings I may be teaching anger management, co-parenting, or marriage education throughout Dallas, Fort Worth, and Kaufman, TX. As a CFLE, I get the best of both worlds: I get to teach families and also develop programs that fit the needs of the families I serve. As a CFLE I get to help families prepare for that everyday test of life, and that is when they see the beauty of education. The work that CFLEs do is beautiful because learning is indeed beautiful.

BOX 6.4 APPLICATIONS: SEXUALITY EDUCATION FOR PRESCHOOLERS

Sexuality includes a variety of dimensions, including gender identity, beliefs and feelings about love, intercourse, and reproduction (Darling & Cassidy, 2014; Darling & Howard, 2009; Sciaraffa & Randolph, 2011). Sexuality educators working in the context of FLE will most likely have an understanding of existing approaches to sexuality education, such as abstinence-only, abstinence-based, and comprehensive sexuality education programs.

Guidelines for Comprehensive Sexuality Education written by the Sexuality Information and Education Council of the United States (SIECUS, 2004) include information about sexuality education in an age-appropriate way. Specifically, there are six key concepts about sexuality and family life; these are: (1) human development, (2) relationships, (3) personal skills, (4) sexual behavior, (5) sexual health, and (6) society and culture (SIECUS, 2004). For each topic (e.g., human development), there is developmental information for four age groups. For example, age-appropriate messages for children aged 5 to 8 years include:

- Each body part has a correct name and a specific function.
- A person's genitals, reproductive organs, and genes determine whether the person is male or female.
- A boy/man has nipples, a penis, a scrotum, and testicles.

- A girl/woman has breasts, nipples, a vulva, a clitoris, a vagina, a uterus, and ovaries.
- Some sexual or reproductive organs, such as penises and vulvas, are external or on the outside of the body while others, such as ovaries and testicles, are internal or inside the body.
- Both boys and girls have body parts that feel good when touched.

(SIECUS, 2004, p. 25)

The aforementioned messages are intended for children aged 5 years or older, but are some of these developmental messages appropriate for preschoolers? Most comprehensive sexuality education programs include kindergarten through 12th grade (Darling & Cassidy, 2014; SIECUS, 2004), but some programs may begin in pre-kindergarten (Darling & Cassidy, 2014).

What does sexuality education for preschoolers include? Sexuality education for preschoolers may include naming body parts (Darling & Cassidy, 2014; Sciaraffa & Randolph, 2011), developing healthy attitudes about their bodies (Darling & Cassidy, 2014; Sciaraffa & Randolph, 2011), and exploring the topic of where babies come from (Darling & Howard, 2009; Essa, Walsh, Burnham, & Shipley, 2015; Sciaraffa & Randolph, 2011). Nonetheless, it is challenging for many teachers and parents to address sexuality education with young children (Darling & Howard, 2009; Sciaraffa & Randolph, 2011). Parents should be their child's main sexuality educator; however, they often need support and guidance (SIECUS, 2004).

Below are some considerations for planning an FLE program to empower parents to respond and to address sexuality education and development in young children.

Naming Body Parts

Between 18 and 36 months, children may start to name genitals and other body parts and functions (Sciaraffa & Randolph, 2011). Anatomically correct dolls may provide teachable moments to explore sex differences (Darling & Howard, 2009). To help answer children's questions about their body parts, you may want to share with preschoolers the book called *It's Not the Stork! A Book about Girls, Boys, Babies, Bodies, Families, and Friends* (Harris, 2008).

Developing Healthy Attitudes about Sexuality

Gender Identity

Preschoolers have an emerging understanding of what it means to be female or male. It takes children time to understand that sex is a constant feature and that one cannot switch sex by changing outward appearance and behaviors (Kohlberg, 1966). An environment that includes anatomically correct dolls can help children understand that sex is a constant, and dramatic play areas can help them experience various gender roles.

Of course, some situations are complex. For instance, a preschooler might have a trans parent. Young children are often very rigid in their ideas of male and female and they might not understand this concept until they gain more cognitive strength to understand their own identity and that of others. Much of the existing research on gender identity does not show any differences in gender identity development as a result of their parents' sexual orientation (Patterson, 2000).

William's Doll (Zolotow, 1972) makes cross-gender play in young children acceptable. In this story William wants a doll to play with because he wants to experience what it is like to be a parent. Cross-gendered play helps children break stereotypes for a gender.

Self-Pleasuring and Expectations for Privacy

This type of behavior in young children is often normal and healthy. They may engage in self-pleasuring unless they were specifically taught not to do this (Sciaraffa & Randolph, 2011). The adult can teach the child when it is appropriate to do this and when it is not appropriate to do this. This may also be an opportunity to discuss touches from others and what is appropriate and what is not appropriate.

Exploring Where Do Babies Come From

Children aged 3 to 4 years are interested in knowing where they came from and where other babies come from and they may ask caring adults (Essa et al., 2015; Sciaraffa & Randolph, 2011). These are two different topics and children may share their curiosity when a new baby arrives in the family (Silverberg, 2012) or when a teacher or caregiver is pregnant (Essa et al., 2015) or just in general because they are curious about this sensitive topic.

The storybook *What Makes a Baby* (Silverberg, 2012) may quench children's curiosity about where they came from and where other babies came from. This is a good story because it underscores parts that are necessary to make a baby and the book is also sensitive to diverse situations.

The needs of Lesbian, Gay, Bisexual, Transgender, Queer, and Questioning (LGBTQ) families are often overlooked and FLEs have an opportunity to build inclusive programs or programs that specifically target LGBTQ families (Maurer, 2012). A children's book that talks about assisted reproduction is *A Dream Come True: Talking to Your Child about Assisted Reproduction* (Zouves, 2004).

A Couple of Developmental Considerations about Preschoolers' Learning

Young children benefit from concrete and hands-on learning experiences. Props and visuals help make concepts understandable and meaningful for young children. For instance, you might see a child put a teddy bear under her shirt and pretend to be pregnant. Other cognitive theories suggest that children have a working memory that is much smaller than adults and they do not selectively attend to information as well as older children. This means that a young child might ask where do babies come from, the adult may provide an answer, and the child may move on to something else but might want to revisit the topic at another time.

Ethics

Make sure that parents provide written consent for participating in the FLE program on this topic. Also, if children are going to be part of any sessions it will be helpful to get parent permission forms signed and some parents may want to see somewhat of a script or detailed information about what the sessions with children may include, even though parents plan to be at the session with their child.

Image 6.2 Family Life Educators Can Take Time to Learn about Families' Cultural Values and Parenting Practices (photo by Gilboy Family in care of Bridget Walsh (permission received)).

Thinking about the law in relationship to ethics is important. For instance, FLEs are mandated reporters of abuse and neglect (Palm, 2009). It is essential to honor the law; and, it is also helpful to consider virtue ethics (Palm, 2009).

In Chapter 2, the **virtue ethics** of caring, practical wisdom, and hope/optimism (Palm, 2009) were identified as important to practice as a professional in the area of HDFS. These characteristics are important to FLE. In the context of sexuality education, it is also important to understand the parents' values and attitudes about sexuality and to understand how parent–child communications about sexuality can help the FLE understand how to approach the family as a system (Darling & Howard, 2009). It is also important to create a safe environment to help participants feel comfortable in the FLE program (Darling & Cassidy, 2014).

The NCFR Family Life Educators code of ethics includes several ethical principles that are germane to an FLE program for empowering parents to talk with and to respond to their young children's sexuality development. For instance, one ethical principle is "I will encourage family members to explore their values and promote healthy sexuality in their family" (NCFR, 2012). Another ethical principle example is "I will provide a program environment that is safe and nurturing to all family members" (NCFR, 2012). Finally, "I will support diverse family values by acknowledging and examining parenting practices that support healthy family relationships" (NCFR, 2012).

One ethical consideration when working with LGBTQ people is that historically they have been the focus of efforts that attempt to change their sexual orientation (Maurer, 2012). It will be important to acknowledge this in an FLE session.

LGBTQ Families

You may want to plan a detailed program on sexuality education for young children that is inclusive of LGBTQ families or a separate program for LGBTQ families. One strength of LGBTQ families is that the children are bicultural because they live and negotiate the norms and values of mainstream society and a non-dominant background (Maurer, 2012). It will be helpful to acknowledge this strength with participants and to acknowledge that society is not always friendly to LGBTQ people. It might be helpful to network with LGBTQ leaders in a community or volunteer at existing LGBTQ events (e.g., pride events) as LGBTQ families often have rich word–of–mouth networks and desire to work with professionals that they can trust (Maurer, 2012). FLE programs that work with LGBTQ families are needed and you will want to review existing programs and learn more about this group to provide beneficial FLE sessions.

Educator Characteristics to Be Successful

An FLE that is easy to build rapport with and work with is helpful in any setting and with any topic. To name a few other characteristics, the professional should have an understanding of ethics, research, theory, content areas and practice, and the goal of strong healthy families (Myers–Walls et al., 2011).

Image 6.3 Family Life Educators Can Become Familiar with Policies and Practices Related to All Families to Build Relationships with and Among Families (photo by Harney Family and Friends in Care of Bridget Walsh (permission granted)).

In the context of sexuality education for young children, the FLE will want to understand the dimensions of sexuality, different approaches to sexuality education, be aware about how they learned about sexuality education and evaluate their experiences, be informed on research that evaluates the effectiveness of different approaches to sexuality education, and the type(s) of sexuality education that their state supports (e.g., in Nevada there is currently an "opt-in" approach, which means that parents may choose to have their children attend sexuality education). The FLE will want to embrace that sexuality education is a lifelong task (Darling & Howard, 2009) and be well-versed in developmental considerations for each age group. The FLE will want to be proactive about creating a safe environment for participants and help them to solidify their own values (Darling & Cassidy, 2014).

They will also want to be familiar with basic LGBTQ terminology, the strengths and the needs of LGBTQ families, understanding LGBTQ families through a life-span approach, and what FLE practices work with this group (Maurer, 2012). A successful FLE does not have to be LGBTQ to do effective FLE work with LGBTQ families (Maurer, 2012). Alternatively, a person with a status of LGBTQ does not automatically make them informed and skilled in this area (Maurer, 2012).

PERSONAL PHILOSOPHY OF FLE

It is essential to develop a **personal philosophy for family life education** (Dail, 1984; Darling & Cassidy, 2014). An FLE philosophy develops over time and is never in a final state (Dail, 1984). For example, a student may craft a statement of philosophy in an FLE course and then the statement may evolve upon further coursework and experiences. Furthermore, in a student's last semester or after graduation, he or she might become a CFLE-provisional and make further changes as more experiences with individuals and families are questioned, evaluated, and reflected upon. The personal philosophy is a direction but there is always the possibility of considering alternate routes as an FLE continues to travel (Dail, 1984). Why should students in an FLE course or professionals in FLE have a personal philosophy about FLE?

> A family-life educator who has taken the time, made the effort, and received the guidance which is necessary to the development of a personal philosophy is a unique individual in possession of uncommon understanding about the meaning of family in the society as well as the meaning of family for the individual. This is a family-life educator who, because of this knowing, is able to work to strengthen families, to educate them for better, more productive and more satisfying lives, and to assist them in developing positive community and social relationships.
>
> (Dail, 1984, p. 149)

An FLE personal philosophy can address a variety of topics. For example, if you specialize in working with LGBTQ families or design programs that are at least inclusive of LGBTQ families, this should be included in your statement. As a facilitator, you can include the personal philosophy statement on your website, display it in your office, or have it available to participants during the welcome session.

BOX 6.5 SAMPLE OF AN FLE PERSONAL PHILOSOPHY

This personal philosophy statement aims to address the following:

* "Beliefs about the family and the quality and nature of family life" (Dail, 1984, p. 148).
* "Beliefs about the purpose of family-life education" (Dail, 1984, p. 149).
* "Beliefs about the content of family-life education" (Dail, 1984, p. 149).
* "Beliefs about the process of learning for families and individuals within families" (Dail, 1984, p. 149).

What might you address in your FLE personal philosophy? The below sample was written by a CFLE. It is her third iteration and there will be more updates and changes in the future!

I believe that there are a variety of groups that comprise a family. While this may include legal and/or genetic ties, a family can extend beyond these definitions. For example, fictive kin can be included in the definition of a family. I think individuals and groups are the best source of information for telling you who comprises their family and how they define their relationships. For instance, it might appear to a facilitator that two individuals are half-siblings; however, if you ask them about their relationship they refer to each other as sisters because of their emotional ties.

Family processes matter more than structure for individual and family functioning (Walsh, 1996). Family processes, such as flexibility, communication, cohesion, and problem solving, are essential to family functioning and wellbeing (Walsh, 1993). Different families have different processing needs and strengths (Walsh, 1996).

As a humanist, I believe that all people share commonalities and all individuals have the same basic needs. Specifically, these needs include: physiological needs (e.g., need for food), safety and security (e.g., being protected), love and belonging (e.g., feeling loved as a family member), esteem (e.g., being respected by family and community), and self-actualization or fulfilling one's potential while appreciating all humans (Maslow, 1954). As a developmental scientist, I believe that beyond these basic needs, an individual's needs differ depending upon their age and stage. For example, an infant needs sensitive and responsive caregiving, whereas an elder desires respect and someone to listen to his or her life review. Family systems theory and the bioecological model, among others, are also important to consider when planning FLE programs.

Theory and research provide coherence and truth that help to guide how families learn and grow. A needs assessment, solidifying a vision, goals, objectives, and planning and implementing an interactive introduction session, several core sessions with objectives, and a closing session with processing questions and an evaluation are also all important components of FLE design.

The program must be culturally appropriate to respect and understand the audience. For example, I am currently planning an FLE program for ELL college students and their families. I have compiled research and demographic data on this group and have taught diversity courses at the college level. I have partnered with a native Spanish speaker to help me deliver the sessions. I think the collaboration of an FLE with a native Spanish-speaking faculty member is what should occur because it will help to engage all members of the audience in the program.

I believe that FLEs should pursue and maintain the CFLE certification. I will always work to renew my CFLE status. I think breadth and depth of the 10 content areas will help a professional be an effective FLE in practice. Because of my breadth and depth in the content areas, I am comfortable being an expert in some areas and a supporter and collaborator on other topics.

I think it is important to target as many members of a family as possible for FLE sessions and to consider a variety of contextual factors that influence the family and vice versa. This helps the FLE understand the system but also encourages positive change throughout the system. Introduction sessions, core sessions, and closing sessions should be interactive and include a variety of modes (e.g., lectures, discussions, media, independent reflection). In accord with the bioecological model, it is important to consider the importance of context. For example, I'm planning an FLE program for college students and their families. In addition to empowering students and families with skills, I also plan to target office staff and faculty on campus in order to address many parts of the system.

WHO WILL YOU BE AS AN FLE?

As you think about FLE and grow a foundation in it, you will be considering forming a professional identity as an FLE. Below are some points to consider:

- Will you have an understanding of all the content areas and depth in one area in particular? Will you gain this depth by participating in an undergraduate research project, doing an internship in this area, or taking several courses in an area?
- How will you become a CFLE? Will you take the exam or apply through the coursework option?
- Will you take an expert approach and transmit knowledge and skills to families? Will you be a facilitator and draw on the knowledge and motivation that participants have within them? Will you adopt a collaborator approach and maintain some control but allow participants active control over the objectives and activities as well? Perhaps, you will take an eclectic approach and adopt a variety of identities depending on the context? For a discussion of approaches and identities in FLE, please see Duncan and Goddard (2011).
- Will you work in an educational setting, faith-based setting, hospital or health care settings, military bases, start your own business, community settings, or other?
- Will you attend local or national conferences to network with other family professionals and to stay current in your field? Will you present at local or national conferences to share information about an FLE program or research-based FLE work?
- What would your 30-second elevator speech on FLE include?
- Will you find personal and professional satisfaction in your work as an FLE?

These are a few questions to consider as you learn more about the content areas of FLE and consider becoming an FLE who truly makes a difference.

Summary

1 The domains of family practice model captures the similarities and differences between FLE, family therapy, and FCM.
2 The NCFR Family Life Educators code of ethics is a guide for CFLEs' ethical thinking and professional growth.

3   Key components of FLE programs include the following:

A   staying current on information about the program topic and preparing for the program;
B   indirect and direct assessments;
C   creating a vision, goals, objectives, outcomes, and impacts;
D   planning and implementing a welcome session, three core sessions, and a goodbye session;
E   processing and evaluation questions.

4   There are 10 content areas of FLE and each content area has practice guidelines that capture what skills and competencies a CFLE should possess.
5   A personal philosophy of FLE is a working document and states the FLE's beliefs that are germane to working with and collaborating with families.
6   A professional identity as an FLE will start to develop as you discover what coursework and professional approaches, settings, and opportunities are most appealing to you.

Key Terms

direct assessment
domains of family practice
dual relationships
Family Life Educators code of ethics
goals
goodbye session
impacts
indirect assessment
NCFR content areas
objectives
objective sessions and activities
outcomes
personal philosophy for family life education
processing and evaluation questions
staying current and preparing
virtue ethics
vision
welcome session

Challenge: Integration

This section suggests watching two movies to prompt thinking about concepts and ideas presented in this chapter.

1   Watch *Still Alice* (2015). *Still Alice* (2015) captures the journey of a professor diagnosed with early onset Alzheimer's disease. Family relationships are tested throughout the movie. Alice needs a caregiver in the advanced stages of the disease.
2   Discuss how individuals and families handle the diagnosis.
3   What are the strengths of the family? Why?
4   Talk about how the ABC-X model of family stress can be applied to this situation or in helping the family handle adversity. The A is used to reference the stressor event, B refers to family resources, C is centered on the family's awareness of the event, and, lastly, X refers to the outcome (see Tornatore & Grant, 2002).
5   Imagine implementing an FLE program with the children and the father. Discuss how the role of FLE is distinct from family therapy. What ethical considerations might an FLE need to be cognizant of in this context?

1   Watch *Race to Nowhere: The Dark Side of America's Achievement Culture* (2010). This film underscores America's achievement culture.
2   Discuss what America's achievement culture means. Discuss the difference between learning and performing. Discuss what may make school-age children happy and motivated to learn. Discuss what may make adolescents in high school happy and motivated to learn.
3   What family theories could be applied to plan a family education program for some children and families featured in the film?
4   What is a possible stance on personal wellbeing that an FLE might have to promote family wellbeing and balanced brains?
5   What ethical issues might you face when implementing an FLE program in a high-achieving educational setting?

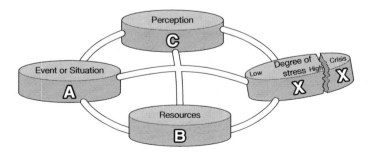

Figure 6.2 ABC-X Model of Family Crisis (Bush, Price, Price, & McKenry, 2017).

Journal Questions

1 What does FLE mean to you?
2 You recently became a CFLE and received funding to design and implement an FLE program. What broad topic would the FLE program address? Why?
3 What components of FLE methods seem most interesting to you? Why?
4 What ethical principles in the NCFR Family Life Educators code of ethics seem natural to you? Alternatively, what ethical principles might you need more training in to demonstrate ethical decision-making?

SUGGESTED RESOURCES

Darling, C. A., & Cassidy, D. (2014). *Family life education: Working with families across the lifespan* (3rd ed.). Long Grove, IL: Waveland.

Duncan, S. F., & Goddard, H. W. (2011). *Family life education: Principles and practices for effective outreach* (2nd ed.). Thousand Oaks, CA: Sage Publications.

Gausman, B., Maher, M., & Allen, B. (2012). *Ethical thinking and practice for family education professionals* [Archived NCFR Webinar]. Retrieved from www.ncfr.org/professional-resources/archived-webinars/ethical-thinking-and-practice-webcast.

Myers-Bowman, K. S., Ballard, S. M., Myers-Walls, J. A., & Darling, C. A. (2013, May 30) *The domains of family practice model: Differentiating the roles of family professionals* [Archived NCFR Webinar]. Retrieved from www.ncfr.org/professional-resources/archived-webinars/family-life-education-practice-webinars/domains-family-prac.

Silverberg, C. (2012). *Talking to your kids about sex: Tips for the modern parent.* Retrieved from http://itsconceivablenow.com/2012/03/02/talking-to-kids-about-sex/.

REFERENCES

Alfaro, E. C., Umaña-Taylor, A. J., & Bámaca, M. Y. (2006). The influence of academic support on Latino adolescents' academic motivation. *Family Relations, 55*, 279–291.

American Psychiatric Association. (2013). *Diagnostic and statistical manual of mental disorders* (5th ed.). Arlington, VA: American Psychiatric Publishing.

Bronfenbrenner, U. (1989). Ecological systems theory. *Annals of Child Development, 6*, 187–249.

Bush, K. R., Price, C. A., Price, S. J., & McKenry, P. C. (2017). Families coping with change: A conceptual overview. In C. A. Price, K. R. Bush, & S. J. Price (Eds.), *Families & change: Coping with stressful events and transitions* (5th ed., pp. 3–23). Thousand Oaks, CA: Sage.

Crosswhite, J. (n.d.). *Family life education* [Syllabus]. Department of Family Studies, University of Nebraska-Kearney, Kearney, NE.

Dail, P. W. (1984). Constructing a philosophy of family-life education: Educating the educators. *Family Perspectives, 18*, 145–149.

Darling, C. A., & Cassidy, D. (2014). *Family life education: Working with families across the lifespan* (3rd ed.). Long Grove, IL: Waveland.

Darling, C. A., Fleming, W. M., & Cassidy, D. (2009). Professionalization of family life education: Defining the field. *Family Relations, 58*, 330–345.

Darling, C. A., & Howard, S. (2009). Human sexuality. In D. J. Bredehoft & M. J. Walcheski (Eds.), *Family life education: Integrating theory and practice* (pp. 141–151). Minneapolis, MN: NCFR.

Doherty, W. J. (2009). Boundaries between parent and family education and family therapy: The levels of family involvement model. In D. J. Bredehoft & M. J. Walcheski (Eds.), *Family life education: Integrating theory and practice* (pp. 253–260). Minneapolis, MN: NCFR.

Duncan, S. F., & Goddard, H. W. (2011). *Family life education: Principles and practices for effective outreach* (2nd ed.). Thousand Oaks, CA: Sage Publications.

Essa, E. L., Walsh, B. A., Burnham, M. M., & Shipley, J. (2015). Heike's belly project: Three-year-olds' inquiry of their teacher's pregnancy. *Childhood Explorer, 2*, 23–27.

Harris, R. H. (2008). *It's not the stork! A book about girls, boys, babies, bodies, families, and friends.* Somerville, MA: Candlewick Press.

Kohlberg, L. (1966). A cognitive-developmental analysis of children's sex-role concepts and attitudes. In E. Maccoby (Ed.), *The development of sex differences* (pp. 82–173). Stanford, CA: Stanford University Press.

Maslow, A. H. (1954). *Motivation and personality.* New York: Harper.

Maurer, L. (2012). Family life education with lesbian, gay, bisexual, and transgender families. In S. M. Ballard & A. C. Taylor (Eds.), *Family life education with diverse populations* (pp. 255–283). Thousand Oaks, CA: Sage.

Myers-Walls, J. A., Ballard, S. M., Darling, C. A., & Myers-Bowman, K. S. (2011). Reconceptualizing the domain and boundaries of family life education. *Family Relations, 60*, 357–372.

NCFR. (2009). Certified family life educator (CFLE) exam content outline. In D. J. Bredehoft & M. J. Walcheski (Eds.), *Family life education: Integrating theory and practice* (2nd ed., pp. 261–263). Minneapolis, MN: Author.

NCFR. (2012). *Family life educators code of ethics.* Retrieved from www.ncfr.org/sites/default/files/downloads/news/cfle_code__of_ethics_2012.pdf.

NCFR. (2014). *Family life education content areas: Content and practice guidelines.* Retrieved from www.ncfr.org/sites/default/files/downloads/news/fle_content_and_practice_guidelines_2014_0.pdf.

Palm, G. (2009). Professional ethics and practice. In D. J. Bredehoft & M. J. Walcheski (Eds.), *Family life education: Integrating theory and practice* (2nd ed., pp. 191–197). Minneapolis, MN: NCFR.

Patterson, C. (2000). Family relationships of lesbians and gay men. *Journal of Marriage and the Family, 62*, 1052–1096.

Sciaraffa, M., & Randolph, T. (2011). "You want me to talk to children about what?" Responding to the subject of sexuality development in young children. *Young Children, 66*, 32–38.

SIECUS. (2004). *Guidelines for comprehensive sexuality education, Kindergarten–12th grade* (3rd ed.). Retrieved from http://sexedu.org.tw/guideline.pdf.

Silverberg, C. (2012). *What makes a baby.* New York: Seven Stories Press.

Tornatore, J. B., & Grant, L. A. (2002). Burden among family caregivers of persons with Alzheimer's disease in nursing homes. *Gerontologist, 4*, 497–506.

Walsh, B. A., Sánchez, C., & Burnham, M. M. (2016). Shared storybook reading in Head Start: Impact of questioning styles on the vocabulary of Hispanic dual language learners. *Early Childhood Education Journal, 44*, 263–273.

Walsh, B. A., Cromer, H., & Weigel, D. (2014). Classroom to home connections: Young children's experiences with a technology-based parent involvement tool. *Early Education and Development, 25*, 1142–1161.

Walsh, F. (1993). Conceptualization of normal family processes. In F. Walsh (Ed.), *Normal family processes* (pp. 3–69). New York: Guilford Press.

Walsh, F. (1996). The concept of family resilience: Crisis and challenge. *Family Processes, 35*, 261–281.

Zolotow, C. (1972). *William's doll.* HarperCollinsPublisher.

Zouves, C. (2004). *A dream come true: Talking to your child about assisted reproduction.* Daly City, CA: Zouves Fertility Center.

CHAPTER 7

Professional Development and Ethics

One of the core concepts of HDFS is that humans grow and change throughout the life-span. This applies to the individuals and families we both study and serve, but it also applies to ourselves as professionals in the field of HDFS. As we interact with people, gain new experiences, and acquire new knowledge, our perspectives often evolve. From our earliest days as emerging professionals through retirement we gain expertise, but more importantly we develop and refine our own identities as professionals. A **professional identity** can be described as how we define ourselves in a professional role. It can encompass interests, knowledge and expertise, adoption of **professional dispositions**, or shared attitudes, values, beliefs, and behaviors, and ethics of individuals in a given profession (Trede, Macklin, & Bridges, 2012). Given the broad nature of HDFS as a field of study and practice, our professional identities are often as diverse as our interests and aspirations.

INTERESTS

For many, one of the earliest steps in forming a professional identity in HDFS is to explore and identify foundational areas of interest. Over the course of your academic and professional career, you may discover that you have a strong preference for either human development or family studies. It may also be that you discover passion for both. If development excites you, which lifespan stages (e.g., early childhood, adolescence), developmental domains (e.g., physical, emotional), or contexts (e.g., education, mental health) do you find most intriguing? For those feeling the pull toward family studies, which topics grab and sustain your attention? If you had to choose between prevention work, intervention work, research, or policy, where would you focus your efforts? Do you have a specific career goal? There is no expectation that you have the answers to these types of questions today, but they are questions worth thinking about as you progress through your undergraduate program and launch your career. In an attempt to ignite this process, we will explore several areas of study and practice in Chapters 8 through 12.

ACQUIRING KNOWLEDGE AND EXPERTISE

Another potentially obvious step in developing a professional identity is the acquisition of knowledge and expertise in a particular area of study or practice (Cornelissen & van Wyk, 2007). As college students, this is often accomplished through coursework. While some HDFS programs encourage or require students to choose an area of concentration within the major, others facilitate specialization in an area by offering a range of courses in different areas to fulfill many of the major's requirements. Regardless of the approach utilized by your institution, you may find it beneficial to take the courses most aligned with your future career interests or goals.

Coursework is not the only means to acquiring knowledge or building expertise, nor is it always the best. In many instances, undergraduate coursework—particularly lower division—is necessarily broad. For example, Lifespan Development courses typically cover development from conception through aging or death in a single academic term. These types of courses may help you to identify interests, but the sheer amount of material often prohibits the exploration of any one concept in depth as part of the course requirements. However, that does not mean that you need to wait until upper division or graduate coursework to pursue knowledge and expertise in areas of interest. As discussed below, there are several additional methods for acquiring knowledge and expertise that are often accessible to all whom are interested, regardless of academic standing or experience.

Reading

Staying on top of current issues in research, practice, policy, and events relevant to your area(s) of interest is not only critical to developing knowledge and expertise, but can also help to form and refine your professional identity. As an undergraduate student, you will undoubtedly be assigned foundational readings as part of course requirements. However, you will also likely have opportunities to select readings on your own, whether in conjunction with course assignments or for personal interest. In general, there is an expectation that published works used to inform course assignments, including papers, come from **scholarly sources**. Scholarly sources may include peer-reviewed journals, reports published by government agencies, reports published by reputable non-governmental organizations, and some books or book chapters (see Table 7.1). Although most undergraduate students in the social sciences report using search engines like Google as their most common tool for seeking information (Kim & Sin, 2007), you likely have access to scholarly sources through your institution's library system. This is important, given the vast amount of non-credible information available online. If you have not done so already, consider participating in a library orientation session to learn how to maximize its use.

HDFS is an **applied discipline**, meaning much of what we study relates to actual real-world practice. Furthermore, HDFS is a unique discipline in that examples or

Image 7.1 Staying on Top of Current Issues in Research, Practice, Policy, and Events Relevant to Your Area of Interest Can Help to Form and Refine Your Professional Identity (photo by Dmitriy Shironosov/Depositphotos, Inc.).

Table 7.1 Scholarly Sources of Information

Publication type	Features
Peer-reviewed journals	Journals are a type of periodical that includes collections of original articles, typically written by academic scholars and researchers, that describe research findings, advance theory, or provide reviews of scholarly literature. In peer-reviewed journals, all articles are reviewed by other scholars and an editorial board before publishing.
Government reports	Government reports often include summaries of data, but can also summarize findings of publicly funded research studies.
Non-governmental reports	Reports issued by some non-governmental agencies are considered scholarly and appropriate for use in academic work. Examples of such agencies would be those that are nonpartisan, nonprofit, and have a strong history of sound research, policy, and/or advocacy.
Books	Edited or authored books written by scholars established in that content area may be considered scholarly. See Box 7.1 for guidelines on how to evaluate the credibility of the source.

applications of the content we cover are readily available via mainstream media on a daily basis. For example, the following is a sample of real headlines that were published over the course of just a few days in 2016:

- "Are You Addicted to Work?" (East, 2016);
- "Embrace the Ways of the New Millennial Dad" (Quigley, 2016);
- "Finding Common Ground in Interfaith Marriage" (Miller, 2016);
- "Giving Students a Second Chance" (Lantigua-Williams, 2016);
- "Marriage May Improve Chances of Surviving a Heart Attack, Say Researchers" (Sample, 2016);
- "Parenting is Now Officially Impossible" (Cunha, 2016);

- "Preschool Suspensions Are Made Worse by Racial Disparities" (Davidson, 2016);
- "The 'Traditional' Definition of Marriage Isn't Really All That Traditional" (Lester, 2016);
- "These 4 Startups Are Taking the Pain Out of Parenting" (Jain, 2016);
- "Think Mothering Young Kids Is Hard? Get Ready for Even Tougher Times" (Lombrozo, 2016);
- "Why Are Millennials Putting Off Marriage? Let Me Count the Ways" (Barkho, 2016).

In some ways, staying informed about current events and issues via the mainstream media may be just as important to developing your identity as a professional as continuous review and exploration of scholarly sources. Current events afford both the opportunity to think about issues from a developmental and/or family science perspective and can provide insight as to diverse perspectives on issues among the general population. Often, when research findings are published in scholarly sources, an accompanying press release is distributed that allows mainstream news outlets to report the highlights of the research without the technical details. In many instances, this allows consumers to get the essence of what was found without having to decipher a highly specialized research article. However, this is where knowing how to evaluate sources is critical! Many articles, particularly those found online, may appear as news, but the content can range from small distortions from the truth to outright falsehoods often for the purpose of advancing a given agenda. Stories that go viral can often be checked for accuracy using websites such as www.factcheck.org, www.snopes.com, www.truthorfiction.com, and www.politifact.com. Additional methods for evaluating sources are provided in Box 7.1.

Presentations, Trainings, Workshops, and Webinars

Another effective method of acquiring knowledge and expertise in an area of interest is to attend presentations, trainings, workshops, and/or webinars conducted by experts in that area. Unlike courses that span the length of an academic term and have a tendency to cover a broad range of content, these are typically much shorter in duration and focus on a very specific topic. The difference between presentations, trainings, workshops, and webinars is largely semantic, as each involves listening to someone with some degree of expertise. The term *presentation*, or *talk*, is often used in academic settings where there is a focus on research or theory. Often, research-oriented presentations are more current than other published scholarly sources of information. This is because it can take several years for research findings to be published in journals or books, but presentations can be prepared quickly. *Trainings* and *workshops* have a tendency to focus on application, or learning "how to," and are often more interactive than presentations. *Webinars* can focus on research, theory, and/or application, but differ from traditional presentations, trainings, and workshops because they are conducted online. Like trainings and workshops, it is common for live webinars to have an interactive component as well.

Participation in presentations, trainings, workshops, and webinars is an encouraged practice in many HDFS-related professions. Although not necessarily required at the undergraduate level, we would argue that there are benefits to starting early. Not only might it help steer your professional identity in terms of interests, but the professional

BOX 7.1 EVALUATING SOURCES OF INFORMATION

We live in an age where it has become increasingly difficult to evaluate the credibility of information. Whether it is something posted online, published in print, or even shared via video, with the right software, nearly all published work can seem legitimate. So how do we know what is credible? The following suggestions have been adapted from the library guide at Johns Hopkins University.*

- *Evaluate the Credibility of the Author Who Wrote It.* Is this person a known scholar in this particular field, a reporter, or someone else? If you are not sure, conduct a search for that person using your library database and/or an internet search engine like Google. If the author is someone in academia, what is their institutional affiliation? Be wary of online postings that do not provide information about the author. Essentially, engage in due diligence to make sure that the author either has the authority to write the piece, or a history of reputable journalism. Ensuring that authors do not have a personal stake in the study's outcome is also important.
- *Evaluating the Accuracy.* What kind of information is being reported? Is it fact, opinion, propaganda, or research? Cross-checking the information presented with other sources can be a useful strategy in making this determination. Can the information reported be verified elsewhere? Does the author provide references? If it is a summary of a research study, the methodology should be clearly described. In general, research summaries are considered more trustworthy when published in peer-reviewed periodicals.
- *Evaluate the Credibility of the Publishing Body.* In addition to checking authorship credentials, it is also a good idea to evaluate the publisher credentials. Who published the piece in question? A professional organization? An academic publishing house? Is the name of any organization given on the document you are reading, or the website you are viewing? If yes, is this organization recognized in the field in which you are studying. This can be important, as even similar sounding organizations can have varying degrees of credibility as academic sources. For example, as you have read throughout this text, the NCFR is a well-respected and vetted organization in the field of family science. NCFR publications can generally be accepted as scholarly and credible. In contrast, the Family Research Council (FRC) is a very different organization. Although the names may sound similar, FRC is a conservative Christian lobbying organization whose main causes include restriction of LGBTQ rights, abortion, divorce, stem-cell research, and pornography (FRC, 2016). Given their stated mission of influencing public policy to align with their core causes, FRC publications would likely not be accepted as scholarly. The same would be true for other lobbying organizations. Regardless, all sources of information should be evaluated for potential bias.
- *Evaluate the Credibility of the Piece Itself.* Credible writing often includes a review or overview of relevant literature, research, technique, and/or theory. Opposing perspectives are described and explained, and references are provided.

* The full library guide is available at http://guides.library.jhu.edu.

connections that are often made through participation can be invaluable. Many states and professional organizations that issue occupational licenses, such as for counseling or teaching, require their licensees to participate in a minimum number of **continuing education** hours or units each year. CFLEs, described in Chapters 1 and 6, are required to complete 100 hours of continuing education every 5 years to maintain certification (NCFR, 2016). This means they must participate in 100 hours of further relevant education over that time period. While some professionals meet their continuing education requirements by enrolling in a graduate program or by taking additional college coursework, many meet this requirement by attending presentations, trainings, workshops, or webinars.

Conferences are an excellent resource for finding presentations, trainings, and workshops to attend. Conferences may be international, national, statewide, regional, or local, and tend to be sponsored by professional organizations, governmental or private agencies, or educational institutions. They can, and often do, have a research focus, but many conferences are geared toward emerging and established practitioners (see Chapter 2). It is not uncommon for conference sponsors to offer discounted registration and lodging for students. A list of well-known conferences relevant to HDFS is presented in Table 7.2; however, finding conferences that work for you is often as simple as a quick internet search.

Colleges and universities, perhaps your own or a neighboring institution, are also potentially good sources for finding professional development opportunities in the form of presentations, trainings, and workshops. Departments and student organizations often sponsor research talks, and many colleges and universities are involved with providing continuing education events for various licensed professions. Check your campus calendar, and consider asking your instructors for additional methods of finding out about such events on or near your campus.

Finally, webinars are gaining in popularity. In many instances, participation is free. Typically, a webinar will be scheduled on a specified date and time, and then registered participants are given a link to join. During the webinar, the presenter or presenters will

Table 7.2 Major Conferences Relevant to HDFS

Name of conference	Sponsoring organization	Frequency
AERA Annual Meeting	American Educational Research Association	Every year
APA Annual Convention	American Psychological Association	Every year
ASA's Annual Aging in America Conference	American Society on Aging	Every year
NAEYC Annual Conference	National Association for the Education of Young Children	Every year
National Research Conference on Early Childhood	Administration for Children and Families	Every year
NCFR Annual Conference	National Council on Family Relations	Every year
SRA Biennial Meeting	Society for Research on Adolescence	Even years
SRCD Biennial Meeting	Society for Research in Child Development	Odd years
Zero to Three Annual Conference	Zero to Three	Every year

Image 7.2 Webinars Are Conducted Online and Gaining in Popularity (photo by Nikita Leushin/ Depositphotos, Inc.).

often use media such as slides or video to lecture on the given topic, and attendees are often able to ask questions or engage in discussion via chat. Perhaps the best way to find out about upcoming webinars is to sign up to receive email updates from sponsoring agencies or search their sites. A few agencies that regularly offer webinars on HDFS-related topics to the public include:

- Administration for Children and Families: Early Childhood Learning and Knowledge Center, https://eclkc.ohs.acf.hhs.gov/hslc/tta–system/ehsnrc/multimedia/webinars;
- American Society on Aging, www.asaging.org/web–seminars;
- Early Childhood Investigations, www.earlychildhoodwebinars.com;
- Futures Without Violence, www.futureswithoutviolence.org/resources–events/ webinars/;
- National Council on Family Relations, www.ncfr.org/events/upcoming-ncfr-webinars;
- U.S. Department of Education, www.ed.gov.

Also note that many agencies publicly archive their webinars, meaning they are available for viewing indefinitely.

Professional Experiences

Finally, gaining professional experience through practica, internships, volunteer work, service learning, and/or paid work is an excellent way to acquire knowledge and expertise that will be vital to developing a professional identity. As discussed in both Chapter 2 and Appendix A, practica, internships, and other field experiences are likely to be part of your undergraduate program. However, obtaining experience beyond that required for your major may prove beneficial for at least a few reasons. First, each experience strengthens your resume, making you that much more competitive in the postgraduation job market or when applying to graduate school. Second, with each experience, you have the

Image 7.3 Volunteer Work Can Be an Appealing Professional Experience Given the Flexibility in Level of Commitment (photo by Mauricio Jordan de Souza Coelho/Depositphotos, Inc.).

potential to meet and make connections with other professionals. Building a professional network can be invaluable as you build your career. Last, but not least, the more experience you gain, the more you will be able to refine who you are and who you want to be as a professional, and the type of work you think you ultimately want to do.

Volunteer work, service learning, and paid work each have advantages and disadvantages. Which is the best choice for you is a personal decision. Volunteer work can be appealing to some, given the relative flexibility in level of commitment. Some volunteer opportunities, like those with Court Appointed Special Advocates (CASA, www.casa forchildren.org) or Big Brothers, Big Sisters (www.bbbs.org) may be more structured in that volunteers are generally expected to make a commitment for an extended period of time, and for so many hours per week. However, other volunteer opportunities can be less structured, possibly entailing a one-time commitment or offering flexibility in terms of hours per week or overall duration. Websites such as www.volunteermatch.org or www.idealist.org are good resources for finding volunteer opportunities nearby, abroad, and even online. Alternatively, you can always contact schools, agencies, and organizations that you are interested in to inquire about opportunities.

Service learning, also referred to as community engagement, is a method of teaching and learning that incorporates community service with instruction and opportunities for meaningful reflection (Bandy, 2016). Although there is much diversity as to what this may look like, in an academic setting, it often involves taking a course with some type of community-based volunteer work or project embedded within as an option or requirement. Research has shown that participation in service learning is associated with student gains in critical thinking, communication skills, civic responsibility, and academic achievement (Bandy, 2016; Finley, 2012; Prentice & Robinson, 2010). One likely advantage of choosing service learning over independent volunteer work is having the support and guidance of an instructor and peers. A possible disadvantage is that service learning options and requirements may be more constrained.

Finally, paid work is another option for gaining professional experience. According to one large study recently conducted by Georgetown University's Center on Education and the Workforce, the primary reasons students give for seeking paid employment while in school include needing the financial support, to gain useful skills and experiences, to build or maintain a professional network, and to complement or reinforce what they are learning in school (Carnevale, Smith, Melton, & Price, 2015, p. 23). However, although a reported 70–80% of college students work, more than half hold jobs in sales, office support, the food and beverage industry, or in personal services (e.g., hair salons). Such occupations may provide needed financial support, but they are not necessarily aligned with many college majors, including HDFS. If you are one of the students who wants or needs to work while in school, know that many entry level jobs in HDFS-related occupations do not require a college degree. For those with an interest in children, early childhood education centers, after school programs, and tutoring programs may be a viable source of early career employment. If scheduling is a concern, or for those interested in other age groups, consider applying to work at human service facilities that serve clients 24 hours a day. Examples might include group homes, medical facilities, residential treatment, or shelters/living facilities for children, youth, women, families, seniors, homeless, or some other demographic in need. Alternatively, you may want to look into HDFS-related jobs on campus.

PROFESSIONAL DISPOSITIONS

Not all professionals in the field of HDFS think and behave exactly alike, nor is the goal to make them do so. However, understanding and adhering to some basic norms within the field is often essential to being taken seriously as a professional. How you present yourself to others matters, and we argue that it matters early. Rather than thinking about undergraduate education as consisting of teachers, students, and school—basically an extension of K–12—consider a different conceptualization. We propose that college, particularly in a major like HDFS, is a place where experienced professionals and scholars come together with emerging professionals and scholars to share knowledge and encourage growth. As such, there is an expectation of professionalism from the onset. As discussed later in this section, professional behavior and responsibility for faculty is often delineated through the ethics codes put forth by the professional organizations to which they belong. But, what does professionalism entail for the HDFS emerging professional while pursuing undergraduate education?

Professionalism in the College Classroom

Many faculty lay out their own expectations for student behavior in the courses they teach. These may be articulated in the course syllabus, or made explicit during class. While the specifics vary by instructor, we share five general guidelines here.

First, *be present and punctual*. Enrolling in a course is a commitment. In traditional courses, it is a commitment to be at a specified place at a specified time for a specified duration, as well as a commitment to complete all course-related activities as assigned by the instructor. In online courses, it is a commitment to set aside enough time each week to complete assigned readings, viewings, discussions, and other course activities by their due dates. In flipped and hybrid courses, the commitment is often all of the above.

Image 7.4 Full Participation Includes Contributing to Discussions and Group Activities, and Allowing Others to Contribute as Well (photo by Monkey Business/Depositphotos, Inc.).

Regardless of the course format, your presence is an important part of professionalism. It demonstrates to others that you care about the discipline, that you care about becoming a knowledgeable professional, and that you care about your professional development. The findings from one recent **meta-analysis**, or an analysis that combines data from multiple studies, suggest that class attendance is one of the strongest predictors of individual course grades and overall college GPA—stronger than SAT scores, high school GPA, study habits, and study skills (Credé, Roch, & Kieszczynka, 2010).

Second, *participate and allow others to participate.* Full participation involves more than simply showing up to class or logging on to a course website. At minimum, it includes going to class or entering web-based discussions prepared, paying attention during lectures and presentations, and minimizing disruptions and distractions. It also includes contributing to discussion and group activities, and allowing others to contribute to those same discussions and activities. It is not uncommon for HDFS courses to cover sensitive or sometimes controversial topics from multiple perspectives, which can be greatly enhanced when students have the opportunity to share their own views and listen to those of others. As such, contributing to a **safe classroom climate** is critical. Safe classroom climates are those that facilitate honest discussion and sharing of ideas and experiences (Gayle, Cortez, & Preiss, 2013). Essentially, all members treat each other with respect and without judgment, even when there is disagreement. Classrooms with safe climates are conducive to personal and professional growth, as students are challenged to think beyond their own values and experiences (Holley & Steiner, 2005).

Third, *engage in critical thought, reflection, and dialogue.* A safe classroom environment is not the same thing as an always comfortable classroom environment. On the contrary, safe classroom climates make it possible for course content and discussion to venture into topics that can be very uncomfortable for some, particularly when deeply held personal values or beliefs are challenged or otherwise contradicted. However, this type of dialogue helps us grow both developmentally and professionally. Not only are sharing and listening important, thinking and reflecting are also vital for personal and professional growth

(Boostrom, 1998). Take the time to think and reflect about what you read, what you hear in lectures, and what your classmates are saying. Ask yourself,

- What does it mean?
- Is it fact or opinion?
- How might it apply to my own life?
- How might it apply to others?
- How does it connect (or not connect) to what I've learned in my coursework?
- Do I agree or disagree, and why?
- What am I missing?

Seek clarity and understanding by asking questions, and take the time to play devil's advocate. Finally, engage in healthy dialogue. Respectfully challenge ideas, criticize theory, and offer counterarguments, but refrain from personal attacks.

Fourth, *take responsibilities seriously*. Completing course assignments is another primary responsibility for HDFS undergraduates. Course assignments are generally not meant to be busy work. On the contrary, they are typically designed to support or measure the student learning objectives for the course. As a professional working with individuals and families, you will likely be expected to complete paperwork, write reports, conduct assessments, facilitate trainings, and the like. As with coursework, there will likely be parameters guiding your work, required collaborations with colleagues, and non-negotiable deadlines. Thus, approaching assignments seriously is good career practice! For all assignments, take care to thoroughly read the instructions, preferably before emailing your instructor with questions. Often, you will find the answer has already been provided. Attention to detail is often considered a desired trait for graduate students and employees. Demonstrate your ability to pay attention to details by reading instructions carefully, and then following them. Proofread your assignments before submitting them. Additionally, honor your commitments. This can be especially important in group projects. For group projects to be successful, all members need to pull their weight. Recognize that each member brings unique strengths, and capitalize on those.

Finally, *communicate professionally*. Strong communication skills are considered important by employers in nearly all professions. However, for many, developing strong communication skills is not something that just comes naturally. It requires practice, guidance, and a degree of self-awareness. Communication involves speaking and listening, writing and reading, and is often transactional in nature. It also includes facial expressions, tone of voice, and body language.

At the most general level, communication is both receptive and expressive. **Receptive communication** involves the ability to understand what someone else is trying to say, be it verbally or in writing. Receptive communication requires careful listening or reading to understand both the actual words and the context in which those words are expressed. It involves paying attention to facial expressions, tone of voice, and body language, as well as following lines of logic and asking questions for clarity. **Expressive communication**, on the other hand, involves the ability to use language, either oral or written, such that you are understood as intended. In your undergraduate program and subsequent career, the ability to speak and write clearly and with concision, the ability to stay on point, to present information in a logical and truthful way, and to make adjustments in communication style based on context, audience, or conversation partners is important. As an undergraduate student, you will have many opportunities to strengthen your receptive and expressive communication skills. Participation in class discussions, presentations, and even lectures can all help to develop and refine listening and speaking skills, and course assignments will likely help to improve reading and writing skills.

Regardless of current skill level, it is the responsibility of HDFS students to demonstrate maturity and respect in their communications with others. This often means thinking before speaking, and drafting, re-reading, and editing emails or other written communication before sending. Recognize the difference between thinking out loud and thinking before speaking, and when each might be most appropriate. For example, thinking out loud may be quite useful when engaged in collaborative problem solving, but not as much during a presentation. Think twice before shooting off important emails from your cell phone or leaving voicemails without thinking through what you want to say and how. As a professional, think about word choices, tone of voice, and the amount of information and level of detail that is appropriate to share. Refrain from using profanity. In addition, be sure to use proper grammar, spelling, punctuation, and capitalization in all professional correspondence.

Professionalism Outside of the College Classroom

Many of the guidelines for the college classroom also apply to field experiences, as employers tend to value similar skills when hiring recent college graduates (National Association of Colleges and Employers, 2015). Whether experiences are volunteer, part of a course requirement, or paid employment, these are all situations in which a strong performance can only help you, thus should be taken seriously. For some, field experiences lead to job offers. For others, field supervisors are often later used as professional references for other jobs or graduate school applications. Demonstrate responsibility, leadership, and value by showing up on time every time, participating in collaborative work or meetings, paying attention to detail, doing your job well, and, above all, by treating supervisors, colleagues, and clients with respect.

Online is another context where professionalism matters. We live in a digital age, and most of us have accumulated at least the beginnings of a **digital identity**. A digital identity, also sometimes called a digital footprint or web presence, consists of all of the information available about a given individual online. This can include information available via public records, websites, blogs, news reports, and social media sites. According to one recent survey, 45% of employers now conduct internet searches on prospective hires and 43% of employers examine applicants' presence on social media prior to offering positions (CareerBuilder, 2014). Essentially, they report screening digital identities for the purpose of assessing professional and personal character. For example, applicants who post content to social media sites that is considered sexually provocative or inappropriate, discriminatory, poorly written, unprofessional (e.g., badmouthing previous employers), or that contains details or photographs about drug or alcohol use are less likely to be considered for positions than those with a more positive social media presence.

ETHICS

The final component of professional identity development that we address here is that of **ethics**, specifically moral principles or standards used to guide professional behavior. Presumably, you already have a personal set of ethics that dictates how you behave and the choices you make in a variety of settings. Essentially it is your moral code of what you perceive as right and wrong. In professional settings, however, there are often multiple perspectives to take into account. Consider the following scenarios:

- Julie has been employed providing in-home intervention services to children with special needs for the past 2 years. Although she has developed warm relationships with all of her families, she especially looks forward to Tuesdays, when she works with Jack. Jack is a 4-year-old with cerebral palsy, who is cared for by his single father, Mark. Julie thinks Mark is an amazing father. He's loving, attentive, and funny. It also does not hurt that she finds him very attractive. One Tuesday, as she is packing up to leave, Mark asks her out on a date.
- Devon is working as a student intern in the counseling office of a local high school. While meeting with 17-year-old Braden, he learns that Braden's girlfriend, also 17, is pregnant. It is currently March, but Braden insists that they are going to wait to tell their parents until after graduation. Braden also states that although his girlfriend has yet to see a doctor, she has been taking prenatal vitamins and otherwise taking good care of herself. The age of sexual consent in their state is 16, so no laws have been broken.
- Sarah is completing her HDFS practicum assignment at the ABC preschool, a subsidized center that provides free or low-cost child care to mostly Chinese-American families. The center itself is nice enough, with plenty of toys and stimulating materials, and most of the staff seem great. However, there is one teacher who is making Sarah uncomfortable. While the teacher is great with the children, and respectful to the families as best as Sarah can tell, Sarah has heard this teacher make disparaging and stereotypical comments about Chinese people and culture on multiple occasions. It does not seem that the teacher is intentionally trying to be hurtful; nonetheless, Sarah worries about how hearing such messages may affect the children.

Each one of these scenarios has the potential to represent an **ethical dilemma**, which occurs when one must make a decision on how to weigh competing morals. Is it okay for Julie to date Mark, or is that not allowed given their professional relationship? Does Devon have an obligation to tell someone that Braden's girlfriend is pregnant and not receiving prenatal care, or is that a breach of confidentiality? What should Sarah do about her concerns? What are her options, and what might be the potential consequences of each? Many professionals in HDFS face ethical dilemmas throughout the course of their careers. Developing both an understanding of ethical standards within your chosen profession and the skills to engage in ethical thinking and decision-making is vital to professional development.

Several professional organizations have developed **ethical codes of conduct** or ethical standards to guide the behavior and decision-making of their members. Such codes are useful in that they outline professional responsibilities and collective core values within a given field (Feeney, 2010; Palm, 2015). While the specifics are unique to each organization, shared features typically include a description of the responsibilities and expected behavior of professionals in relation to diversity, equity, power, confidentiality, assessment, and more. Examples of such documents in professions relevant to HDFS include:

Professional organization	Title*	Target professionals
American Counseling Association	*2014 ACA Code of Ethics*	Professional counselors, counselor educators
APA	*Ethical Principles of Psychologists and Code of Conduct*	Psychologists, including practitioners and researchers
NAEYC	*Code of Ethical Conduct and Statement of Commitment*	Early childhood educators
NCFR	*Ethical Principles and Guidelines for Family Scientists*	Family science practitioners and educators
National Education Association	*Code of Ethics*	P–12 administrators, teachers, and paraprofessionals
NOHS	*Ethical Standards for Human Service Professionals*	Professionals and paraprofessionals who provide direct services to individuals in diverse settings

* Links to each of these are available in the Suggested Resources section at the end of this chapter.

As you develop your professional identity, we suggest familiarizing yourself with the ethical codes or principles most relevant to your future career goals. Doing so will not only provide you with a sense of the professional expectations that lie ahead, but also a sense of direction as you face dilemmas and engage in problem solving in your field experiences (Corey, Corey, & Callanan, 1998; Palm, 2015). However, it is important to recognize that ethical codes have their limitations (Brophy-Herb, Kostelnik, & Stein, 2001; Corey et al., 1998; Herlihy & Corey, 2014; Palm, 2015). Ethical codes provide broad guidelines for professional behavior. They do not prescribe specific action to deal with individual situations, nor is there guidance for all potential dilemmas professionals will face. In some cases, the need to abide by the law or institutional policy will dictate behavior, regardless of ethical codes (Palm, 2015; see Box 7.2 for an example). Rather than conceptualizing a code of ethics as a set of rules to learn, memorize, and rigidly adhere to, it may be more helpful to think of it as a tool for thinking and problem solving. Throughout your HDFS program, you should have ample opportunity to gain additional tools to guide your ethical decision-making.

Finally, it should be noted that ethical thinking and behavior also extends to your role as a student. Similar to the ethical codes described above, most institutions of higher education also hold students responsible to a code of conduct specific to the institution. While student codes of conduct often address a range of behavior, including drug and alcohol use, hazing, possession of firearms, sexual misconduct, and the like, we focus here on standards of academic integrity. Academic integrity refers to the honesty and responsibility with which one approaches scholarly endeavors. For

BOX 7.2 CHILD ABUSE AND NEGLECT: LAW AND ETHICS

We would all likely agree that knowingly allowing a child to be abused or neglected without reporting it is unethical, particularly as members of a field committed to promoting the wellbeing of individuals and families. However, identifying abuse or neglect is not always straightforward. Abuse and neglect can take many forms, and can vary greatly in severity and persistence. Sometimes it occurs intentionally, but often abuse and neglect occurs as a byproduct of diminished mental health, inadequate resources, social isolation, or misguided or otherwise unconventional beliefs about what is best for children. Furthermore, incidences of abuse and neglect are often discovered during the course of a family or individual seeking help or treatment for those very issues. Our individual perceptions of what constitutes abuse or neglect, and when we think it is necessary to report it are often influenced by our personal values, beliefs, experiences, and even relationships with perpetrators and victims. To address some of this ambiguity, all U.S. states and territories have adopted statutes as to what each considers abuse or neglect (Child Welfare Information Gateway, 2013). A searchable database of all statutes by state or territory is available at www.childwelfare.gov/topics/systemwide/laws-policies.

Additionally, all states and territories of the United States have laws specifying who *must* report suspicion of child abuse and neglect in that state or territory (Child Welfare Information Gateway, 2015). Persons who are required by law to report suspected instances of child abuse or neglect are referred to as **mandated reporters**. As a professional in the field of HDFS, it is imperative that you develop an understanding of both the laws articulating what constitutes child abuse and neglect in your state, and who is required to report it, as nearly all states have designated specific professions, many in the field of HDFS, as mandated reporters. In other states, all adults are considered mandated reporters. For mandated reporters, adherence to law supersedes, but does not completely disregard, other possible ethical obligations when faced with ethical dilemmas involving child abuse or neglect (Palm, 2015).

students, behaviors considered academically dishonest typically include **cheating** and **plagiarism**.

For many students, acts of cheating are often readily identifiable, and generally include behaviors that somehow serve the purpose of giving one student an advantage over another. For example, copying someone else's exam or assignment responses, using unauthorized notes or materials on an exam, and fraudulently changing a grade would all likely be considered cheating. Consequences for cheating vary by institution, and even by course, but often range from a failing grade on the assignment or exam in question through academic expulsion, depending on the seriousness of the infringement.

Plagiarism, on the other hand, involves misrepresenting someone else's intellectual property, including knowledge, thoughts, words, and ideas, as your own. This can be a deliberate act, such as submitting an assignment or paper written by someone else, or

Image 7.5 For Students, Cheating and Plagiarism Are Behaviors that Are Considered Academically Dishonest (photo by Dmytro Zinkevych/Depositphotos, Inc.).

copying text verbatim and without proper citations. However, plagiarism often occurs unintentionally, particularly among students who may not completely understand what constitutes plagiarism, and how to circumvent it (Guillifer & Tyson, 2014). This is unfortunate, as the consequences for plagiarizing can be just as severe as those for cheating.

The key to avoiding plagiarism in your writing is to exercise diligence in your use of citations. If it is not 100% your own idea stated in your own words, you must credit the original source by providing the citation. Learning when and how to use citations is part of the professional development process. For those still learning to recognize and avoid plagiarism, Indiana University provides a very good online tutorial geared toward students. The tutorial is available at www.indiana.edu/~academy/firstPrinciples/index.html.

In HDFS and across the social and behavioral sciences, we adhere to the guidelines set forth by the APA for how to credit sources in our written work. The most current guidelines appear in the *Publication Manual of the American Psychological Association, 6th edition* (APA, 2010), often referred to as the *APA Manual*. The *APA Manual* covers much more than just citations. It is a writing style guide, with instructions on everything from formatting, to grammatical preferences, to strategies for reducing bias in our language. From an ethical perspective, it is critical that you learn when and how to credit sources. From an academic and professional perspective, it is also important to learn the APA writing style as a whole (see Box 7.3).

BOX 7.3 APA AS PART OF THE HDFS PROFESSIONAL IDENTITY

A message from Dr. Maureen McBride, Director of the University Writing Center and Northern NV Writing Project, University of Nevada, Reno

Since many of our professional communications happen through writing, via email, text, reports, articles, etc., developing your written professional identity is important. Part of the written identity is developed through adherence to a particular style, such as APA. Many students often view citation styles as arbitrary rules that guide punctuation, capitalization, and fonts. While style handbooks do provide information about such usage, they also give students an entry point to present their writing in a way that is accepted and expected within the field. Basically, following the APA style guidelines demonstrates your willingness to be a professional member contributing to your field because your writing demonstrates the professional norms of the community. Following the expected patterns also establishes you as a professional member whose ideas are the focus—not the form in which the ideas are presented. So, instead of viewing APA style guidelines as hoops to jump through, understand that these guidelines lead you to think and to present your thinking as part of the community in which you are engaging.

Summary

1   From our earliest days as emerging professionals through retirement we develop and refine our professional identities:

   A   Professional identities encompass interests, knowledge and expertise, adoption of professional dispositions, and ethics.

2   Identifying foundational areas of interest is important to the development of a professional identity within HDFS.

3   In addition to coursework, there are multiple effective strategies for acquiring knowledge and expertise as an HDFS student:

   A   Continuous reading of both scholarly and mainstream publications in areas of interest provides further knowledge and expertise, as well as opportunities to think about issues from an HDFS perspective.

      a   Knowing how to evaluate the credibility of sources is critical.

   B   Presentations, trainings, workshops, and webinars provide opportunities to develop more specialized knowledge or expertise with limited commitment.

   C   Practica, internships, volunteer work, service learning, and paid work are all potential methods for students to acquire real-world experience in HDFS-related professions.

4   Understanding and adhering to shared attitudes, values, beliefs, and behaviors within the field of HDFS is important for being taken seriously as a professional:

    A   As an HDFS student, professionalism can be demonstrated in the classroom through attendance and participation in courses, the engagement in critical thought, reflection, and dialogue, approaching responsibilities seriously, and by communicating professionally.

    B   Professionalism in field experiences involves demonstrating responsibility, leadership, and value by being present and punctual as scheduled, participating in collaborative work or meetings, being detail-oriented, doing your job well, and by treating others with respect.

    C   In the current digital age, professionalism also extends to online profiles. Many prospective employers evaluate applicants' digital identities as part of their selection process.

5   Engaging in ethical thinking, decision-making, and behavior is important as a student and emerging professional in HDFS:

    A   Developing skills to engage in ethical thinking and decision-making is essential for solving ethical dilemmas faced over the course of a career working with individuals and families.

    B   Many professional organizations provide ethical codes of conduct or guiding principles that outline the collective responsibilities and core values of its members.

    C   Student codes of conduct recognize cheating and plagiarism as additional forms of unethical behavior.

        a   Plagiarism can be avoided by providing appropriate citation in your work, using the guidelines of the *APA Manual, 6th edition*.

Key Terms

applied discipline
cheating
continuing education
digital identity
ethical codes of conduct
ethical dilemma
ethics
expressive communication

mandated reporter
meta-analysis
plagiarism
professional dispositions
professional identity
receptive communication
safe classroom climate
scholarly sources

Challenge: Integration

Given the potential influence of digital identities on career opportunities, it is wise to start thinking about crafting your digital identity sooner rather than later. This can mean two things: (1) taking measures to control what is already available about you online, and (2) to alter your online presence going forward, such that internet or social media searches conducted on you generate a profile of a professional.

A good starting point is to conduct an internet search for yourself using multiple search engines, as well as on any social media platform you may use. Search using your name, email address, and other potentially identifiable information. As you examine your current digital identity, ask yourself

- What information about me is already available?
- What messages does my online presence portray about me, my interests, and my lifestyle?
- Am I satisfied with my current digital identity, both in terms of the quality and quantity of publicly available content?

If applicable, consider changing your social media settings to private, and even still, hiding or removing postings that may hurt your professional image down the road.

Next, think about beginning or continuing the process of increasing your online visibility from a professional perspective. Start with your email address. While fun, cute, or otherwise clever email addresses may be appropriate for your personal life, for professional purposes, an email address that uses your name or initials is generally standard. If needed, create an email account for professional and academic use. Once you have a professional email account, consider elevating your professional visibility by creating professional profiles on social media sites such as Facebook, Twitter, and LinkedIn, and possibly even creating a personal website, webpage, or electronic portfolio to highlight your interests and accomplishments. Continue to add and revise throughout your career.

Journal Questions

1   Within HDFS, which foundational areas of interest are currently most appealing or intriguing to you? Why?
2   How would you characterize both your current professional identity, and the professional identity you hope to develop? What steps can you take as an undergraduate to realize your professional identity goals and values?
3   For each of the ethical dilemmas presented on p. 149, how might you choose to proceed? Describe the factors that should be taken into consideration prior to acting, as well as the potential consequences of your actions.

SUGGESTED RESOURCES

American Counseling Association. (2014). *2014 ACA code of ethics.* Retrieved from www.counseling.org/resources/aca-code-of-ethics.pdf.
APA. (2010). *Ethical principles of psychologists and code of conduct.* Retrieved from www.apa.org/ethics/code/.
NAEYC. (2011). *Code of ethical conduct and statement of commitment.* Retrieved from www.naeyc.org/files/naeyc/file/positions/Supplement%20PS2011.pdf.
NCFR. (1998). *Ethical principles and guidelines for family scientists.* Retrieved from www.ncfr.org/sites/default/files/downloads/news/ncfr_ethical_guidelines_0.pdf.
National Education Association. (1975). *Code of ethics.* Retrieved from www.nea.org/home/30442.htm.
NOHS. (2015). *Ethical standards for human service professionals.* Retrieved from www.nationalhumanservices.org/ethical-standards-for-hs-professionals.

REFERENCES

APA. (2010). *Publication manual of the American Psychological Association* (6th ed.). Washington, DC: APA.
Bandy, J. (2016). *What is service learning or community engagement?* Vanderbilt University, Center for Teaching. Retrieved from https://cft.vanderbilt.edu/guides-sub-pages/teaching-through-community-engagement/.
Barkho, G. (2016, June 6). Why are millennials putting off marriage? Let me count the ways. *Washington Post.* Retrieved from www.washingtonpost.com/news/soloish/wp/2016/06/06/why-are-millennials-putting-off-marriage-let-me-count-the-ways/.
Boostrom, R. (1998). "Safe spaces": Reflection on educational metaphor. *Journal of Curriculum Studies, 30,* 397–408.
Brophy-Herb, H. E., Kostelnik, M. J., & Stein, L. C. (2001). A developmental approach to teaching about ethics using the NAEYC Code of Ethical Conduct. *Young Children, 56,* 80–84.
CareerBuilder. (2014). *Number of employers passing on applicants due to social media posts continues to rise, according to new CareerBuilder survey.* Retrieved from www.careerbuilder.com/share/aboutus/pressreleasesdetail.aspx?sd=6%2F26%2F2014&id=pr829&ed=12%2F31%2F2014.

Carnevale, A. P., Smith, N., Melton, M., & Price, E. W. (2015). *Learning while earning: The new normal*. Georgetown University, Center on Education and the Workforce. Retrieved from https://cew.georgetown.edu/cew-reports/workinglearners/.

Child Welfare Information Gateway. (2013). *What is child abuse and neglect? Recognizing the signs and symptoms*. Retrieved from www.childwelfare.gov/pubs/factsheets/whatiscan/.

Child Welfare Information Gateway. (2015). *Mandatory reporters of child abuse and neglect*. Retrieved from www.childwelfare.gov/topics/systemwide/laws-policies/statutes/manda/.

Corey, G., Corey, M. S., & Callanan, P. (1998). *Issues and ethics in the helping professions* (5th ed.). Pacific Grove, CA: Brooks/Cole Publishing Company.

Cornelissen, J. J., & van Wyk, A. S. (2007). Professional socialisation: An influence on professional development and role definition. *South African Journal of Higher Education, 21*, 826–841.

Credé, M., Roch, S. G., & Kieszczynka, U. M. (2010). Class attendance in college: A meta-analytic review of the relationship of class attendance with grades and student characteristics. *Review of Educational Research, 80*, 272–295.

Cunha, D. (2016, June 8). Parenting is now officially impossible. *Time*. Retrieved from http://time.com/4357166/parenting-social-media/.

Davidson, J. (2016, June 12). Preschool suspensions are made worse by racial disparities. *Washington Post*. Retrieved from www.washingtonpost.com/politics/preschool-suspensions-are-made-worse-by-racial-disparities/2016/06/12/c9601318-30bf-11e6-95c0-2a6873031302_story.html.

East, S. (2016, June 12). Are you addicted to work? *CNN*. Retrieved from www.cnn.com/2016/06/12/health/work-addiction-adhd-norway/.

Family Research Council. (2016). *Marriage and family*. Retrieved from www.frc.org/Marriage-and-Family.

Feeney, S. (2010). Ethics today in early care and education: Review, reflection, and the future. *Young Children, 65*(2), 72–77.

Finley, A. (2012, January). *A brief review of the evidence on civic learning in higher education*. Paper distributed at the American Association of American Colleges and Universities Annual Meeting. Washington, DC. Retrieved from www.aacu.org/sites/default/files/files/crucible/CivicOutcomesBrief.pdf.

Gayle, B. M., Cortez, D., & Preiss, R. W. (2013). Safe spaces, difficult dialogues, and critical thinking. *International Journal for the Scholarship of Teaching and Learning, 7*(2), 1–8.

Guillifer, J. M., & Tyson, G. A. (2014). Who has read the policy on plagiarism? Unpacking students' understanding of plagiarism. *Studies in Higher Education, 39*, 1202–1218.

Herlihy, B., & Corey, G. (2014). *ACA ethical standards casebook*. Alexandria, VA: American Counseling Association.

Holley, L. C., & Steiner, S. (2005). Safe space: Student perspectives on classroom environment. *Journal of Social Work Education, 41*, 49–64.

Jain, S. (2016, June 9). These 4 startups are taking the pain out of parenting. *Entrepreneur*. Retrieved from www.entrepreneur.com/article/277218.

Kim, K-S., & Sin, S-C. J. (2007). Perception and selection of information sources by undergraduate students: Effects of avoidant style, confidence, and personal control in problem-solving. *Journal of Academic Librarianship, 33*, 655–665.

Lantigua-Williams, J. (2016, June 10). Giving students a second chance. *Atlantic*. Retrieved from www.theatlantic.com/politics/archive/2016/06/fair-chance-education-pledge/486518/.

Lester, C. (2016, June 9). The "traditional" definition of marriage really isn't all that traditional. *Public Radio International*. Retrieved from www.pri.org/stories/2016-06-09/traditional-definition-marriage-really-isnt-all-traditional.

Lombrozo, T. (2016, June 6). Think mothering young kids is hard? Get ready for even tougher times. *National Public Radio*. Retrieved from www.npr.org/sections/13.7/2016/06/06/480906083/think-mothering-young-kids-is-hard-get-ready-for-even-tougher-times.

Miller, J. (2016, June 9). Finding common ground in interfaith marriage. *New York Times*. Retrieved from www.nytimes.com/2016/06/12/fashion/weddings/interfaith-marriage.html?_r=0.

National Association of Colleges and Employers. (2015). *Job outlook 2016: Attributes employers want to see on new college graduates' resumes*. National Association of Colleges and Employers. Retrieved from www.naceweb.org/s11182015/employers-look-for-in-new-hires.aspx.

NCFR. (2016). *5-year recertification*. NCFR. Retrieved from www.ncfr.org/cfle-certification/maintain-your-certification/5-year-recertification.

Palm, G. F. (2015). Professional ethics and practice. In M. J. Walcheski and J. S. Reinke (Eds), *Family life education: The practice of family science* (3rd ed., pp. 235–241). Minneapolis, MN: NCFR.

Prentice, M., & Robinson, G. (2010). *Improving student outcomes with service learning*. Washington, DC: American Association of Community Colleges.

Quigley, M. W. (2016, June 9). Embrace the ways of the new millennial dad. *AARP*. Retrieved from www.aarp.org/home-family/friends-family/info-2016/millennials-dadsfathers-mq.html.

Sample, I. (2016, June 7). Marriage may improve chances of surviving a heart attack, say researchers. *Guardian*. Retrieved from www.theguardian.com/society/2016/jun/08/marriage-may-improve-chances-of-survivinga-heart-attack-say-researchers.

Trede, F., Macklin, R., & Bridges, D. (2012). Professional identity development: A review of the higher education literature. *Studies in Higher Education, 37*, 365–384.

PART VI

What Are the Key Areas within HDFS?

CHAPTER 8

Family and Early Years

While not all families include children, many do. The decision to raise a child can be immensely personal, and the circumstances that bring adults to choose parenthood vary widely. Whereas many children are planned, such as when an adult or couple intentionally attempt to conceive or adopt, others are unexpected. An unplanned pregnancy, falling in love with someone who is already a parent or pregnant, or stepping in to care for children who have lost their parent or parents to incarceration, substance abuse, mental health issues, or death all represent circumstances in which families are created or extended unexpectedly. Regardless, nearly all individuals are raised in some family context, and characteristics of that family context often have implications for development. Likewise, characteristics of individuals can also affect family context and functioning, both in **families of orientation**, or the families we are born into or raised by, and in **families of procreation**, or the families we create ourselves. As explained in Chapter 1, understanding these multidirectional relationships is central to the study of HDFS. Over the next five chapters, we provide a preview of some of the concepts and issues you will likely explore as an HDFS major. Chapters 8 through 10 focus on the lifespan stages of early childhood through adolescence, and Chapters 11 and 12 focus on early through late adulthood. Within each chapter, we highlight some of the major developmental milestones of the lifespan stage, as well as current areas of research and study. Policy issues, career options associated with each lifespan stage, and strategies for specializing in each as both an area of study and future career are also presented. In Chapters 13 and 14, we shift our focus to families, specifically family diversity and family strengths. We begin here, however, with early childhood.

THE EARLY YEARS

For families with a child or children under age 5, life can feel a bit overwhelming. In addition to the constant care and supervision young children require, many families face stress related to expenses, isolation, and parenting in general. New parents must often renegotiate roles and responsibilities, older siblings may experience jealousy or resentment, and all family members make adjustments with each new addition to the family unit. This stress can be amplified for single parents, working parents, and other parents lacking adequate supports or resources. Among married parents, it is common for marital satisfaction to decline over those early years, often due to the changes young children bring to an existing relationship (Khajehei, 2016). The sheer multitude of potential issues and decisions faced by parents of young children might make one wonder why anyone bothers having children at all. Yet, most parents don't regret having children, and many voluntarily do it again. Decisions related to family planning and the effects of children on marital relationships will be discussed in more detail in Chapter 11. In this chapter, we provide an overview of early childhood and families as an area of study and practice, starting with an introduction to the development of young children from birth through age 5.

PHYSICAL HEALTH AND DEVELOPMENT

Healthy physical growth and development begins before birth, and arguably even before conception. Factors such as the age and health of the mother, genes, chromosomes, nutrition, and prenatal exposure to substances that can harm fetal development, such as alcohol or drugs, can influence children's physical health and development even before they take their first breath. Fortunately, in the United States, widespread access to prenatal care and education in conjunction with advances in medicine, technology, and science more generally, has led to both an increase in newborn health and a very low infant mortality rate, with over 99.99% of infants surviving their first year of life (Centers for Disease Control and Prevention (CDC), 2016b).

Image 8.1 Life Can Feel a Little Bit Overwhelming in Families with Children under 5 (photo by Dmitry Kalinovsky/Depositphotos, Inc.).

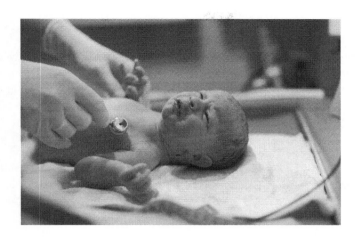

Image 8.2 Babies Born More than 3 Weeks Early Are Considered Preterm (photo by Marcin Sadlowski/Depositphotos, Inc.).

Height and weight can be used as one indicator of physical health throughout early childhood and beyond. At birth, however, we are typically more concerned with weight. Newborns weighing less than 5.5 pounds (or 2,500 grams) are considered **low birthweight**, and are generally at higher risk for illness, developmental problems, and infant death than children born weighing more (Child Trends, 2015). The smaller the baby, the higher the immediate and long-term risks. In the United States, slightly less than 10% of newborns are low birthweight (CDC, 2016b). Some of these babies are small because they are born **preterm**, meaning more than 3 weeks early. They may be tiny, but they weigh pretty much what they should, given their **gestational age**, or the number of weeks since conception. Many children born preterm do just fine after giving everyone an initial scare, but they are at higher risk for developmental delays and learning disabilities. Other low birthweight newborns, referred to as **small-for-gestational age (SGA)**, weigh less than they should, given their gestational age. Regardless of whether the SGA baby is born full-term or not, the fact that they are smaller than they should be is cause for concern, as something has prevented them from developing *in utero* as expected. A few common culprits include maternal smoking, drug use, malnutrition during pregnancy, and, in the case of multiples, sharing the womb with at least one other sibling (Stanford Children's Health, 2016). SGA babies are more likely to catch infections, have brain damage, and die during infancy than children born at a healthy weight for their gestational age, thus careful monitoring throughout early childhood is recommended (Tsai, Chen, Tsou, & Mu, 2015).

Babies born a healthy weight for their gestational age tend to grow rapidly over the first year. By their first birthday, most children in the United States have nearly tripled their birthweight, and have grown almost a foot (CDC, 2016a). Growth continues steadily, such that by age 6, the average child weighs between 40 and 50 pounds, and is at least 3.5 feet tall (CDC, 2016a).

Good nutrition is essential for optimal physical health and development. In most cases, and for a number of reasons, medical professionals recommend feeding children breast milk or infant formula only for the first 6 months, and then mixing breast milk or formula with cereals and other foods until children are one (American Academy of

Pediatrics, 2016a). By age 2, most children can eat the same types of foods as adults. Young children are remarkably good at regulating their own food intake, meaning they know when they are hungry and when they are full. To support healthy eating habits and proper nutrition, the American Academy of Pediatrics (2016b) recommends that parents provide children with a range of healthy food options, but let children decide what and how much to eat.

Sleep is critical for healthy physical, intellectual, and emotional development. According to the National Sleep Foundation (2016), most children spend about 40% of their childhood asleep. This percentage is even higher in early childhood. Newborns need an average of 16 hours of sleep per every 24 hours, although there is certainly individual variation. In general, children need fewer hours of sleep as they get older, but even 5-year-olds need between 11 and 13 hours each night. Ensuring young children get adequate sleep can present challenges to parents. Not only do many young children resist going to sleep or wake frequently at night, busy schedules and competing demands sometimes mean disruptions to important routines around naps and bedtimes.

Physical development also includes the development of motor skills. **Gross motor skills** are those that involve large body movements, and in early childhood include milestones such as rolling over, sitting, standing, walking, running, and jumping. The age at which each skill emerges varies considerably, and is typically influenced by environmental factors (Kaplan & Dove, 1987). For example, in some families young children are encouraged to be independent. As such, infants may be held less, affording them more opportunity to move their bodies and practice their developing skills. Compared to infants from families where babies are almost always held, we would expect to see earlier mastery of many early gross motor skills (Super, 1976). Gross motor skills tend to occur in sequence, with sitting occurring before crawling, crawling before walking, and walking before running. Each new motor skill builds on the previous skills, but the pace of progression differs by child. Some infants may go from crawling to walking so quickly, it seems they never crawled at all. Others may crawl for months before taking those first steps. Both are normal and indicative of healthy development.

A second type of motor skills that develop throughout early childhood are **fine motor skills**. Fine motor skills are those movements that require small muscles, especially those of the hands and fingers. Infants use fine motor skills to grasp fingers and toys, wave bye-bye, and eat finger foods. Over the next few years, young children will learn how to use utensils, build with blocks, draw, write, and possibly even tie their own shoes as their fine motor skills become highly developed. As with gross motor skills, opportunity for practice is important.

INTELLECTUAL DEVELOPMENT

The study of young children's intellectual development has been approached from a number of disciplines within the cognitive sciences. In HDFS, we often focus on cognitive development, or understanding how individuals think and learn across time. The study of cognitive development includes, but is not limited to, perception, attention, memory, language, and brain development.

Research on infant cognition has shown that very young infants demonstrate several noteworthy cognitive competencies. For example, over their first 6 months, babies begin

Image 8.3 Gross Motor Skills Develop with Practice (photo by Lydia DeFlorio).

to demonstrate an understanding of **object permanence**, meaning they recognize that objects continue to exist even when out of sight (Ruffman, Slade, & Redman, 2005), they can match small numbers of sounds with small numbers of objects (Kobayashi, Hiraki, & Hasegawa, 2005), and demonstrate memory capacity, as even 3-month-olds have some ability to remember things they have seen 3 months later (Campanella & Rovee-Collier, 2005). These and other early competencies continue to develop, such that by age 3 there are marked differences in cognitive ability as compared to infancy.

Language development during the first 2 years of life is generally associated with cognitive development, as language is the most clear evidence of children being capable of **symbolic thought**, or the ability to think using words or images. Although infants and toddlers are able to learn any language, the sequence at which language is acquired during the first 2 years is essentially universal. Newborns cry as a form of communication. Although initially they may cry to indicate discomfort, such as when they are hungry, tired, or wet, it is not long before they display cries with seemingly different meanings. For example, an infant may have a distinct cry for hunger, a distinct cry for pain, and a distinct cry for boredom. By the time they are 2 or 3 months old, most babies can also coo, fuss, smile, and make repetitive vowel sounds. At around 6 months, babbling begins. Babbling involves making simple consonant/vowel sounds repeatedly, such as *ba-ba-ba* or *ma-ma-ma*. Around age 1, many children say their first word.

For most children, vocabulary growth is rapid from about age 18 months through early childhood. By first grade, most children know anywhere from 5,000 to 20,000 words (Moats, 2001). Over this same time period, children develop the ability to string words together into sentences. Whereas 2-year-olds tend to speak in very short sentences, by kindergarten, many children speak much like adults, demonstrating a progressively sophisticated mastery of grammar and syntax. Although there are several theories about how language is learned, children's exposure to language is important. Unfortunately, not all children benefit from comparable exposure. It is estimated, for example, that poor children hear 30 million fewer words by age 3 than children from higher income families (Hart & Risley, 2003). This "word gap" is believed to at least partially explain the pronounced differences seen in later reading achievement between poor and non-poor elementary students (Hindman, Wasik, & Snell, 2016).

The first 5 years of life are also particularly important for brain development. Newborns are born with billions of **neurons**, or nerve cells capable of receiving and sending electrical and chemical signals throughout the central nervous system. Each neuron has one **axon** and many **dendrites**. Axons are used to transmit signals to other cells, and dendrites are used to receive signals from other cells. Axons and dendrites communicate across small gaps between neurons called **synapses**. Everyday experiences create the formation of dendrites, and, subsequently, synapses in the brains of young children, at a rate unparalleled at any other time in life. Synapses that are used regularly become stronger, and those that are not wither and die as part of a process known as **pruning**.

Myelination is another important process occurring in the brain during early childhood. Myelination involves the coating of axons with a fatty substance, called myelin, which speeds up transmission between neurons. Myelination is like adding insulation around wires to make conduction more efficient. The more efficient the transmission between neurons, the more automated processes become. To illustrate, suppose a young child is learning how to kick a ball. The first several attempts might appear kind of awkward. The child may kind of walk into the ball, trip over it, or miss completely. However, the same neurons are going to be responsible for coordinating vision and movement for each attempt. As this sequence of neurons is repeatedly activated, the connections become stronger and performance begins to improve. Once myelinated, however, kicking a ball becomes an effortless activity.

One part of the brain that myelinates rapidly during the preschool years is the corpus callosum, which is made up of the nerve fibers that connect the left and right sides of the brain. The left and right sides of our brains are set up to do different things. The left side of our brain controls the right side of our body and, for many, contains the parts of the brain dedicated to language and logic. The right side of the brain controls the left side of the body and is often called the "creative" side of the brain. During the preschool years, the two hemispheres become more specialized and better coordinated, thus children are better able to use both at the same time.

As an HDFS student, you can expect to learn much more about brain development in your introductory and advanced development courses, including how maturation of specific regions or structures within the brain correspond to human behavior. The important thing to remember at this point is that early experiences matter. Without stimuli, synapses are not formed or maintained. Young children need routine interaction with people, and exposure to a variety of places and things. This does not mean that families must enroll young children in special classes, purchase special toys, or take them to travel the world. On the contrary, much of the stimulation necessary for optimal brain growth occurs naturally through reading, talking, running errands, trips to the park, visits with family and friends, routine caregiving tasks, and play (see Box 8.1).

BOX 8.1 PLAY

Of the many experiences that contribute to healthy child development, one of the most important is play. In fact, play is so important it has been declared a universal right of children by the United Nations High Commissioner for Human Rights (1989). Play contributes to children's development across the physical, intellectual, and emotional domains in a multitude of ways (White, 2013). Examples include:

Physical benefits:

- contribute to children's gross and fine motor development;
- contribute to healthier bodies, including endurance, strength, and growth of muscles and organs, and reduces risk of childhood obesity.

Intellectual benefits:

- promote the development of language and literacy, problem-solving skills, creativity, and math and science knowledge;
- provide opportunities for exploration, experimentation, and hypothesis-testing.

Social benefits:

- help children develop social competencies, such as cooperation, negotiation, compromise, rule-following, and advocating for self and others;
- allow children to practice adult roles, work through fears, and master imaginary worlds with little risk of failure.

As an HDFS student, you will likely learn a lot about play, including types of play, social aspects of play, and how to promote play in home and classroom settings.

EMOTIONAL DEVELOPMENT

Positive social interactions with parents and caregivers not only stimulate healthy brain development, but, relatedly, they are the foundation on which emotional development occurs. It is through early social interactions that infants learn whether the world is a safe place, and whether they can count on their needs being met. When parents or caregivers consistently tend to their young children's needs, keep them safe, and show them love, infants develop secure attachments to those adults (see Attachment Theory in Chapter 5). Conversely, when care is inconsistent or harsh, infants often develop insecure attachments. This is important because these early attachments provide children with internal working models about relationships and the availability of caregivers during times of need that they then use as the basis for relationships with others throughout childhood and beyond (Bowlby, 1988). Infants with secure attachments are generally more comfortable exploring and interacting with people and things in their environments. They trust the adults in their life to keep them safe. As they get older, children with secure attachments tend to do better in school, have positive relationships with others, and are more likely to someday become parents with securely attached infants themselves (Aviezer, Sagi, Resnick, & Gini, 2002; Englund, Kuo, Puig, & Collins, 2011; Kretchmar & Jacobvitz, 2002). On the other hand, infants with insecure attachments are more likely to be withdrawn, irritable, and/or fearful. As they get older, they demonstrate lower levels of social competence, and may be more vulnerable to stress associated with negative life events (Dallaire & Weinraub, 2007; Groh et al., 2014).

The extent to which parents are sensitive and responsive to their young children's needs greatly influences attachment quality. Children are unlikely to develop secure attachments to parents who are abusive or absent, for example. But that does not mean that many, or even most, children with insecure attachments are somehow maltreated, as there are many other reasons that early care might be inconsistent or insensitive even when love is strong. Factors such as substance abuse, mental illness, and stress associated with work, marriage, parenting other children, and poverty can all result in diminished parenting, as parents' attention may be focused elsewhere (Farmer & Lee, 2011; Joshi & Bogen, 2007; Kahng, Oyserman, Bybee, & Mowbray, 2008; Mayes & Truman, 2002). Furthermore, some children are just harder to parent.

Temperament refers to innate dispositions held by individuals that influence their emotions and behaviors (see Box 8.2). In general, when parents talk about how "easy" their child is, or how "difficult" one child is compared to another, they are often talking about temperament. Easy children are generally happy, and easily distracted or comforted when upset. They are interested in new people and things, and can often self-entertain when needed. They live more-or-less on a predictable schedule, but also adjust well to changes in routine. Parents of easy children often feel competent, experience less stress, and get more sleep than those with less easy children (Sorondo & Reeb-Sutherland, 2015). Studies of infant temperament suggest that about 40% of children are rated by their parents as easy (Thomas & Chess, 1980). The remaining 60% may demonstrate a variety of more challenging temperamental features. They may have difficulty establishing feeding and sleeping schedules, adjusting to changes in routine or new people, or being soothed when upset (Thomas, Chess, & Korn, 1982). They may also become overstimulated or become distressed easily. Consequently, their parents may feel

BOX 8.2 DIMENSIONS OF TEMPERAMENT

According to Alexander Thomas and Stella Chess, pioneers in the field of infant development, temperament comprises nine dimensions (Thomas, Chess, & Birch, 1970).

- *Activity level*, or the ratio of an infant's active periods to inactive periods. How active is the child?
- *Rhythmicity*, or body rhythms. Are the child's sleep, feeding, and excretion patterns fairly predictable?
- *Distractibility*. Is the child easily distracted, particularly when upset?
- *Approach/withdrawal*. How does the child respond to new things, places, and people?
- *Adaptability*. How does the child respond to a change in routine?
- *Attention span and persistence*. How much time and effort does a child devote to a toy or activity?
- *Intensity of reaction*. To what extent does a child respond emotionally to various stimuli? How happy, sad, hurt, or angry does the child appear?
- *Threshold of responsiveness*. How much stimulation is required for the child to invoke an emotional response?
- *Quality of mood*. Is the child generally happy or fussy?

frustrated or lack confidence in regards to caregiving tasks, particularly when parents perceive their infants' behavior as an indication that they are somehow parenting wrong (Verhage, Oosterman, & Schuengel, 2015).

Parental self-efficacy, or parents' beliefs about their own ability to parent effectively, influences the quality of parenting behavior. Whereas parents with high self-efficacy tend to be more sensitive, responsive, and generally in-tune with their children's needs, parents with lower self-efficacy are less consistent. There is some evidence to suggest that young children with difficult temperaments are the ones most sensitive to the quality of the caregiving they receive (Stright, Gallagher, & Kelley, 2008). For example, one study showed that infants with difficult temperaments who consistently received warm and responsive caregiving had fewer behavior problems as children in first grade when compared to babies with similar caregiving experiences but easier temperaments (Bradley & Corwyn, 2007). Such findings highlight the importance of providing education and support to parents of young children.

Also critical to healthy social and emotional functioning in early childhood and across the lifespan is children's increasing awareness of self through the formation of a **self-concept** and **theory of mind**. Self-concept refers to the ideas or images we hold about ourselves. Self-concept not only affects our self-esteem, but, as discussed in Chapter 10, is important for identity development as well. Theory of mind, on the other hand, is the understanding that other people have thoughts, feelings, ideas, plans, and beliefs different from our own. Such understanding is essential for both expressive and receptive communication (see Chapter 7), and, subsequently, for developing and maintaining healthy relationships with others.

Image 8.4 Children Do Not Become Aware that They Are Looking at Themselves in the Mirror, and Not Another Child, Until About 18–24 Months (photo by Aynur Shauerman/ Depositphotos, Inc.).

The development of self-awareness begins early in life. Young infants, even newborns, have a basic understanding that they are a separate entity from everything else (Filippetti, Johnson, Lloyd-Fox, Dragovic, & Farroni, 2013; Rochat, 2003). However, it is not really until they are a little over 1 year that they become aware of their own physical features. For example, it takes until about 18–24 months for most children to become aware that they are looking at themselves, and not another child, when looking in the mirror (Bard, Todd, Bernier, Love, & Leavens, 2006; Nielsen, Dissanayake, & Kashima, 2003). Around this same time, most children in the United States also become capable of expressing emotions such as embarrassment, guilt, shame, or pride, all of which are early indications that they recognize that other people have feelings and thoughts about them and what they do (Lewis, 2013).

By age 2 or 3, most typically developing children have a relatively sophisticated self-awareness as compared to during infancy. They typically understand the difference between "you" and "me," and they can describe themselves at a very basic level, as in "I am a boy" (Stipek, Gralinski, & Kopp, 1990). They can even be observed demonstrating empathy toward others (Taylor, Eisenberg, Sprinrad, Eggum, & Sulik, 2013). Between the ages of 3 and 5, children are most likely to define themselves based on observable characteristics, such as their names, their ages, toys they own, things they can do on their own, and the people in their family (Keller, Ford, & Meacham, 1978). They can also define themselves in terms of their emotions and attitudes. Children's understanding of others is also becoming increasingly sophisticated, such that they begin to understand the motives and reasons behind their emotions and behaviors. They understand that a friend may be upset because he broke his toy, or that a parent may get angry when their child misbehaves. By about age 4, most healthy children also understand that people can be fooled into believing something untrue. For some children this manifests as practical jokes and other forms of harmless trickery, and for others as behavior more likely characterized as lying. Either way, the ability to engage in deception is indicative of a healthy theory of mind, as it requires a complex understanding that the thoughts of others are not only different from our own, but can be manipulated as well. Helping parents to understand that some of the more challenging or less-desirable behaviors exhibited by children are often a sign of healthy development is one of the core responsibilities of many HDFS professionals.

MAJOR AREAS OF RESEARCH AND STUDY

The lifespan stage of early childhood has received considerable empirical and scholarly attention for decades, thus the potential areas of research and study are seemingly infinite. At the broadest level, physical, intellectual, and emotional development can certainly be considered major areas of research and study. Within each of these domains, there are numerous subdomains, or subareas, of study (see Table 8.1). For example, scholars may have a broad interest in intellectual development, but a more specific interest in perception or language. Others may be interested in how two or more subdomains are interrelated, such as understanding the relationship between sleep and memory. Given the applied nature of HDFS in conjunction with the vast amount of research that has already been done on early childhood, much of the current research in HDFS aims to better understand the often complex relationships between domains (or subdomains) of development and the contexts (or subcontexts) in which development occurs. Table 8.2 provides examples of various developmental contexts and subcontexts frequently studied.

Table 8.1 Examples of Subdomains of Research and Study in Early Childhood

Physical development	Intellectual development	Emotional development
Health	Attention	Aggression
Illness	Brain development	Attachment
Injury/trauma	Creativity	Behavior
Motor skills	Decision-making	Development of emotions
Nutrition	Developmental disabilities	Emotional regulation
Prematurity	Imitation	Empathy
Reflexes	Information processing	Friendships
Sensory development	Inhibition	Gender development
Sleep	Intelligence	Moral development
Weight	Language	Motivation
	Learning	Personality
	Literacy	Play
	Memory	Self-awareness/understanding
	Metacognition	Self-concept
	Number sense	Self-esteem
	Object permanence	Separation anxiety
	Perception	Social competency
	Problem solving	Stranger anxiety
	Reasoning	Temperament
	Spatial development	Theory of mind
	Symbolic thought/representation	

Table 8.2 Examples of Contexts and Sub-Contexts of Research and Study in Early Childhood

Individual	*Family*	*School/child care*	*Institutional*
Ability	Abuse and neglect	Academic achievement	Discrimination
Age	Adoption and foster care	Bullying/victimization	Privilege/power
Gender	Discipline practices	Classroom quality	Public policy/laws
Health status	Divorce and remarriage	Curriculum and instruction	Social service involvement
Individual characteristics	Domestic violence	Early childhood education	
Prematurity	Family composition/structure	Early intervention	
	Family decision-making	Parent involvement	
	Family dynamics	Pedagogical orientations	
	Family functioning	Peer interactions	
	Family resources	Special education	
	Family strengths	Teacher characteristics and qualifications	
	Family stress	Teacher–child interactions	
	Gender roles and socialization		
	Homelessness	Teacher training	
	Immigration experiences	Time spent in school/ child care settings	
	Intergenerational relationships		
	Marital relationships		
	Military families		
	Neighborhood influences		
	Parent–child relationships		
	Parenting		
	Race/ethnicity/culture		
	Religion/spirituality		
	Risk and resilience		
	Sibling relationships		
	Social support		
	Socioeconomic status/poverty		
	Teen parenting		
	Transition to parenthood		

Although research can focus on potentially any combination of domains and/or contexts, and at varying degrees of specificity (e.g., subdomains and subcontexts), we focus briefly here on the contexts of family and child care and their developmental correlates.

Family and Early Development

Understanding early development within a wide range of family contexts is fundamental to the study of early childhood. Parents and primary caregivers play a large role in creating these contexts, particularly through their knowledge, attitudes, beliefs, and practices, which, in turn, often have implications for young children's outcomes. For example, within the domain of physical development, research has shown that parent behaviors such as monitoring, pressuring children to eat, and restricting food intake are consistently associated with their children's weight and eating habits (Clark, Goyder, Bissell, Blank, & Peters, 2007; Faith, Scanlon, Birch, Francis, & Sherry, 2004). Within the intellectual domain, both parents' beliefs about young children's mathematical abilities and the accuracy of those beliefs predict children's actual math skills at the end of preschool (DeFlorio & Beliakoff, 2015). In the emotional domain, we have already highlighted how parenting practices influence young children's attachment quality. There are many more examples across domains found in the research literature, many with the common finding being that parenting matters.

Understanding how other factors within the home environment, such as family functioning and stress, affect both parents' ability to parent and children's outcomes is also a focus of current research. We know that children from homes with high conflict or stress are at considerable risk for a range of developmental problems, including but not limited to lower school readiness competencies, behavioral problems, and less-developed social competencies more generally (Cabrera, Scott, Fagan, Steward-Streng, & Chien, 2012; Minze, McDonald, Rosentraub, & Jouriles, 2010; Nigrelli & Brennan, 2014). These problems are exacerbated when factors such as poverty, child maltreatment, or parent substance abuse are also present (Magnuson & Duncan, 2002; Mayes & Truman, 2002; Azar, 2002). Current research not only focuses on understanding why and how parenting and the home environment influence children's outcomes, but also on effective methods of prevention and intervention within these various contexts.

Child Care and Early Development

Although nearly all children develop within the context of a family, approximately one-third of children also spend a significant portion of their early years in non–relative child care (U.S. Census Bureau, 2013). Many children need out-of-home care so their parents can work, but some also attend early childhood education programs for personal enrichment, including opportunities for socialization or to promote school readiness. The effects of child care on children's development has long been an area of study in HDFS, particularly in regards to how the quality of care, including characteristics of the caregiver–child relationship, relates to children's development (e.g., Abner, Gordon, Kaestner, & Korenman, 2013; Mortensen & Barnett, 2015). This continues to be an area of study, albeit at an increasingly nuanced level.

There has also been an increased focus on promoting school readiness among at-risk children, particularly those living in poverty. In 2002, the U.S. Department of Education, Institute for Education Sciences, funded several large-scale research projects to evaluate the effects of 14 different preschool curricula when implemented with low-income children (Preschool Curriculum Evaluation Research Consortium, 2008). The findings, which revealed that many of the curricula commonly used in programs serving low-income children had no discernible effects on children's literacy, math, or socioemotional skills, highlighted the need for effective curricula for use in early childhood programs, thus curriculum development and efficacy testing has become a popular area of research and study among early childhood education scholars.

AREAS OF PRACTICE

Career opportunities working with young children and/or their families often involve some element of education and support, be it the education and support of the child, the parents, or the family. For those considering a career working with young children and/ or their parents or families, we provide an overview of some of the possibilities for HDFS graduates.

Early Childhood Education

Numerous programs throughout the country provide early childhood education services to children from birth through prekindergarten, and in some instances through the primary grades. Some programs, such as Head Start, Early Head Start, and state pre-school, are publicly funded, meaning they are free or low cost to parents, and tend to be geared toward promoting school readiness among low-income children. Other programs are privately operated, and funded through tuition paid to parents. Similar to publicly funded programs, many private programs also have an explicit school readiness focus. However, in the private sector, there tends to be more variation in what it means to be "ready for school," as some programs focus more heavily on academic content, some on socioemotional development, and still others embrace specific educational philosophies over the development of specific skills (e.g., Montessori, Reggio Emilia, Waldorf). The range of career options for HDFS graduates may vary between publicly funded and pri-vately funded programs. While teacher and administrator positions are typically options in both types of programs, Head Start, Early Head Start, and some state preschool pro-grams may have more opportunities for those interested in working with teachers in a professional development capacity, or with families in more of a case management role, as opposed to teaching or being responsible for daily operations. Given the vast variation in types of programs, educational philosophies, ages and populations served, and even in things such as operating days and hours, pay, and opportunities for advancement, you may find it worthwhile to do some research on programs in your area prior to applying to ensure the programs you are applying to are the best fit for you.

Image 8.5 Numerous Programs Are Available that Provide Early Childhood Education Services to Children from Birth through Prekindergarten (photo by Sergiy Nykonenko/ Depositphotos, Inc.).

Special Education/Early Intervention

The field of early childhood special education as an area of practice has been steadily growing over recent years, as the importance of early intervention becomes more widely acknowledged. While many children with special needs attend mainstream early childhood education programs, they often do so with additional supports in the form of special education teachers or instructional aides provided by school districts, regional centers for individuals with disabilities, and other community-based agencies. Other children may have needs that are potentially better met through self-contained programs where all children demonstrate similar need. Therapeutic preschools represent one example of a self-contained program. Although there is variation by program, therapeutic preschools generally provide mental health and behavioral services to young children and their families in a preschool-like setting. Very often the children have experienced some sort of early trauma, and most have, or are at very high risk for, social, emotional, and behavioral problems.

Parent Education

HDFS graduates may also find parent education a career area of interest. As the name implies, parent education involves teaching skills or content to parents of young children, typically for the purpose of promoting healthy development in one or more domain. The range of potential topics addressed by a parent educator is infinite, but may include things like prenatal development, infant health nutrition, safety, child discipline, how to support early learning, or how to co-parent effectively after a separation or divorce. Parent educators may be employed by school districts, county offices overseeing child welfare services and/or child care programs, regional centers for individuals with disabilities, early childhood education programs, hospitals, and other community agencies.

Home Visiting

Finally, home visiting may be a viable career option for HDFS graduates. Home visiting encompasses elements of early childhood education, early intervention, and parent education, but services are provided in families' homes, as opposed to a classroom setting. During each home visit, which in many programs occur weekly, the home visitor and parent work together on goals related to health, parenting, child development, and school readiness. The home visitor may be responsible for conducting developmental assessments on the children, and then suggest activities for parents and children to do together to promote further development based on those assessments. Home visitors often provide resources and referrals to other services families may need, and they often work in collaboration with professionals from school districts and social service agencies to ensure that the needs of the children and families are met. Home visiting programs are often paid for through grants awarded by the U.S. Department of Health and Human Services to state and local governments, school districts, and community service agencies. Information on home visiting programs being implemented in each state can be found at http://mchb.hrsa.gov/maternal-child-health-initiatives/home-visiting/home-visiting-program-state-fact-sheets. Additional links to some of the more common home visiting models can be found in the Suggested Resources section at the end of this chapter.

Strategies for Specialization

HDFS students with a specific interest in working with young children and their families tend to have many options for building expertise and gaining experience as undergraduates. Introductory and advanced coursework in infant/toddler development, early child development, and parenting will provide you with a solid foundation for understanding this lifespan stage, but can be further enhanced with coursework addressing topics such as abuse prevention, early childhood education, childhood nutrition, and special needs. Field work experiences are also important. Even if teaching is not your long-term goal, spending time in early childhood education programs through volunteer work, service-learning projects, practicum or internship experiences, or as a paid employee provides the opportunity to observe development across those early years and possibly better understand family experiences over those same years. Professional organizations such as the NAEYC often have chapters at the state or regional level, which may offer avenues for becoming involved in local initiatives related to young children, thus we recommend exploring whether a membership is something of interest to you.

Summary

1   Families with young children often experience stress related to parenting demands:

    A   This stress may be amplified for single parents, working parents, and others lacking adequate supports or resources, but most parents do not regret having children and many voluntarily have more.

2   Healthy physical growth and development begins far before birth:

    A   Factors such as the age and health of the mother, genes, chromosomes, nutrition, and prenatal exposure to substances that can harm fetal development can influence prenatal development.
    B   Birthweight is an indicator of newborn health. Infants weighing less than 5.5 pounds are considered low birthweight, and are at higher risk for illness, developmental problems, and infant death compared to children weighing more at birth.

        a   Some infants are low birthweight because they are born preterm, and others are SGA.

C   Growth is rapid over the first year, and then tapers such that by age 6, the average child weighs between 40 and 50 pounds, and is at least 3.5 feet tall.

3   Good nutrition is important for physical health and development. Breast milk or infant formula should be the main staple of children's diets through the first year of life, after which, parents should provide children with a healthy range of food options.

4   Most children spend about 40% of their childhood asleep. Newborns need an average of 16 hours of sleep per 24 hours. The amount of sleep needed for healthy development decreases as children get older, but even 5-year-olds need between 11 and 13 hours each night.

5   Early childhood is marked by significant advances in gross and fine motor skills. Some gross motor developments include sitting, standing, walking, running, and jumping. Fine motor skills progress from grasping and waving to eating with utensils, building with blocks, drawing, writing, and even tying one's shoes.

6   Children make significant advances in cognitive development over the first 5 years. Cognitive development includes, but is not limited to, perception, attention, memory, language, and brain development:

A   Language is the clearest evidence of children being capable of symbolic thought.

B   The sequence at which language is acquired is universal. Infants progress from crying as their only form of communication, to cooing, smiling, and fussing, to babbling, to ultimately saying their first word. Vocabulary growth is rapid from about 18 months through early childhood.

C   Brain growth and development is rapid over the first 5 years, as synapses are created and pruned, axons are myelinated, and the brain becomes better connected. The stimulations necessary for optimal brain growth occurs naturally through reading, talking, running errands, trips to the park, visits with family and friends, routine caregiving tasks, and play.

7   Social interactions with parents and caregivers are the foundation on which emotional development occurs:

A   Children who experience responsive and sensitive caregiving on a consistent basis learn that the world is a safe place, and subsequently develop secure attachments to others. Children who do not experience responsive and sensitive care develop insecure attachments, which can negatively affect development.

B   The quality of caregiving can be affected by many factors, including substance abuse, mental illness, stress, and infant temperament.

C   Children with difficult temperaments are often most affected by the quality of caregiving.

8   Also important to children's emotional development is increasing self-awareness, as evidenced by the development of self-concept and theory of mind:

A   Self-concept refers to the ideas or images we hold about ourselves.
B   Theory of mind is the understanding that other people have thoughts, feelings, ideas, plans, and beliefs different from our own.

9   The potential areas of research and study are seemingly infinite. Some scholars may have a broad interest in a domain of development, but specialize in a subdomain. Others may be focused on the relationship between two domains or subdomains. Much of the current research in HDFS focuses on understanding relationships between domains of development and contexts of development. Two examples of contexts of interest include the family and child care.

10   HDFS graduates wanting to pursue a career with young children and/or their families have several options:

A   Within early childhood education, HDFS graduates may consider careers in teaching, administration, teacher professional development, and FCM.
B   Employment through special education and early intervention programs, such as therapeutic preschool, represent potential career paths for HDFS graduates with an interest in helping children with special needs.
C   Parent education, or teaching skills or content to parents of young children, is another career option for HDFS graduates. Potential employers may be school districts, local government, regional centers, early childhood education programs, hospitals, and other community agencies.
D   Home visiting encompasses elements of early childhood education, early intervention, and parent education, but services are provided in families' homes, as opposed to a classroom setting.

11   HDFS students wishing to specialize in early childhood or in families with young children should pursue coursework in early development, parenting, and other relevant topics. Field work experiences with young children also provide the opportunity to observe development and better understand family experiences.

Key Terms

axons
dendrites
family of orientation
family of procreation
fine motor skills
gestational age
gross motor skills
low birthweight
myelination
neurons
object permanence
parental self-efficacy
preterm
pruning
self-concept
small-for-gestational age
symbolic thought
synapses
theory of mind

Challenge: Integration

Many young children spend a significant amount of time being cared for in an early childhood education program, the quality of which can vary widely. The purpose of this assignment is to provide you with a better understanding of what quality in early childhood education means, as well as to give you the opportunity to observe children in an early learning environment.

Schedule an appointment with an early childhood education program to observe in a classroom for about an hour. Explain to the program director that this observation is for a course assignment, and ask to observe in a classroom serving an age group of interest to you. The observation should occur during a time when children are awake and participating in the more structured parts of their day (i.e., do not observe at lunch or nap). You will need a few minutes to speak to the teacher, so be sure to plan for that as well.

After your observation, document your experience by answering the following questions and prompts:

1   Where and when did your observation take place? Which type of program or classroom did you choose, and what age were the children (e.g., Head Start/3-year-old classroom, campus child care program/infants)?
2   Why did you choose this program or classroom?
3   Briefly describe what was happening during your observation (e.g., children participated in a circle time activity, snack, and then small-group activities).
4   Describe the quality of the classroom in relation to the:

   a   *Physical setting.* Did the classroom appear physically safe? Was the classroom clean? How was the lighting and ventilation? Did there feel like there was enough space, or did the classroom feel crowded? Was there outdoor space for children to use? What was your general impression of the quality of the physical environment?
   b   *Materials and equipment.* What kinds of things did you see in the room? How were the walls decorated? Were the materials (toys, books, play structures) in good condition? Did the amount of materials available to children seem appropriate (i.e., not too many or too few)? Did the materials seem appropriate given the age of the children? What was your general impression about the quality and appropriateness of the materials and equipment?
   c   *Adult–child ratio.* How many adults were present in the room? How many children? Were the adults (or was the adult) able to attend to every child that needed them? What was your general impression about the ratio in the class you observed?
   d   *Daily activities.* Describe the daily routine in the class you observed (you may need to ask a teacher). Did the class follow a strict schedule or routine (e.g., from 8:30–8:45 take attendance, from 8:45–9:05 have a class meeting, from 9:05–9:20 in centers), or was the schedule more flexible? Which activities did you observe? Did the children appear interested and engaged in the activities or were they bored and restless? What was your general impression about the daily activities in the classroom?
   e   *Interactions between adults and children.* How did the teacher act toward the children? Was he/she warm and responsive or cold and indifferent? Did he/she seem comfortable or overwhelmed? Did the teacher treat all of the children the same, or did she seem to prefer some over others? Did the children seem happy? What was your general impression about the interactions between the adults and children?

f   *Teacher qualifications.* Ask the teacher about his/her qualifications. How long have they been teaching overall? How long have they been teaching this age group? How much education do they have (e.g., 12 ECE units, a child development permit, a teaching credential, an emergency credential, a master's degree)? Do you feel the teacher was qualified to teach the class he/she was in?

g   *Relationship with parents.* Were there any parents in the classroom while you were there? Ask the teacher about parent participation. How do/can parents participate in that classroom? How many actually do? Are parents encouraged to visit the classroom during the day? Does the teacher hold parent–teacher conferences? If yes, are they offered to all parents, or just parents of children who are struggling? What was your general impression about the teacher's or program's relationship with parents?

5   What was your overall impression of the classroom or program you visited? What did you like best or were you most impressed with? What did you like least or were not impressed by? Would you put your own children in this classroom or program (or recommend it to parents of children you care about)? Would you want to work in this program? Explain.

Journal Questions

1   Of the areas of research, study, and practice discussed in this chapter, which do you find most interesting? Would you be interested in pursuing a career working with young children and/or their families? Explain.

2   Review the nine dimensions of temperament described in Box 8.2. For each dimension, explain how being exceptionally high or low might contribute to a difficult temperament in infancy. What challenges might each present to parents?

3   Describe your personal thoughts and values regarding child care and early childhood education programs for young children. Would you be open to putting your own children in such programs, and, if yes, under what circumstances? If no, why not? Describe the features of an acceptable program that would be most important to you.

SUGGESTED RESOURCES

Early Childhood Learning and Knowledge Center: https://eclkc.ohs.acf.hhs.gov/hslc.
Early Head Start: https://eclkc.ohs.acf.hhs.gov/hslc/tta-system/ehsnrc.
Healthy Families America: www.healthyfamiliesamerica.org/.
NAEYC: www.naeyc.org/.
Office of Head Start: www.acf.hhs.gov/ohs.
Parents and Teachers: www.parentsasteachers.org/resources/federal-home-visiting-program.
Zero to Three: www.zerotothree.org/.

REFERENCES

Abner, K. S., Gordon, R. A., Kaestner, R., & Korenman, S. (2013). Does child-care quality mediate associations between type of care and development? *Journal of Marriage and Family, 75,* 1203–1217.

American Academy of Pediatrics. (2016a). *Infant food and feeding.* Retrieved from https://ihcw.aap.org/Pages/infantfeeding.aspx.

American Academy of Pediatrics. (2016b). *Preschooler food and feeding.* Retrieved from www.aap.org/en-us/advocacy-and-policy/aap-health-initiatives/HALF-Implementation-Guide/Age-Specific-Content/Pages/Preschooler-Food-and-Feeding.aspx.

Aviezer, O., Sagi, A., Resnick, G., & Gini, M. (2002). School competence in young adolescence: Links to early attachment relationships beyond concurrent self-perceived competence and representations of relationships. *International Journal of Behavioral Development, 26,* 397–409.

Azar, S. T. (2002). Parenting and child maltreatment. In M. H. Bornstein (Ed.), *Handbook of parenting* (Vol. 4, pp. 361–388). Mahwah, NJ: Lawrence Erlbaum Associates.

Bard, K. A., Todd, B. K., Bernier, C., Love, J., & Leavens, D. A. (2006). Self-awareness in human and chimpanzee infants: What is measured and what is meant by the mark and mirror test? *Infancy, 9,* 191–219.

Bowlby, J. (1988). *A secure base: Parent–child attachment and healthy human development.* New York: Basic Books.

Bradley, R. H., & Corwyn, R. F. (2007). Infant temperament, parenting, and externalizing behavior in first grade: A test of the differential susceptibility hypothesis. *Journal of Child Psychology and Psychiatry, 49*(2), 124–131.

Cabrera, N. J., Scott, M., Fagan, J., Steward-Streng, N., & Chien, N. (2012). Coparenting and children's school readiness: A mediational model. *Family Process, 51,* 307–324.

Campanella, J., & Rovee-Collier, C. (2005). Latent learning and deferred imitation at three months. *Infancy, 7,* 243–262.

CDC. (2016a). *Individual growth charts.* Retrieved from www.cdc.gov/growthcharts/charts.htm.

CDC. (2016b). *Infant health.* Retrieved from www.cdc.gov/nchs/fastats/infant-health.htm.

Child Trends. (2015). *Low and very low birthweight infants: Indicators on children and youth.* Retrieved from www.childtrends.org/?indicators=low-and-very-low-birthweight-infants.

Clark, H. R., Goyder, E., Bissell, P., Blank, L., & Peters, J. (2007). How do parents' child-feeding behaviours influence child weight? Implications for childhood obesity policy. *Journal of Public Health, 29,* 132–141.

Dallaire, D. H., & Weinraub, M. (2007). Infant–mother attachment security and children's anxiety and aggression at first grade. *Journal of Applied Developmental Psychology, 28,* 477–492.

DeFlorio, L., & Beliakoff, A. (2015). Socioeconomic status and preschoolers' mathematical knowledge: The contribution of home activities and parent beliefs. *Early Education and Development, 26,* 319–341.

Englund, M. M., Kuo, S. I-C., Puig, J., & Collins, W. A. (2011). Early roots of adult competence: The significance of close relationships from infancy to early adulthood. *International Journal of Behavioral Development, 35*, 490–496.

Faith, M. S., Scanlon, K. S., Birch, L. L., Francis, L. A., & Sherry, B. (2004). Parent–child feeding strategies and their relationships to child eating and weight status. *Obesity Research, 12*, 1711–1722.

Farmer, A. Y., & Lee, S. K. (2011). The effects of parenting stress, perceived mastery, and maternal depression on parent–child interaction. *Journal of Social Service Research, 37*, 516–525.

Filippetti, M. L., Johnson, M. H., Lloyd-Fox, S., Dragovic, D., & Farroni, T. (2013). Body perception in newborns. *Current Biology, 23*, 2413–2416.

Groh, A. M., Fearon, R. P., Bakermans-Kranenburg, M. J., Van IJzendoorn, M. H., Steele, R. D., & Roisman, G. I. (2014). The significance of attachment security for children's social competence with peers: A meta-analytic study. *Attachment and Human Development, 16*, 103–136.

Hart, B., & Risley, T. R. (2003). The early catastrophe: The 30 million word gap by age 3. *American Educator, 27*, 4–9.

Hindman, A. H., Wasik, B. A., & Snell, E. K. (2016). Closing the 30 million word gap: Next steps in designing research to inform practice. *Child Development Perspectives, 10*, 134–139.

Joshi, P., & Bogen, K. (2007). Nonstandard schedules and young children's behavioral outcomes among working low-income families. *Journal of Marriage and Family, 69*, 139–156.

Kahng, S. K., Oyserman, D., Bybee, D., & Mowbray, C. (2008). Mothers with serious mental illness: When symptoms decline does parenting improve? *Journal of Family Psychology, 22*, 162–166.

Kaplan, H., & Dove, H. (1987). Infant development among the Ache of eastern Paraguay. *Developmental Psychology, 23*, 190–198.

Keller, A., Ford, L. H., & Meacham, J. A. (1978). Dimensions of self-concept in preschool children. *Developmental Psychology, 14*, 483–489.

Khajehei, M. (2016). Parenting challenges and parents' intimate relationships. *Journal of Human Behavior in the Social Environment, 26*, 447–451.

Kobayashi, T., Hiraki, K., & Hasegawa, T. (2005). Auditory-visual intermodal matching of small numerosities in 6-month-old infants. *Developmental Science, 5*, 409–419.

Kretchmar, M. D., & Jacobvitz, D. B. (2002). Observing mother–child relationships across generations: Boundary patterns, attachment, and the transmission of caregiving. *Family Process, 41*, 351–374.

Lewis, M. (2013). *The rise of consciousness and the development of emotional life.* New York: Guilford Press.

Magnuson, K. A., & Duncan, G. J. (2002). Parents in poverty. In M. H. Bornstein (Ed.), *Handbook of parenting* (Vol. 4, pp. 95–121). Mahwah, NJ: Lawrence Erlbaum Associates.

Mayes, L. C., & Truman, S. (2002). Substance abuse and parenting. In M. H. Bornstein (Ed.), *Handbook of parenting* (Vol. 4, pp. 329–359). Mahwah, NJ: Lawrence Erlbaum Associates.

Minze, L. C., McDonald, R., Rosentraub, E. L., & Jouriles, E. N. (2010). Making sense of family conflict: Intimate partner violence and preschoolers' externalizing problems. *Journal of Family Psychology, 24*, 5–11.

Moats, L. (2001). Overcoming the language gap. *American Educator, 25*(2), 4–9.

Mortensen, J. A., & Barnett, M. A. (2015). Teacher–child interactions in infant/toddler child care and socioemotional development. *Early Education and Development, 26*, 209–229.

National Sleep Foundation. (2016). *Children and sleep.* Retrieved from https://sleepfoundation.org/sleep-topics/children-and-sleep/.

Nielsen, M., Dissanayake, C., & Kashima, Y. (2003). A longitudinal investigation of self–other discrimination and the emergence of mirror self-recognition. *Infant Behavior and Development, 26*, 213–226.

Nigrelli, C., & Brennan, C. (2014). Minimizing the effects of chronic stress on infants and toddlers. *Exchange, 217*, 52–53.

Preschool Curriculum Evaluation Research Consortium. (2008). *Effects of preschool curriculum programs on school readiness* (NCER 2008–2009). Washington, DC: National Center for Education Research, Institute of Education Sciences, U.S. Department of Education. Washington, DC: U.S. Government Printing Office.

Rochat, P. (2003). Five levels of self-awareness as they unfold early in life. *Consciousness and Cognition, 12*, 717–731.

Ruffman, T., Slade, L., & Redman, J. (2005). Young infants' expectations about hidden objects. *Cognition, 97*, B35–B43.

Sorondo, B. M., & Reeb-Sutherland, B. C. (2015). Associations between infant temperament, maternal stress, and infants' sleep across the first year of life. *Infant Behavior and Development, 39*, 131–135.

Stanford Children's Health. (2016). *Small for gestational age*. Retrieved from www.stanfordchildrens.org/en/topic/default?id=small-for-gestational-age-90-P02411.

Stipek, D. J., Gralinski, J. H., & Kopp, C. B. (1990). Self-concept development in the toddler years. *Developmental Psychology, 26*, 972–977.

Stright, A. D., Gallagher, K. C., & Kelley, K. (2008). Infant temperament moderates relations between maternal parenting in early childhood and children's adjustment in first grade. *Child Development, 79*, 186–200.

Super, C. M. (1976). Environmental effects on motor development: the case of "African infant precocity." *Developmental Medicine and Child Neurology, 18*, 561–567.

Taylor, T. E., Eisenberg, N., Spinrad, T. L., Eggum, N. D., & Sulik, M. J. (2013). The relations of ego-resiliency and emotion socialization to the development of empathy and prosocial behaviour across early childhood. *Emotion, 13*, 822–831.

Thomas, A., & Chess, S. (1980). *The dynamics of psychological development*. New York: Brunner-Mazel.

Thomas, A., Chess, S., & Birch, H. G. (1970). The origin of personality. *Scientific American, 223*, 102–109.

Thomas, A., Chess, S., & Korn, S. J. (1982). The reality of difficult temperament. *Merrill-Palmer Quarterly, 28*, 1–20.

Tsai, L-Y., Chen, Y-L., Tsou, K-I., & Mu, S-C. (2015). The impact of small-for-gestational-age on neonatal outcome among very-low-birth-weight infants. *Pediatrics and Neonatalogy, 56*, 101–107.

United Nations High Commissioner for Human Rights. (1989). *Convention on the rights of the child.* General Assembly Resolution 44/25. Retrieved from www.ohchr.org/en/professionalinterest/pages/crc.aspx.

U.S. Census Bureau. (2013). *Who's minding the kids? Child care arrangements: Spring 2011.* Retrieved from www.census.gov/library/publications/2013/demo/p70-135.html.

Verhage, M. L., Oosterman, M., & Schuengel, C. (2015). The linkage between infant negative temperament and parenting self-efficacy: The role of resilience against negative performance feedback. *British Journal of Developmental Psychology, 33*, 506–518.

White, R. E. (2013). *The power of play: A research summary on play and learning.* Retrieved from www.google.com/url?sa=t&rct=j&q=&esrc=s&source=web&cd=1&cad=rja&uact=8&ved=0a hUKEwiczefPjI7PAhWD24MKHUxcB10QFggcMAA&url=http%3A%2F%2Fwww.childrens museums.org%2Fimages%2FMCResearchSummary.pdf&usg=AFQjCNH-kFu9Xi7JqhgI11 ptvSS6KJ2g7g&sig2=w7gfr3xJ8aiW7N8WSvlNEg.

CHAPTER 9

Family and Childhood

My greatest joys have been watching this little person blossom into a determined kid, with a definite sense of humor. His gifts, likes, and dislikes are starting to really show, and he has the words to express what is going on in his head. It's like I am finally meeting the person that he is. He is incredibly kind, forgiving, and has a huge capacity to love. Sometimes he causes me to look at myself and try to be a better person when I'm feeling frustrated.

(Sylvia, mother of an 8-year-old)

For many families, middle childhood, the ages between roughly 6 and 12, is marked with a sense of wonderment and relative ease. In comparison with early childhood and adolescence, middle childhood is often a time of considerable calm, when parental demands can be less strenuous. Children in this lifespan stage demonstrate increasing self-sufficiency, often able to take on many tasks of self-care, including those related to health and hygiene. From the beginning of elementary school, their social worlds and responsibilities to non-family members expand considerably, yet remain largely within parental control. Advances in brain development and language allow for the expression of thoughts, personality traits, and behavior in a manner unparalleled at earlier ages. This chapter provides an introduction to elementary school-age children's development, areas of study, and areas of practice.

PHYSICAL DEVELOPMENT

At age 6, most children weigh between 40 and 50 pounds and stand about between 43 and 47 inches tall (CDC, 2000). Growth over the next 5 or 6 years is relatively slow in comparison to early childhood and adolescence. On average, boys are slightly taller and heavier than girls until around age 9, when girls' bodies spurt up in preparation for puberty. Boys will typically start their pre–puberty growth spurt a little later, around age 11. For both boys and girls, the bottom half of the body grows much faster than the top half, so parents often find themselves having to replace pants and shoes much more frequently than tops and jackets. By age 12, the average boy weighs between 90 and 120 pounds and is between 58 and 63 inches tall (CDC, 2000). The average girl weighs between 80 and 110 pounds and is between 58 and 62 inches tall (CDC, 2000). Although genes certainly play an important role in determining growth patterns for children, environmental influences matter as well. Children's nutrition can affect weight and height, as can exposure to toxins like lead (Schwartz, Angle, & Pitcher, 1986). Family norms around food, such as eating meals together, influence children's dietary behaviors and subsequent body mass index (BMI; Gable, Chang, & Krull, 2007; Meade et al., 2014).

Childhood **overweight** and **obesity** rates among school–aged children in the United States have risen dramatically over the last 50 years. Individuals are considered overweight when their BMI reaches the 85th percentile, and obese when their BMI reaches the 95th percentile. In the 1960s, only about 4% of children ages 6 to 11 were overweight or obese (Ogden & Carroll, 2010). By 2008, the number increased to just over 19% (Ogden & Carroll, 2010). One recent study conducted on children in the Pacific Northwest found that approximately 31% of kindergarteners and 44% of fifth graders had a BMI at or above the 85th percentile (Moreno, Johnson–Shelton, & Boles, 2013).

Physical activity is essential for healthy growth during middle childhood. Not only can it prevent childhood obesity and its related health issues, but physical activity benefits children's cognitive and emotional growth as well. Exercise and physical play is associated with increased academic performance, self–esteem, positive emotions, and mood (Rasmussen & Laumann, 2013), and may help to improve attention, memory, and classroom behavior (Strong et al., 2005). Both the CDC and World Health Organization (WHO) recommend that children participate in a minimum of 60 minutes of physical activity per day for optimal health (CDC, 2016b; WHO, 2010). However, in the United States, only 42% of children ages 6–12 actually meet that recommendation (Troiano et al., 2008). This drops to a little more than one–third among children who are already overweight or obese (Kunin–Batson et al., 2015).

Image 9.1 Physical Activity Is Essential for Healthy Growth during Middle Childhood (photo by Anatoily Samara/Depositphotos, Inc.).

There are many reasons underlying the diminished amount of physical activity children are getting. For example, schools across the country have reduced the amount of time dedicated to recess and physical education in exchange for more time devoted to academics or to divert financial resources elsewhere (Harman, 2004). Additionally, children in general spend more free time engaged in sedentary activity than ever before, in part due to a change in broader culture that promotes technology use and discourages unsupervised, unstructured free play outdoors (Lou, 2014). Regardless, play and physical activity remain important throughout middle childhood.

Perhaps one of the most impressive physical changes in middle childhood is that of improved motor skills. Increased muscle strength, combined with brain maturation, lead to advances in children's gross motor skills, allowing children to run faster, climb higher, turn cartwheels, and cross monkey bars. There is also marked improvement in children's fine motor skills. By early elementary school, most children are able to hold a pencil, type on a keyboard, use a mouse, tie their shoes, zip their coats, and pour a glass of juice. Increased hand–eye coordination not only makes sports, games, art, and writing possible at a level not seen in early childhood, but also allows and facilitates children's independence in that they do not have to rely on adults to do as many things for them.

INTELLECTUAL DEVELOPMENT

In the United States, the middle childhood years loosely correspond with elementary school, recognizing that elementary schools typically serve children from kindergarten through fifth or sixth grade. However, as even the lay person without any formal education in child development has likely observed, first graders think and behave very differently from fifth graders. As children progress through their elementary school years, maturation of the brain leads to better and more complex reasoning and problem-solving skills, more efficient processing of information, increased memory capacity, and the improved ability to pay attention and demonstrate inhibitory control (Bridges, Fox, Reid, & Anderson, 2014; Piekny & Maehler, 2013; Simonds, Kieras, Rosario, & Rothbart, 2007). Collectively, these skills or abilities are referred to as **executive functions**. As you might imagine, executive functions are related to academic achievement from the earliest grades through adolescence (Best, Miller, & Naglieri, 2011).

Advances in both language development and cognition create young individuals who are increasingly able to express themselves and participate in meaningful conversation. Not only do we see marked growth in vocabulary and mastery of grammar across the elementary school years, but typically developing children also become more skilled at the **pragmatics** of language, or the ability to intentionally use and alter language according to need and context. The American Speech-Language-Hearing Association (2016) describes pragmatics as involving three major communication skills: (1) the ability to use language for different purposes (e.g., greeting, informing, demanding), (2) the ability to change language as needed or expected according to social conventions (e.g., speaking differently to infants and adults, or in a classroom compared to on the playground), and (3) the ability to follow socially constructed rules about conversations and storytelling (e.g., turn-taking, body language, eye contact). Although personality traits have likely been evident to some extent since infancy, parents of school-age children may find themselves surprised to learn that their children are quite funny, as it is during middle childhood that children's joke-telling and sarcasm emerge (Glenwright & Pexman, 2010; Kielar-Turska & Bialecka-Pikul, 2010).

Elementary school is often also the time when learning disabilities or other special needs are first identified, marking the beginning of special education services for many families. Thought to arise from neurological differences, learning disabilities affect an individual's ability to learn specific skills or information (Cortiella & Horowitz, 2014). The two most common learning disabilities are **dyslexia** and **dyscalculia**, but there are others as well. Individuals with dyslexia have difficulty with reading, and individuals with dyscalculia have difficulty with math. Although not a learning disorder, an estimated 6.4 million children in the United States have been diagnosed as having **attention deficit/ hyperactivity disorder** (**ADHD**), which is another neurological difference that can make learning difficult (CDC, 2016a). Children with ADHD often have difficulty staying focused, are hyperactive, and find themselves easily distracted. Nearly two-thirds of parents of children with learning disabilities or ADHD report struggling with or feeling conflicted about their children's diagnoses (Cortiella & Horowitz, 2014). Some may doubt their ability to help their children succeed in school, while others report feeling overwhelmed or anxious more generally.

Many studies have shown that **parental involvement** in children's education has a positive influence on children's academic achievement, behavior in school, and overall educational attainment (Barnard, 2004; El Nokali, Bachman, & Vortruba-Drzal, 2010; Lee & Bowen, 2006). Parent involvement can take many forms, but typically includes engaging in parenting practices that support children as students, communicating with teachers, volunteering to work in the classroom or for other school events, providing learning opportunities for children at home to reinforce what is being taught at school, participating in the PTA/PTO or other decision-making entities, and engaging in community service activities as a family (Epstein et al., 2002). Current research in the area of parental involvement focuses on better understanding the relationship between specific types of parent involvement and child outcomes, as well as identifying effective strategies for increasing parent involvement across demographics and grade levels (e.g., Hoglund, Jones, Brown, & Aber, 2015; McNeal, 2015; Topor, Keane, Shelton, & Calkins, 2010).

Image 9.2 Parental Involvement in Children's Education Has a Positive Influence on Children's Academic Achievement (photo by Karel Miragaya/Depositphotos, Inc.).

EMOTIONAL DEVELOPMENT

Although school-age children demonstrate increasing independence from their families, parent–child attachments remain important. Similar to early childhood, older children with secure attachments to their parents or caregiver experience a host of academic, psychological, and social benefits. Having that secure base affords children the confidence to engage with people and things in the environment, thus increasing their opportunities to learn. In middle childhood, attachment quality has been associated with children's academic skills and achievement, cognitive development, levels of exploration and engagement, social skills, behavior, friendship quality, and emotional wellbeing (Bergin & Bergin, 2009; Jacobsen & Hofmann, 1997; Kerns, Tomich, Aspelmeier, & Contreras, 2000; McCormick, O'Connor, & Barnes, 2016; Moss & St-Laurent, 2001; O'Connor, Scott, McCormick, & Weinberg, 2014; West, Mathews, & Kerns, 2013). Many children depend on parents to facilitate opportunities for developing friendships (Johnston & Fletcher, 2015). For example, children may rely on their parents to enroll them in school, arrange playdates, and register them for afterschool activities. Parents may make introductions, or give advice on how to approach potential friends, repair relationships, and the like, but the actual process of making and keeping friends is often the responsibility of the child.

Friendships in middle childhood are qualitatively different from those of early childhood. Whereas in early childhood, friendships are often characterized by proximity and shared interests, during middle childhood, features such as intimacy, loyalty, and supportiveness become increasingly important (Blair et al., 2014). Friendships also become voluntary, as children can choose to dissolve them if they so wish. Children who are able to both make and keep friends tend to be more prosocial and have higher levels of popularity amongst their peers (Wojslawowicz Bowker, Rubin, Burgess, Booth-LaForce, & Rose-Krasnor, 2006). Conversely, children who are unable to maintain friendships are at greater risk for loneliness, aggression, and peer rejection (Ellis & Zarbatany, 2007).

Children's self-concept is strongly influenced by both family and peers. Advances in cognitive development mean children are increasingly able to infer the thoughts and beliefs of others. They develop a sense of what is expected or desired from them, and then use those expectations to evaluate themselves (Davis-Kean, Jager, & Collins, 2009). They engage in **social comparison**, or the tendency to assess one's abilities, achievements, social status, and other attributes by measuring them against those of other people, especially peers. When children feel they are not living up to the expectations of others, or they are somehow inferior to others, their self-esteem tends to decrease. Even the healthiest children tend to exhibit a decrease in self-esteem from early to middle childhood, primarily because their beliefs about their own abilities become more realistic as they compare themselves to peers and get feedback from others. Whereas preschool children often believe they can do anything, elementary school children are more aware of their limitations. Ideally, children reach a place where their self-esteem is not unrealistically low or unrealistically high, as both are related to higher rates of aggression (Diamantopoulou, Rydell, & Henricsson, 2008; Menon et al., 2007).

Ultimately, it is the relationships children have with their families during middle childhood that may have the greatest impact on their overall psychological and emotional wellbeing, as a positive home life, regardless of composition or structure, can often serve as a buffer to adversity faced elsewhere. When parents continuously demonstrate warmth

Image 9.3 The Relationships Children Have with Their Families May Have the Greatest Impact on Their Wellbeing (photo by Robert Churchill/Depositphotos, Inc.).

and responsiveness, and hold their children to high, but age-appropriate, standards of responsibility and behavior, most children thrive. The challenge for parents is often finding where that balance lies (see Box 9.1).

MAJOR/CURRENT AREAS OF RESEARCH

Much of the developmental research on middle childhood focuses on the school context. Perhaps one of the largest areas of ongoing research is in **curriculum and instruction**, a broad umbrella term that includes research on the best practices for increasing individual achievement.

Curriculum and Instruction

Researchers in curriculum and instruction have a diverse range of interests, from identifying *what* children should be learning and *when*, to understanding the nuances affecting *how* individual or groups of children learn best and *why*. Some develop and test new instructional approaches or curriculum, and others focus on assessment. Still others focus on teacher training or professional development. Facilitating the development of literacy and numeracy skills has long been one of the primary responsibilities of elementary education, as these skills lay the foundation for later learning in school, but also provide a means to self-learning. Unfortunately, many children in the United States, particularly those from low-income families, minoritized racial and ethnic groups, and non-English-speaking households, are below grade-level proficiency in both subjects (National Education Association, 2015). These achievement gaps are present at kindergarten entry, and not only persist but widen over time, meaning students are falling further behind with

BOX 9.1 CHILDHOOD AND PARENTING IN THE 21ST CENTURY: ONE FUTURE DIRECTION FOR RESEARCH

Many adults over the age of 40 would agree that childhood looks a lot different today from when they were growing up. Gone are the days when many children were free to roam the neighborhood until dinnertime, playing with whomever they might encounter along the way. In many communities across the country, childhood has become more structured, scheduled, and supervised than perhaps ever before. Children, particularly in middle-class communities, are shuttled from home to school, school to after-school lessons or activities if applicable, and back home again—all the while under adult supervision. For some, their weekly schedule may include a supervised "playdate" or two, but, for many, opportunities for unstructured, unscheduled, and unsupervised activity outside of the home alone or with peers are rare. Parents who reject these changing norms, often labeled "free-range parents" in the media, have not only been subjected to public criticism, but in some cases charged with child neglect or endangerment for things such as allowing their school-age children to play outside unsupervised, walk to or from the park alone or with other children, or in one famous case, ride the subway alone.

The reasons underlying this cultural shift in parenting norms are not yet well understood, nor are the implications for children's development. It may be that children do benefit from increased structure, scheduling, and adult supervision throughout middle childhood. For example, having an adult always present may be associated with lower rates of injury, or closer parent–child relationships. However, it is also possible that too much structure, scheduling, and supervision leads to psychological harm as children have fewer opportunities to develop autonomy and self-reliance. The reality is, we don't yet know, but research is clearly needed.

each passing year (Cameron, Grimm, Steele, Castro-Schilo, & Grissmer, 2015). Reducing or eliminating such achievement gaps is widely viewed as a priority among researchers and scholars in curriculum and instruction, thus prevention and intervention efforts are a major focus of research.

Although the pendulum can and does swing in regards to societal ideas about additional roles and responsibilities of the primary education system, in recent years there has been an increased emphasis on encouraging critical thinking and problem solving in the classroom, and a decrease in the importance of rote memorization of information. This is perhaps most evident in the Common Core State Standards, released in 2010 and subsequently adopted by 42 states (Common Core State Standards Initiative, 2016; see Box 9.2). A current goal within the K–12 system is to produce graduates who are both college and career ready, a process that begins in childhood. Unpacking how to accomplish this effectively is a current area of research and study.

Of course increasing student achievement involves much more than a set of standards, a good curriculum, and an effective approach to teaching. Achievement does not occur in a vacuum, and there are many more variables of potential importance. For example, in addition to the quality of teacher training, some researchers seek to understand how

BOX 9.2 COMMON CORE STATE STANDARDS: Q & A

Whether you are a recent high school graduate, a parent or caregiver to a K–12 student, or someone who follows headlines related to education, chances are that you have heard about the Common Core, a set of academic standards for K–12 that has been adopted by 42 states and the District of Columbia since their release in 2010. As with most large-scale education initiatives, there has been quite a bit of confusion and controversy as to what the standards are, and what they mean for education. Below is a set of questions and answers meant to provide clarity.

Q: *What are the Common Core State Standards, and which subjects do they cover?*

A: The Common Core State Standards are a set of education standards for grades K–12. Essentially, the standards include the concepts and skills students are expected to learn by the end of each grade. Standards have been developed for English language arts and mathematics only.

Q: *Who developed the Common Core State Standards and why?*

A: The Common Core State Standards Initiative was led by state governors and State Department of Education officials, and written in collaboration with teachers, higher education faculty, and other education experts from around the country. Early proponents of the Common Core recognized a need for one common set of academic standards that would (1) adequately prepare students for college, career, and life, (2) ensure that graduates of schools in the United States would have the skills to be competitive in a global market, and (3) provide consistency across states, allowing resources to be shared. Prior to the development and adoption of the Common Core Standards, each state had their own set of standards with varying degrees of rigor. For example, what fourth graders were expected to know in one state could be completely different from what fourth graders were expected to know in another. By design, high school graduates from different states may have been differentially prepared for college. Separate standards for each state also meant that each state needed its own set of textbooks, standardized tests, professional materials, and the like.

Q: *What makes the Common Core State Standards different from previous standards?*

A: Aside from being uniform across states, the Common Core State Standards are supported by research, aligned with college and career expectations, competitive with other high-performing countries in terms of rigor, and focus on the application of knowledge rather than memorization of knowledge. For some states, this represents a significant change. For others, perhaps not so much.

Q: *What is the relationship between the Common Core State Standards and the curriculum used by teachers?*

A: The Common Core State Standards are not a curriculum. They do not tell teachers how to teach, only what to teach. Curriculum decisions are typically made at the individual state or school district level.

> Q: *Where can I read the Common Core State Standards?*
>
> A: A copy of the Common Core State Standards is available at www.corestandards. org. There are also free apps available for mobile phones and tablets through your preferred app store.
>
> Source: adapted from www.corestandards.org.

teachers' personal beliefs, values, attitudes, and practices affect children's experiences in the classroom (e.g., Polly et al., 2015; van den Bergh, Denessen, Hornstra, Voeten, & Holland, 2010). Similarly, others focus exclusively on the home environment, examining how things like family structure, relationship quality, neighborhood conditions, family income, and parents' beliefs, values, attitudes, and practices might impact children's achievement (e.g., Carlson & Cowen, 2015; Mulvaney & Morrissey, 2012; Swanson, Valiente, & Lemery-Chalfant, 2012). The influence of peer relationships on children's developmental and academic outcomes is yet another area of interest.

Bullying and Peer Victimization

One aspect of peer relationships that is receiving considerable empirical attention is that of bullying and peer victimization. **Bullying** involves the repeated infliction of verbal, relational, or physical aggression toward a less powerful individual. Bullying can occur in person, such as at school, or online, referred to as **cyberbulling**. Research has shown that both children who engage in bullying behavior and those who are bullied are at higher risk for both immediate and long-term psychological, emotional, and behavioral problems (Brunstein Klomek, Sourander, & Elonheimo, 2015; Golmaryami et al., 2016; Jiang, Walsh, & Augimeri, 2011). Current research focuses on identifying who is most at risk for becoming either a bully or a victim, how to prevent bullying behavior, and how to effectively intervene.

Children and Technology

Another current area of research on middle childhood involves that of technology use, both for educational and leisure purposes. As technology use becomes more integrated into our daily lives, understanding how technology use affects children's development and relationships with others is important. Whereas some research focuses on the potentially negative consequences of technology use, such as whether there is an association between aggression and exposure to violence on television or through video games (Bushman, Gollwitzer, & Cruz, 2015; Ferguson, 2015), there is also significant interest in understanding how technology might enhance children's outcomes. For example, several studies have shown that video game use is associated with increases in attention, perception, creativity, problem-solving skills, and other executive functions (Boot, Kramer, Simons, Fabiani, & Gratton, 2008; Green & Bavelier, 2012; Jackson et al., 2012). Consequently, some researchers are investigating how video games may be used

Image 9.4 Understanding How Technology Use Affects Children's Development and Relationships with Others Is Important (photo by Hongqi Zhang/Depositphotos, Inc.).

to help children with learning disabilities or other special needs. Although more research is needed, findings thus far indicate that action video games may be helpful for children with dyslexia (Franceschini et al., 2013). For school-aged children with Down syndrome, *Wii Sports* appears more effective at improving motor skills and perceptual abilities than several more traditional measures of occupational therapy (Wuang, Chiang, Su, & Wang, 2011). Of course, technology is not limited to video games, thus children's use of the internet, computers, and smart phone or tablet apps is also of interest to researchers. As with video games, some scholars focus on the benefits to children and others are concerned with the perils. Understanding how different technologies influence development will likely be an active area of research for the foreseeable future.

AREAS OF PRACTICE

Although many individuals interested in working with school-age children choose to pursue teacher certification, there are several career options for those who do not aspire to teach. However, as described below, many of the more common occupations working with this age group are located on elementary school campuses or within school districts, regardless of whether the school district is the actual employer.

School Districts. Many school districts have a number of positions for which a teaching credential or certification is not necessary. Many districts refer to these as "classified" positions in their job announcements. Classified positions typically include every job within a district that does not require teacher or administrator certification. Classified positions include everything from school bus drivers and custodians to upper management, and everything in between. For college graduates with a degree in HDFS or related field, classified positions associated with parent education programs, behavioral interventions, case management, after-school programs, or special education may be of interest. While most districts post their open job positions on their own websites, it may be fruitful to search www.edjoin.org for positions of interest to you. Edjoin.org allows

Image 9.5 Child and Youth Development Programs Promote Social and Emotional Wellbeing through Participation in Activities (photo by James Steidl/Depositphotos, Inc.).

for the search of open positions in thousands of educational organizations across the United States by state, region, or district.

Child and Youth Development Programs. For those looking to make a difference in the lives of children, but outside of the classroom, child and youth development programs may be an avenue worth pursuing. Child and youth development programs are programs designed and offered for the purpose of promoting social and emotional wellbeing through participation in activities during non-school hours. Examples of some of the more well-known programs include the Boys and Girls Clubs of America, Scouts, Big Brothers Big Sisters of America, and 4-H, but can also include other afterschool or extracurricular programs, such as those focusing on youth sports, art, music, technology, religion, skateboarding, martial arts, leadership, or the development of social justice or moral responsibility. Although such programs are often located on school campuses, only some are actually operated by school districts. The others are often operated by private non-profit groups, or even through local municipal parks and recreation departments. If this type of career experience interests you, position announcements may appear on school district websites, city government websites, and perhaps the more general career-search websites in your area. Another alternative is to use the resources provided in Chapter 7 to identify private, non-profit agencies that provide child and youth development programs, and visit the career section of their websites.

Therapeutic Behavioral Services (TBS). Although sometimes referred to by other names, TBS are often components of mental health programs for children with severe behavioral problems or emotional disturbance, including but not limited to children with autism spectrum disorders. As part of a treatment team, TBS counselors or technicians are charged with working individually with children on specified behavioral goals for the purpose of alleviating the need for a more restrictive level of full-time care. Services are generally provided in the child's environment, thus TBS professionals often work with children in their homes, classrooms, and community settings (e.g., soccer practice). Potential employers may include county mental health or social service departments, private, non-profit mental health agencies, and other organizations that provide behavioral health services. Additionally, some school districts offer similar positions, but typically only focused on the school environment.

Social Services. Although a degree in social work is generally required to become a licensed social worker, there are often positions within the child welfare system for HDFS graduates. In many counties, for example, child protective service workers are required to have a 4-year degree in social work or related field, which HDFS is generally considered. Similarly, there are often opportunities in case management, parent education, or direct care working with families who are receiving social services, or with children who have been placed in emergency shelters or foster care. Most professionals employed in social services are hired either through county government or private, non-profit agencies. However, it is important to note that upward career mobility in social services often means needing to pursue graduate studies, typically in social work or counseling.

Research. It is true that some students enter college with aspirations of a career in research and/or completing a doctoral-level research degree, but for many, an interest in research or graduate studies develops as a result of coursework or other experiences as an undergraduate student. Graduates wanting to either build a career in research or gain more research experience prior to applying to graduate school may want to consider seeking employment as a bachelor-level research assistant at a university or research institution. Common job responsibilities at the entry level include assisting with subject recruitment, data collection, and data entry, but can grow with experience. University websites are a good resource for learning about open positions on grants or projects within each institution, but also check more mainstream job websites, as not all research is physically conducted at universities and efforts may have been made to recruit qualified professionals elsewhere. Private research agencies such as Mathematica Policy Research (www.mathematica-mpr.com), SRI International (www.sri.com), WestEd (www.wested. org), and Westat (www.westat.com) typically have numerous large-scale HDFS-related research projects in progress, thus may also have positions of interest.

STRATEGIES FOR PURSUING SPECIALIZATION OR CAREERS IN MIDDLE CHILDHOOD

As you may have inferred while reading this chapter, much of the research and scholarship on middle childhood has been approached from an educational rather than developmental perspective. Likewise, many of the courses that focus on this age group are found in elementary education programs. If you are so fortunate as to have a middle childhood specialization within your HDFS program, following the prescribed coursework for that specialization should prepare you well for a career with this age group. However, if your program does not have a middle childhood option for specialization, you may choose to supplement your core coursework (in which middle childhood will likely be covered to at least some extent) with electives focusing on your potential career interests. For example, if you are interested in social services, then learning about the child welfare system, abuse and neglect, and developmental psychopathology may prove beneficial. If you are interested in working within the school system, then perhaps coursework in elementary education makes sense. Also, consider supplementing your coursework with field experiences working with school-age children. Such experience can be gained through paid or volunteer work in the schools, or through child or youth development programs. As discussed in Chapter 7, there are numerous ways to develop expertise in an area of interest.

Summary

1 Middle childhood is largely regarded by parents as a time of considerable calm, when parental demands can be less strenuous:

    A Children not only demonstrate increasing self-sufficiency, but advances in brain development and language allow for children's individual expression.

2 Physical growth and development throughout middle childhood is relatively slow, compared to early childhood and adolescence, and are influenced by both genetic and environmental factors:

    A Childhood overweight and obesity rates have been steadily increasing over recent decades, largely due to family norms around food combined with a decrease in physical activity.

    B Increased muscle strength, combined with brain maturation, contribute to advances in both fine and gross motor skills, affording children greater independence.

3 Intellectual development in middle childhood includes advances in cognition and language:

    A Maturation of the brain leads to improved executive functions, or reasoning skills, problem-solving skills, processing of information, memory capacity, attention, and inhibitory control.

    B Children typically exhibit marked growth in vocabulary, grammar, and become more skilled at the pragmatics of language, which allows for communication and expression unparalleled in early childhood.

    C Learning disabilities, including dyslexia and dyscalculia, and ADHD, are often first diagnosed during elementary school.

    D Parents' involvement in children's education often has a positive effect on children's academic achievement, behavior in school, and overall educational attainment.

4 Families and peer groups play a crucial role in children's emotional development:

    A Parent–child attachment quality has been associated with children's academic skills and achievement, cognitive development, levels of exploration and engagement, social skills, behavior, friendship quality, and emotional wellbeing.

    B Friendships in middle childhood are generally characterized by features such as intimacy, loyalty, and supportiveness, and having friends is important for children's emotional wellbeing.

C   Children's self-concept is influenced by family and peers, as children learn what is expected from them. They engage in social comparison, which in turn influences both self-concept and self-esteem.

D   Positive family relationships and parenting practices serve as a buffer to adversity faced in other contexts.

5   Examples of major areas of research on middle childhood include curriculum and instruction, bullying and peer victimization, and children and technology:

A   Research conducted under the umbrella of curriculum and instruction focuses on identifying and understanding what children should be learning and when, as well as how individuals or groups of children learn and why.

B   Current research on bullying and peer victimization often focuses on identifying who is at risk for becoming a bully or victim, the prevention of bullying, and bullying interventions.

C   Research in the area of children and technology is concerned with identifying the potential benefits and risks associated with technology use.

6   There is a range of career opportunities for those interested in working with school-aged children and their families:

A   A variety of classified positions within school districts may be of interest to HDFS graduates.

B   Child and youth development programs are another option for employment, and span a wide range of foci.

C   Graduates with a mental health interest may want to consider pursuing a position in TBS, or individual behavioral coaching to children with severe emotional disturbance.

D   There are often positions available within the social services and/or child welfare system for HDFS graduates. These may include non-licensed social work, case management, parent education, or direct care with children or families receiving social services.

E   Careers in HDFS-related research are also an option, and can provide experience prior to applying to graduate school.

7   HDFS students wanting to work with the middle childhood population should take coursework in middle childhood to the extent possible. They can also build expertise through course assignments and field experiences.

Key Terms

attention deficit/hyperactivity disorder
bullying
curriculum and instruction
cyberbullying
dyscalculia
dyslexia
executive functions
obesity
overweight
parental involvement
pragmatics
social comparison

Challenge: Integration

Interviewing parents can be a powerful means of acquiring expertise about diverse children and families from a parenting perspective. The assignment here is to conduct a short interview (five to seven questions) with a parent of a 6–11 year old child, and then write a one to two page response to the prompts below. The purpose is to learn more about their experiences as parents of a school-aged child.

Sample interview questions might include:

- Information about the child

  - What types of things does your child like to do? What is he/she really good at?
  - Describe your child's personality. Has he/she always been that way, or have you noticed a change at some point?
  - What does a typical weekday look like for your child? What about a weekend day?
  - How has your child's school experience been so far? What have been some of the highlights of elementary school? Have there been any challenges?
  - Do you have any concerns about your child?

- Information about parenting

  - How is parenting an elementary-age child similar to and different from parenting an infant, toddler, or preschooler? What do you enjoy most about parenting now? What do you enjoy least?

- Describe yourself as a parent. What kinds of expectations do you have for your child? How do you approach discipline? What kinds of things do you do with your child for fun?
- What advice would you give parents of younger children about parenting school-aged children?

Prompts:

1 What did you learn from this experience?
2 What did you find the most interesting?
3 What was most unexpected?
4 How does this person's experience compare to what you've learned in your courses, read, and/or have experienced or observed in your personal life?
5 Describe at least two ways their experience is similar to what you have learned/read/experienced.
6 Describe at least two ways their experience is different from what you have learned/read/experienced.
7 How do you think the interview went?
8 Do you feel the person was being open and upfront in terms of his/her responses, or was the person guarded?
9 How did you feel during the interview process? Were there any moments that were uncomfortable for you? Explain.
10 What are your general thoughts about this interview experience?

Journal Questions

1 Of the areas of research, study, and practice discussed in this chapter, which do you find most interesting? Would you be interested in pursuing a career working with school-aged children? Explain.
2 Describe your thoughts on children and technology use. In your opinion, is technology use a good thing during elementary school, or do you see it as potentially harmful? Explain.
3 Box 9.1 raises the issue of how much independence should be granted to school-aged children. Thinking back to your own childhood experiences, how does it compare in terms of structure, schedules, and supervision to children's experiences today? If applicable, do you see these changes as positive, negative, or both? Explain.

SUGGESTED RESOURCES

Childhood Obesity Prevention Coalition: www.copcwa.org.
Common Core State Standards: www.corestandards.org.
National Association of Parents with Children in Special Education: www.napcse.org.
National Parent-Teacher Association: www.pta.org.
The Bully Project: www.thebullyproject.com.

REFERENCES

American Speech-Language-Hearing Association. (2016). *Social language use (pragmatics)*. Retrieved from www.asha.org/public/speech/development/Pragmatics/.

Barnard, W. M. (2004). Parent involvement in elementary school and educational attainment. *Children and Youth Services Review, 26*, 39–62.

Bergin, C., & Bergin, D. (2009). Attachment in the classroom. *Educational Psychology Review, 21*, 141–170.

Best, J. R., Miller, P. H., & Naglieri, J. A. (2011). Relations between executive function and academic achievement from ages 5 to 17 in a large, representative national sample. *Learning and Individual Differences, 21*, 327–336.

Blair, B. L., Perry, N. B., O'Brien, M., Calkins, S. D., Keane, S. P., & Shanahan, L. (2014). The indirect effects of maternal emotion socialization on friendship quality in middle childhood. *Developmental Psychology, 50*, 566–576.

Boot, W. R., Kramer, A. F., Simons, D. J., Fabiani, M., & Gratton, G. (2008). The effects of video game playing on attention, memory, and executive control. *Acta Psychologica, 129*, 387–398.

Bridges, C. R., Fox, A. M., Reid, C. L., & Anderson, M. (2014). The differentiation of executive functions in middle and late childhood: A longitudinal latent-variable analysis. *Intelligence, 47*, 34–43.

Brunstein Klomek, A., Sourander, A., & Elonheimo, H. (2015). Bullying by peers in childhood and effects of psychopathology, suicidality, and criminality in adulthood. *Lancet Psychiatry, 2*, 930–941.

Bushman, B. J., Gollwitzer, M., & Cruz, C. (2015). There is a broad consensus: Media researchers agree that violent media increase aggression in children, and pediatricians and parents concur. *Psychology of Popular Media Culture, 4*, 200–214.

Cameron, C. E., Grimm, K. J., Steele, J. S., Castro-Schilo, L., & Grissmer, D. W. (2015). Nonlinear Gompertz curve models of achievement gaps in mathematics and reading. *Journal of Educational Psychology, 107*, 789–804.

Carlson, D., & Cowen, J. M. (2015). Student neighborhoods, schools, and test score growth: Evidence from Milwaukee, Wisconsin. *Sociology of Education, 88*, 38–55.

CDC. (2000). *Clinical growth charts*. Retrieved from www.cdc.gov/growthcharts/clinical_charts.htm#Set1.

CDC. (2016a). *Attention-deficit/hyperactivity disorder: Data and statistics*. Retrieved from www.cdc.gov/ncbddd/adhd/data.html.

CDC. (2016b). *How much physical activity do children need?* Retrieved from www.cdc.gov/physicalactivity/basics/children/index.htm.

Cortiella, C., & Horowitz, S. H. (2014). *The state of learning disabilities: Facts, trends and emerging issues*. New York: National Center for Learning Disabilities.

Davis-Kean, P. E., Jager, J., & Collins, W. A. (2009). The self in action: An emerging link between self-beliefs and behaviors in middle childhood. *Child Development Perspectives, 3*, 184–188.

Diamantopoulou, S., Rydell, A-M., & Henricsson, L. (2008). Can both low and high self-esteem be related to aggression in children? *Social Development, 17,* 682–698.

El Nokali, N. E., Bachman, H. J., & Vortruba-Drzal, E. (2010). Parent involvement and children's academic and social development in elementary school. *Child Development, 81,* 988–1005.

Ellis, W. E., & Zarbatany, L. (2007). Explaining friendship formation and friendship stability: The role of children's and friends' aggression and victimization. *Merrill-Palmer Quarterly, 53,* 79–104.

Epstein, J. L., Sanders, M. G., Simon, B. S., Salinas, K., Clark, J., Rodriguez, N., & Van Voorhis, F. L. (2002). *School, family, and community partnerships: Your handbook for action* (2nd ed.). Thousand Oaks, CA: Corwin Press, Inc.

Ferguson, C. J. (2015). Do angry birds make for angry children? A meta-analysis of video game influences on children's and adolescents' aggression, mental health, prosocial behavior, and academic performance. *Perspectives on Psychological Science, 10,* 646–666.

Franceschini, S., Gori, S., Ruffino, M., Viola, S., Molteni, M., & Facoetti, A. (2013). Action video games make dyslexic children read better. *Current Biology, 23,* 462–466.

Gable, S., Chang, Y., & Krull, J. L. (2007). Television watching and frequency of family meals are predictive of overweight onset and persistence in a national sample of school-aged children. *Journal of the American Dietetic Association, 107,* 53–61.

Glenwright, M., & Pexman, P. M. (2010). Development of children's ability to distinguish sarcasm and verbal irony. *Journal of Child Language, 37,* 429–451.

Golmaryami, F. N., Frick, P. J., Hemphill, S. A., Kahn, R. E., Crapanzano, A. M., & Terranova, A. M. (2016). The social, behavioral, and emotional correlates of bullying and victimization in a school-based sample. *Journal of Abnormal Child Psychology, 44,* 381–391.

Green, C. S., & Bavelier, D. (2012). Learning, attentional control, and action video games. *Current Biology, 22,* R197–R206.

Harman, K. (2004). *An update on the status of physical education in schools worldwide: Technical report for the World Health Organization.* Geneva: WHO.

Hoglund, W. L. G., Jones, S. M., Brown, J. L., & Aber, J. L. (2015). The evocative influence of child academic and social-emotional adjustment in inner-city schools. *Journal of Educational Psychology, 107,* 517–532.

Jackson, L. A., Witt, E. A., Games, A. I., Fitzgerald, H. E., von Eye, A., & Zhao, Y. (2012). Information technology use and creativity: Findings from the children and technology project. *Computers in Human Behavior, 28,* 370–376.

Jacobsen, T., & Hofmann, V. (1997). Children's attachment representations: Longitudinal relations to school behavior and academic competency in middle childhood and adolescence. *Developmental Psychology, 33,* 703–710.

Jiang, D., Walsh, M., & Augimeri, L. K. (2011). The linkage between childhood bullying behaviour and future offending. *Criminal Behaviour and Mental Health, 21,* 128–135.

Johnston, C. A., & Fletcher, A. C. (2015). Prediction of maternal use of friendship facilitation strategies in middle childhood. *Journal of Social and Personal Relationships, 32,* 946–966.

Kerns, K. A., Tomich, P. L., Aspelmeier, J. E., & Contreras, J. M. (2000). Attachment-based assessments of parent–child relationships in middle childhood. *Developmental Psychology, 36,* 614–626.

Kielar-Turska, M., & Bialecka-Pikul, M. (2010). Generating and understanding jokes by five- and nine-year-olds as an expression of theory of mind. *Polish Psychological Bulletin, 40,* 163–169.

Kunin-Batson, A. S., Seburg, E. M., Crain, L., Jaka, M. M., Langer, S. L., Levy, R. L., & Sherwood, N. E. (2015). Household factors, family behavior patterns, and adherence to dietary and physical activity guidelines among children at risk of obesity. *Journal of Nutrition Education and Behavior, 47,* 206–215.

Lee, J-S., & Bowen, N. K. (2006). Parent involvement, cultural capital, and the achievement gap among elementary school children. *American Educational Research Journal, 43,* 193–218.

Lou, D. (2014). *Sedentary behaviors and youth: Current trends and the impact on health.* San Diego, CA: Active Living Research. Retrieved from www.activelivingresearch.org.

McCormick, M. P., O'Connor, E. E., & Barnes, S. P. (2016). Mother–child attachment styles and math and reading skills in middle childhood: The mediating role of children's exploration and engagement. *Early Childhood Research Quarterly, 36*, 295–306.

McNeal, R. B. (2015). Parent involvement and school performance: The influence of school context. *Educational Research for Policy and Practice, 14*, 153–167.

Meade, R., Colby, S., White, A., Matthews, D., Yerxa, K., Franzen-Castle, L., Krehbiel, M., Kattelmann, K., Kabala, M., Olfert, J., & White, J. (2014). iCook 4-H: Childhood BMI is associated with family meal frequency. *Journal of the Academy of Nutrition and Dietetics, 114*(9), A64.

Menon, M., Tobin, D. D., Corby, B. C., Menon, M., Hodges, E. V. E., & Perry, D. G. (2007). The developmental costs of high self-esteem for antisocial children. *Child Development, 78*, 1627–1639.

Moreno, G., Johnson-Shelton, D., & Boles, S. (2013). Prevalence and prediction of overweight and obesity among elementary school students. *Journal of School Health, 83*, 157–163.

Moss, E. & St-Laurent, D. (2001). Attachment at school age and academic performance. *Developmental Psychology, 37*, 863–874.

Mulvaney, M. K., & Morrissey, R. A. (2012). Parenting beliefs and academic achievement across African-American and Caucasian family contexts. *Early Child Development and Care, 182*, 1105–1124.

National Education Association. (2015). *Understanding the gaps: Who are we leaving behind and how far?* Retrieved from www.nea.org/home/AchievementGaps.html.

O'Connor, E. E., Scott, M. A., McCormick, M. P., & Weinberg, S. L. (2014). Early mother–child attachment and behavior problems in middle childhood: The role of the subsequent caregiving environment. *Attachment and Human Development, 16*, 590–612.

Ogden, C., & Carroll, M. (2010). Prevalence of obesity among children and adolescents: United States, trends 1963–1965 through 2007–2008. *Centers for Disease Control and Prevention.* Retrieved from www.cdc.gov/nchs/data/hestat/obesity_child_07_08/obesity_child_07_08.htm.

Piekny, J., & Maehler, C. (2013). Scientific reasoning in early and middle childhood: The development of domain-general evidence evaluation, experimentation, and hypothesis generation skills. *British Journal of Developmental Psychology, 31*, 153–179.

Polly, D., McGee, J., Wang, C., Martin, C., Lambert, R., & Pugalee, D. K. (2015). Linking professional development, teacher outcomes, and student achievement: The case of a learner-centered mathematics program for elementary school teachers. *International Journal of Educational Research, 72*, 26–37.

Rasmussen, M., & Laumann, K. (2013). The academic and psychological benefits of exercise in healthy children and adolescents. *European Journal of Psychological Education, 28*, 945–962.

Schwartz, J., Angle, C., & Pitcher, H. (1986). Relationship between childhood blood lead levels and stature. *Pediatrics, 77*, 281–288.

Simonds, J., Kieras, J. E., Rosario, R. M., & Rothbart, M. K. (2007). Effortful control, executive attention, and emotional regulation in 7–10-year-old children. *Cognitive Development, 22*, 474–488.

Strong, W. B., Malina, R. M., Blimkie, C. J., Daniels, S. R., Dishman, R. K., Gutin, B., Hergenroeder, A. C., Must, A., Nixon, P. A., Pivarnik, J. M., Rowland, T., Trost, S., & Trudeau, F. (2005). Evidence based physical activity for school-age youth. *Journal of Pediatrics, 146*, 732–737.

Swanson, J., Valiente, C., & Lemery-Chalfant, K. (2012). Predicting academic achievement from cumulative home risk: The mediating roles of effortful control, academic relationships, and school avoidance. *Merrill-Palmer Quarterly, 58*, 375–408.

Topor, D. R., Keane, S. P., Shelton, T. L., & Calkins, S. D. (2010). Parent involvement and student academic performance: A multiple mediational analysis. *Journal of Prevention and Intervention in the Community, 28*, 183–197.

Troiano, R. P., Berrigan, D., Dodd, K. W., Masse, L. C., Tilert, T., & McDowell, M. (2008). Physical activity in the United States measured by accelerometer. *Medicine and Science in Sports and Exercise, 40*, 181–188.

van den Bergh, L., Denessen, E., Hornstra, L., Voeten, M., & Holland, R. W. (2010). The implicit prejudiced attitudes of teachers: Relations to teacher expectations and the ethnic achievement gap. *American Educational Research Journal, 47*, 497–527.

West, K. K., Mathews, B. L., & Kerns, K. A. (2013). Mother–child attachment and cognitive performance in middle childhood: An examination of mediating mechanisms. *Early Childhood Research Quarterly, 28*, 259–270.

Wojslawowicz Bowker, J. C., Rubin, K. H., Burgess, K. B., Booth-LaForce, C., & Rose-Krasnor, L. (2006). Stable and fluid best friendship patterns in middle childhood. *Merrill-Palmer Quarterly, 52*, 671–693.

WHO. (2010). *Global recommendations on physical activity for health.* Geneva: World Health Organization Press.

Wuang, Y-P., Chiang, C-S., Su, C-Y., & Wang, C-C. (2011). Effectiveness of virtual reality using Wii gaming technology in children with Down syndrome. *Research in Developmental Disabilities, 32*, 312–321.

CHAPTER 10

Family and Adolescence

Adolescence, or roughly the second decade of life, represents a period of the lifespan in which family relationships necessarily, and perhaps dramatically, change. For many families, this is a time characterized by the paradoxes of great anxiety and excitement, and increased closeness and conflict. Adolescents strive for increasing **autonomy**, or independence. Parents are charged with the often complex task of facilitating their teen's successful transition to adulthood, while simultaneously protecting them from the risks associated with engaging in adult behavior too soon. This chapter begins with an overview of some of the developmental changes central to understanding these changing relationships, with a focus on promoting healthy teens and families.

PHYSICAL CHANGES

Adolescence is the lifespan stage in which individuals become capable of sexual reproduction. From a physical maturation perspective, individuals enter this period as children and exit as adults. This transformation is called **puberty**. Puberty is marked by a physical growth spurt, affecting height, weight, and body composition, and the development of primary and secondary sex characteristics. **Primary sex characteristics** are those directly related to reproduction, such as maturation of the sex organs, including **menarche**, or the onset of menstruation, and **spermarche**, or the onset of the ability to ejaculate sperm. **Secondary sex characteristics** are the more visible changes that accompany puberty but do not affect reproduction. Increases in height and weight, skin changes, body hair growth, the development of breasts (for females), and facial hair (for males) are all examples of secondary sex characteristics.

The age in which children begin puberty appears to be influenced by both genes and environment, and varies widely (Ge, Natsuaki, Neiderhiser, & Reiss, 2007; Mustanski, Viken, Kaprio, Pulkkinen, & Rose, 2004). Genes provide a predisposition toward a

Image 10.1 Adolescence Is the Lifespan Stage in which Individuals Become Capable of Sexual Reproduction (photo by Lev Dolgachov/Depositphotos, Inc.).

particular timetable, providing a window constraining the earliest and latest times puberty may occur, and environmental factors influence when during that window it actually does occur. Environmental factors such as nutrition and health can affect the timing of puberty. Children, particularly females, who are malnourished or otherwise underweight are more likely to experience a delayed onset of puberty (Kulin, Bwibo, Mutie, & Santer, 1982). The same is true for children with chronic illness (Pozo & Argente, 2002; Rosen, 1991). Conversely, children who are overweight or obese are more likely to experience an earlier onset of puberty (Ahmed, Ong, & Dunger, 2009; Shalitin & Phillip, 2003).

Puberty does not only affect physical development and reproductive capability, it affects both how adolescents see themselves and how others see them. These changes in perceptions can have implications for their social and emotional health, as well as their relationships with others. Body changes associated with puberty are often accompanied by issues with self-image and body satisfaction as youth adjust to their new and changing physical selves (Chakraborty, 2014; Williams & Currie, 2000). This can be particularly difficult when puberty comes much earlier than expected. Indeed, research shows that adolescents who begin puberty earlier than their peers are more likely to have problems in school, to engage in earlier sexual activity, are at higher risk for earlier experimentation with substance use, and to engage in delinquent behavior (Costello, Sung, Worthman, & Angold, 2007; Kaltiala-Heino, Kovisto, Marttunen, & Fröjd, 2011; Negriff, Susman, & Trickett, 2011). This appears to be due, in part, to how early maturing youth are perceived and treated by their peers. Some early maturing youth find themselves socially rejected or otherwise put off by same-age peers, but accepted by older adolescents who look more like themselves (Negriff, Ji, & Trickett, 2011). This can result in premature exposure to experiences and phenomena that are not otherwise developmentally appropriate for the younger adolescent, thus leading to problems.

Parents also react to their children's maturing physical appearance. Puberty is often associated with a change in parenting practices that consists of less monitoring and supervision, even when the timing of puberty is early or late (Laird & Marrero, 2011). For the early developing child, this can lead to having too much freedom or responsibility too soon, and for the later developing adolescent, not enough. Many parents feel less sure about their own parenting behaviors around the time of puberty (Glatz & Buchanan, 2015). It has long been established that puberty is associated with feelings of increased distance between parents and children (Steinberg, 1987). However, increased distance is not necessarily a negative thing. It is likely driven by the growing teen's need for privacy rather than a reflection of feelings toward the parent. Most parents and adolescents report getting along well throughout adolescence (Steinberg, 2001). The diminished closeness experienced during puberty is not only expected, but perhaps even necessary for children to become healthy and independent adults.

Sleep is another issue affected by puberty. The typical adolescent needs at least 9 hours of sleep per night (National Sleep Foundation, 2016b). However, during puberty, adolescents experience a shift in the circadian rhythm, creating a natural desire to stay awake later at night and sleep in later in the morning (Hagenauer, Perryman, Lee, & Carskadon, 2009). While many teens have no problem finding ways to spend those extra evening hours, including watching television, doing homework, and socializing with friends online, early school start times mean they are not getting enough sleep (see Box 10.1). Inadequate sleep is associated with diminished physical, cognitive, and emotional health, with consequences ranging from weight gain, to poor academic achievement, to substance abuse (Owens, Adolescent Sleep Working Group, & Committee on Adolescence, 2014; Short & Louca, 2015; Winsler, Deutsch, Vorona, Payner, & Szklo-Coxe, 2015). Sleep issues during adolescence may also take their toll on family relationships, as parents find themselves not only no longer able to enforce bedtimes, but also dealing with a sleep–deprived adolescent.

INTELLECTUAL CHANGES

In addition to changing bodies, adolescence is also a time of changing brains. Experiences affect brain development, which in turn leads to changes in both thinking and behavior (Kuhn, 2009). Unlike children, most adolescents are capable of thinking in the abstract

Image 10.2 Inadequate Sleep during Adolescence Is Associated with Poor Academic Achievement (photo by Lev Dolgachov/Depositphotos, Inc.).

BOX 10.1 HELPING TEENS GET ENOUGH SLEEP

Fifteen-year-old Crystal leads a busy life. Monday through Friday, she wakes at 6:00 a.m., has an hour to shower, dress, and eat before catching the bus to school. By 7:30 a.m., she is busy conjugating verbs in Spanish class. Classes end by 2:15 p.m., but her day is far from over. Between softball and student leadership activities, she rarely gets home before 6:00 p.m. After a quick dinner with her family, she still needs at least 2 hours to finish her homework. After 9:00 p.m. seems to be the only time Crystal has for herself—time she uses to watch her favorite shows while catching up with friends on social media. It's usually midnight by the time she gets to bed. Thank goodness for the weekends when she can sleep until noon! If only it wasn't so hard getting back into a routine each Monday morning.

Like over 90% of all adolescents in the United States, Crystal is not getting the minimum 9 hours of sleep recommended by health professionals, and would benefit from changes to her daily routines and sleep habits (Basch, Basch, Ruggles, & Rajan, 2014). Several professional organizations, including the American Academy of Pediatrics, the APA, the American Sleep Association, and others advocate changing secondary school start times such that they are more conducive to adolescents' sleep needs (Schools Start Later, 2016). While it is true that post-poning school start times until at least 8:30 a.m. is associated with higher academic achievement, less depression, and fewer car accidents among adolescent students, change at the institutional level has been slow (Wheaton, Chapman, & Croft, 2016). The majority of school districts continue to start middle and high schools early, often citing issues with bus schedules, teacher contracts, and extracurricular activities as reasons action is not possible (National Sleep Foundation, 2016a). In the meantime, teens continue to have issues with sleep deprivation.

However, there are things parents can do to help their teens get adequate sleep. These include:

* encouraging teens through education, scheduling, and limit-setting to develop consistent sleep and wake times throughout the week, including weekends;
* adopting and enforcing a rule that all screens must be turned off an hour before bedtime—exposure to electronic screens delays the production of melatonin, resulting in even later feelings of sleepiness;
* restricting the use of caffeine and other stimulants after 4:00 p.m.;
* not overscheduling adolescents—the reality is that teens will never get enough sleep if they have too many places to be or things to do;
* setting a good example by practicing healthy sleep habits themselves.

(Smetana & Villalobos, 2009). They think about possibilities and become better at viewing situations and issues from multiple perspectives. Whereas children see things as black or white, right or wrong, or good versus bad, adolescents are more likely to view things as relative. This is a positive and necessary step toward higher order thinking, but can cause tension in family relationships as these shifts in thinking often lead teens to challenge knowledge, decisions, or beliefs espoused by parents (Steinberg, 2016). For these reasons, it is common to see increases in bickering and family conflict in even the healthiest of families, particularly in early adolescence.

During adolescence, there are major changes in the structure and functions of the brain, particularly in regards to the **limbic system** and the **prefrontal cortex**. The limbic system, which is the part of the brain associated with basic emotions and drives, likely reaches full maturity by late adolescence (Steinberg, 2005). In contrast, the prefrontal cortex, or part of the brain associated with higher-level thinking skills such as impulse control, decision-making, and planning, develops much slower, typically not reaching full maturation until around age 25 or later (Steinberg, 2005). This means that the instinctual and emotional areas of the brain develop before the thoughtful and reflective areas. As a result, adolescents are susceptible to acting first and thinking later, often engaging in higher degrees of risk-taking than seen at other stages of the lifespan.

The immaturity of the prefrontal cortex contributes to beliefs commonly held by adolescents that they are somehow invincible, and that bad things only happen to other people. This is referred to as the **invincibility fable**, and underlies many seemingly reckless decisions made during adolescence, such as engaging in unsafe sex, driving too fast, or drinking too much. The consequences of high-risk behavior can be severe, and even fatal. In fact, the leading cause of death in adolescence is unintentional injuries, including car accidents (Ozer & Irwin, 2009). However, the rewards can also be great when the risk pays off. Feelings of invincibility allow adolescents to not only dream big, but to follow those dreams. Encouraging adolescents to pursue healthy risks, such as those facilitated by many extracurricular activities, is important for optimal development.

EMOTIONAL, SOCIAL, AND PSYCHOLOGICAL CHANGES

Adolescence also marks the time when an individual's social world broadens. Teens spend increasingly more time away from family, with friends, at school, engaged in extracurricular activities, and even at work. However, this does not mean that parents are no longer important. On the contrary, parents are still very important. Most teens report feeling close to their parents, which is a good thing because a close relationship, characterized by warmth, communication, and support, is associated with better outcomes, including academic achievement, and social and emotional wellbeing (Moore, Guzman, Hair, Lippman, & Garrett, 2004). Close parent–adolescent relationships that include a reasonable degree of parental monitoring and supervision in conjunction with the affordance of age-appropriate autonomy provide adolescents with a strong home foundation for exploring the broader social world (Hair, Moore, Garrett, Ling, & Cleveland, 2008).

Along this vein, it is during adolescence where we expect to see elevated influence and importance of peer groups. Although teens tend to choose their friends based on mutual interests and values, the roots of those interests and values often lie within the family. For example, adolescents who come from families where academic achievement is highly valued are more likely to choose friends who also value academic achievement (Chen, Dornbusch, & Liu, 2007). Parent–teen relationships also influence the quality of adolescents' peer relationships, as it is through family that we first learn how to relate to others. Whereas in childhood, intimacy is learned from and shared with parents, in adolescence, intimacy is practiced with friends, and later romantic partners. During adolescence, parents often become the role models and advisors about life issues, while peers are the ones who provide feedback on application of those lessons.

A major task of adolescence is **identity formation**, or the process of figuring out who one is and who one wants to become. Although this process continues into adulthood and potentially through the lifespan, in many respects, it is considered an adolescent issue. Beginning in early adolescence, the self-concept becomes differentiated, as teens recognize they are actually quite complex individuals, capable of behaving or thinking in seemingly contradictory ways depending on the context (Cantin & Boivin, 2004; Kuzucu, Bontempo, Hofer, Stallings, & Piccinin, 2014). For example, a teen might recognize that he is very shy and reserved in new settings, but fun and outgoing when with his friends. Throughout adolescence, it is common to see individuals experiment with multiple different identities, perhaps exploring different musical genres, styles of dress, dietary choices, and causes. As you will learn in your development courses, healthy identity development also often involves questioning the values, morals, beliefs, and practices of one's family, and possibly exploring alternatives. This does not mean they must be rejected, only questioned and compared to alternatives before accepted as one's own. Regardless, for many families, conflict can increase.

Through the study of adolescent development, you will learn that many of the stereotypical problems of adolescence are actually indicators of typical and healthy development. Helping teens and families to view these issues as milestones toward adulthood may help to improve family and individual health and overall wellbeing.

AREAS OF RESEARCH AND STUDY

Understanding parent–adolescent relationships is one growing area of research in adolescent development that you will learn about as an HDFS student. In fact, each of the topics already discussed in relation to parent–adolescent relationships is an area of study in its own right (e.g., puberty, sleep, cognition, brain development, risk-taking, peer groups, identity, self-concept, self-esteem). A few additional prominent areas of research and study that are likely to come up in your coursework include adolescent sexuality, academics, and problems of adolescence.

Sexuality

Studying sex during adolescence is not new. For decades, researchers have been interested in the prevalence of sexual activity, characteristics of sexual behavior, the consequences of teen pregnancy, and even the coming out process for sexual minority individuals. However, research along this vein has typically been approached from the assumption that sex during adolescence has largely negative repercussions. In more recent years, it has become clear that having sex as an older adolescent (at least 16) is not usually associated with negative outcomes, nor is it typically affiliated with other problem behavior (Diamond & Savin-Williams, 2009). Hence, there has been a shift in perspective within the larger HDFS field. We now acknowledge and respect that sexual thoughts and behavior are a normal part of adolescence, and that most teens will engage in some sort of sexual behavior. The shift from viewing adolescent sex as problematic to a focus

Image 10.3 The Larger HDFS Field Acknowledges and Respects that Sexual Thoughts and Behaviors Are a Normal Part of Adolescence (photo by Vitaly Valua/Depositphotos, Inc.).

on promoting healthy and responsible sexuality in a very comprehensive way has led to a broadening of scholarship in adolescent studies. Rather than focusing exclusively on sexual behavior and potential consequences, like sexually transmitted infections (e.g., genital herpes or HIV) and pregnancy, recent research and practice have focused on a wide range of topics, including adolescents' knowledge and feelings about puberty, communication about sex between teens and their parents, peers, and potential partners, consent and assertiveness, sex and media, dating violence prevention, sexual satisfaction, and comprehensive sex education (see Box 10.2).

Researchers have long been interested in the characteristics of adolescent dating and romantic relationships. Most younger adolescents report that they are not yet involved in romantic relationships, but, for many, the composition of friendships and peer groups change from predominantly same-sex to mixed-sex (Mehta & Strough, 2009; Molloy, Gest, Feinberg, & Osgood, 2014). Among those who do claim to have a boyfriend or girlfriend, there is often little in the way of intimacy (Connolly & McIsaac, 2009). Relationships may be established and terminated via text messages or social apps (formerly hand-written notes), or through friends, and the relationship is very often in name only and very short lived. Two young preteens or teens may claim to be "going out," but where do they actually go? Often nowhere, or, if they do, it is most often in a group setting. In mid-adolescence, we expect intimacy to grow, such that "going out" actually means something, and perhaps relationships last months. However, we still expect that "dating activities complement, rather than replace, time spent with same-sex friends" (Connolly & McIsaac, 2009, p. 117). Later in adolescence, relationships have the potential to become more adult-like in terms of intimacy. Relationships may last a year or

BOX 10.2 COMPREHENSIVE SEXUALITY EDUCATION: MUCH MORE THAN THE "BIRDS AND THE BEES"

Promoting positive sexual health through education is a value shared by many professionals in the field of HDFS. Comprehensive sexuality education is one such approach. Unlike other approaches to sex education that perhaps focus only on reproductive biology, abstinence, or disease prevention, comprehensive sexuality education encompasses the sociocultural, biological, psychological, and spiritual dimensions of sexuality needed to become a sexually healthy adult.

What constitutes a sexually healthy adult, one might ask? SIECUS (2004) has identified 37 behaviors indicative of healthy sexuality in adulthood. A few examples of such behaviors include the ability to:

- express love and intimacy in appropriate ways;
- develop and maintain meaningful relationships;
- practice effective decision-making;
- express one's sexuality in ways that are congruent with values;
- discriminate between life-enhancing sexual behaviors and those that are harmful to self and/or others;
- engage in sexual relationships that are consensual, non-exploitative, honest, pleasurable, and protected;
- practice health-promoting behaviors, such as regular check-ups, breast and testicular self-exam, and early identification of potential problems;
- use contraception effectively to avoid unintended pregnancy;
- avoid contracting or transmitting a sexually transmitted disease, including HIV (pp. 16–17).

The Guidelines for Comprehensive Sexuality Education (SIECUS, 2004) represent a valuable resource for promoting positive sexual health from early childhood through adolescence. A link to the full document is located in the Suggested Resources section at the end of this chapter.

more, and can often be quite serious, although not necessarily leading to marriage. For the most part this is non-problematic in terms of development. Dating or romantic involvement throughout adolescence is not necessary for healthy psychosocial development, but it does provide opportunity for youth to learn about and practice participating in relationships. When dating or romantic involvement does occur, it is important that relationships are age and maturity-level appropriate. When we see younger adolescents in serious relationships more typical of older adolescents, this is reason for concern, as involvement in serious intimate romantic relationships too early is associated with poor academic achievement and substance abuse (Orpinas, Horne, Song, Reeves, & Hsieh, 2013).

There is considerable variation as to when in the dating or romantic involvement process sexual activity begins. According to the CDC (2016b), 41% of high school students report being sexually active. Current research suggests that sexual activity in adolescence does not appear to be psychologically harmful provided it does not occur too early, prior to 16, it is consensual, and it does not lead to pregnancy or disease (Diamond & Savin-Williams, 2009). Whereas some adolescent sexual activity occurs in the context of dating, we are seeing an increase in sexual activity between non-dating individuals (Manning, Giordano, & Longmore, 2006; Rowley & Hertzog, 2016). Known as "hooking up," or "friends with benefits," teens' motivations for engaging in these relationships, their desired or expected outcomes, and their potential psychosocial consequences represent an additional area of study in HDFS. It should be noted, however, that there is no evidence that hooking up is the new normal for teens, and further research is needed to gauge prevalence.

There has also been increased interest among researchers in sexual identity formation, particularly when it comes to LGBTQ individuals. In the past, sexual identity was seen as more of an adult issue, as most LGBTQ persons did not come out, or publicly self-identify as LGBTQ, until adulthood (Dunlap, 2016; Pew Research Center, 2013). However, changing the landscape in terms of public opinion, as well as exposure to more LGBTQ adults in real life and in the media has contributed to more individuals self-identifying as LGBTQ at younger ages, hence making sexual identity an adolescent, as opposed to adult-only, issue (Dunlap, 2016). While some of the research on LGBTQ youth focuses on the coming out process, many recent studies have been more concerned with their psychosocial outcomes or wellbeing (e.g., Bird, Kuhns, & Garofalo, 2012; Hatzenbuehler & Keyes, 2013; Page, Lindahl, & Malik, 2013). Others, such as the Family Acceptance Project at San Francisco State University, conduct research and community outreach focused on promoting family and community acceptance of LGBTQ youth (Ryan, 2010). The link to their website is located in the Suggested Resources section at the end of this chapter.

Academics

Although high school is often said to be the "time of our lives," many individuals face a range of academic challenges during adolescence. Even historically "good" students are at risk for diminished performance and increased stress, depression, or behavior problems as they transition into high school (Benner, 2011). By age 18, a full 6.5% of students will drop out of school completely, thus potentially altering their life-course permanently (U.S. Department of Education, 2016b). As such, adolescent scholars and educators are particularly interested in how to best promote academic success in secondary, or middle and high school, education.

What is it about a secondary school that makes students thrive? Researchers have explored a number of characteristics, including school size, perceived safety, curriculum, and school climate. Research examining the importance of school size has yielded mixed results (Newman, Garrett, & Elbourne, 2006). While some studies suggest that students do better in more intimate settings (e.g., Stewart, 2009), others find the opposite (e.g., Terling Watt, 2003). Regardless of school size, students perform better when they feel safe at school, as evidenced by higher academic achievement among students who attend schools where bullying, victimization, and other violent incidents or hostile climates are perceived to be low (Ripski & Gregory, 2009). Perhaps counterintuitively, measures like the use of metal detectors, security cameras, and police presence make students feel less safe, even in schools where community violence is high (Tanner-Smith & Fisher, 2016).

Image 10.4 Higher Academic Achievement Is Found among Students who Attend Schools Where Bullying, Victimization, and Other Violent Incidents Are Low (photo by Mandy God-behear/Depositphotos, Inc.).

Research has also focused on curriculum, in an attempt to identify not only what should be taught in secondary schools, but how students best learn the material. Ideally, the high school curriculum should be engaging, but also provide students with the skills to be college or career ready upon graduation. This represents a challenge, as clearly not all students share similar interests, goals, or learning styles. One strategy for addressing this challenge is to educate similar students together, as seen in magnet schools, charter schools, and career academies. In the end, however, what may matter most for adolescents is **school climate** (Kutsyuruba, Klinger, & Hussain, 2015). Similar to the classroom climate discussed in Chapter 7, the school climate refers to the quality and character of a given school, as experienced by its members (Cohen, McCabe, Michelli, & Pickeral, 2009). It includes the norms, values, rules, expectations, relationships, practices, and organizational structures (National School Climate Center, 2016). Positive school climates promote physical and emotional safety, as well as inclusivity, and are linked to higher academic achievement (Hopson, Schiller, & Lawson, 2014). Schools with a positive climate have administrators, teachers, parents, and students who are both engaged and committed to a shared vision. Relationships between adults and youth tend to be warm and responsive, but the standards and expectations are held high. The curriculum is engaging and meaningful, and teachers promote cooperation rather than competition in the classroom. Much of the current research in this area focuses on either better understanding the relationship between school climate and adolescent outcomes, or on specific strategies for improving the climate within schools.

Problems of Adolescence

In general, adolescence is one of the physically healthiest stages of the lifespan. Most of the "problems" teens face are actually quite normal, and some even necessary for becoming a healthy adult. However, a minority of teens will develop more serious problems, including problems with depression, substance abuse, and/or antisocial behavior. In

Image 10.5 Depression Is the Most Common Psychological Problem among Adolescents (photo by Anastasia Tepikina/Depositphotos, Inc.).

HDFS, identifying and understanding who is most at risk, how to prevent such problems from occurring, and how to most effectively intervene when they do is a major area of research and study.

Depression. Depression is the most common psychological problem among adolescents (Graber & Sontag, 2009). Symptoms can range from mild to severe, and have the potential to affect an individual's mood, self-esteem, self-worth, concentration, thoughts, motivation, sleep, appetite, and behavior. As you will learn about in your HDFS coursework, the **diathesis–stress model** is often offered as a potential explanation for depression. At the simplest level, diathesis is another word for a predisposition, and stress refers to the negative impact of circumstances or events. According to this model, it takes the combination of a diathesis and stress to trigger a depressive reaction (Lewinsohn, Joiner, & Rohde, 2001). Stressors might include transitions (e.g., school, puberty, moving, divorce/remarriage), family conflict, romantic relationships, problematic peer relationships, victimization, or other adversities.

Consequences of depression can be severe, and might include a disruption in family and peer relationships, failing grades or other trouble in school, self-injurious behavior, and/or **suicidal ideation**, or thinking about committing suicide. Suicide is the second leading cause of death in adolescence in the United States per year (Ozer & Irwin, 2009). In 2015, nearly 18% of high school students admitted to thinking about suicide, and roughly half of those said they had made at least one attempt (CDC, 2016a). The majority of completed suicides are first attempts. This means that (1) intervention is critical before an attempt is actually made, and (2) suicide is often a spontaneous act, not a persistent one. Thus, early identification and intervention with those at risk is critical.

Substance Abuse. Research suggests that some experimentation with alcohol or soft drugs, like marijuana, is not necessarily always associated with negative outcomes (Englund, Siebenbruner, Oliva, Egeland, & Chung, 2013). This is good news, as 58% of high school seniors report having used alcohol at least once over the preceding year, and about 35% report having used marijuana over that same time period (National Institute on Drug Abuse, 2016). Very few teens report drinking alcohol or smoking marijuana daily. In general, these "experimenters" tend to have good social skills, and engage in more social activities with opportunities for substance use compared to teens who abstain from alcohol and drug use completely (Tucker, Ellickson, Collins, & Klein, 2006). However, this does not mean that we do not need to worry about them, as there are risks associated with even minor experimentation (e.g., driving under the influence, lowered inhibition), and experimentation can always evolve into more frequent use and/ or use of harder drugs.

Both frequent use of soft substances or any use of hard substances are associated with a range of negative consequences. Frequent or hard substance abuse is associated with problems at school (e.g., grades, truancy, behavior), depression, involvement in criminal or delinquent behavior, unprotected sexual activity, car accidents, accidental overdose, and long-term physical health problems, including addiction (National Institute on Drug Abuse, 2014). Although most teen substance abusers are not addicts and most will not become addicts, many adult addicts began their substance use as adolescents.

Antisocial Behavior/Delinquency. Across the social sciences, the term **antisocial** is used to describe a pattern of behavior that disregards the rights and wellbeing of others. Although there are other definitions of the word, in this context being antisocial has nothing to do with how outgoing or reclusive a person is. We would consider most criminal behavior to be antisocial, including grand theft, vandalism, arson, and assault. **Delinquency**, on the other hand, is a term more often used to describe engagement in minor crimes, including status offenses (i.e., engaging in behavior that is illegal only for persons under a certain age, like drinking alcohol), shoplifting, graffiti, and truancy. However, as you may find through your HDFS coursework, these terms are sometimes used interchangeably in the literature. Although many adolescents may engage in the occasional delinquent act, most do not exhibit a consistent pattern of delinquent or anti-social behavior. For those who are involved in persistent delinquent or antisocial activity, interventions targeting family and individual mental health can often help.

AREAS OF PRACTICE

Professionals aspiring to work with adolescents and/or their families have multiple options in the education, community, and mental health sectors. As discussed in Chapter 1, HDFS provides a strong foundation for students who wish to pursue graduate studies in any of these fields, but there are also career possibilities in each of these areas where a graduate degree or license is not typically required. We will discuss some of these here.

Education. Teens in the United States spend an average of 36 hours per week at school or engaged in school-related activities (U.S. Department of Health and Human Services, 2016). While teachers, counselors, and administrators must typically be licensed, there are other opportunities to work with adolescents in the secondary school setting.

College preparation programs, especially those targeting first generation college students, are growing throughout the country and represent a potential source of employment for HDFS graduates. Examples of federally funded programs include Upward Bound, Talent Search, the Student Support Services Program, and GEAR UP (U.S. Department of Education, 2016a). Although the specifics vary by program, common features of such programs include tutoring, mentoring, and instruction on things like the college application process, financial aid, and college success. Often, participants of such programs are selected in middle school, and remain in the program through college entry or beyond.

Teen parent programs are another service often provided by school districts or other educational agencies. In some cases these are funded through Early Head Start, and in others funding comes from elsewhere. Occupations in such programs might include parent education, case management, and home visiting. Depending on the structure of the program, either the young child or the teen parent may be the official "client," but, regardless, a strong background in early childhood development, adolescent development, and parenting is often needed to be effective in these roles.

There are also often employment opportunities within school districts to provide support services to students with designated physical, intellectual, or emotional special needs. Federal law mandates that all students are entitled to a free and appropriate education in the least restrictive environment possible (Individuals with Disabilities Education Act, 2004). For many students, having an extra support person to assist them means they are able to stay in regular classrooms. For others, instruction in regular classrooms is not immediately possible, but having that support is integral to being able to access the curriculum.

Community. Areas of practice within the community are diverse, as agencies and programs tend to reflect the needs of the specific community they serve. Many communities have programs to teach IL skills to foster youth who will be aging out of the foster care system, programs for homeless youth, youth with substance abuse issues, crisis hotlines or centers, and teen centers. Agencies such as Planned Parenthood may provide services such as sexual health education and counseling, and still others may provide support or resources for teens grappling with other issues. The internet can be a valuable source of information about the resources and programs offered in your community, either by searching for specific resources in an area of interest and then viewing job opportunities on individual websites, or by browsing non-profit or human service jobs on your favorite job boards. Additionally, many counties across the country maintain a listing of their community resources that is accessible through www.211.org. Although designed to connect people in need with resources, browsing the site can give you an idea of the types of programs (and potential employers) in your area.

Mental Health. For HDFS graduates interested in pursuing employment in adolescent mental health, one option is to explore careers in residential treatment. Residential treatment is an intensive mode of therapy that occurs outside of the home, typically because the youth has either been court-ordered to receive such service or because lesser restrictive forms of intervention have not been successful. In residential treatment, youth typically live in a group home, unlocked treatment center, or locked psychiatric facility with other youth who have similar behavioral issues for an extended period of time. Typically designed to treat aggression, antisocial behavior, substance abuse, sexual offending, and psychiatric disorders, youth in residential treatment participate in individual, group, and family counseling, as appropriate. Licensed and graduate-level staff are generally responsible for providing clinical services, but B.A./B.S.-level counselors oversee the residential component of the program, working one-on-one with the youth throughout the day. Working with these youth as part of preventative or aftercare services is also a possibility.

STRATEGIES FOR PURSUING SPECIALIZATION OR CAREERS IN ADOLESCENCE

HDFS students wishing to pursue a career working with adolescents should seek out coursework and field experiences focusing on teenagers. Many HDFS programs offer courses specific to adolescence, but if your program does not, check to see if there are approved courses you can take in other majors that may be relevant. Psychology, Sociology, Social Work, Education, and Criminal Justice are a few majors that may offer coursework specific to adolescence. Consider joining professional organizations with an adolescence focus. The SRA and the SRCD are good places to start. Attend a conference if you are able, and participate in webinars. Field experiences, including paid employment, are often available in college mentorship programs, Early Head Start or teen parenting centers, and adolescent mental health programs prior to graduation. Alternatively, some students gain initial experience with adolescents through coaching, leading religious-based youth groups, or otherwise facilitating some other adolescent extracurricular activity.

Summary

1   Family relationships change over the course of adolescence:

    A   Parents must balance their teens' needs for autonomy with protecting them from risks associated with engaging in adult behaviors too soon.

2   During adolescence, individuals undergo a physical transformation in which they become physically capable of sexual reproduction. This physical transformation is called puberty:

    A   Puberty is marked by a physical growth spurt, and the development of primary and secondary sex characteristics.

    B   The age at which individuals begin puberty is influenced by both genes and the environment.

        a   Health and nutrition are important environmental factors influencing the timing of puberty.

    C   Puberty affects how adolescents see themselves, and how they are seen by others.

        a   Many youth experience issues with body image and satisfaction around the time of puberty.

        b   Early puberty is associated with a higher risk of academic problems, early sexual activity, early experimentation with alcohol and drugs, and delinquency. This likely has to do with peer group choices combined with less supervision and monitoring by parents.

3   Sleep is also affected by puberty, with most adolescents finding themselves unable to sleep until later at night, and needing to sleep later in the morning:

A   Most teens do not get enough sleep, often due to staying up late and needing to be awake early for school.

B   Sleep deprivation in adolescence is associated with diminished physical, cognitive, and emotional health, thus putting teens who do not get enough sleep at risk for problems with weight, academics, behavior, and relationships.

4   Brain maturation during adolescence leads to changes in the way adolescents think. Thinking becomes more abstract, multidimensional, and relative:

A   The limbic system, or instinctual and emotional part of the brain, develops more rapidly than the prefrontal cortex, or the part of the brain responsible for higher order thinking. As such, adolescents are more likely to engage in impulsive or risky behavior compared to adults.

5   Throughout adolescence, individuals spend increasingly more time with peers, at school, engaged in extracurricular activities, and work. However, family, especially parents, remain important:

A   For many, parents serve as role models and advisors as adolescents learn how to negotiate a larger world.

B   In many respects, adolescence marks the beginning of identity formation. As teens think about who they are and who they want to become, family values, morals, beliefs, and practices may be challenged, sometimes leading to increased family conflict.

6   Examining issues related to sexuality, academics, and problems of adolescence are all areas of current research and study:

A   Areas of study related to adolescent sexuality include understanding the functions and features of dating, romantic relationships across adolescence, and sexual activity.

B   Researchers who study academic issues are often interested in characteristics of schools, including size, safety, curriculum, and climate, that are associated with higher academic achievement.

C   A minority of teens will develop serious psychosocial problems, including depression, substance abuse, and/or antisocial behavior. Understanding who is at risk, and developing effective prevention and intervention measures is another area of study within adolescent development.

7   There are a number of career options for individuals with 4-year degrees to pursue working with adolescents:

A   In the education sector, college preparation programs, teen parent programs, and support services for students with physical, intellectual, or emotional special needs are viable sources of employment.

B   Community-based employment may be found at programs for youth aging out of the foster care system, programs for homeless youth, programs for youth with substance abuse issues, crisis hotlines or centers, and teen centers.

C   For those interested in careers in mental health, working with youth in residential treatment, or in preventative or aftercare services, is a possibility.

8   HDFS students wishing to pursue a career working with adolescents should pursue coursework and field experiences focused on teenagers.

Key Terms

antisocial
autonomy
delinquency
diathesis-stress model
identity formation
invincibility fable
limbic system
menarche
prefrontal cortex
primary sex characteristics
puberty
secondary sex characteristics
spermarche
suicidal ideation

Challenge: Integration

Research on adolescent development can have implications for public policy. One example includes the application of the findings from neuroscientists that the brain is not fully mature until around age 25 to the issue of to what degree juveniles and young adults who commit crimes should be held accountable for their actions. In other words, should juveniles and young adults who commit crimes be punished similarly to adults, even though science shows that the part of the brain responsible for planning, decision-making, and causal reasoning is not fully developed?

To gain a better understanding of the issues, evidence, and arguments, read the following two articles (both are available online). Then, respond to the prompts below.

Articles:

Buchen, L. (2012). Arrested development. *Nature, 484*, 304–306. Retrieved from www.nature.com/news/science-in-court-arrested-development-1.10456.

Requarth, T. (2016). Neuroscience is changing the debate over what role age should play in the courts. *Newsweek, 166*(16). Retrieved from www.newsweek.com/2016/04/29/young-brains-neuroscience-juvenile-inmates-criminal-justice-449000.html.

Prompts:

1   Briefly summarize the main arguments given for treating juveniles and young adults who commit crimes different from and similar to older adults who commit the same types of crimes.
2   Do you believe that juveniles, under the age of 18, should receive the same punishment as adults (including life sentences) if they commit a serious crime? Explain your reasoning.
3   Do you believe that young adults, ages 18–25, should receive the same punishment as older adults (including life sentences) if they commit a serious crime? Explain your reasoning.
4   As HDFS professionals who care about prevention and intervention efforts, describe your ideas as to how we might go about keeping individuals from committing serious crimes in the first place.

Journal Questions

1   Of the areas of research, study, and practice discussed in this chapter, which do you find most interesting? Would you be interested in pursuing a career working with adolescents? Explain.

2   Based on your own experience, describe the characteristics of adults who are well liked and trusted by adolescents. What kind of qualities do such adults share, and what is it that makes them seemingly effective at working with teens? Do you see yourself as possessing these qualities? Explain.

3   Looking back at your own adolescence, discuss the positives and negatives from a professional perspective. In other words, if you were a professional who worked with your adolescent self, which areas of development would you say were healthy or typical, and which areas would raise concern? Explain.

SUGGESTED RESOURCES

Family Acceptance Project, San Francisco State University: https://familyproject.sfsu.edu/.
Inside the Teenage Brain, PBS Frontline: www.pbs.org/video/2365601861/.
National School Climate Center: www.schoolclimate.org.
Planned Parenthood, Resources and Tools for Educators: www.plannedparenthood.org/educators/resources.
SIECUS Guidelines for Comprehensive Sexuality Education: www.siecus.org.
Suicide Prevention Resource Center: www.sprc.org.

REFERENCES

Ahmed, M. L., Ong, K. K., & Dunger, D. B. (2009). Childhood obesity and the timing of puberty. *Trends in Endocrinology and Metabolism, 20*(5), 237–242.

Basch, C. E., Basch, C. H., Ruggles, K. V., & Rajan, S. (2014). Prevalence of sleep duration on an average school night among four nationally representative successive samples of American high school students, 2007–2013. *Preventing Chronic Disease, 11*(E216), 1–5.

Benner, A. D. (2011). The transition to high school: Current knowledge, future directions. *Educational Psychology Review, 23*, 299–328.

Bird, J. D. P., Kuhns, L., & Garofalo, R. (2012). The impact of role models on health outcomes for lesbian, gay, bisexual, and transgender youth. *Journal of Adolescent Health, 50*, 353–357.

Cantin, S., & Boivin, M. (2004). Change and stability in children's social network and self-perceptions during transition from elementary to junior high school. *International Journal of Behavioral Development, 28*, 561–570.

CDC. (2016a). *Trends in the prevalence of suicide-related behavior, National YRBS: 1991–2015.* Retrieved from www.cdc.gov/healthyyouth/data/yrbs/results.htm.

CDC. (2016b). *Youth risk behavior surveillance: United States, 2015.* Retrieved from www.cdc.gov/healthyyouth/data/yrbs/pdf/2015/ss6506_updated.pdf.

Chakraborty, R. (2014). Body image and its relation with the concept of physical self among adolescents and young adults. *Psychological Studies, 59*, 419–426.

Chen, Z., Dornbusch, S. M., & Liu, R. X. (2007). Direct and indirect pathways between parental constructive behavior and adolescent affiliation with achievement-oriented peers. *Journal of Child and Family Studies, 16*, 837–858.

Cohen, J., McCabe, E., Michelli, N., & Pickeral, T. (2009). School climate: Research, policy, practice, and teacher education. *Teachers College Record, 111*, 180–213.

Connolly, J. A., & McIsaac, C. (2009). Romantic relationships in adolescence. In R. Learner & L. Steinberg (Eds.), *Handbook of adolescent psychology* (3rd ed., Vol. 2, pp. 104–151). New York: Wiley.

Costello, E. J., Sung, M., Worthman, C., & Angold, A. (2007). Pubertal maturation and the development of alcohol use and abuse. *Drug and Alcohol Dependence, 88*(S1), S50–S59.

Diamond, L. M., & Savin-Williams, R. C. (2009). Adolescent sexuality. In R. Learner & L. Steinberg (Eds.), *Handbook of adolescent psychology* (3rd ed., Vol. 2, pp. 479–523). New York: Wiley.

Dunlap, A. (2016). Changes in coming out milestones across five age cohorts. *Journal of Gay and Lesbian Social Services, 28*, 20–38.

Englund, M. M., Siebenbruner, J., Oliva, E. M., Egeland, B., & Chung, C-T. (2013). The developmental significance of late adolescent substance use for early adult functioning. *Developmental Psychology, 49*, 1554–1564.

Ge, X., Natsuaki, M. N., Neiderhiser, J. M., & Reiss, D. (2007). Genetic and environmental influences on pubertal timing: Results from two national sibling studies. *Journal of Research on Adolescence, 17*, 767–788.

Glatz, T., & Buchanan, C. M. (2015). Change and predictors of change in parental self-efficacy from early to middle adolescence. *Developmental Psychology, 51*, 1367–1379.

Graber, J. A., & Sontag, L. M. (2009). Adolescent and young adult health. In R. Learner & L. Steinberg (Eds.), *Handbook of adolescent psychology* (3rd ed., Vol. 2, pp. 642–682). New York: Wiley.

Hagenauer, M. H., Perryman, J. I., Lee, T. M., & Carskadon, M. A. (2009). Adolescent changes in the homeostatic and circadian regulation of sleep. *Developmental Neuroscience, 31*(4), 276–284.

Hair, E. C., Moore, K. A., Garrett, S. B., Ling, T., & Cleveland, K. (2008). The continued importance of quality parent–adolescent relationships during late adolescence. *Journal of Research on Adolescence, 18*, 187–200.

Hatzenbuehler, M. L., & Keyes, K. M. (2013). Inclusive anti-bullying policies and reduced risk of suicide attempts in lesbian and gay youth. *Journal of Adolescent Health, 53*(Supplement), S21–S26.

Hopson, L. M., Schiller, K. S., & Lawson, H. A. (2014). Exploring linkages between school climate, behavioral norms, social supports, and academic success. *Social Work Research, 38*, 197–209.

Individuals with Disabilities Education Act, 20 U.S.C. § 1400 (2004).

Kaltiala-Heino, R., Kovisto, A-M., Marttunen, M., & Fröjd, S. (2011). Pubertal timing and substance abuse in middle adolescence: A 2-year follow-up study. *Journal of Youth and Adolescence, 40*, 1288–1301.

Kuhn, D. (2009). Adolescent thinking. In R. Learner & L. Steinberg (Eds.), *Handbook of adolescent psychology* (3rd ed., Vol. 2, pp. 152–186). New York: Wiley.

Kulin, H. E., Bwibo, N., Mutie, D., & Santer, S. J. (1982). The effect of chronic malnutrition on pubertal growth and development. *American Journal of Clinical Nutrition, 36*, 527–536.

Kutsyuruba, B., Klinger, D. A., & Hussain, A. (2015). Relationships among school climate, school safety, and student achievement and well-being: A review of the literature. *Review of Education, 3*, 103–135.

Kuzucu, Y., Bontempo, D. E., Hofer, S. M., Stallings, M. C., & Piccinin, A. M. (2014). Developmental change and time-specific variation in global and specific aspects of self-concept in adolescence and association with depressive symptoms. *Journal of Early Adolescence, 34,* 638–666.

Laird, R. D., & Marrero, M. D. (2011). Mothers' knowledge of early adolescents' activities following the middle school transition and pubertal maturation. *Journal of Early Adolescence, 31,* 209–233.

Lewinsohn, P. M., Joiner, T. E., & Rohde, P. (2001). Evaluation of cognitive diathesis-stress models in predicting major depressive disorder in adolescents. *Journal of Abnormal Psychology, 110,* 203–215.

Manning, W. D., Giordano, P. C., & Longmore, M. A. (2006). Hooking up: The relationship contexts of "nonrelationship" sex. *Journal of Adolescent Research, 21,* 459–483.

Mehta, C. M., & Strough, J. (2009). Sex segregation and normative contexts across the lifespan. *Developmental Review, 29,* 201–220.

Molloy, L. E., Gest, S. D., Feinberg, M. E., & Osgood, D. W. (2014). Emergence of mixed-sex friendship groups during adolescence: Developmental associations with substance use and delinquency. *Developmental Psychology, 50,* 2449–2461.

Moore, K. A., Guzman, L., Hair, E., Lippman, L., & Garrett, S. (2004). Parent–teen relationships and interactions: Far more positive than not. *Child Trends Research Brief* (publication no. 2004–25). Retrieved from www.childtrends.org/wp-content/uploads/2014/10/2004-25Parent_TeenRB.pdf.

Mustanski, B. S., Viken, R. J., Kaprio, K., Pulkkinen, L., & Rose, R. J. (2004). Genetic and environmental influences on pubertal development: Longitudinal data from Finnish twins at ages 11 and 14. *Developmental Psychology, 40,* 1188–1198.

National Institute on Drug Abuse. (2014). *Principles of adolescent substance use disorder treatment: A research-based guide.* Retrieved from www.drugabuse.gov/publications/principles-adolescent-substance-use-disorder-treatment-research-based-guide/introduction.

National Institute on Drug Abuse. (2016). *DrugFacts: High school and youth trends.* Retrieved from www.drugabuse.gov/publications/drugfacts/high-school-youth-trends.

National School Climate Center. (2016). *School climate.* Retrieved from www.schoolclimate.org/climate/.

National Sleep Foundation. (2016a). *Eight major obstacles to delaying school start times.* Retrieved from https://sleepfoundation.org/sleep-news/eight-major-obstacles-delaying-school-start-times.

National Sleep Foundation. (2016b). *Sleep and teens: Biology and behavior.* Retrieved from https://sleepfoundation.org/ask-the-expert/sleep-and-teens-biology-and-behavior.

Negriff, S., Ji, J., & Trickett, P. K. (2011). Exposure to peer delinquency as a mediator between self-report pubertal timing and delinquency: A longitudinal study of mediation. *Development and Psychopathology, 23,* 293–304.

Negriff, S., Susman, E. J., & Trickett, P. K. (2011). The developmental pathway from pubertal timing to delinquency and sexual activity from early to late adolescence. *Journal of Youth and Adolescence, 40,* 1343–1356.

Newman, M., Garrett, Z., & Elbourne, D. (2006). Does secondary school size make a difference? A systematic review. *Educational Research Review, 1,* 41–60.

Orpinas, P., Horne, A. M., Song, X., Reeves, P. M., & Hsieh, H-L. (2013). Dating trajectories from middle to high school: Association with academic performance and drug use. *Journal of Research on Adolescence, 23,* 772–784.

Owens, J., Adolescent Sleep Working Group, & Committee on Adolescence. (2014). Insufficient sleep in adolescents and young adults: An update on causes and consequences. *Pediatrics, 134,* 921–932.

Ozer, E. M., & Irwin, C. E. (2009). Adolescent and young adult health. In R. Learner & L. Steinberg (Eds.), *Handbook of adolescent psychology* (3rd ed., Vol. 2, pp. 618–641). New York: Wiley.

Page, M. J. L., Lindahl, K. M., & Malik, N. M. (2013). The role of religion and stress in sexual identity and mental health among lesbian, gay, and bisexual youth. *Journal of Research on Adolescence, 23,* 665–677.

Pew Research Center. (2013). *A survey of LGBT Americans.* Retrieved from www.pewsocial-trends.org/2013/06/13/a-survey-of-lgbt-americans/.

Pozo, J., & Argente, J. (2002). Delayed puberty in chronic illness. *Best Practice and Research in Clinical Endocrinology and Metabolism, 16,* 73–90.

Ripski, M. B., & Gregory, A. (2009). Unfair, unsafe, and unwelcome: Do high school students' perceptions of unfairness, hostility, and victimization in school predict engagement and achievement? *Journal of School Violence, 8,* 355–375.

Rosen, D. S. (1991). Pubertal growth and sexual maturation for adolescents with chronic illness or disability. *Pediatrician, 18*(2), 105–120.

Rowley, R. L., & Hertzog, J. L. (2016). From holding hands to having a thing to hooking up: Framing heterosexual youth relationships. *Marriage and Family Review, 52,* 548–562.

Ryan, C. (2010). Engaging families to support lesbian, gay, bisexual, and transgender youth: The family acceptance project. *Prevention Researcher, 17*(4), 11–14.

Schools Start Later. (2016). *Position statements and resolutions on sleep and school start times.* Retrieved from www.startschoollater.net/position-statements.html.

SIECUS. (2004). *Guidelines for comprehensive sexuality education* (3rd ed.). Retrieved from www.siecus.org.

Shalitin, S., & Phillip, M. (2003). Role of obesity and leptin in the pubertal process and pubertal growth: A review. *International Journal of Obesity, 27,* 869–874.

Short, M. A., & Louca, M. (2015). Sleep deprivation leads to mood deficits in healthy adolescents. *Sleep Medicine, 16,* 987–993.

Smetana, J. G., & Villalobos, M. (2009). Social cognitive development in adolescence. In R. Learner & L. Steinberg (Eds.), *Handbook of adolescent psychology* (3rd ed., Vol. 2, pp. 187–228). New York: Wiley.

Steinberg, L. (1987). Impact of puberty on family relations: Effects of pubertal status and pubertal timing. *Developmental Psychology, 23,* 451–460.

Steinberg, L. (2001). We know some things: Parent–adolescent relationships in retrospect and prospect. *Journal of Research on Adolescence, 11,* 1–19.

Steinberg, L. (2005). Cognitive and affective development in adolescence. *Trends in Cognitive Science, 9,* 69–74.

Steinberg, L. (2016). *Adolescence* (11th ed.). New York: McGraw-Hill.

Stewart, L. (2009). Achievement differences between large and small schools in Texas. *Rural Educator, 30*(2), 20–28.

Tanner-Smith, E. E., & Fisher, B. W. (2016). Visible school security measures and student academic performance, attendance, and postsecondary aspirations. *Journal of Youth and Adolescence, 45,* 195–210.

Terling Watt, T. (2003). Are small schools and private schools better for adolescents' emotional adjustment? *Sociology of Education, 76,* 344–367.

Tucker, J. S., Ellickson, P. L., Collins, R. L., & Klein, D. J. (2006). Are drug experimenters better adjusted than abstainers and users? A longitudinal study of adolescent marijuana use. *Journal of Adolescent Health, 39,* 488–494.

U.S. Department of Education. (2016a). *Office of postsecondary education: Federal trio programs.* Retrieved from http://www2.ed.gov/about/offices/list/ope/trio/index.html.

U.S. Department of Education. (2016b). *The condition of education 2016* (NCES 2016–144). Retrieved from https://nces.ed.gov/fastfacts/display.asp?id=16.

U.S. Department of Health and Human Services. (2016). *America's adolescents: A day in the life.* Retrieved from www.hhs.gov/ash/oah/adolescent-health-topics/americas-adolescents/day.html.

Wheaton, A. G., Chapman, D. P., & Croft, J. B. (2016). School start times, sleep, behavioral, health, and academic outcomes. *Journal of School Health, 86*, 363–381.

Williams, J. M., & Currie, C. (2000). Self-esteem and physical development in early adolescence: Pubertal timing and body image. *Journal of Early Adolescence, 20*(2), 129–149.

Winsler, A., Deutsch, A., Vorona, R. D., Payner, P. A., & Szklo-Coxe, M. (2015). Sleepless in Fairfax: The difference one more hour of sleep can make for teen hopelessness, suicidal ideation, and substance use. *Journal of Youth and Adolescence, 44*, 362–378.

CHAPTER 11

Family and Adulthood

Adulthood begins roughly in the third decade of life and stretches until late adulthood. In this chapter we will focus on the experiences of those in young adulthood (about ages 20–40) and middle adulthood (roughly ages 40–60). We spend the majority of our lives in adulthood and continue to grow and develop during these years. From a lifespan per-spective, gains as well as losses take place during adulthood (Staudinger & Bluck, 2001). During adulthood individuals may take on a variety of new roles including entering into long-term romantic partnerships (perhaps even getting married), joining the workforce full-time, and possibly becoming a parent. There is a tremendous amount of variability found in adulthood and while previous generations characterized adulthood by getting married and starting a family, there is no singular path for adults today.

Image 11.1 Arnett Argued that in Our Current Society, Individuals Aged 18–30 Are Neither Adolescents Nor Young Adults, and There Is a Distinct Development Period Called Emerging Adulthood (photo by Andres Rodriguez/Depositphotos, Inc.).

Reflected in this variability is debate around whether there is a distinct developmental period in between adolescence and young adulthood called **emerging adulthood**. Arnett (2000) argued that in our current society, individuals aged 18–30 are neither adolescents nor young adults as they have achieved a number of significant developmental milestones but are still exploring possible life directions. In emerging adulthood, Arnett (2000) argues there is a great amount of instability and variability as individuals delay responsibilities and prepare themselves for careers, long-term relationships, and parenthood. Many individuals in this age group do not consider themselves to be adults (Staudinger & Bluck, 2001) and currently more 18–34 year olds are living with their parents than other living arrangements (Fry, 2016). According to the emerging adulthood framework, it is now normative for individuals in their 20s to use this time period for continued development prior to launching into adulthood. However, some have critiqued this idea of emerging adulthood as a distinct developmental stage since many individuals diverge from this path of exploration. Not all individuals attend college and delay entering the workforce and parenthood (Mitchell & Syed, 2015). Because emerging adulthood may only describe the experiences of some individuals, it is questionable whether this is a distinct developmental period.

There is also debate about when middle adulthood ends and late adulthood begins with many agreeing that about age 60 or 65 is the beginning of late adulthood (Staudinger & Bluck, 2001). However, as individuals retire later and live longer perhaps adulthood is also stretching out longer than previous generations. These dialogues highlight that adulthood is more complex to define compared to adolescence and childhood. There are not the same obvious developmental milestones and transitions, and it is more difficult to make clear demarcations when one developmental period begins and ends.

PHYSICAL CHANGES

A number of physical changes occur during adulthood although the rate and timing of physical changes will depend on psychological and environmental factors (Whitbourne, 2001). It is also important to note that not all physical changes during adulthood are inevitable and individuals may accelerate or slow down the aging process through a variety of lifestyle factors. Skin begins to wrinkle and discolored areas may begin to appear although this depends on sun exposure and usage of sunscreen throughout the lifetime. Skin may also begin to sag as it loses elasticity. Hair may begin to grey as early as the 20s and both men and women may experience hair loss, but this loss is most evident in men. Typically there also changes in body weight during adulthood. Starting in the early 20s and until about the mid-50s, weight tends to increase and then after the mid-50s weight tends to decline as part of the aging process (Whitbourne, 2001). Exercise in adulthood becomes increasingly important and participation in both aerobic exercise and resistance training helps to strengthen muscles, protect bones, and maintain a healthy weight. Smoking, alcohol use, and a poor diet will exacerbate these physical changes and accelerate the aging process. Exercise, having a healthy diet, and refraining from drinking and smoking also protects the heart and lungs. Sleep continues to be important as individuals age and 7 to 9 hours are recommended although as individuals go through adulthood they often prefer going to bed and waking earlier compared to childhood and adolescence (Whitbourne, 2001).

Estrogen begins to decline in the mid–30s and by the early to mid–50s women will cease to have menstrual cycles (Whitbourne, 2001). It is unlikely that a woman will become pregnant in the years preceding **menopause**, the permanent cessation of menstrual cycles, and pregnancy is impossible following menopause. Women who wish to become pregnant have a wider fertility window than is commonly believed although by the early 40s it becomes more difficult to get pregnant. Dunson, Baird, and Colombo (2004) found 82% of 35–39-year-old women having sex at least twice a week get pregnant within a year, compared to 86% for 27–34-year-old women and 92% for 19–26-year-old women. These data indicate that women are certainly most fertile in their 20s but there is a relatively high level of fertility for women in their 30s too. Importantly, it appears that male age is also linked to fertility (Dunson et al., 2004) even though men do not go through a similar process, like menopause, in which fertility ceases.

INTELLECTUAL DEVELOPMENT

Adults experience both declines and gains in intellectual functioning as they age and some of these changes are associated with individual and lifestyle factors (Sternberg, Grigorenko, & Oh, 2001). **Crystallized abilities** are defined as concrete, accumulated knowledge whereas **fluid abilities** are more closely associated with creativity and flexible thinking required when facing a new and novel situation. Most adults show an increase in fluid thinking between ages 20 and 30 and then have fairly stable patterns of fluid thinking until their 60s (Sternberg et al., 2001). We see increases in crystallized intelligence throughout adulthood as individuals accumulate more information and knowledge. Speed of mental processes begins to decline during midlife but adults also gain skills with regards to integrating cognitive, interpersonal, and emotional thinking which allows for a deeper understanding of their families, relationship partners, the self, and their broader world (Sternberg et al., 2001).

Most individuals in adulthood continue to possess good memory skills. Middle–aged adults tend to perform somewhat between younger adults and older adults on memory skills tests, with younger adults performing the best. These findings indicate there is some mild decline in memory during middle adulthood (Dixon, De Frias, & Maitland, 2001). However, most research indicates that there is no functional decline in memory processes during middle adulthood. Any small declines which are observed are typically lapses in short-term memory, the capacity for holding on to small pieces of information for a short period of time (Dixon et al., 2001).

IDENTITY, PERSONALITY, AND EMOTIONAL DEVELOPMENT

By adulthood we have a relatively set identity although there is evidence that our identity continues to evolve. According to the identity process model, identities are reinforced and refined through **assimilation** and **accommodation** (Lachman & Bertrand, 2001). Assimilation is the process through which we incorporate new information into our existing identity whereas accommodation is the process through which individuals alter their identity based on new experiences. For example, when an individual starts their first full-time job, accommodation may occur as individuals begin to view themselves as a person with a career. It is ideal when a balance is struck between the two processes (Lachman & Bertrand, 2001). Particularly as individuals go through middle age they must recognize what they are or are not capable of doing (waking early to care for a sick child vs. staying up all night at a party). As individuals take on new roles, such as husband/wife or parent, we expect changes in identity as well. A stable but shifting identity allows individuals to alter expectations for themselves. Additionally, self-esteem increases during young and middle adulthood and reaches a peak around age 60 (Orth, Trzesniewski, & Robins, 2010).

Personality traits are relatively stable during adulthood although there is evidence that some change does occur. For example, openness to new experiences declines somewhat with age as does extraversion (Lachman & Bertrand, 2001). Overall, research suggests that personality does not radically shift as individuals age but personality is not static either. In other words, an individual who is extraverted will be an extravert their entire life but they may be less outgoing or thrill seeking as an adult in midlife. We also can see that there is great variability in personality at all ages so there is no one personality profile that defines individuals at any age group (Noftle & Fleeson, 2010).

Research indicates that as individuals age, neuroticism (emotional instability) appears to decline, indicating that adults become less anxious and self-conscious as they mature (Lachman & Bertrand, 2001). Additionally, positive affect (e.g., being happy, feeling good) increases throughout adulthood and negative affect (e.g., being unhappy, feeling glum) decreases throughout adulthood (Magai & Halpern, 2001). In movies and television shows the midlife crisis is often represented as a common feature of adulthood, particularly among men. A **midlife crisis** is an emotional crisis of identity and self-confidence which may occur in middle age. However, research indicates such crises are not commonplace and, in fact, there is no association between middle age and feelings of turmoil, confusion, and life dissatisfaction (Magai & Halpern, 2001). Some individuals do have an emotional crisis but it appears that individuals who are higher on neuroticism are more likely to experience a midlife crisis (Lachman & Bertrand, 2001). Therefore, it appears that an individual's disposition may be a better predictor of this emotional crisis, rather than age.

AREAS OF RESEARCH AND STUDY

There have been dramatic shifts in family formation and romantic relationship development over the last 50 years. It is important to recognize that there is no one specific way to be an adult. A number of transitions and milestones may take place during adulthood but the absence of specific transitions does not mean development is not transpiring. Adulthood is also characterized by a number of unique challenges and stressors.

Cohabitation, Marriage, and Divorce

In the United States there have been major changes with regards to cohabitation, marriage, and divorce over the last 50–60 years. **Cohabitation** refers to living with a relationship partner outside of the context of marriage. Cohabitation has become an increasingly common relationship pattern over the last 50 years (Cohan, 2013). About

62% of first marriages are preceded by cohabitation (Kennedy & Bumpass, 2008). However, not all cohabitating relationships transition to marriage; some couples remain in long-term cohabitating partnerships whereas other cohabitating relationships end. Using data from the National Survey on Family Growth, Copen, Daniels, and Mosher (2013) found that within 3 years of moving in together, 40% of first time cohabitators were married, 32% remained in a committed relationship, and 27% of relationships ended.

Many couples believe that cohabitating prior to marriage will benefit the relationship in the long run. However, there is no evidence that cohabitation prior to marriage is a protective factor against divorce (Cohan, 2013). In fact, some research indicates that couples who cohabitate prior to having clear marital intentions may actually be at greater risk for later getting divorced (Cohan, 2013). There are a variety of individual, relational, and contextual factors which help to explain this pattern. One popular explanation of this pattern is that how and why individuals entered into a cohabitating relationship can have a significant impact on relationship outcomes (Cohan, 2013). For example, some couples may begin cohabitating as a way to combine household expenses, a very pragmatic reason to move in together. The couple may then slide into becoming parents and marrying without actually developing a stronger emotional attachment to one another (Stanley, Rhoades, & Markman, 2006). This increase in interdependence, without an increase in love and affection, may explain why some cohabitating couples eventually dissolve their relationships.

For some U.S. adults, cohabitation may be a long-term alternative to getting married although many adults express a desire to get married (Cohn, 2013). Currently, the age at first marriage is at a historic high in the United States which lends support for the emerging adulthood framework. In the United States, the median age at first marriage for women is 26 years of age whereas the median age for men is 29 years of age (Copen, Daniels, Vespa, & Mosher, 2012). Furthermore, adults in the United States are getting married at a lower rate compared to previous decades (Copen et al., 2013), and only about 51% of U.S. adults are currently married (Cohn, 2013). Black women are the most likely to have never been married (55%), followed by U.S.-born Hispanic women (49%), Asian women (39%), and White women (34%) (Copen et al., 2013). It is important to note that Black women appear to be more likely to remain in long-term cohabitating relationships compared to White women (Rinelli & Brown, 2010). These findings indicate that although Black women are less likely to be married, many are still in stable, happy, long-term partnerships.

Adults choose to get married for a number of reasons. Love is the most popular reason, followed by making a life-long partnership, companionship, having children, and financial stability (Cohn, 2013). Among never married adults, about 12% of adults say they do not wish to get married and another 27% are not sure about whether they want to get married. These attitudes reflect a broader cultural shift in the United States where marriage is still valued but at the same time there is greater acceptance of alternative pathways. Another change to marriage patterns in the United States is marriage equality. As of 2015, all adults in the United States are legally able to marry regardless of sexual orientation. Whether this public policy change impacts broader marital trends remains to be seen.

Many individuals incorrectly believe that the divorce rates in the United States are increasing. In reality, the divorce rate is certainly higher than it was 50 years ago but the divorce rate has been fairly stable since the 1990s with a slight decline in divorce rates in recent years (Cherlin, 2010). Copen et al. (2013) found that the probability of a first marriage lasting at least 10 years was 68% for women and 70% for men. The researchers found that the probability for a first marriage to last 20 years was 52% for women and 56% for men. The divorce rate has declined for couples in which both spouses have college degrees although the divorce rate has increased slightly for those with less education (Cherlin, 2010). Adults divorce for a variety of reasons with infidelity being the most common reason followed by incompatibility, drinking or drug use, and growing apart (Amato & Previti, 2003).

Parenthood

For most individuals who eventually parent, the transition to becoming a parent occurs in adulthood. For some adults the decision to parent is a conscious choice. For others, becoming a parent may be unplanned or unintended. Women in their 20s actually have the highest unintended pregnancy rate of any age group, and unintended pregnancies are most common among poor women and Black and Hispanic women (Zolna & Lindberg, 2012). These findings suggest a need for continued education and programming, perhaps FLE, to promote safe sex among adults. Not becoming a parent also appears to be a conscious choice for many individuals and more U.S. adults are choosing not to parent (Blackstone, 2014; Umberson, Pudrovska, & Reczek, 2010). Research suggests that not having children has few costs to psychological health and wellbeing, and for some individuals may even be associated with greater wellbeing, although we do see individual variability (Umberson et al., 2010).

Many individuals also wish to become parents but struggle with **infertility**. It is estimated that about 12% of men and 12% of women ages 25–44 experience infertility (Chandra, Copen, & Stephen, 2013). A woman is considered infertile if after 1 year of frequent and consistent sex she is unable to become pregnant, or after 6 months if she is over age 35. There is a less clear definition of infertility for men. Among heterosexual couples with a diagnosable cause of infertility, in about 35% of cases the infertility is due to an issue with the man, 35% of cases are due to an issue with the woman, and the remaining 30% of cases indicate an issue with both partners (Hammound et al., 2012). In both men and women, complications from sexually transmitted infections are a common reason for infertility. Infertility does not necessarily mean an individual is sterile, which means there is zero chance of conception, but it does mean they are having difficulty becoming pregnant.

Becoming a parent is certainly a major life transition regardless of circumstance. Parenthood can be a rewarding experience which encourages personal growth and development (Shannon, Baumwell, & Tamis-LeMonda, 2013). The transition to parenthood can also be a time of significant stress and turbulence for an individual and within a relationship. After the birth of a first child, couples report lower levels of relationship quality (Doss, Rhoades, Stanley, & Markman, 2009). Although this change in relationship quality is typically small, it does appear to persist over time. A number of individual and relational factors impact how couples cope with new parenthood. Communication and sharing in child care impact how parenting is associated with relationship quality (Doss et al., 2009; Galovan, Holmes, Shramm, & Lee, 2014). Couples that continue to engage in

Image 11.2 Couples that Continue to Engage in Leisure Activities after the Transition to Parenthood Are Characterized by Greater Quality and Lower Conflict (photo by Angel Nieto/Depositphotos, Inc.).

leisure activities together following the transition to parenthood are characterized by greater quality and lower conflict (Claxton & Perry-Jenkins, 2008).

It is increasingly common for children to be born to unmarried parents. In 2014, 40% of all children in the United States were born to unmarried parents (Hamilton, Martin, Osterman, Curtin, & Mathews, 2015) and approximately one in three births were to women in cohabiting relationships (U.S. Census Bureau, 2010). Therefore, it is important to consider the variety of contexts children are born into today. As HDFS scholars, we need to recognize the major shifts which have taken place and respect that there are numerous ways adults today create and experience families.

Relationships with Aging Parents

Some adults have the added responsibility of caring for their aging parents. These caregiving responsibilities tend to fall more to adult women compared to adult men due to broader gender norms and socially prescribed family roles regarding caregiving (Putney & Bengston, 2001). For some adults, they are able to easily navigate parental caregiving whereas for others the experience may be quite stressful. Context and timing matters with regards to how adults are able to handle this caregiving. Adults who are still caring for their own children or have significant employment responsibilities may experience high levels of stress. Individuals who must provide prolonged and intensive care may also experience distress and lower levels of wellbeing (Putney & Bengston, 2001). In contrast, adults who only need to provide occasional assistance or have fewer role demands likely navigate the caregiving more easily.

Parent–child relationships continue to be important for most adults and the concept of **intergenerational solidarity** is used to explain the continued links between parents and adult children (Putney & Bengston, 2001). Intergenerational solidarity is a multidimensional concept that examines emotional closeness, agreement in values, time spent together, exchange of emotional and practical support, expectations of support, and

Image 11.3 Intergenerational Solidarity Is Used to Explain the Continued Links between Parents and Adult Children (photo by Lydie Salaun/Depositphotos, Inc.).

structural factors (geographic location, health status) which facilitate interactions. Although there is substantial variability with regards to levels of intergenerational solidarity, it appears that having some continued integration with parents is beneficial to adults (Putney & Bengston, 2001). Not surprisingly, higher levels of intergenerational solidarity are also associated with greater parental caregiving. With modern technology, including cell phones and video chatting, we can see that it is now easier to remain in contact and boost intergenerational solidarity (Cooney & Dykstra, 2013).

Work–Life Balance

Nowadays, the majority of adult men and women are employed outside of the home. For adults in partnerships, who are parenting, who are managing a household, and/or caring for an aging parent, there can be significant demands on individuals' time which may make balancing all one's personal and professional activities difficult. Research on **work–life balance** is a large and growing body of literature, and there are many lenses with which to explore how adults today may struggle to meet the demands of work and other life domains (Perry-Jenkins & MacDermid, 2013). Work–life balance refers to the equilibrium individuals attempt to achieve by meeting all their professional and personal responsibilities. There are different demands on individuals depending on type of employment and personal responsibilities. For example, parents who do shift work and have schedules which change each week may face greater work–life conflict compared to parents who work a more consistent 8 a.m. to 5 p.m. work schedule.

BOX 11.1 UNDERSTANDING PAID FAMILY AND MEDICAL LEAVE POLICIES

A major struggle many adults experience is not only balancing their time but affording time away from the workplace upon the birth or adoption of a new child, a serious medical illness, or caring for an older family member. The United States lags behind all other developed countries with regards to formal policies which mandate paid family leave (Appelbaum & Milkman, 2011). As of writing this textbook, some American workers are covered by the Family and Medical Leave Act (FMLA) of 1993 (2006), which guarantees workers up to 12 weeks of leave per year to care for family members. However, this leave is unpaid and many individuals and families cannot afford to miss out on a weekly paycheck.

Particular concern is given to the lack of maternity/paternity leave laws in the United States (Appelbaum & Milkman, 2011). There is no federal policy which mandates that mothers or fathers receive paid leave upon the arrival of a new child. Because of the lack of policy at both state and federal levels, many new mothers and fathers are unable to remain home and prioritize parent–infant bonding. For mothers who go through pregnancy and labor, rushing back to work does not permit them to physically recover from the pregnancy and childbirth process.

Employers in the United States are able to set their own standards and often individuals in professions with higher pay are those who have access to better paid maternity/paternity leave. Therefore, parents who likely most need paid leave are the ones who are less likely to have access to paid leave. Currently, three states— California, New Jersey, and Rhode Island—guarantee paid family and medical leave. Research suggests that these state level paid leave policies have been beneficial for families (National Partnership for Women and Families, 2016). Specifically, there appear to be physical and mental health benefits for the parents. Mothers with access to paid leave are more likely to breastfeed, which has a number of health benefits for the child. Paid leave for fathers is also linked with greater participation in child care (National Partnership for Women and Families, 2016). In the 2016 election, presidential candidates from both the Republican and Democratic parties proposed policies to provide some levels of maternity leave. Hillary Clinton's (the Democratic presidential candidate) proposed policy also includes paid leave for fathers. It remains to be seen which, or if any, policy is implemented in the near future.

Other researchers are concerned with examining and explaining observed gender differences with regards to work–life balance. Research continues to demonstrate that even for heterosexual couples in which both partners work, a larger share of household and child-care responsibilities are undertaken by women (Perry-Jenkins & MacDermid, 2013). Although men have certainly increased their activity in these domains, women continue to do more household labor, a phenomenon known as the **second shift** (Hochschild & Machung, 2012). The second shift refers to the finding that many women who work outside of the home come home to significant household and child-care responsibilities

Image 11.4 Modern Technology Plays a Role in Work–Life Conflict (photo by Uriy Rudyy/ Depositphotos, Inc.).

which equate to another shift of work. This inequitable division of labor can lead to **role strain**. Adults typically occupy multiple roles defined by social norms and statuses. Role strain is when individuals have difficulty fulfilling multiple role demands and research suggests women may be more vulnerable to experiencing role strain (Perry-Jenkins & MacDermid, 2013). Given that there is only so much time in a day, there is a reasonable constraint on every individual's time.

Modern technology also plays a role in work–life conflict. Nowadays, many individuals have smartphones and seemingly are able to access emails, text, and receive calls at all hours of the day. The boundaries between home and work can be significantly blurred now that we can always be in contact with employers. In fact, many corporations issue company smartphones, laptops, and tablets to their employees with the expectation that the employee be accessible even during non-work hours.

Relationship Violence

HDFS scholars recognize that families and relationships may not always be a safe space for individuals. Unfortunately, a significant proportion of adults have experienced physical violence in their relationships. **Intimate partner violence** refers to violence perpetrated by a romantic relationship partner. Some individuals use the term domestic violence but in HDFS the terminology intimate partner violence is generally preferred. Intimate partner violence is the more commonly used term because it highlights that partners do not need to share a home for violence to be present in a relationship. Additionally, in the past, violence was viewed as a private issue since it occurred in the private (domestic) sphere. In removing the word domestic, we also highlight that violence is a major public issue. Among adult women in the United States, 31.5% report having experienced intimate partner violence in their lifetime and 27.5% of U.S. adult men have experienced intimate partner violence (Breiding et al., 2014). Physical violence is any form of hitting, slapping, kicking, punching, or throwing of an object at the partner.

Johnson (2011) makes the important argument that there are actually three types of intimate partner violence which display gendered patterns. The first type of violence identified by Johnson (2011) is intimate terrorism. Intimate terrorism is characterized by prolonged and severe physical, sexual, psychological, and emotional violence. Perpetrators of intimate terrorism use a variety of coercive tactics in order to control their partners along with physical violence. Intimate terrorists will humiliate, put down, threaten, and withhold economic resources so victims feel unable to safely leave the relationship. Some victims of intimate terrorism will eventually be killed by their partners and are most at risk when attempting to leave the relationship. Overwhelmingly, perpetrators of intimate terrorism are male and the victims are female. The second type of violence identified by Johnson (2011) is violent resistance in which a victim of violence fights back in response to an attack. Such resistance often does not mitigate the violence and, in fact, can make an episode of violence worse. Women are most likely to engage in violent resistance. The third type of violence identified by Johnson (2011) is situational couple violence. Situational couple violence is by far the most common form of intimate partner violence and is characterized by sporadic, less severe episodes of violence. Essentially, violence is not a defining quality of the relationship and no emotional or psychological violence is present. Men and women engage in situational couple violence at approximately equal rates which is why when we look at general rates of violence, men and women report similar lifetime incidences.

Services which help victims of intimate partner violence are typically geared toward female victims of intimate terrorism since these are the most damaging and prolonged patterns of violence (although men can be victims of intimate terrorism as well and need help too). Although most programs are aimed to help victims of intimate terrorism, any type of violence is never justified regardless of whether you are a man or a woman. There is no reason why any individual should physically harm a partner and all forms of physical violence are against the law. In your HDFS courses you will learn a wide variety of positive communication tactics which help you to navigate conflict in a healthy manner. Your HDFS coursework can also help prepare you to work with and help victims of intimate partner violence.

AREAS OF PRACTICE AND CAREERS

Relationship and Parenting Education

Relationship education and parenting education courses are typically aimed at preventing problems before any arise. Different relationship education programs may target various types of romantic relationships and populations. Some programs focus on pre-marital counseling whereas other programs are for individuals who have been in long-term relationships. Programs may also target particular populations, such as low socioeconomic families, rural families, etc. Ideally, all prevention programs should be grounded in evidence-based approaches (Halford, Markman, Kline, & Stanley, 2003). Marriage-education courses have been found to be effective in building skills necessary for healthy marriages and promoting relationship satisfaction. However, there is a call for greater diversity and more perspectives within relationship and parenting education courses (Randles, 2016). Many programs were designed with middle-class, two-parent families in mind which does not reflect the majority of families nowadays. Concerns have also been raised about how some programs reinforce, or fail to problematize, gender roles which are actually detrimental to relationships and parenting (Randles, 2016). If you are interested in becoming a relationship or parenting educator you should consider becoming a CFLE. Additionally, each U.S. state has a cooperative extension program which is affiliated with that state's land grant university. Cooperative extension is meant to be the outreach arm of the university and serve the local community. Many cooperative extension programs offer relationship and parenting education. Programs may also be offered in affiliation with religious groups, family courts, and schools.

Marriage and Family Therapy

Marriage and family therapists, as introduced in Chapter 1, typically provide short-term counseling for individuals, couples, and families (AAMFT, 2016). MFTs utilize a family systems perspective (see Chapter 5) and while they may treat individuals, will contextualize issues based on relationships with partners, parents, and other family members. MFTs are licensed to diagnose and treat mental and emotional disorders. MFTs often help families navigate relationship distress and parent–child issues, and will typically work with children, adolescents, and adults. MFTs can also work with victims and perpetrators of intimate partner violence. The main difference between MFTs and clinical and counseling psychologists is the systems perspective utilized by MFTs. In order to be an MFT, you will need to go to graduate school. You can earn a master's degree or a doctoral degree in marriage and family therapy, and there are a number of accredited programs in North America. It is important to investigate early the licensing and education requirements where you plan to live and practice.

Family Coaching

Family coaching is a new area. "Broadly defined, it is a process–driven relationship between a family system (as represented by an individual or familial group) and a family practitioner designed to foster the achievement of family-identified goals" (Allen & Huff, 2015, p. 61). It is different from FLE because it uses coaching techniques, such as providing continuous feedback (Allen & Huff, 2015). Family functioning increases when coaching is used (Allen & Huff, 2015). HDFS graduates can pursue accreditation in coaching to gain a further credential.

Substance Abuse Counselor

Drug and alcohol abuse was discussed in Chapter 10; however, the abuse of alcohol and narcotics continues to be a concern during adulthood. Adults between the ages of 18 and 25 report the highest levels of drug use and drug use appears to be increasing among individuals in their 50s and 60s (National Institute on Drug Abuse, 2015). Marijuana is the most commonly used drug among adults and rates of methamphetamine use and prescription drug abuse are increasing as well (Schulden, Thomas, & Compton, 2009). There is great concern because there is a "treatment gap" currently in the United States.

Image 11.5 The Abuse of Alcohol and Narcotics Continues to Be a Concern during Adulthood (photo by Sasin Tipchai/Depositphotos, Inc.).

It is estimated that about 22.7 million Americans would benefit from alcohol or drug treatment but only about 2.5 million people have received treatment (National Institute on Drug Abuse, 2015). Substance abuse counselors may work in private practice, schools, hospitals, rehabilitation centers, as well as other sites. There are multiple educational routes you can take to become a substance abuse counselor. You will need to pursue some form of licensure in order to work as a substance abuse counselor. One of the most common certifications is a Licensed Chemical Dependency Counselor (LCDC). Each state has its own process for obtaining certification and licensure. For some types of certification and licensure, you will be eligible to begin the process with relevant coursework as an undergraduate student. For other more advanced certifications, you will need to pursue graduate education. You should begin looking into these requirements early in your college career so you can be sure to take any needed coursework.

STRATEGIES FOR PURSUING SPECIALIZATION OR CAREERS IN ADULTHOOD

If you are interested in working with adults, you may take courses related to parenting, intimate relationships, sexuality, and family dynamics as an HDFS student. Some HDFS programs offer specific classes on development in adulthood. If you are interested in working in substance abuse or becoming a therapist you should investigate if your college offers any courses on addictions or clinical experiences for undergraduate students. You will also want to keep in mind that some of these careers will require you to earn a graduate degree and/or a license. Applying for graduate school can be extremely competitive so it is important that you earn good grades and establish relationships with your professors. Any type of clinical work or prevention education requires a great deal of maturity, excellent communication skills, and respect for diverse individual and family experiences. You will want to demonstrate that you possess all these qualities so your professors are able to write detailed recommendation letters for you. One good way to get to know your professors better is to work as a research assistant. Most professors run their own programs of research and rely on undergraduate research assistants for help.

Many colleges allow students to work as an undergraduate research assistant for course credit. Sometimes students are even able to get paid for their work as a research assistant. This firsthand research experience will be helpful for gaining admittance to graduate school and forming relationships with your professors.

Summary

1   Adulthood is typically viewed as happening between the ages of 20 and 60:

  A   A developmental stage termed emerging adulthood has been proposed. In emerging adulthood, individuals aged 18–30 are able to delay major responsibilities and explore potential careers, partnerships, and identities.

  B   Some researchers have argued that only some individuals are able to delay responsibilities and go on this journey of exploration. Because of this, some scholars question the emerging adulthood framework.

  C   There is also debate about when adulthood ends and late adulthood begins. Changes in the life course exacerbate this fuzzy boundary between developmental stages.

2   There are a number of physical changes which occur during adulthood:

  A   Changes with regards to weight, and bone and muscle strength may be delayed with lifestyle factors such as exercise, good diet, and refraining from drinking and smoking. Other changes include greying hair, hair loss, wrinkles, and the loss of skin elasticity.

  B   Fertility ceases for women when they go through menopause.

  C   Fertility is highest in women's 20s although women have fairly high fertility rates until about age 40.

  D   Men also experience declines in fertility as they age.

3   Adults continue to experience high levels of cognitive functioning. Small lapses in memory are common as individuals age. Increases in crystallized abilities (knowledge) are also found as individuals age.

4   Adults have relatively stable levels of identity. Identity continues to evolve though as the adult continues to develop and take on new roles:

  A   Personality traits are also relatively stable throughout adulthood although we do see some small changes as individuals mature.

  B   Most adults do not experience a midlife crisis, a period of emotional turmoil and identity crisis during midlife. Higher levels of emotional instability are associated with the likelihood of experiencing a midlife crisis.

5   There is now great variability in how adults live their lives in the United States. There is no one normative pathway.

6   Cohabitation refers to romantic partners who reside together outside of the context of marriage:

   A   Many individuals believe that cohabitation prior to marriage is beneficial to reduce the likelihood of divorce. Research does not support this conclusion.

   B   Instead, we see that for some individuals cohabitation prior to marriage actually increases the risk for divorce.

7   Marriage rates in the United States have declined. The median age of first marriage has also increased. Marriage is not a normative transition in adulthood currently although most adults hope to marry:

   A   Individuals get married for a variety of reasons including love, commitment, and companionship.

   B   The divorce rate in the United States has been fairly stable since the 1990s. Individuals with higher levels of education have actually seen their likelihood of getting divorced decrease.

8   In adulthood some individuals make a conscious choice to parent and others make a conscious choice to not parent. Unintended pregnancies occur at a high rate during young adulthood:

   A   More U.S. adults are opting to not become parents. For most individuals, not having children is not associated with lower wellbeing and psychological health.

   B   Infertility can be a challenge for about 12% of adults. These are individuals who wish to parent but are having difficulty conceiving.

   C   The transition to parenthood can be a stressful experience for individuals and couples. Communication, sharing in child care, and sharing in leisure activities appear to buffer adults from the small drops in relationship quality associated with becoming a parent.

9   Some adults have the added responsibilities of taking care of older parents:

   A   Some adults may have to offer prolonged, intensive care for older family members whereas others only need to provide occasional support.

   B   Families that are higher on intergenerational solidarity offer greater levels of support as parents age.

10 As adults take on multiple professional and personal responsibilities it is not uncommon for them to experience work–life conflict:

   A   Work–life conflict may look different depending on the types of demands individuals have.

B   Work–life conflict appears to particularly impact women as they continue to perform the majority of household and child-care responsibilities even if they themselves work full-time.

11 A sizable proportion of adults have experienced intimate partner violence:

A   There are different types of intimate partner violence and intimate terrorism is the most extensive and severe. Most often men are the perpetrators and women are the victims of intimate terrorism.

B   There are a number of programs and services which help victims of intimate partner violence.

C   Violence in relationships is never acceptable and is an unhealthy pattern of behavior.

12 Individuals working with adults may find employment as relationship and parenting educators, MFTs, and substance abuse counselors. These are only a few of the positions available to HDFS students who wish to work with adults:

A   Be aware early of whether you will need to go to graduate school or obtain a certification. You will be able to ensure that you take the necessary coursework and form relationships with professors and other professionals.

Key Terms

accommodation
assimilation
cohabitation
crystallized abilities
emerging adulthood
fluid abilities
infertility
intergenerational solidarity
intimate partner violence
marriage and family therapist
menopause
role strain
second shift
work–life conflict

Challenge: Integration

Watch the Ted Talk by Dr. Meg Jay, "Why 30 Is Not the New 20" online at www.ted.com/talks/meg_jay_why_30_is_not_the_new_20?language=en. Dr. Jay argues that 80% of our life defining moments happen before age 35. She acknowledges that marriage, career, and parenthood are coming later in life but through her clinical practice is concerned that twentysomethings need to reclaim their adulthood.

Prompts:

1 How do the concerns raised by Dr. Jay fit into the emerging adulthood framework? Does her talk support the existence of emerging adulthood? Do you agree or disagree with the existence of an emerging adulthood developmental period?
2 What are the three main pieces of advice Dr. Jay offers to young adults in their 20s?
3 Do you agree or disagree with Dr. Jay's concerns and advice? What are the benefits of emerging adulthood? What are the drawbacks?
4 What do you hope to achieve in your 20s? If you are already past your 20s, how do you feel about your accomplishments?

Journal Questions

1 Of the areas of research, study, and practice discussed in this chapter, which do you find most interesting? Would you be interested in pursuing a career working with adults? Explain.
2 Based on the research discussed in this chapter, would you recommend cohabitation? Why or why not?
3 What workplace policies could we put into place to support work–life balances? What do you think are the greatest needs?

SUGGESTED RESOURCES

AAMFT: www.aamft.org/.
Cooperative Extension: https://extension.org/.
Lachman, M. E. (Ed.). *Handbook of midlife development.* New York: Wiley.

REFERENCES

Allen, K., & Huff, N. L. (2015). Family coaching: An emerging family science field. In M. J. Walcheski & J. S. Reinke (Eds.), *Family life education: The practice of family science* (pp. 61–72). Minneapolis, MN: NCFR.

Amato, P. R., & Kane, J. B. (2011). Life-course pathways and the psychosocial adjustment of young adult women. *Journal of Marriage and Family, 73*, 279–295.

Amato, P. R., & Previti, D. (2003). People's reasons for divorcing: Gender, social class, the life course, and adjustment. *Journal of Family Issues, 24*, 602–626.

AAMFT. (2016). *About marriage and family therapists.* Retrieved from www.aamft.org/imis15/AAMFT/Content/About_AAMFT/Qualifications.aspx?hkey=2d5f6fac-24c6-40fd-b74f-5f3eaf214e55.

American Society for Reproductive Medicine. (2012). *Age and fertility: A guide for patients.* Retrieved from www.asrm.org/BOOKLET_Age_And_Fertility/.

Appelbaum, E., & Milkman, R. (2011). *Leaves that pay: Employer and worker experiences with paid family leave in California.* Retrieved from http://cepr.net/documents/publications/paid-family-leave-1-2011.pdf.

Arnett, J. J. (2000). Emerging adulthood: A theory of development from the late teens through the twenties. *American Psychologist, 55*, 469–480.

Blackstone, A. (2014). Doing family without having kids. *Sociology Compass, 8*, 52–62.

Breiding, M. J., Smith, S. G., Basile, K. C., Walters, M. L., Chen, J., & Merrick, M. T. (2014). Prevalence and characteristics of sexual violence, stalking, and intimate partner violence victimization: National Intimate Partner and Sexual Violence Survey, United States, 2011. *Morbidity and Mortality Weekly Report, 63*. Retrieved from www.cdc.gov/mmwr/preview/mmwrhtml/ss6308a1.htm?s_cid=ss6308a1_e.

Chandra, A., Copen, C. E., & Stephen, E. H. (2013). Infertility and impaired fecundity in the United States, 1982–2010: Data from the National Survey of Family Growth. *National Health Statistics Reports, 67*. Retrieved from www.cdc.gov/nchs/data/nhsr/nhsr067.pdf.

Cherlin, A. J. (2010). Demographic trends in the United States: A review of research in the 2000s. *Journal of Marriage and Family, 72*, 403–419.

Claxton, A., & Perry-Jenkins, M. (2008). No fun anymore: Leisure and marital quality across the transition to parenthood. *Journal of Marriage and Family, 70*, 28–43.

Cohan, C. L. (2013). The cohabitation conundrum. In M. A. Fine & F. D. Fincham (Eds.), *Handbook of family theories: A content-based approach* (pp. 105–122). New York: Routledge.

Cohn, D. (2013). *Love and marriage.* Retrieved from www.pewsocialtrends.org/2013/02/13/love-and-marriage/.

Cooney, T. M., & Dykstra, P. A. (2013). Theories and their empirical support in the study of intergenerational family relationships in adulthood. In M. A. Fine & F. D. Fincham (Eds.), *Handbook of family theories: A content-based approach* (pp. 356–380). New York: Routledge.

Copen, C. E., Daniels, K., & Mosher, W. D. (2013). First premarital cohabitation in the United States: 2006–2010. *National Health Statistics Reports, 64*. Retrieved from www.cdc.gov/nchs/data/nhsr/nhsr064.pdf.

Copen, C. E., Daniels, K., Vespa, J., & Mosher, W. D. (2012). First marriages in the United States: Data from the 2006–2010 National Survey of Family Growth. *National Health Statistics Reports, 49*. Retrieved from www.cdc.gov/nchs/data/nhsr/nhsr049.pdf.

Dixon, R. A., De Frias, C. M., & Maitland, S. B. (2001). Memory in midlife. In M. E. Lachman (Ed.), *Handbook of midlife development* (pp. 248–275). New York: Wiley.

Doss, B. D., Rhoades, G. K., Stanley, S. M., & Markman, H. J. (2009). The effect of the transition to parenthood on relationship quality: An 8-year prospective study. *Journal of Personality and Social Psychology, 96*, 601–619.

Dunson, D. B., Baird, D. D., & Colombo, B. (2004). Increased infertility with age in men and women. *Obstetrics & Gynecology, 103*(1), 51–56.

Family and Medical Leave Act of 1993, 29 U.S.C. §§ 2601–2654 (2006).

Fry, R. (2016). *For first time in modern era, living with parents edges out other living arrangements for 18–34 year olds.* Retrieved from www.pewsocialtrends.org/2016/05/24/for-first-time-in-modern-era-living-with-parents-edges-out-other-living-arrangements-for-18-to-34-year-olds/.

Galovan, A. M., Holmes, E. K., Schramm, D. G., & Lee, T. R. (2014). Father involvement, father–child relationship quality, and satisfaction with family work: Actor and partner influences on marital quality. *Journal of Family Issues, 35*, 1846–1867.

Halford, W. K., Markman, H. J., Kline, G. H., & Stanley, S. M. (2003). Best practices in couple relationship education. *Journal of Marital & Family Therapy, 29*, 385–406.

Hamilton, B. E., Martin, J. A., Osterman, M. J. K., Curtin, S. C., & Mathews, T. J. (2015). *Births: Final data for 2014.* Hyattsville, MD: National Vital Statistics Reports web release.

Hammound, A. O., Meikle, A. W., Reis, L. O., Gibson, M., Peterson, M., & Carrell, D. T. (2012). Obesity and male infertility: A practical approach. *Seminar in Reproductive Medicine, 30*, 486–495.

Hochschild, A. R., & Machung, A. (2012). *The second shift: Working parents and the revolution at home* (Rev. ed.). London: Penguin Books.

Johnson, M. P. (2011). Gender and types of intimate partner violence: A response to an anti-feminist literature review. *Aggression and Violent Behavior, 16*, 289–296.

Kennedy, S., & Bumpass, L. (2008). Cohabitation and children's living arrangements: New estimates from the United States. *Demographic Research, 19*, 1663–1692.

Lachman, M. E., & Bertrand, R. M. (2001). Personality and the self in midlife. In M. E. Lachman (Ed.), *Handbook of midlife development* (pp. 279–309). New York: Wiley.

Magai, C., & Halpern, B. (2001). Emotional development during the middle years. In M. E. Lachman (Ed.), *Handbook of midlife development* (pp. 310–344). New York: Wiley.

Mitchell, L. L., & Syed, M. (2015). Does college matter for emerging adulthood? Comparing developmental trajectories of educational groups. *Journal of Youth and Adolescence, 44*, 2012–2027.

National Institute on Drug Abuse. (2015). *Drug facts: Nationwide trends.* Retrieved from www.drugabuse.gov/sites/default/files/drugfacts_nationtrends.pdf.

National Partnership for Women and Families. (2016). *Paid leave works in California, New Jersey, and Rhode Island.* Retrieved from www.nationalpartnership.org/research-library/work-family/paid-leave/paid-leave-works-in-california-new-jersey-and-rhode-island.pdf.

Noftle, E. E., & Fleeson, W. (2010). Age differences in big five behavior averages and variabilities across the adult life span: Moving beyond retrospective, global summary accounts of personality. *Psychology and Aging, 25*, 95–107.

Orth, U., Trzesniewski, K. H., & Robins, R. W. (2010). Self-esteem development from young adulthood to old age: A cohort-sequential longitudinal study. *Journal of Personality and Social Psychology, 98*, 645–658.

Perry-Jenkins, M., & MacDermid, S. M. (2013). The state of theory in work and family research at the turn of the twenty-first century. In M. A. Fine & F. D. Fincham (Eds.), *Handbook of family theories: A content-based approach* (pp. 381–397). New York: Routledge.

Putney, N. M., & Bengston, V. L. (2001). Families, intergenerational relationships, and kinkeeping in midlife. In M. E. Lachman (Ed.), *Handbook of midlife development* (pp. 528–570). New York: Wiley.

Randles, J. M. (2016). Redefining the marital power struggle through relationship skills: How US marriage education programs challenge and reproduce gender inequality. *Gender & Society, 30*(2), 240–264.

Rinelli, L. N., & Brown, S. L. (2010). Race differences in union transitions among cohabitors: The role of relationship features. *Marriage & Family Review, 46*, 22–40.

Schulden, J. D., Thomas, Y. F., & Compton, W. M. (2009). Substance abuse in the United States: Findings from recent epidemiologic studies. *Current Psychiatry Reports, 11*(5), 353–359.

Shannon, J. D., Baumwell, L., & Tamis-LeMonda, C. S. (2013). Transition to parenting within context. In M. A. Fine & F. D. Fincham (Eds.), *Handbook of family theories: A content-based approach* (pp. 249–262). New York: Routledge.

Stanley, S. M., Rhoades, G. K., & Markman, H. J. (2006). Sliding versus deciding: Inertia and the premarital cohabitation effect. *Family Relations, 55*, 499–509.

Staudinger, U. M., & Bluck, S. (2001). A view on midlife development from life-span theory. In M. E. Lachman (Ed.), *Handbook of midlife development* (pp. 3–39). New York: Wiley.

Sternberg, R. J., Grigorenko, E. L., & Oh, S. (2001). The development of intelligence at midlife. In M. E. Lachman (Ed.), *Handbook of midlife development* (pp. 217–247). New York: Wiley.

Umberson, D., Pudrovska, T., & Reczek, C. (2010). Parenthood, childlessness, and well-being: A life course perspective. *Journal of Marriage and Family, 72*, 612–629.

U.S. Census Bureau. (2010). *Fertility of American women: 2008.* Retrieved from www.census.gov/newsroom/releases/archives/fertility/cb10-167.html.

Whitbourne, S. K. (2001). The physical aging process in midlife: Interactions with psychological and sociocultural factors. In M. E. Lachman (Ed.), *Handbook of midlife development* (pp. 109–155). New York: Wiley.

Zolna, M., & Lindberg, L. (2012). *Unintended pregnancy: Incidence and outcomes among young adult unmarried women in the United States, 2001 and 2008.* Retrieved from www.guttmacher.org/report/unintended-pregnancy-incidence-and-outcomes-among-young-adult-unmarried-women-united-states.

CHAPTER 12

Family and Late Adulthood

With Jencie M. LeJeune

The population of older adults in the United States was estimated to be 43.1 million in 2012 (slightly under 15% of the total population) and is projected to almost double to 83.7 million by 2050 (over 20% of the total population; Ortman, Velkoff, & Hogan, 2014). For comparison, residents aged 65 and older numbered only 9.8% of the population in 1970 (Ortman et al., 2014). This changing proportion of older adults is due to increases in life expectancy and the movement of the "baby boom" generation into the stage of late adulthood.

In late adulthood, family takes on new meaning and purpose. Individuals in late adulthood may be reviewing and making meaning of their lives (Cierpka, 2012). With retirement, older adults have expanded possibilities for varied activities, family, and other social

Image 12.1 Family Takes on New Meaning and Purpose for Individuals in Late Adulthood (photo by Monkey Business/Depositphotos, Inc.).

engagement. They may be participating in their adult children's and perhaps grandchildren's lives, in their partner's life, as well as in ongoing social networks. Older adults are feeling the impacts of **senescence** in all domains of development, and thus may need to make accommodations to address these changes. With advances in technology and medicine, individuals in late adulthood are leading more active, longer, and healthier lives than ever before. As we'll see, older adults are increasingly more likely to experience "**successful aging**," defined as freedom from disability and disease, high cognitive and physical functioning, and social engagement (Rowe & Kahn, 1987).

PHYSICAL CHANGES

In late adulthood, individuals experience declines in each of the senses. Eyesight becomes worse for most older adults, and disease of the eyes is increasingly likely to occur (for example, cataracts, glaucoma; Berger, 2014). Advances in medicine and technology, however, have minimized the impact of these problems. For example, cataract surgery is largely successful and minimally invasive as an outpatient procedure. The strength of corrective lenses will likely change over the late adulthood years, thus compensating for most changes in eyesight.

Hearing is another sense that experiences a general decline in late adulthood. Hearing acuity decreases, and high frequencies may not be perceived as readily. Men experience earlier and faster decreases in hearing sensitivity compared to women (National Institute on Aging, 2008). Nonetheless, advances in hearing aid technology can largely compensate for these declines.

In addition to these changes in hearing and vision, older adults experience changes in skin elasticity, increasing wrinkles, a decline in bone density, and loss of muscle strength (Dziechciaz & Filip, 2014). Sleep changes occur with normal aging as well as with various diseases that increase with age. Research has found that total sleep time, sleep efficiency, and slow-wave sleep all decrease with age, while the number of awakenings at night increases with age (Ohayon, Carskadon, Guilleminault, C., & Vitiello, 2004). The sleep of older adults becomes lighter, and the circadian rhythm shifts so that they tend to go to bed and wake up earlier than do adults earlier in the lifespan.

The effects of many of these declines associated with **primary aging** can be minimized with attention to continued exercise and health habits. Continued physical activity helps immensely with both quality of life and minimizing disease in older adulthood (Depp, Vahia, & Jeste, 2010). In fact, the greatest predictors of subsequent disability are smoking, BMI, and exercise patterns (Vita, Terry, Hubert, & Fries, 1998).

COGNITIVE CHANGES

Although many people of all ages fear cognitive declines with age as inevitable, the truth is much less daunting. Some cognitive tasks do get more demanding with age, such as the older adult's ability to keep several items in mind at the same time in **working memory** (Nyberg & Backman, 2011). The plasticity of the brain remains remarkable into older adulthood, however, which means that as brain declines occur, the brain itself is able to largely compensate for these changes (Rodrigue & Kennedy, 2011).

Some aspects of memory do change with age, while others remain remarkably intact. For example, implicit memory, the memory of how to do something that has been learned such as writing or driving, remains largely untouched. **Explicit memory**, memory involved with recalling facts, and working memory, that involved with the momentary holding of information until evaluation occurs, do experience declines (Berger, 2014). With compensation, however, such as allowing for longer processing time, the normal memory declines experienced can be minimized.

The prevalence of neurocognitive disorders such as **Alzheimer's disease** and vascular dementia does increase with age. Plassman and colleagues (2007) report that only 5% of adults in their 70s experience any form of dementia, while a little over 35% of adults in their 90s do so. Thus, while the likelihood of experiencing neurocognitive disorders does increase with age, it is by no means inevitable that older adults will suffer from such disorders even in very old age.

An aspect of successful aging with regard to cognitive changes is the existence of **cognitive reserve** (Depp et al., 2010). Cognitive reserve refers to the brain's "ability to adapt to damage, such as via compensation and recruitment of alternative brain regions to perform tasks" (Depp et al., 2010, pp. 535–536). Cognitive reserve is increased with higher education levels, mentally demanding work, having developed an area of expertise, and maintenance of cognitively stimulating activities (Stine, Soederberg, & Morrow, 1996). Physical, particularly aerobic, activity also plays a role in decreasing the impact of cognitive declines (Park & Bischof, 2011). Keeping mentally and physically active can play a critical role in increasing the quality of later life.

Aging is not only associated with declines in cognition. Many researchers and theorists have proposed, and research supports, the idea that older adults display a "more mature stage of cognition" during this phase of life, characterized by increases in wisdom and a greater ability to synthesize ideas (Woodruff-Pak, 1997, p. 207). This is consistent with the theory of Erik Erikson, which proposed that older adults seek integrity in their lives by sorting through their life memories and synthesizing them into a meaningful whole (Woodruff-Pak, 1997). It is also consistent with the concept of the "**life review**," in which the older adult reminisces about her past. Woodruff-Pak (1997) reports that the life review can result in "developing a sense of serenity, feeling pride in accomplishment, and gaining a feeling of having done one's best" (p. 232). She points out that while it may be difficult for younger family members to listen to the older adult's legacies, listening thoughtfully is important, as the life review process is a necessary and healthy one for older adults as they prepare for the end of life.

SOCIAL AND EMOTIONAL CHANGES

In the social and emotional domains of development, older adults tend to fare well if they have adjusted to previous emotional and social challenges earlier in life. The prevalence of psychological disorders is no greater in older adulthood than it is in earlier stages of life (Woodruff-Pak, 1997). Only about 5% of older adults experience major depression. Older adults do experience potential stressors in the social and emotional realm, however.

One example of a source of stress in later adulthood is the experience of the death of one's spouse and other significant others, such as siblings and good friends. Because women tend to live longer and heterosexual women tend to marry men who are slightly older, women are more likely to experience spousal **bereavement** than are men (Berger, 2014). Various definitions related to loss are provided in Figure 12.1. The death of a spouse remains one of the most stressful life experiences, causing loneliness, depression, reevaluation of identity, and role changes (de Vries, 2012). It can also result in positive transformative change as the individual can experience personal growth, a renewed sense of strength, and a newfound appreciation of continuing relationships (de Vries, 2012). Box 12.1 contains a poignant interview with an older adult on her personal experiences with caregiving of her spouse at the end of life, exemplifying both the trials of caregiving and the positive outcomes. Although it was once considered necessary for a spouse to detach from his/her lost loved one in order to move on positively in life, recent evidence suggests that bereavement is much more complex. Rather than letting go of the bond with a lost spouse, the "continuing bonds" theory points out that the relationship can be constructively reorganized (de Vries, 2012). As seen in the story told in Box 12.1, a continuing psychological relationship with the deceased, through memories and comforting thoughts, is not pathological, but perfectly healthy in the coping process.

Experiencing the death of a sibling (or siblings) is also a stressful experience for older adults and is more common, making up almost three-quarters of the deaths among close relatives (de Vries, 2012). De Vries (2012) quotes a reaction of one sibling after the death of her brother: "there was a part of my childhood that went. There were things I couldn't verify … suddenly I was alone with my memories" (p. 438). Again, through this loss, there is a great possibility for growth as older adults may emerge from their grief with a greater appreciation of life and relationships.

Another common experience potentially impacting the social and emotional functioning of older adults is the experience of **retirement**. In 2010, more than two-thirds of women aged 55 to 59 were in the labor force, compared to about 20% of women aged 65 and over (Szinovacz, Ekerdt, Butt, Barton, & Oala, 2012). Retirement considerations include when to retire, whether or not to retire jointly with a spouse or partner, and what to do during the postretirement years. Individuals who are single tend to retire later than

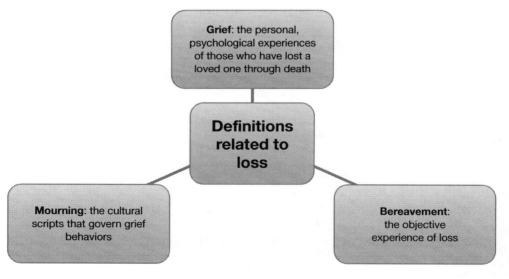

Figure 12.1 Definitions Related to Loss (de Vries, 2012).

Image 12.2 The Death of a Loved One Is a Source of Stress in Later Adulthood (photo by Diego Cervo/Depositphotos, Inc.).

BOX 12.1 SPOUSAL CAREGIVING IN LATER ADULTHOOD

Q1: *Briefly describe your marriage. How many years were you married? Did you have any children? How would you describe the general quality of your marriage?*

A: My husband and I had been married over 45 years when he died. We had two children during the first few years of our marriage, a girl and a boy. Like all long-term relationships, our marriage had its ups and downs, but overall we were deeply in love in a way that grew over the years. One way to summarize our marriage, I think, is to say that we fully trusted each other in every way. I never doubted that he placed our family above everything else and I know he trusted me explicitly. I always knew this without actually articulating it as such in my mind, but the reality of his total trust in me became very evident as his final illness progressed.

Q2: *Could you describe the context that led to your caring for your spouse?*

A: My husband developed dementia, a terrible disease for such an intelligent, bright person as he was. I'm not sure when the disease actually started; it sort of snuck up on us. In retrospect, I can think of signs I noted but did not really pay close attention to at the time over at least 10 years before he died. However, about 7 years before his death it became evident that something was clearly wrong. We visited a neurologist and got confirmation of what we suspected.

My husband had already retired by that time though I kept on working. It gradually became evident that being alone all day long was not a good thing for him, so I asked some friends who had had similar experiences and ended up hiring a woman who came for 5 hours a day, 3 days a week. After a while his inability to take care of some routine tasks grew and I decided that we needed a full-time professional caregiver (not just a companion) during the hours I was away from home. I again asked around and, through the Gerontology Center at our university, was given the name of a caregiving agency. Through this agency we had a series of very caring and competent people who both my husband I liked very much. Thus, for several years a caregiver was at our house from 9:00 a.m. to 5:00 p.m. while I was at work, and I was "on duty" from 5:00 p.m. to 9:00 a.m.

On a number of occasions, friends asked me whether I had considered putting my husband into an assisted living facility. I knew without hesitation that I could never do that to him. He would have been miserable in such a place. Furthermore, who understood him as well as I did? In our home, he was surrounded by things he loved, and this, I felt, was also important. He knew our home, which we had lived in for over 40 years, and could get around without feeling lost. I do have to add, however, that during the last few months of his life, my husband was disoriented at home and I had to help him find his way to the kitchen or bathroom or bedroom because he could not remember where they were.

Q3: *What factors made this experience more difficult? Did anything make it easier?*

A: I think the most difficult part of this experience was the loss of my husband. I'm not referring to his death but to the gradual erosion of the person I had known and admired for so many years. It was terribly painful to see him struggle to remember common, everyday things or to recall how to do simple tasks. Perhaps the epitome of this change came one day when he said to me, "What is your position here?" I was rather dumbfounded but quickly answered, "We're married. I'm your wife." His answer was, "Oh, that's nice." This exchange made me indescribably sad, though I also saw the humor that often emerged from his almost childlike, innocent remarks.

One of the most difficult periods during my husband's later decline was his inability to sleep for more than a short period of time. For several months I was getting increasingly more sleep deprived. This made me irritable and, as result, I spent many hours feeling guilty for getting upset with my husband for constantly waking me. I knew he could not control his sleep–wake pattern, and I hated how it affected me. It actually took me several years to rid myself of my feelings of guilt.

On the other hand, there were many factors that made things easier for me. In many ways, the fact that I kept on working was one of those things. I'm not sure I could have handled a 24/7 schedule. Work became a refuge, although things were in flux in my work environment and, as a result, very stressful on their own. But, on balance my ability to get out of the house for 8 hours a day was very helpful.

Having a supportive family and friend network was also immensely helpful. Our son lived close by and he and his wife were often at our house and helped with running errands. I felt that I was able to rely on my son and daughter-in-law for help when I needed it. For example, one time I felt a strong need to get away to a relaxing place, only just for a day or two. A friend offered to take me to her cabin in the nearby forest. Our son stayed with his father for the two nights while I was gone and I got a much needed respite and rest. Our daughter lives in another state and was not able to be here, though she visited as often as she could and we talked on the phone a lot. I always appreciated our children's support for both their father and me. This was very comforting. Another family visit came from abroad, when one of my husband's nephews and his wife came to the United States just to see their uncle for what, they rightly assumed, would be their last chance to do so.

My friends from work were also a wonderful support network. We laughed a lot and also cried a bit together. At times we held meetings at my house rather than at work, which made it easier for me. My husband enjoyed their visits, though he had no idea who they were. Other, non-work-related friends also stayed in touch and visited often. One friend, knowing how much my husband always loved flowers, made a point of stopping by with a bouquet of flowers from her garden on several occasions. Just knowing there were people around whom I could share what was going on and know they were there for us was enormously important.

Q4: How did you cope with the shifts you experienced in the relationship as the disease progressed?

A: Probably the hardest thing I had to cope with was the dramatic change in the person who was such a big part of me. He had always been my strength and support but now he totally relied on me. I had to take over all the things he had always taken responsibility for. Somehow, I developed a strength I did not know I had within me. I didn't think about it much at the time, but in the years since my husband's death I have pondered over how my role and, along with it, my behaviors, had changed. In many ways I became more tender and solicitous. I often felt as if I were dealing with a very young child.

There was one additional thing that helped me cope with the changing nature of my relationship with my husband. About 2 years before his death, I started keeping a journal. It was comforting to share my reactions and his behaviors in this written format—a mode of communication I felt very comfortable with. I have reread my journal entries often, both before and after his death, though I have never shared this journal with anyone else. I probably never will because it is so personal. Some of the entries are painful to read but many others are humorous and amusing. They help me put into perspective the difficult years and see the enduring nature of our love.

Q5: You seem to have arrived at a positive outcome, enjoying your independence and taking advantage of opportunities for growth and adventure. To what do you attribute this positive transition?

A: You are right in recognizing that I have become a different person since my husband's death. For some time, both before and after his death, I felt like I was two people. Inside me was someone in great pain while outwardly I carried on my daily functions much as I had before. It took me several months before I was able to think about my husband's illness and all that involved, dwell more seriously on my feelings, and eventually face the pain inside me. I had a couple of close friends who had experienced similar losses and who were very supportive in helping me articulate and better understand my feelings.

> Gradually, I recognized that I probably still had many years to live and that I could shape what that time might look like. I made a number of fairly major changes in my life, such as retiring from my job, buying a new house, having a couple of major surgeries, and taking sizable trips. I made choices about friendships and have become close to several people in a way very different from the couple-relationships my husband and I enjoyed for many years. I gained a grandchild along the way and find enormous joy in watching this new life unfold and being able to participate in her upbringing. She has made me much more aware of and philosophical about the passage of time and the continuity among generations.
>
> I think about my husband all the time. There are times when I am driving along a street or listening to a song or engaging in an everyday activity and suddenly, out of the blue, a memory of the two of us together overcomes me. Even now, more than 8 years after his death, such moments cause a catch in my throat and tears in my eyes. I believe that he is here with me and I talk with him often. I have come to realize that he and I will always be together, even if his presence is only in my mind at this time. I also know that he wants me to find as much enjoyment out of life as I can, and I will try to continue doing so.

those who are married, and married individuals tend to make the choice to retire jointly (Szinovacz et al., 2012). Adaptation to retirement is influenced by whether one has a spouse or partner, children and grandchildren, and/or has surviving siblings and parents (Szinovacz et al., 2012). Older adults tend to adjust best when they have a significant other, when retirement allows them time to engage in activities that correspond to their identities, and when it reduces stress associated with work–related role strain.

Several aspects of older adults' personality and the presence of social supports are related to successful aging (Depp et al., 2010). For example, Depp and colleagues (2010) report that individuals who are adaptable, have positive attitudes, and are optimistic tend to live longer and more healthily than their counterparts. The presence of social supports, in the form of a spouse, close relatives and friends, religious community, and/or participation in social organizations, buffers against stress and is a "central determinant of successful aging" (Depp et al., 2010, p. 538). Emotionally close sibling relationships also play a potentially supportive role in promoting social and emotional health (Connidis & Campbell, 1995). In order to promote successful aging in older adults, some studies have reported success with social interventions such as pairing older adults with children who are struggling in math or reading in public schools (Depp et al., 2010). Mindfulness meditation also has been successful in promoting older adults' emotional regulation and stress reduction (Depp et al., 2010).

AREAS OF RESEARCH AND STUDY

There are a number of existing and emerging areas of research that relate to this period of the lifespan. Many have been discussed in this chapter already, such as changes associated with primary vs. secondary aging and the impact of social supports on the aging process. Further emerging areas of research will be briefly reviewed here.

Contextual Influences on Individual Aging

What aspects of one's existing and former environments and experiences have an impact on his/her experience of aging? There is compelling evidence to suggest that individual outcomes are not equivalent across contexts. An individual living in poverty, for example, has fewer cumulative opportunities across life, and may have experienced factors early in life that are compounded over time, such as poor health care or asthma induced by living in an impoverished environment. This individual will experience different outcomes from his counterpart who grew up with access to resources and healthy environments. There are many possible areas of research looking into the impact of context on the process and experience of aging. Examining the physical and societal contexts within which individuals age is a ripe area for more research.

Intersectionality and Aging Families

As noted in the previous section, context matters. The theoretical lens of **intersectionality** brings into focus the multiple contexts that interact and impact individuals disproportionately. Systems of inequalities exist, which describe relationships "of privilege and oppression based on group membership" such as gender, race and ethnicity, class, sexuality, and age (Calasanti & Kiecolt, 2012, p. 213). For example, there is compelling evidence that an individual's sex, race, and socioeconomic status create advantages and disadvantages throughout life, and these impacts are both multifaceted and cumulative (Berger, 2014). The effects of poverty may be magnified by gender, ethnicity, and age, thus influencing many people's access to postretirement income, adequate housing, and appropriate health care. The embeddedness of these inequalities into social institutions make them both difficult to see, especially for those in dominant groups, and difficult to shift. Although intersectionality is a perspective that has been used to frame research in the social sciences more generally, it has not been used as much to frame research on aging families (Calasanti & Kiecolt, 2012). Thus, there is a rich opportunity for family scholars to engage in research using the lens of intersectionality.

Structurally Diverse Family Forms

While diversity of family form is certainly prominent in the United States today, with increases in single parent families, legalization of same-sex marriage, child-free couples, and various configurations of adoptive and foster parenting, research on structurally diverse family forms in later adulthood is scarce (Bedford & Blieszner, 2012). Bedford and Blieszner (2012) bring up a number of provocative research and policy questions, such as: What are the long-term trajectories for increasingly diverse forms of repartnerships, whether the repartnered persons are older adults or family members of older adults? Can chosen and fictive kin be given legal decision-making rights for older adult family members? Research into the benefits and challenges of being part of a family with a diverse structure or form, from the perspective of an older adult with relatives in a diverse structure or from the perspective of an older adult *in* the diverse structure, would provide more insight into these complex questions.

Quality of Relationships

Bedford and Blieszner (2012) also point out the need for research that acknowledges the impact of the quality of adult relationships in examining their impact on older adults. For example, most research suggests that a rich social network is important in impacting older adults positively. However, the presence or absence of a relationship is not sufficient in determining its impact. The quality of that relationship is important in impacting outcomes. If an older adult has a sibling with whom he hasn't spoken in 10 years, that relationship will have a different level of potential support than a sibling relationship wherein the two see or speak with each other daily and consider each other an important source of social support.

Current research is exploring the link between social isolation and health outcomes in late adulthood. **Social isolation**, or the degree to which a person lacks belonging, social contacts and does not have quality relationships is linked to increased risk for many diagnoses associated with aging (Nicholson, 2009). Thus, the quality of relationships and feelings of connectedness to friends, family, and community can increase the overall physical health of adults as they age and functions as a protective factor that merits deeper research. Findings suggest that it is not the number of relationships, but the quality of relationships in late adulthood that serve as a psychosocial buffer against physical and cognitive decline (Nicholson, 2012).

Transdisciplinary Research

A final area of research is that which integrates a number of different perspectives in order to gain stronger discoveries. Research teams comprising sociologists, economists, family scientists, and/or developmental scholars have the potential to ask new questions and discover nuances in results that are informed by the strengths of the approaches of multiple disciplines (Bedford & Blieszner, 2012). For example, family sociologists may bring to the table a strength in knowledge of social structural influences on family relationships while

Image 12.3 Most Research Suggests that a Rich Social Network Impacts Older Adults Positively (photo by Scott Griessel/Depositphotos, Inc.).

psychologists may bring to the table a strength in knowledge of individual level development and interactional levels of expertise (Bedford & Blieszner, 2012).

POLICY/PRACTICE

Public policy issues relating to families and late adulthood are multifaceted and complex. Advocates point to three main issues facing the aging: health care services, economic security, and social justice. While these topics can seem unrelated, the reality for most families is that they are powerfully interwoven and function together to create a landscape where it is increasingly difficult for families to care for their aging members.

What is the bottom line for those considering how public policy impacts adults over 65 and their families? Essentially, the question is, how much support is necessary to keep seniors independent for as long as possible and are we creating policies that support the best interest of our aging population over time?

1   *Health care.* As the aging population grows, those over the age of 65 will be the largest consumers of health care in the United States changing the demographic of patients, care practices, and increasing the cost of care nation-wide (Health and Aging Policy Fellows, 2016; Orszag, 2008). Within the health care industry more geriatricians and skilled workforce are needed to provide quality service particularly for older adults with mental and/or behavioral health needs. Effective policy that supports diverse delivery models of care rather than a one-size-fits-all strategy will ensure the most appropriate and least restrictive practices are available. Flexible

Image 12.4 Aging Adults Are at a Financial Disadvantage and Economically Insecure (photo by Pantilimon Ion Jinga/Depositphotos, Inc.).

service delivery models allow medical practitioners, families, and the caregiving workforce to individualize care to aging seniors within the context of their cultural and family needs.

2   *Economic security.* Aging adults are increasingly at financial disadvantage. Over 25 million adults over age 60 are economically insecure with income below $29,425, or 250% of the federal poverty level (FPL) (National Council on Aging, 2015). Seniors living on a low, fixed income often cannot afford the rising cost of living and health care despite Social Security and Medicaid benefits. Many older adults are underwater on their home loans or have no equity leading to housing insecurity, which can compound other financial risk factors. Policy that provides relief to adults struggling to pay their bills and comprehensive retirement planning for those entering this stage is needed.

3   *Social justice.* Elder abuse can take several forms: physical, sexual, verbal, financial, and neglect. An estimated one in ten seniors over the age of 60 is the victim of elder abuse each year (U.S. Department of Justice, 2016). This number is alarming, particularly considering that elder abuse is vastly underreported. Contributing to this crisis, older adults experience higher risks for developing chronic disease, and have increased rates of cognitive decline, memory loss, and dementia (Plassman et al., 2007). Some seniors also have behavioral health needs that make them difficult to care for placing a heavy load on families and caregivers. Families who are caring for older adults may also become isolated and thus unable to or unwilling to seek services highlighting the importance of family and community relationships. When attempting to address social policy that can reduce incidence of elder abuse, we must consider how we ensure that social policies support the best interest of the aging and whether existing policies unintentionally reinforce practices that take advantage of the aging. To combat elder abuse we must have laws in place to protect seniors and systematic ways of enforcing them.

These issues are infrequently addressed in major policy reform at the local, state, and federal levels. Ensuring that our health care industry is prepared for the shifting demographics of care, that we have a skilled/educated workforce to care for the aging, that elders are economically secure and less susceptible to elder abuse are paramount to the quality of our society and to the healthy functioning of families. Students with degrees in HDFS with a focus on older adults are well stationed to support this healthy functioning.

STRATEGIES FOR PURSUING SPECIALIZATION OR CAREERS IN OLDER ADULTHOOD

Students interested in the study of older adults should consider taking developmental coursework in aging and gerontology, as well as family coursework that uses a lifespan or life course perspective. Look for minors available across your campus. Occasionally, you can find a minor or certificate program in **gerontology** to supplement your HDFS degree. If your undergraduate program has an internship requirement or has internship credits available for students independently, consider signing up as you near the end of your degree program. Internships in adult care facilities or with non–profit organizations designed to facilitate healthy and successful aging would be particularly well suited as internship sites.

Summary

The way we define late adulthood is beginning to take on a different meaning in the context of our current population demographics. It used to be that those over 65 were retiring and approaching end of life. Now, due to increased life expectancy, many are experiencing a full 20+ years of life after entering this "final" life stage.

Adults over the age of 65 experience the effects of primary aging in the decline of each of their senses, reduction of skin elasticity causing wrinkles and sagging, and shifts in their circadian rhythms changing their wake–sleep cycles. Changes in cognition include reductions in explicit and working memory that are compensated for by brain plasticity and through the mechanisms of selective optimization with compensation. The prevalence of neurocognitive disorders increases, with Alzheimer's disease and vascular dementia impacting adults at greater rates as they approach their 90th year. While this is worrisome, most older adults do not experience any form of dementia and habits associated with healthy aging can protect the brain against age-related decline. Social–emotional health is as important as ever and takes on a protective factor in late adulthood. As we approach the end of life, many adults take on a life review to chronicle their contributions to society and family throughout their lives. Depression is not more common in late adulthood, but many find themselves facing the passing away of loved ones which increases stress, loneliness, and can prompt role changes or reevaluation of identity.

Current areas of research highlight the importance of individual context and quality relationships in late adulthood on healthy aging. The larger societal forces that predict access to and quality of services throughout the lifespan can compound in late adulthood, either limiting or granting access to quality services. Family structure and feelings of connectedness can additionally influence how one ages. Policy interacts with these areas of research to create a sociopolitical system that is either prepared for the growing aging population or is ill prepared to meet the needs of the aging. Policy related to health care, mental health, community services, economic security of the population, and social justice interact dynamically to form a landscape that has the potential to encourage or discourage healthy aging practices.

Those looking to pursue a career working with older adults face a growing industry with immense need for qualified and passionate professionals. Degrees in Gerontology combined with coursework in family studies can be particularly valuable.

Key Terms

Alzheimer's disease
bereavement
cognitive reserve
explicit memory
gerontology
intersectionality
life review
primary aging
retirement
senescence
social isolation
social justice
successful aging
working memory

Challenge: Integration

Visit the websites below to find out more information on the complex policy issues facing aging adults and their families. Then, respond to the prompts below.

National Council on Aging: www.ncoa.org
Health and Aging Policy Fellows: www.healthandagingpolicy.org

Prompts:

1   Briefly summarize the general content of each website.
2   After exploring these websites, what would you say are the top policy issues facing aging adults and their families?
3   Have you had any personal experience with any of these policy issues?
4   How can HDFS professionals work toward justice and fair/kind treatment of elders in our communities?
5   Is elder care a family issue or a societal issue? Briefly outline an argument for each perspective.

Journal Questions

1   Of the areas of research, study, and practice discussed in this chapter, which do you find most interesting? Would you be interested in pursuing a career working with older adults? Explain.
2   Based on what was discussed in this chapter, what are the benefits of aging?
3   If you were asked to recommend a program or policy to reduce the incidence of elder abuse, what would be your focus? Explain.

SUGGESTED RESOURCES

Alzheimer's Association: www.alz.org.
American Society on Aging: www.asaging.org.
Family Caregiver Alliance: www.caregiver.org.
International Network for the Prevention of Elder Abuse: www.inpea.net.
National Council on Aging: www.ncoa.org.
National Institute on Aging: www.nia.nih.gov.

REFERENCES

Bedford, V. H., & Blieszner, R. (2012). New directions for family gerontology: Where do we go from here? In R. Blieszner & V. Bedford (Eds.), *Handbook of families and aging* (2nd ed., pp. 448–458). Santa Barbara, CA: Praeger.
Berger, K. S. (2014). *The developing person through the lifespan* (9th ed.). New York: Worth.
Calasanti, T., & Kiecolt, K. J. (2012). Intersectionality and aging families. In R. Blieszner & V. Bedford (Eds.), *Handbook of families and aging* (2nd ed., pp. 213–231). Santa Barbara, CA: Praeger.
Cierpka, A. (2012). Narrative identity in late adulthood. *Psychology of Language and Communication, 16*(3), 237–252.
Connidis, I. A., & Campbell, L. D. (1995). Closeness, confiding, and contact among siblings in middle and late adulthood. *Journal of Family Issues, 16*(6), 722–745.
de Vries, B. (2012). Turning points in later life: Grief and bereavement. In R. Blieszner & V. Bedford (Eds.), *Handbook of families and aging* (2nd ed., pp. 429–446). Santa Barbara, CA: Praeger.
Depp, C., Vahia, I. V., & Jeste, D. (2010). Successful aging: Focus on cognitive and emotional health. *Annual Review of Clinical Psychology, 6,* 527–550.
Dziechciaz, M., & Filip, R. (2014). Biological physiological and social determinants of old age: Bio-psycho-social aspects of human aging. *Annals of Agricultural and Environmental Medicine, 21*(4), 835–838.
Health and Aging Policy Fellows. (2016). *What do we mean by health and aging policy?* Retrieved from www.healthandagingpolicy.org/health-and-aging-policy/.
National Council on Aging. (2015). *Economic security for seniors facts.* Retrieved from www.ncoa.org/news/resources-for-reporters/get-the-facts/economic-security-facts/.
National Institute on Aging. (2008). Healthy aging: Lessons from the Baltimore Longitudinal Study of Aging. Bethesda, MD: Author.

Nicholson, N. (2009). Social isolation in older adults: An evolutionary concept analysis. *Journal of Advanced Nursing, 65*, 1342–1352.

Nicholson, N. R. (2012). A review of social isolation: An important but under-assessed condition in older adults. *Journal of Primary Prevention, 33*(2–3), 137–152.

Nyberg, L., & Backman, L. (2011). Memory changes and the aging brain: A multimodal imaging approach. In K. W. Schaie & S. L. Willis (Eds.), *Handbook of the psychology of aging* (7th ed., pp. 121–131). Burlington, MA: Elsevier.

Ohayon, M., Carskadon, M. A., Guilleminault, C., & Vitiello, M. V. (2004). Meta-analysis of quantitative sleep parameters from childhood to old age in healthy individuals: Developing normative sleep values across the human lifespan. *Sleep, 27*, 1255–1273.

Orszag, P. (2008). *Growth in health care costs: testimony before the Committee on Budget United States Senate.* Retrieved from www.cbo.gov/sites/default/les/01-31-healthtestimony.pdf.

Ortman, J. M., Velkoff, V. A., & Hogan, H. (2014). *An aging nation: The older population in the United States* (Current Population Reports, P25–1140). Washington, DC: U.S. Census Bureau.

Park, D. C., & Bischof, G. N. (2011). Neuroplasticity, aging, and cognitive function. In K. W. Schaie & S. L. Willis (Eds.), *Handbook of the psychology of aging* (7th ed., pp. 109–119). Burlington, MA: Elsevier.

Plassman, B. L., Langa, K. M., Fisher, G. G., Heeringa, S. G., Weir, D. R., Ofstedal, M. B., Burke, J. R., Hurd, M. D., Potter, G. G., Rodgers, W. L., Steffens, D. C., Willis, R. J., & Wallace, R. B. (2007). Prevalence of dementia in the United States: The aging, demographics, and memory study. *Neuroepidemiology, 29*(1–2), 125–132.

Rodrigue, K. M., & Kennedy, K. M. (2011). The cognitive consequences of structural changes to the aging brain. In K. W. Schaie & S. L. Willis (Eds.), *Handbook of the psychology of aging* (7th ed., pp. 73–91). Burlington, MA: Elsevier.

Rowe, J. W., & Kahn, R. L. (1987). Human aging: Usual and successful. *Science, 237*, pp. 143–149.

Stine, E. A. L., Soederberg, L. M., & Morrow, D. G. (1996). Language and discourse processing through adulthood. In F. Blanchard-Fields & T. M. Hess (Eds.), *Perspectives on cognitive change in adulthood and aging* (pp. 255–290). New York: McGraw-Hill.

Szinovacz, M. E., Ekerdt, D. J., Butt, A., Barton, K., & Oala, C. R. (2012). Families and retirement. In R. Blieszner & V. Bedford (Eds.), *Handbook of families and aging* (2nd ed., pp. 366–387). Santa Barbara, CA: Praeger.

U.S. Department of Justice. (2016). *Elder Justice Initiative: researcher resources.* Retrieved from www.justice.gov/elderjustice/research/.

Vita, A. J., Terry, R. B., Hubert, H. B., & Fries, J. F. (1998). Aging, health risks, and cumulative disability. *New England Journal of Medicine, 338*(15), 1035–1041.

Woodruff-Pak, D. S. (1997). *The neuropsychology of aging.* Malden, MA: Blackwell.

CHAPTER 13
Diverse Families

In Chapters 8 through 12, we provided an introduction to the field of HDFS largely from the perspective of the individual, or the individual's development within a family context. We now shift our focus to the family. As a student of HDFS, you will likely have the opportunity to learn about a wide range of topics and issues encompassed by family science, including, but not limited to, family history, family theories, partner selection, love, communication in relationships, human sexuality, cohabitation, marriage, family planning, parenting, work–life balance, family stress and crisis, family resilience, relationship violence, and public policy. For many students, exploring these topics in relation to their own family experience leads to a sense of personal growth and self-understanding. However, it is your ability to understand these issues as they apply to both yourself and others that will enable you to work effectively with diverse individuals and families in professional settings.

Diversity is a term you will likely encounter often as an HDFS student. Although there are many definitions of diversity, in the context of HDFS, the definition given by the NCFR is appropriate. According to NCFR (2016b), diversity is a term used to describe the variety of dynamic and evolving backgrounds and contexts that people experience, including:

- Ability and disability
- Aboriginal, mixed, immigrant
- Age
- Bilingualism and multiculturalism/English language learners
- Body size and condition
- Customs and traditions
- Educational, disciplinary, or career status
- Ethnicity, race, national origin, or cultural identity
- Gender, gender identity, and gender expression

- Geographical background and location
- Marital status, relational status (including singlehood), and family structure or identity
- Objective and subjective worldviews and standpoints
- Political ideologies and affiliations
- Religion/no religion, spirituality and affiliations, and faith
- Sexual orientation, identities, and expressions
- Socioeconomic status, residential status, social class, employment, and national service

(p. 1)

Essentially, diversity encompasses the many characteristics that may or may not contribute to the way we experience and act within our social worlds. Many colleges and universities now have diversity requirements, meaning all students may be required to take courses often for the purpose of learning about a historically disenfranchised or minoritized group of people. Within HDFS programs, you can expect to learn about and examine a perhaps broader range of diversity through your coursework and field experiences, as the ability to understand, respect, appreciate, and work with the diverse populations we serve represents a core value within our field (see Box 13.1).

UNDERSTANDING FAMILY DIVERSITY

As a professional in the field of HDFS, you will almost inevitably work with a range of individuals and families from diverse backgrounds and/or with diverse circumstances, including many of those listed above. Working with families effectively often requires the ability to read social cues, to interpret behavior, to understand context, and to identify potential sources of strength and stress. In some instances, you may work with families who look and behave very much like your own, or families with whom you share values, beliefs, goals, and experiences, making each of these responsibilities potentially more straightforward. However, there are also bound to be times when you have less in common. Unless adequately prepared, you may find your interactions with families seemingly different from your own uncomfortable or confusing. Nonetheless, it is your responsibility as the professional to make sure all families you serve not only receive the services they need, but that they feel valued, respected, and understood throughout the process (Lynch, 2011b). Learning about family diversity is an important first step in developing the knowledge and skill set needed to ensure that you are effective in your professional role.

Although families may present with any number and combination of characteristics and circumstances, we attend here to two broad dimensions of family diversity: structural variations, and cultural variations. Our purpose is not to "teach family diversity," but to highlight some of the types of diversity you will likely encounter, and provide a preview of the range of topics and considerations that you are likely to examine as an HDFS student.

BOX 13.1 PROFESSIONAL STANDARDS AND DIVERSITY

As discussed in Chapter 7, professional organizations often develop ethical codes of conduct or ethical standards for the purpose of outlining professional responsibilities and collective core values within a given field. Of those organizations most closely tied to HDFS, all include positions, standards, and/or guiding principles reflecting our commitment to working respectfully and effectively with diverse individuals and families. Although not an exhaustive list, a few examples are provided here.

NAEYC (2011, pp. 3, 4), *Code of Ethical Conduct and Statement of Commitment*:

- "P-1.5 We shall support children's well-being by promoting connections with their culture and collaborating with communities to ensure cultural consistency between the program and families' childrearing practices."
- "P-2.1 We shall work to create a respectful environment for and a working relationship with all families, regardless of family members' sex, race, national origin, immigration status, preferred home language, religious belief or affiliation, age, marital status/family structure, disability, or sexual orientation."

NCFR (2016a, pp. 1, 2), *Family Life Educators Code of Ethics*:

- "I will respect cultural beliefs, backgrounds and differences and engage in practice that is sensitive to the diversity of child-rearing values and goals."
- "I will support diverse family values by acknowledging and examining parenting practices that support healthy values."

NOHS (2015), *Ethical Standards for Human Service Professionals*:

- "STANDARD 11 Human service professionals are knowledgeable about their cultures and communities within which they practice. They are aware of multiculturalism in society and its impact on the community as well as individuals within the community. They respect the cultures and beliefs of individuals and groups."
- "STANDARD 26 Human service professionals seek the training, experience, education and supervision necessary to ensure their effectiveness in working with culturally diverse individuals based on age, ethnicity, culture, race, ability, gender, language preference, religion, sexual orientation, socioeconomic status, nationality, or other historically oppressive groups. In addition, they will strive to increase their competence in methods which are known to be the best fit for the population(s) with whom they work."
- "STANDARD 34 Human service professionals are aware of their own cultural backgrounds, beliefs, values, and biases. They recognize the potential impact of their backgrounds on their relationships with others and work diligently to provide culturally competent service to all of their clients."

STRUCTURAL VARIATIONS

Family structure refers to the organization of a family unit. It includes its form (e.g., stepfamily), **family composition**, or the makeup of its members, and operational rules or patterns as they pertain to member roles and responsibilities.

It is often tempting to think about families as being either traditional or non-traditional, with traditional meaning **nuclear families**, or families that consist of a father, mother, and children, often with clearly defined **gender roles**, or expectations of what males and females do (i.e., the father provides the income, while the mother cares for the children and the home), and non-traditional families being everything else. However, this way of thinking is not only erroneous, but implies that one type of family is in some way superior to other types of families by their mere composition and responsibilities. The reality is that there is no traditional family. Families have always existed in diverse forms, albeit for different reasons from those that are common today. Previous generations had much shorter life expectancies than those of today, and it was not uncommon for a parent to die from accident, illness, or childbirth while children were still young. Remarriage was generally expected, and even necessary, as two adults were often needed to manage work and family life, thus many children grew up in stepfamilies (Wilson, 2014). In situations where children lost both parents, they were often raised by extended family members, including grandparents, aunts, and uncles. Circumstances such as out-of-wedlock pregnancy, desertion, and divorce resulted in a variety of family forms as well.

Rather than characterize families as traditional or non-traditional, it is important to recognize that there is a multitude of varying family types that can and do function effectively. Nuclear families are one such type, but so too are stepfamilies, intergenerational families, single parent families, transnational families, cohabiting families, co-parenting families, conditionally separated families, adoptive families, foster families, single child families, childless families, and the like (see Box 13.2 for definitions). Within each of these family forms, there is also considerable variation in terms of composition. For example, families may include two parents of the opposite sex, two parents of the same sex, one or more transgender parent, and in the case of binuclear, polygamous, or

Image 13.1 There Is No Such Thing as a "Traditional" Family Structure (photo by Maria Dubova/Depositphotos, Inc.).

BOX 13.2 FAMILY FORMS

Families may take many diverse forms. Some of the terms commonly used to describe these forms are defined here.

adoptive families. Families that include one or more members (typically children) who are related through legal or informal adoption.

binuclear families. Two families consisting of married or otherwise partnered parents who share a common child. This typically occurs when two biological parents separate or divorce and remarry, but share physical custody of at least one child.

childless families. Families that do not have children, either by choice or circumstance.

cohabitating families. Families that consist of two adults who are in a committed and intimate relationship together, but who are not legally married.

conditionally separated families. Families that consist of two adults who are temporarily separated due to external circumstances, such as military deployment.

co-parenting families. Families where parenting is shared by two adults, often biological parents, who do not live together and who are not involved in a romantic relationship with each other.

foster families. Families that include one or more foster children.

nuclear families. Families headed by two married parents who live together.

polyamorous families. Families that consist of two or more adults, where all partners retain the option of openly becoming involved in intimate, sexual, and committed relationships with more than one person. In some instances, the structure of polyamorous families resembles a group marriage, where three, four, or more individuals live together, pool resources, share responsibility, and engage in sexually expressive relations. However, there are several other variations (for examples, see http://polyliving.net/2013/04/polyamory-combinations/).

polygamous families. Within polygamous families, marriage occurs to more than one person simultaneously, such as the case of a man having multiple wives (polygyny), or a women having multiple husbands (polyandry). In theory, polygamy represents one form of polyamory, with one adult being the focal point of each relationship. However, the term polygamy has generally been associated with practices stemming from religious or cultural beliefs that restrict multiple marriages to either males or females.

single child families. Families consisting of one child.

single parent families. Families that consist of only one parent and one or more children.

stepfamilies. Families that include one or more children from at least one partner's previous relationship.

transnational families. Families whose immediate members live in more than one country, often meaning lengthy separations. For example, a parent may move to another country for employment, but the other members stay behind.

polyamorous families, more than two parents. Families may also be headed by a mother, father, or other guardian only. Although individuals may personally place more value on some family types over others, there has been little in the way of empirical evidence to suggest that family form or composition influences the overall wellbeing of a family or its members (e.g., Bos, Knox, Gelderen, & Gartrell, 2016; Lansford, Ceballo, Abbey, & Stewart, 2001; Phillips, 2012).

There is also wide variation in regards to roles and responsibilities within families, particularly in regards to gender. For some families, ideas about the roles and responsibilities of males versus females are very rigid. In such families, it is common for males to be viewed as the providers and protectors of the family, and females as the homemakers. In other families, roles and responsibilities are more flexible, in that they are subject to modification based on the needs of the family and/or desires of its members. For example, some families are headed by male and female partners who both contribute to the family income. This may be due to economic necessity or because both partners choose to work. In some cases, the domestic chores, including parenting, are shared between the two working partners, and, in others, one partner continues to hold the primary responsibility. We are also seeing a small but growing number of families where the female has assumed the role of provider, and the male takes care of the home (Livingston, 2014).

Of these various role patterns, one might wonder which is the most common in the United States today? According to one national survey conducted in 2012, among families with children headed by married heterosexual parents, each of whom may or may not be biologically related to the children, more than half, or 56%, consist of two working parents (Cohen, 2014). Approximately 36% consist of a working father and stay-at-home mother, and 7% of a working mother and stay-at-home father. Less than 1% of families indicated that neither parent worked. In regards to domestic chores, including things like cleaning, laundry, shopping, cooking, and child care, gender roles and responsibilities are also becoming more flexible, but remain a long way from being equitable (Austin Institute, 2014). While males are participating in more domestic chores at higher rates than ever before, women still do the majority of tasks related to housework and child care. Among same-sex couples, both work and domestic responsibilities are more likely to be shared (Goldberg, Smith, & Perry-Jenkins, 2012; Patterson, Sutfin, & Fulcher, 2004). Whether or not family roles and responsibilities play a role in things like marital satisfaction and overall wellbeing has less to do with who actually does what, but more to do with the degree to which roles are perceived as fair according to gender ideologies held by each partner (Greenstein, 1996).

CULTURAL VARIATIONS

Although the terms diversity and **culture** are often used interchangeably, they are not necessarily the same thing. Whereas diversity refers to the variation in human experience, at the most general level, culture refers to the similarities within groups. Culture is the unpublished book of rules and options that dictates much of how we live our lives. Culture influences the types of food we eat, the languages we speak, the types of music we listen to, our choice of hobbies, interests, careers, and partners, whether we make eye contact with strangers, whether we stand for the national anthem, how often we talk to our grandparents, and so much more. Culture is often shaped by our family experiences, which in turn have been influenced by the social forces of race, ethnicity, nationality, language, religion, socioeconomic status, and potentially any other social group to which we belong.

The degree to which we can identify and articulate our own cultural influences is often related to the amount and degree of exposure we have had to cultures much different from our own, as without a point of comparison, our own ways of thinking, being, and doing may be viewed simply as "normal" or not something we think about at all (Lynch, 2011a). When asked to share about their own cultures or cultural influences, for example, many of our students have struggled to provide concrete descriptions. We have observed a tendency among some to highlight family history in relation to a family member's immigration experience at some point in the past, but then seem lost other than to say they are "American," or "don't really have a culture." Responding to this same question may be less abstract for students who have traveled internationally, particularly in study abroad programs or as part of service learning projects or humanitarian work, as well as for some students with cultural backgrounds or experiences vastly different from those of the majority culture. Regardless, we are all influenced by culture, whether we recognize it or not. The world is a very big place, and, despite its power, the United States is but one country, with norms and other ways of doing and being that are distinctly different from others. When we travel or live abroad, our "American" culture is evident, often regardless of race, ethnicity, religion, language, or socioeconomic status.

Image 13.2 Surface Culture Includes Customs and Celebrations (photo by Anuruk Parai/Deposit-photos, Inc.).

We become the ones who look different, speak different, dress different, and behave in ways that are not always easily understood.

One common analogy used for the purpose of understanding culture is that of an iceberg. Icebergs are large masses of ice, often formed over thousands of years, which float in bodies of water. Because only about 10% of the iceberg is visible above the water and the remaining 90% lies below, it is impossible to know the true size, shape, and other features without examining what lies beneath the surface. In some respects, culture may be thought of in the same way. There is a part of culture that is easy to recognize because it is easily observed. Things like language, food, dress, music, art, literature, customs, symbols, and holidays are examples of **surface culture**, or culture that exists, at least partially, within view of others. For some families, elements of surface culture are very important, as they are reflective of deeply held values or beliefs. For example, some may exercise religious beliefs through diet or dress. For others, surface culture holds less significance. Regardless, the most salient features of culture represent only a small proportion of who we are, what we think, and how we behave; the majority of culture lies below the surface, often at the unconscious level (Hall, 1976). **Deep culture** includes things like learned patterns of communication, value systems, orientation toward time and personal space, beliefs about roles, responsibilities, and competencies, and approaches to things such as religion, marriage, sexuality, parenting, and problem solving, all of which can have profound implications on family life.

Within the United States, both surface culture and deep culture can vary significantly, particularly, but by no means exclusively, along racial and ethnic lines. These differences can be found in communication patterns, attitudes toward marriage, and parenting practices, to name but just a few (e.g., Bornstein, 2015; Shearman & Dumlao, 2008; Yahya & Boag, 2014). For many of us, our very definitions of whom should be considered family members and which family members should live in a household together are often influenced by our racial or ethnic backgrounds. For example, many families of Western European descent consider family to include parents, children, siblings, and any other relatives from either parent's side who may be involved in their lives (Hanson, 2011). To the extent economically feasible, families of Western European descent tend to live in

Image 13.3 Many Asian American Families Trace Family through the Male Line of Descent (photo by Wong Yu Liang/Depositphotos, Inc.).

Image 13.4 Religion Can Be a Powerful Influence on Culture (photo by James Steidl/Depositpho-
tos, Inc.).

households consisting only of parents (one or two) and their dependent children, with
the expectation that children establish their own residence soon after they reach adulthood. In contrast, both American Indian and African American families tend to define
family more broadly, often extending full membership to individuals who are not legally
related but important nonetheless (Goode, Jones, & Jackson, 2011; Joe & Malach, 2011).
While many American Indian and African American households also comprise parents
and their dependent children, intergenerational households are also common. Still,
among other groups, family may be more rigidly defined. Many, but not all, Asian
American groups, for example, consider the immediate family to include parents, their
unmarried daughters, their married and unmarried sons, and their sons' families (Chan &
Chen, 2011). Upon marriage, their daughters will leave their family to join the family of
the husband. Asian American families are more likely to live in intergenerational households than any other race or ethnic group in the United States (Cohn & Passel, 2016).
Although beyond the scope of this chapter, these ideas about family and household often
have deep historical roots (Chan & Chen, 2011; Goode et al., 2011).

Race, ethnicity, religion, and socioeconomic status can also influence other ideas we
have about family, including our attitudes and beliefs about the roles, responsibilities, and
appropriate treatment of family members. Ideas about children and child–rearing, for
example, vary widely and encompass everything from determining which family
members are responsible for raising children, to which values and behaviors are considered important to instill, and what is the best process for going about teaching those
values. Among some groups, child–rearing is considered a shared responsibility of the
larger family or even community network, but, for others, the responsibility of raising
children lies predominantly with the parents (e.g., Goode et al., 2011; Joe & Malach,
2011). Often, the values and behaviors we hope to instill in our children are influenced
by our own orientations toward **collectivism** and **individualism** (Tamis–LeMonda et
al., 2008). Collectivist values are those that emphasize the importance of the group to
which one belongs. The needs of the family are generally accepted as more important
than the needs of its individual members. In contrast, individualist values are those that
prioritize the needs and wants of the individual over what is best for the entire group.

Families with a predominantly collectivist orientation often value traits such as obedience, conformity, security, and reliability, while families with a predominantly individualistic orientation are more likely to encourage independence, exploration, creativity, and self-reliance (Triandis, 2001). Families instill these values using a wide range of approaches.

Any and all of the diverse backgrounds and contexts listed at the beginning of this chapter can contribute to culture, and which is most influential will vary from family to family. For some families, race or ethnicity represents the strongest influence on culture, but, in others, religious affiliation, military background, socioeconomic status, sexual identity, political orientation, or geographic location may be more important. Throughout your college career, we encourage you to take advantage of opportunities to examine issues of privilege, power, discrimination, and racism from both a historical and contemporary perspective, as none of us are untouched. It is also important to remember that the identities of families and their members are complex. We typically belong to more than one social group, thus culture is shaped by multiple forces. As such, attempting to understand a family through a singular lens (e.g., race or religion) will often provide an incomplete picture at best. Box 13.3 introduces the concept of intersectionality, which is essential to consider when working with families.

WORKING RESPECTFULLY AND EFFECTIVELY WITH FAMILIES

Learning to recognize, understand, and value the many variations of families and family life is critical for working effectively with families and their individual members. In HDFS, one of our core priorities is to help families be the healthiest and strongest versions of themselves, such that they are functioning well by their own definitions and in accordance with their own priorities and value systems. As professionals in this field, developing cultural competence allows us to support families in appropriate and sensitive ways.

Cultural competence is a set of congruent behaviors, attitudes, and policies that come together in a system, agency, or among professionals and enable that system, agency, or those professionals to work effectively in cross-cultural situations. The word "culture" is used because it implies the integrated pattern of human behavior that includes thoughts, communications, actions, customs, beliefs, values, and institutions of a racial, ethnic, religious, or social group. The word "competence" is used because it implies having the capacity to function effectively. A culturally competent system of care acknowledges and incorporates—at all levels—the importance of culture, the assessment of cross-cultural relations, vigilance toward the dynamics that result from cultural differences, the expansion of cultural knowledge, and the adaptation of services to meet culturally unique needs (Cross, Bazron, Dennis, & Isaacs, 1989, p. 13).

Culturally competent professionals do not hold values or engage in behaviors that are destructive or dehumanizing to others, be it intentionally or unintentionally (Cross et al., 1989). They do not proclaim "**blindness**" toward diverse groups by suggesting that they do not see differences, that differences do not or should not matter, or that they simply treat everyone as they would like to be treated. Although the intentions underlying blindness may come from a good place, this philosophy has the consequence of not only devaluing, but ignoring human experience that differs from one's own. Instead, culturally

BOX 13.3 WHAT IS INTERSECTIONALITY IN HDFS?

By Adrienne L. Edwards, Ph.D.

Human beings have different social identities that influence their lives. Social identities include many facets of who we are such as our race, gender, sexual orientation, religion, disability, socioeconomic status, and geographic location. Crenshaw (1993) used the term **intersectionality** to explain how our social identities work together to influence how we view and experience the world. In HDFS, intersectionality can be used as a way of analyzing how our linked social identities influence our development as well as how we form and maintain family relationships. When using an intersectionality perspective, family professionals can better understand family diversity and how to address multiple levels of a family's needs. Let's look at the family in the vignette below from an intersectionality perspective.

- Kendra and Debbie are a married, African American lesbian couple. They have a son named Anthony who is in the third grade. The family lives in a Southern state. Anthony is Kendra's biological son from her first marriage to an African American man named Keith. Anthony has not seen Keith since his parents' divorce 3 years ago. Kendra's and Debbie's parents do not support their marriage and have stopped all contact with the couple. Anthony has been diagnosed with ADHD and a learning disability in reading. Anthony loves his parents very much but lately he has wanted to spend more time with Keith. Anthony's inattentiveness has increased and his grades have dropped at school.

In order to effectively work with this family, professionals should analyze how the intersecting social identities of the family members influence their life experiences. We may start our analysis by asking some thought-provoking questions.

- *What are the experiences of African American lesbian women in the South?*
  An intersectionality perspective highlights how African American and White lesbian women have different experiences. Further, being a lesbian in the South, where Christian, conservative views are dominant, may influence the couples' experiences.
- *What kinds of disadvantages in society may Anthony experience as an African American child with disabilities?*
  Anthony may be discriminated against because of his disabilities. As an African American male, he may encounter racism and discrimination because of his race and gender.

While these questions do not address all of the issues raised in the vignette, they are an initial start at using an intersectionality perspective to analyze the family. By asking these questions, professionals can gain insight into how to work with this family. These questions also highlight how racism and discrimination operate in different ways in the lives of children and families. Intersectionality provides a way to examine children and families that provides a more comprehensive view into their experiences in society. Professionals should consider using an intersectionality perspective to explore the nuances of family diversity.

competent individuals demonstrate acceptance, respect, and even esteem for differences. They approach diverse families without judgment, continuously and intentionally monitor their own level of sensitivity in their interactions with others, and recognize that there is always more to learn.

Becoming a culturally competent professional is an ongoing and deliberate process. There is no magic course one can take to become fully competent in a day, week, or semester, nor is it something that just naturally happens over time. Our own socialization forces are typically too strong, and our own values, beliefs, customs, and behaviors too ingrained for competency to effortlessly unfold. This is particularly true for the aspects of our own culture that are shared by, and often taken for granted by, the larger society in which we live (Hall, 1976). Although there is no silver bullet, developing cultural competency typically requires a thorough identification and examination of one's own values, beliefs, customs, and behaviors, as well as learning about the values, beliefs, customs, and behaviors of others (Cross et al., 1989; Hall, 1976; Lynch, 2011b). It involves learning about the history and experiences shared by people belonging to demographic or social groups, both those to which one does and does not also belong, and using that knowledge to better understand families and inform practice.

Summary

1   Diversity encompasses the many characteristics that may or may not contribute to the ways we experience and act within our social worlds.

2   As a professional in the field of HDFS, working with individuals and/or families from diverse circumstances or from diverse backgrounds is inevitable:

    A   Developing the knowledge and skill set necessary to work with diverse families is necessary to ensure that families receive the services they need, and feel valued, respected, and understood throughout the process.

3   Family structure refers to the organization of a family unit, and includes its form, composition, and operational patterns and procedures as related to roles and responsibilities:

    A   There are many types of family forms. No one type of family is "traditional" or inherently superior to any other.

    B   There is also significant variation in family composition, or who is considered part of the family unit.

    C   Neither family form nor family composition is indicative of healthy or unhealthy family functioning.

    D   Roles and responsibilities differ among families, particularly in regards to gender roles. Ideas about gender roles may be rigid, flexible, or somewhere in between. In regards to marital satisfaction and wellbeing, it matters less who actually does what in the home and more whether each partner perceives the arrangement as fair.

4   Culture refers to the similarities within groups of people that influence nearly all aspects of their daily lives:

   A   Surface culture includes things like language, food, dress, music, art, literature, customs, symbols, and holidays.

   B   Deep culture includes things like learned patterns of communication, value systems, orientation toward time and personal space, beliefs about roles, responsibilities, and competencies, and approaches to things such as religion, marriage, sexuality, parenting, and problem solving.

   C   Race, ethnicity, religion, and socioeconomic status contribute to family culture, which in turn influences our attitudes and beliefs about the roles, responsibilities, and appropriate treatment of family members. Identification with other social groups may also influence culture.

5   Learning to recognize, understand, and value the many variations of families and family life is critical for working effectively with families and their individual members:

   A   Developing cultural competence allows HDFS professionals to support families in appropriate and sensitive ways.

   B   Becoming culturally competent is an ongoing an intentional process that includes examining the values, beliefs, customs, and behaviors held by the self and others, as well as learning about the history and experiences shared by people belonging to a range of demographic or social groups.

Key Terms

adoptive families
binuclear families
blindness
childless families
cohabitating families
collectivism
conditionally separated families
co-parenting families
cultural competence
culture
deep culture
diversity

family composition
family structure
foster families
gender roles
individualism
intersectionality
nuclear families
polyamorous families
polygamous families
single child families
single parent families
stepfamilies
surface culture
transnational families

Challenge: Integration

Among other things, becoming culturally competent involves self-examination of one's own values. Although our values are shaped by many people and experiences, our families often are most influential. Along this vein, look at the topics listed below and then answer the following questions.

Topics:

- gender
- race/ethnicity
- poverty
- education
- sexual orientation
- marriage/divorce
- religion

Questions:

1   Briefly describe the messages you received from your family growing up about each topic. Were these messages explicitly stated (i.e., verbally), or were they more subtle?
2   Where do you think these values came from? What may have influenced older generations of family members to adopt these values and choose to pass them on to their children?

3   What would have happened (or would happen) if you or another family member behaved in a manner that went against these values?

4   Do you see these values being shared by the next generation of children in your family as they grow and reach adulthood? Explain.

5   If you choose to have children, what is one family message or value that you want to pass on to them? Why?

6   If you choose to have children, what is one family message or value that you will not pass on to them? Why?

7   Of each of the values or messages identified, which would be the hardest for you to put aside when working with families who do not share that same value. Why?

Journal Questions

1   The beginning of the chapter lists a number of backgrounds and contexts that may or may not contribute to our individual and family identities. Which of these, or others, contribute most to your personal and family identity? Explain.

2   How would you describe your own family form and composition? Which family types have you had the most exposure to, and which have you had the least? Describe some strategies you might use to learn more about families whose forms or composition is less familiar or comfortable to you.

3   Read through the vignette presented in Box 13.3. Imagine that the family has come to you, an HDFS professional, for advice. How many potential levels or dimensions of diversity might a culturally competent professional take into consideration in trying to assess the situation and experiences of the family members?

SUGGESTED RESOURCES

Lynch, E. W., & Hanson, M. J. (Eds.). (2011). *Developing cross-cultural competence: A guide for working with children and their families*. Baltimore, MD: Brookes Publishing.
The Cultural Iceberg (eLearning module): www.languageandculture.com/cultural-iceberg.

REFERENCES

Austin Institute for the Study of Family and Culture. (2014). *Modern family: Division of labor, perception, and reality*. Retrieved from www.austin-institute.org/research/modern-family-division-of-labor-perception-and-reality/.

Bornstein, M. H. (2015). Culture, parenting, and zero-to-threes. *Zero to Three, 35*, 2–9.

Bos, H. M. W., Knox, J. R., Gelderen, L. V. R., & Gartrell, N. K. (2016). Same-sex and different-sex parent households and child health outcomes: Findings from the national survey of children's health. *Journal of Developmental and Behavioral Pediatrics, 37*, 179–187.

Chan, S., & Chen, D. (2011). Families with Asian roots. In E. W. Lynch & M. J. Hanson (Eds.), *Developing cross-cultural competence: A guide for working with children and their families* (pp. 234–318). Baltimore, MD: Brookes Publishing.

Cohen, P. (2014). *Family diversity is new normal for America's children*. Retrieved from https://contemporaryfamilies.org/the-new-normal/.

Cohn, D., & Passel, J. (2016). *A record 60.6 million Americans live in multigenerational households*. Pew Research Center. Retrieved from www.pewresearch.org/fact-tank/2016/08/11/a-record-60-6-million-americans-live-in-multigenerational-households/.

Crenshaw, K. (1993). Demarginalizing the intersection of race and sex: A Black feminist critique of antidiscrimination doctrine, feminist, theory and antiracist politics. In D. Weisberg (Ed.), *Feminist legal theory: Foundations* (pp. 383–411). Philadelphia: Temple University Press.

Cross, T. L., Bazron, B. J., Dennis, K. W., & Isaacs, M. R. (1989). *Toward a culturally competent system of care* (Vol. 1). Washington, DC: Georgetown University Child Development Center, CASSP Technical Assistance Center.

Goldberg, A. E., Smith, J. Z., & Perry-Jenkins, M. (2012). The division of labor in lesbian, gay, and heterosexual new adoptive parents. *Journal of Marriage and Family, 74*, 812–828.

Goode, T. D., Jones, W., & Jackson, V. (2011). Families with African American roots. In E. W. Lynch & M. J. Hanson (Eds.), *Developing cross-cultural competence: A guide for working with children and their families* (pp. 140–189). Baltimore, MD: Brookes Publishing.

Greenstein, T. N. (1996). Gender ideology and perceptions of the fairness of the division of household labor: Effects on marital quality. *Social Forces, 74*, 1029–1042.

Hall, E. T. (1976). *Beyond culture*. Garden City, NY: Anchor Press/Doubleday.

Hanson, M. J. (2011). Families with Anglo-European roots. In E. W. Lynch & M. J. Hanson (Eds.), *Developing cross-cultural competence: A guide for working with children and their families* (pp. 80–109). Baltimore, MD: Brookes Publishing.

Joe, J. R., & Malach, R. S. (2011). Families with American Indian roots. In E. W. Lynch & M. J. Hanson (Eds.), *Developing cross-cultural competence: A guide for working with children and their families* (pp. 110–139). Baltimore, MD: Brookes Publishing.

Lansford, J. E., Ceballo, R., Abbey, A., & Stewart, A. J. (2001). Does family structure matter? A comparison of adoptive, two-parent biological, single-mother, stepfather, and stepmother households. *Journal of Marriage and Family, 63*, 840–851.

Livingston, G. (2014). *Growing number of dads home with the kids*. Pew Research Center. Retrieved from www.pewsocialtrends.org/2014/06/05/growing-number-of-dads-home-with-the-kids/.

Lynch, E. W. (2011a). Conceptual framework: From culture shock to cultural learning. In E. W. Lynch & M. J. Hanson (Eds.), *Developing cross-cultural competence: A guide for working with children and their families* (pp. 20–40). Baltimore, MD: Brookes Publishing.

Lynch, E. W. (2011b). Developing cross-cultural competence. In E. W. Lynch & M. J. Hanson (Eds.), *Developing cross-cultural competence: A guide for working with children and their families* (pp. 41–77). Baltimore, MD: Brookes Publishing.

NAEYC. (2011). *Code of ethical conduct and statement of commitment*. Retrieved from www.naeyc.org/files/naeyc/file/positions/Supplement%20PS2011.pdf.

NCFR. (2016a). *Family life educators code of ethics*. Retrieved from www.ncfr.org/sites/default/files/downloads/news/ncfr_ethical_guidelines_0.pdf.

NCFR. (2016b). *National Council on Family Relations' definition of diversity*. Retrieved from www.ncfr.org/about/inclusion-and-diversity/ncfr-definition-diversity.

NOHS. (2015). *Ethical standards for human service professionals*. Retrieved from www.national humanservices.org/ethical-standards-for-hs-professionals.

Patterson, C. J., Sutfin, E. L., & Fulcher, M. (2004). Division of labor among lesbian and heterosexual parenting couples: Correlates of specialized vs. shared patterns. *Journal of Adult Development, 11,* 179–189.

Phillips, T. M. (2012). The influence of family structure vs. family climate on adolescent well-being. *Child and Adolescent Social Work Journal, 29,* 103–110.

Shearman, S. M., & Dumlao, R. (2008). A cross-cultural comparison of family communication patterns and conflict between young adults and parents. *Journal of Family Communication, 8,* 186–211.

Tamis-LeMonda, C. S., Way, N., Hughes, D., Yoshikawa, H., Kalman, R. K., & Niwa, E. Y. (2008). Parents' goals for children: The dynamic coexistence of individualism and collectivism in cultures and individuals. *Social Development, 17,* 183–209.

Triandis, H. C. (2001). Individualism-collectivism and personality. *Journal of Personality, 69,* 907–924.

Wilson, L. (2014). *A history of stepfamilies in early America*. Chapel Hill: University of North Carolina Press.

Yahya, S., & Boag, S. (2014). Till faith do us part…: Relation between religious affiliation and attitudes toward cross-cultural and interfaith dating and marriage. *Marriage and Family Review, 50,* 480–504.

CHAPTER 14

Family Strengths

With Jennifer A. Mortensen

A prerequisite to building strengths is a core belief in the capacity to grow and flourish ... family members want to know we actually care about them, and that how they fare makes a difference. They want us to listen and treat them with respect—regardless of their history. But most of all, clients want us to know that we believe they can surmount adversity and begin the climb toward transformation and growth. We refuse to accept problems as a fixed state but search for the hidden strengths in every family.

(Hatter, 2014, p. 6)

Consider Christine's story: Christine is 23 years old, and is the mother of twin boys. Christine works as a waitress at a local restaurant. Her minimum wage job qualifies her for services at a local Early Head Start program, where her twin boys attend regular child care. Christine loves spending time with her sons, but feels stressed by constant economic hardship, especially since her boyfriend Luis lost his job and moved into her apartment. Christine's mother helps with babysitting and groceries when she can, and the staff at Early Head Start connect her with local food banks. Recently Christine and Luis have been using alcohol to help manage their stress.

Reading Christine's story, it is easy to focus on the problems. Christine is a single mother who is dealing with poverty, potential substance abuse, and a romantic partner who is adding to the financial strain and stress. Understanding these challenges is important, but it is only one part of the picture. We can also consider the strengths of this family. For example, Christine loves her children and finds joy in spending time with them; she has a steady job, and the social support of her own mother, as well as her local Early Head Start program to connect her with community resources. As a professional, if you were to work with this family, wouldn't it be more productive to focus on what's right, instead of what's wrong? An important perspective in HDFS is that families have many inner strengths to draw on, especially in times of stress and adversity.

WHY FOCUS ON FAMILY STRENGTHS?

All over the world, individuals use family life as the preferred way of joining together for survival (Day, 2010). Human life is family life, therefore family wellbeing is inextricably linked to the health and development of all individuals. Infants thrive when they are raised by parents who love and care for them. Children accomplish more in school when parents are happy and healthy. Adults benefit from quality romantic relationships and close social bonds with family members. The connections between family functioning and individual wellbeing are endless. Strong families benefit the larger society as well, both socially and economically. Strong families produce happy, healthy citizens that are productive members of the community (Etzioni, 1993). It is in the interest of researchers, policy-makers, and all citizens to understand how to maximize the strengths of all families.

Family strengths encompass the relationships, patterns of interaction, and support systems that protect families, especially during times of hardship. Family strengths help individual family members thrive, as well as maintain the cohesion of the family unit (Moore, Chalk, Scarpa, & Vandievere, 2002). HDFS differs from other fields in that a large focus is placed on understanding and maximizing strengths and competencies within families as a means of preventing problems. Of course, problems that need remedying do arise. In these cases, professionals focus on the strengths and competencies families bring to the situation as a starting point for intervention and assistance.

Focusing on family strengths (i.e., a **strengths-based** perspective) is a shift in perspective for many. Simply put, it is easier to focus on what is wrong with people than what is right. Researchers have historically concentrated their efforts on studying problems families face, such as poverty, divorce, substance abuse, mental health issues, and others (Krysan, Moore, & Zill, 1990). It is quite common to discuss "dysfunctional families." While it is important to understand how families navigate difficult issues that they face, a purely **deficit-based** perspective ignores the many supports and inner strengths families already have at their disposal. As researchers describe,

> obscured behind this seemingly endless litany of troubles is the compelling evidence that many families—including those living in difficult circumstances—have inner strengths that enable them to do a good job of raising their children and supporting one another.
>
> (Moore et al., 2002, n.p.)

A strengths-based perspective helps professionals move away from the idea that it is their job to "fix" families and instead focus on all the resources, relationships, and supports families already have to draw from. This perspective is exemplified in the philosophy of FLE (see Box 14.1).

BOX 14.1 STRENGTHS-BASED FLE

FLE brings a strengths-based perspective to working with families. The primary goal of FLE is to work with families to build inner strengths and capacities to prevent problems before they arise. Professionals in the field, or CFLEs, achieve this through education on different topics related to family functioning. CFLEs may work in schools, community agencies, or for other family service providers. CFLEs assist families with issues related to all areas of family functioning, such as parenting, romantic relationships, connections to community resources, among others (Darling & Cassidy, 2014).

In their work, CFLEs emphasize collaboration with families, rather than doing things for families (Petkus, 2015). This represents a shift in thinking for many professionals. "Doing for" families has good intentions. Professionals want to help families and believe that their way can help. However, this perspective puts the professional in the position of the "expert." Experts may think they know what is best for families (after all, they are the "expert"!), but their advice often leaves out the values and goals of the families themselves. What does the family want to accomplish? What is important to them? Professionals who view themselves as experts may never stop to ask these questions. Instead, "collaboration with" families places families and professionals as equal partners. Families are part of the process and have a voice in their needs.

This shift in thinking may seem small, but embracing it leads to a view of families as strong and capable, which has important consequences for everyday interactions with families.

CHARACTERISTICS OF STRONG FAMILIES

When you think of a "strong" family, what comes to mind? Do you think of family members who all get along and care for each other? Do you think of a family that raises children who do well in school? Perhaps you think of a family who is involved in local community or cultural events. Or perhaps you simply think of a family in which everyone gets along and members are happy and healthy. Researchers have tried to capture the idea of a "strong family" with a variety of definitions. For example, you could define a strong family by the emotional support family members provide one another, or the degree to which the family creates a supportive environment to raise children (Lewis & Looney, 1983). Establishing a positive **family identity**, in which family members share values and beliefs, and work together for the good of the family unit, could also define a strong family (Stinnett, Chesser, & DeFrain, 1979). Working in HDFS-related professions, you will likely develop your own ideas about what constitutes a "strong family." As you do, it is important to be aware of the various research-based characteristics that contribute to family wellbeing.

Image 14.1 There Are Many Ways to Define a "Strong Family" (photo by Elizabeth Christensen).

Individual Characteristics

Families comprise individuals, and the personal characteristics of each individual play an important role in how family members get along and build relationships. Personality is an important factor. Having a naturally calm disposition (i.e., temperament), confidence, and a positive outlook when interacting with others and for the future help families interact with one another in ways that help them achieve positive outcomes (Allison et al., 2003). Families also get along better when family members are loving, caring, and happy toward one another. Family wellbeing is supported when family members provide encouragement and appreciation toward each other, and describe themselves as generally happy people (Krysan et al., 1990; Moore et al., 2002).

The traits and characteristics of individual family members are important, but researchers and practitioners agree that the heart of family strength lies in family processes. **Family processes** are the relationships and patterns of interactions that families engage in as they go about their day-to-day routines (Roehlkepartain & Syvertsen, 2014).

Relationships

Family members who love and support one another lay the foundation for a strong family unit. The American Family Assets Study, a nationwide survey of approximately 1,500 families with children (ages 10 to 15) from socioeconomically and culturally diverse backgrounds, developed a framework that describes elements of nurturing relationships that contribute to family strength (Roehlkepartain & Syvertsen, 2014). Important components include family members that respectfully listen and speak to one another, show warmth and affection, and are emotionally available and supportive (Table 14.1). Parents build family strength when they interact with their children with sensitive and responsive behaviors and encourage children to express themselves emotionally. Parents also set their children up for success when they act as a healthy model for handling stress and problems, and when they encourage their children to build relationships with peers and other adults who are emotionally available (Allison et al., 2003). Family wellbeing is also supported when parents maintain a balance of praise and positive communication toward their children with reasonable control and guidance over behavior problems (Moore et al., 2002).

Family Interactions

How family members interact with one another on a day-to-day basis builds patterns of interaction that define how a family functions over time. These patterns of interaction themselves serve as a source of strength. For example, families function better with clear roles, expectations, and boundaries for the individuals and relationships within the family

Table 14.1 Research-Based Family Strengths Related to Positive Parent and Youth Outcomes

Strong families:	*By means of:*
Build nurturing relationships	• Positive communication • Affection • Emotional availability • Support for ideas and interest
Establish routines	• Family meals • Shared activities • Meaningful traditions • Dependability
Maintain expectations	• Openness about tough topics • Fair rules • Clear boundaries and expectations • Meeting each other's needs
Adapt to challenges	• Managing daily commitments • Being flexible and adaptable • Solving problems • Democratic decision-making
Build connections with the community	• Neighborhood cohesion • Relationships with others in community • Engaging in enriching activities • Connection to supportive resources

Source: adapted from Roehlkepartain and Syvertsen (2014).

Image 14.2 Day-to-day Patterns of Family Interactions Serve as a Source of Strength (photo by Jasmin Merdan/Depositphotos, Inc.).

(Allison et al., 2003; Krysan et al., 1990). Families with clear roles have shared understanding of the responsibilities and duties of each family member, which helps families establish clear expectations for acceptable behavior. Well-defined **boundaries** between different family relationships help maintain clear roles and expectations. For example, the parental relationship should maintain a united front that sets it apart from the parent–child relationship. Family functioning is hindered when parents and children become **enmeshed**, meaning that boundaries are unclear, and children are overly involved in issues that should remain within the parental relationship. Clear yet flexible boundaries help everyone understand his or her role within the family unit, providing security and stability but allowing for adaptation when necessary (Jacobvitz, Hazen, Curran, & Hitchens, 2004).

Families who take the time to establish routines and traditions build **cohesion** through shared time together (Roehlkepartain & Syvertsen, 2014). Meaningful traditions such as holidays, rituals, and celebrations are often held close as special and sacred to family members. Basic family routines are also important. For example, families that ritualize sitting down and eating meals together build cohesion through shared conversations about their lives and feelings (Fiese, Foley, & Spagnola, 2006). Parents and children also build cohesion when they simply spend time together doing activities they enjoy. When parents are involved in their children's lives, including safely monitoring their whereabouts, children enjoy spending time with their parents and are more likely to turn to their parents when they are faced with a problem (Moore et al., 2002).

Cultural and Community Characteristics

Culture is inextricably linked to family life. Culture

> patterns our thinking, feeling, and behavior in both obvious and subtle ways, although we are generally not aware of it. Culture plays a major role in determining how we live our lives—how we eat, work, love, raise our families, celebrate, grieve, and die.
>
> (McGoldrick & Ashton, 2012, p. 251)

In the broadest sense, culture includes all family diversity related to race, ethnicity, socio-economic class, gender, sexual orientation, religion, or migration experience (McGoldrick & Ashton, 2012). Strong families tend to have a strong family cultural identity, passing on shared values and beliefs from generation to generation. Families benefit when their family culture is visible and respected in the community and through support services (DeFrain & Asay, 2007). Families also draw on strength from their communities (Roehlkepartain & Syvertsen, 2014). Neighborhood cohesion is built when neighbors help each other out, and families feel close and participate in activities with other community members. As discussed in more detail in later sections, families are able to build on their strengths when they have access to supportive resources in their community.

DEVELOPING FAMILY STRENGTHS

Think back to the story of Christine and Luis presented at the beginning of the chapter. It was easy to view the situation from a deficit-based perspective and see how poverty, unemployment, and substance abuse were making Christine's life harder. Understanding the "secrets" of strong families helps professionals recognize and capitalize on the existing supports families have, even in times of hardship. Looking closer at Christine's story, we can identify her positive emotions toward her children and the social support of her family and community as inner strengths from which to build on and develop. HDFS professionals in community and social service careers may work with families facing a multitude of challenges. To develop family strengths in the face of these challenges, professionals work with families to help them to recognize their own strengths, foster family resilience, as well as connect families to valuable community resources and services.

Fostering Family Resilience

Resilience describes the ability of a family to withstand and rebound from adversity (Luthar, Cicchetti, & Becker, 2000). Adversity may include events such as unemployment, poverty, separation, divorce, illness, death and loss, trauma, stigma and discrimination, among others. The focus on resilience by researchers in recent decades represents a significant shift in thinking. Previously, researchers focused heavily on the problems families faced, without considering the processes involved in positive adaptation to stress. In other words, what kinds of things do families do in times of stress that help them remain relatively stable and positive? Helping families develop the strengths that foster family resilience is a primary goal for many HDFS professionals who work in careers that provide prevention and intervention services. **Prevention** efforts include programs and services that work with families before problems arise. **Intervention** efforts involve programs and services that help families with an existing problem. Fostering family resiliency during prevention and intervention efforts brings a strengths-based approach to this work (Walsh, 2002).

Professionals who work with families in prevention and intervention programs must build a relationship with each family that is based on respect and collaboration. Starting with what the family has, instead of what they are lacking, is the first step in this process (Nichols & Schwartz, 2000). This philosophy is the cornerstone of professional practice

Image 14.3 Resilience Describes a Family's Ability to Withstand and Rebound from Adversity (photo by Edward Bartel/Depositphotos, Inc.).

for CFLEs (see Box 14.1). Without this strengths-based approach to building relationships, families involved in prevention and intervention services may feel threatened or offended when "experts" try to tell them how to "fix" their lives. Collaboration instead places the family as equal partners with professionals. This communicates to the family that they are strong, capable, and know what is best for their own life.

Resilience is fostered in prevention and intervention efforts through relationships (Walsh, 2002). Families build resilience when they develop a shared understanding of the stress they are facing. A shared belief system helps the family make meaning of their situation, which helps develop a more positive, hopeful outlook for the future. Through this process, family members provide one another with more encouragement and reduced feelings of shame and blame regarding their challenges. Professionals are there to guide this process, as well as help the family identify and reinforce the family strengths that will help counter negative feelings toward stress. Professionals can also help foster resilience when they encourage families to openly communicate, be empathetic toward one another, and help them develop a teamwork approach to solving problems. Families and professionals that collaborate in these efforts help families "bounce forward" toward achieving their goals (Walsh, 2002).

As a new professional working with families, it may be overwhelming to think about helping families face challenges, and how exactly to help them develop resilience. Roehlkepartain and Syvertsen (2014) suggest three guiding principles that apply to any professional who encounters families. Holding these principles as guiding values of your professional practice will help you become a supporter of family strengths.

1   *Emphasize relationships.* The interactions and processes between family members are the mechanisms that provide "pathways" for positive growth. Those working with families should constantly be asking themselves questions such as: How are my practices with the family helping strengthen relationships? Which relationships in the family need strengthened? Are there relationships that can be used as a resource for this family? How are the interactions between family members contributing to family functioning?

2   *Recognize both strengths and challenges.* A strengths-based perspective does not mean that stress and challenges are ignored or minimized. Instead the stress each family member is experiencing is recognized and validated, all the while moving toward a focus on inner strength and resilience. Establishing the foundation of trust through fostering a positive relationship with the family is an essential first step before challenges can be addressed.

3   *Start with families' priorities, passions, and capacities.* Families are their own best experts. They know what they like and what they need. In this sense, "the professional task shifts from the expert holder of knowledge to facilitating democracy and shared action" (Roehlkepartain & Syvertsen, 2014, p. 18). Professionals should constantly be checking in with themselves to ensure that they are not overstepping their boundaries and deciding what is "best" for the family. The family's priorities and capacities should guide practice. It is helpful to remember that there is no one "right way" to be a family.

Support Services

Families do not operate in isolation. From an ecological perspective, families are embedded in neighborhoods, communities, political systems, and are influenced by local and national policy and ideologies. Local institutions and the services available in a community have an important impact on family functioning. Family strengths are developed through community-level resources and services that support the health and wellbeing of individuals and support healthy family interactions.

HDFS professionals often work in careers that help connect families with local, state, and federal social services. Over 40 million people in the United States live in poverty (U.S. Census, 2016), approximately 17 million households struggle with keeping food on the table (Coleman-Jensen, Rabbitt, Gregory, & Singh, 2015), and millions of families deal with unstable living conditions, including homelessness (National Alliance to End Homelessness, 2015). These families often qualify for welfare services that help them meet many of their basic needs for food, housing, and medical care. These programs are typically paid for through a combination of federal and state dollars. For example, the Supplemental Nutrition Assistance Program (SNAP) offers economically disadvantaged families assistance with buying food. The Special Supplemental Nutrition Program for Women, Infants, and Children (WIC) is a food assistance program specifically for mothers with young children up to age 5. WIC also provides health care referrals, nutrition education, and support for pregnancy, breastfeeding, bottle-feeding, and other women and infant health needs. For families who need housing assistance, the Temporary Assistance for Needy Families program provides financial assistance for housing, utilities, and other home-related expenses. In terms of medical care, Medicaid and the Children's Health Insurance Program (CHIP) provide health coverage to families and children who do not qualify or cannot afford other health insurance options. As families get older, all retired adults who have contributed are eligible to draw Social Security payments, as well as access health care services with Medicare. Access to these types of social service benefits helps families build strong foundations through assistance with meeting basic needs for health and housing.

Family strengths are also developed through prevention and intervention programs. **Home visiting** support services are offered through a variety of local, state, and federal programs. Home visiting programs involve a trained professional visiting a family's home to work with the family on a variety of topics such as parenting skills, child development, the home environment, access to community resources, parent mental health, or assistance in finding employment or educational opportunities. Most home visiting programs target young women who are pregnant or parents with very young children, hoping to help the family and children make significant improvement in their wellbeing to help children get ready to do well in school. For example, the program Nurse Family Partnership provides home visiting services to first-time mothers with infants (Olds, 2006). Trained nurses work with families to support mothers' mental health and educational goals, as well as monitor child health and safety. Other programs, such as Healthy Families America, target parents facing challenges such as single parenthood or history of maltreatment, substance abuse, or mental health issues (LeCroy & Krysik, 2011). Through home visits, the program provides screenings to determine if the parents are at risk for maltreating (i.e., abusing or neglecting) their children, and routine screenings of child and parent health. Professionals who work as home visitors typically have an educational background in HDFS, nursing, social work, or other related field. Some programs train home visitors from the same population as the families they serve, as these individuals have a better and more empathetic understanding of the challenges the families face (Hiatt, Sampson, & Baird, 1997). No matter the structure of the home visiting program, the interactions that occur during home visits help develop family strengths when they are founded on collaborative partnerships with families. Specific home visiting curriculum programs, such as Parents as Teachers, guide home visitors and parents to work together to build parents' views of themselves as their children's first and most important teachers (Zigler, Pfannenstiel, & Seitz, 2008). Professionals pursuing training and certification in FLE also bring a strengths-based perspective to home visiting practices (see Box 14.1).

Other prevention programs support parents and children through a combination of early care and education, home visiting, and parent support activities. **Head Start** is a federally funded prevention program for families who qualify based on low income (Administration for Children and Families [ACF], 2011). Head Start was developed in 1964 as a strategy to combat poverty by improving children's chances to succeed in school, as well as support their families through the challenges of economic hardship. Head Start serves families with preschool-age children, offering early care and education, home visiting, nutrition, health, and parental wellbeing services. In response to overwhelming research demonstrating the importance of the earliest years of infancy on long-term development, in 1994 policy-makers passed funding to develop **Early Head Start**, extending Head Start services to pregnant women and families with infants and toddlers. Head Start is a "two-generation" program meaning that families are included in the program with the children. This reflects the idea that child wellbeing is supported not only through intervention services, but through improved family wellbeing as well. Parents enrolled in Head Start are required to actively participate in parent support activities and have opportunities for leadership and advocacy roles on parent advisory councils. Head Start approaches work with families from a strengths-based perspective through a framework of Parent, Family, and Community Engagement (PFCE) (ACF, 2011). The details of this framework are highlighted in Box 14.2.

BOX 14.2 PFCE IN HEAD START

Head Start and Early Head Start programs develop family strengths through a PFCE Framework. The framework provides a model for program staff and families to come together to develop the supports and resources necessary for family well-being and children's success. This is achieved through family engagement. Family engagement is based on "building relationships with families that support family well-being, strong relationships between parents and their children, and ongoing learning and development for both parents and children" (ACF, 2011, p. 1).

The PFCE Framework is based on scientific research and provides specific guidelines for how the different components of Head Start programs should work together to meet families' needs in the best way possible. Family engagement in the program comes from the top down. Strong program leadership is necessary to build a staff that is committed to family engagement. Programs encourage family engagement by being welcoming to families. Families' values should be visible and respected. Families are viewed as partners with the staff, conveying the message to parents that they are the best "lifelong educators" for their children. The PFCE Framework also guides programs on serving as a bridge between families and various community health, social service, and school partner services. These opportunities help families build support networks with their peers and community. The end goal of these efforts is to help children be ready for school and make gains in development and learning.

Table 14.2 PFCE Framework

PFCE Framework: positive and goal-oriented relationships develop between families and program staff when family engagement is integrated throughout the program. This results in children who are healthy and ready for school.

Program foundations	Program impact areas	Family engagement outcomes	Child outcomes
• Program leadership • Continuous program involvement • Professional development	• Program environment • Family partnerships • Teaching and learning • Community partnerships	• Family wellbeing • Parent–child relationships • Families as lifelong educators • Families as learners • Family engagement in transitions • Family connections to peers and community • Families as advocates and leaders	• Children are ready for school and sustain development and learning gains through third grade

Source: Administration for Children and Families (ACF) (2011).

Support in School

Aside from their own homes, children spend more time in school than anywhere else. School is obviously an important setting where children learn traditional academic skills in literacy, mathematics, science, and the arts. Research also tells us that schools are where children learn many important social and emotional skills as well (Durlak, Weissberg, Dymnicki, Taylor, & Schellinger, 2011), and that healthy social and emotional development is a critical foundation for academic success (Elias & Haynes, 2008). Many researchers and practitioners now advocate that schools have the opportunity to do more than provide academic training.

One possibility is for schools to serve as **family resource centers** (Dewey & Mitchell, 2014). School is already an important setting in the lives of children and their families, so it is an opportune setting in which to provide more comprehensive family services in addition to traditional academic instruction. In this sense, schools could operate as a "one-stop shop" for a variety of family needs, helping to develop family strengths (Dewey & Mitchell, 2014). Parents that have a history of negative interactions with school are often reluctant to become involved in their own children's schooling. Family resource centers communicate to the family that they are a welcomed part of their child's education and that school is a place that is interested in fostering the best interests of the entire family.

Dewey and Mitchell (2014) propose that in order to develop family strengths, family resource centers in schools should be viewed as a network of prevention and intervention efforts. Professionals should work with the school and community to assess local family needs, as well as work with an advisory council in which community members comprise the majority, giving local families a voice. Other services family resource centers can provide to children and their parents include:

- partnership with community service providers;
- academic tutoring;
- counseling;

Image 14.4 Children Spend More Time in School than Anywhere Else Aside from Their Own Homes (photo by Hemant Mehta/Depositphotos, Inc.).

- high school equivalence testing;
- resources for entering the workforce;
- financial literacy education;
- parent support activities;
- classes supporting dual language learners;
- other health and human services that are important to the specific needs of the community.

These efforts help build **home–school partnerships**, which serve as an important support for family strength. Family wellbeing is supported when parents feel a strong connection to their children's schools, and children thrive developmentally when this strong connection exists (Christenson, 2004). One example, the FirstSchool program, brings this important idea to life. FirstSchool is a coordinated approach to elementary school education for children at risk for school failure, and is implemented in elementary schools around the nation (Gillanders, Iruka, Bagwell, Morgan, & Garcia, 2014). First-School builds home–school partnerships by developing strong two-way communication between the two settings. For example, the school provides many opportunities for families to socialize and network with each other. There are ample opportunities for teachers and parents to come together to discuss goals for the children. The school also serves as a resource-hub for connecting families to community resources. Through these efforts, the school supports families in raising their children (Gillanders et al., 2014).

In sum, family strengths are supported through a variety of social services, prevention and intervention programs, educational settings, and developing family resilience in the face of adversity. There are limits however to what is reasonable to expect families to be able to adapt to or withstand, even with the right supports in place (Seccombe, 2002). Family adversity is personal in nature, but oftentimes it is also impacted by state and federal policies. From an ecological perspective, macro-level influences such as national politics, institutions, and values can work to support family life, or make family life harder. For example, the United States is one of only a few industrialized countries that does not have a national paid **family leave** policy for employees who must take time off work after the birth or adoption of a new baby, or to help care for a sick relative (International Labour Organization, 2014). While some families are able to manage this with vacation days, flexible work schedules, or saved income, many families face considerable stress and tough decisions about balancing work and family life. Families are also affected by national policies and values related to equitable access to health care, availability and affordability of high quality child care and after-school care, economic hardship, sexual education and family planning, community responses to substance abuse, treatment, and recovery, institutionalized discrimination, child abuse and maltreatment, and endless others. Sometimes it takes change in national policies to create the environment in which families can build and develop strengths. This shifts the perspective from "beating the odds" to "changing the odds" (Seccombe, 2002). HDFS professionals are well positioned to serve as advocates for family-friendly state and federal policies.

BRINGING A STRENGTHS-BASED PERSPECTIVE TO PROFESSIONAL PRACTICE

As a professional, you may have a very different personal background from the families with whom you work. This can create challenges and barriers to bringing a strengths-based perspective to your own professional practice. Even with formal education in HDFS, it is sometimes challenging to understand the choices families make. The economic, education, ethnic, and/or cultural backgrounds of individuals all play an important role in all family interactions, and you may have trouble truly understanding the lived experiences of families or what motivates their values and behaviors. In professional settings, this can create friction and get in the way of building professional relationships with families that are based on collaboration and respect.

Your work with families will be enhanced by remembering one piece of critical advice: "It is almost impossible to understand the meaning of behavior unless one is first aware of one's own cultural assumptions, and knows something of the cultural values of the family" (McGoldrick & Ashton, 2012, p. 264). Good professionals take time to examine their own lived experiences. This process helps you understand where your own ideas about individuals and families come from, as well as uncover biases you hold about people who are different from you (Derman-Sparks & Edwards, 2010). Biases about others are deeply rooted, and often it takes efforts more than merely deciding to be objective in your work with families. You will be a better professional if you engage in some self-reflection about your own lived experiences and how they have impacted your beliefs you hold about others (see the Challenge: Integration activity at the end of this

Image 14.5 Good Professionals Take Time to Examine Their Own Lived Experiences (photo by Ralf Cornesse/Depositphotos, Inc.).

chapter to help you reflect on your own ideas about family and confront your own biases about families that differ from your own).

Having a more complete understanding of your own unexamined views about families will help you bring a strengths-based perspective to your professional practice because you will be better prepared to appreciate families' beliefs and values, or **sociocultural practices**, even if they differ from your own. Developing this practice takes time and effort. Below are some practical tips for incorporating families' sociocultural practices into your professional practice (adapted from Gillanders et al., 2014). Valuing a family's sociocultural practices helps families feel visible and respected.

- Obtain information about and validate the beliefs, attitudes, and practices of all families.
- Be open to the idea that unique family beliefs and practices help support family goals.
- Integrate family home life in all aspects of the professional setting.
- Identify existing learning opportunities and sociocultural practices in the home that support family strengths.
- Constantly examine how your own biases and misconceptions affect your interactions with families.

Holding yourself to high professional standards in this area is important. Successful professionals truly view themselves as partners with families and regularly engage in self-reflection and personal growth. Professionals who do this embody a certain set of ethical principles about their work. Committed strengths-based professionals acknowledge and value (Sutton, 2016):

1   the care and respect of all individuals;
2   diverse family patterns;
3   cultural diversity;
4   unique family histories and backgrounds;
5   family respect and empowerment;
6   family strengths, knowledge, and experience;
7   anti-discriminatory practices.

As a new professional, bring an element of curiosity to your work. Your interest in HDFS likely has something to do with the fact that you find fascination in the inner workings of individuals and families. Working with families can be incredibly rewarding, but also challenging. When confronted with new challenges, return to that curiosity. In times of frustration, it is best to remember that all families, no matter the circumstances, want the best for themselves and their children.

Summary

1   An important perspective in HDFS is that families have many inner strengths to draw on, especially in times of stress and adversity.

2   Focusing on family strengths is important because healthy families benefit children, adults, and society as a whole:

   A   Family strengths encompass the relationships, patterns of interaction, and support systems that protect families, especially during times of hardship.

   B   A strengths-based perspective to working with families stands in contrast to a deficit-based perspective that focuses on the problems families face.

3   While there is no exact definition of a "strong family," research shows that many different characteristics contribute to family wellbeing:

   A   Individual personality characteristics of family members, such as positivity and encouragement, are important for family wellbeing.

   B   Nurturing relationships between family members, and parents who are sensitive and responsive with their children, build family strengths.

   C   Family interactions on a day-to-day basis build patterns of interaction that define how a family functions over time. Families function well with clear, yet flexible, boundaries between family members and when they build cohesion through shared time together.

   D   Cultural identity (ethnicity, socioeconomic class, gender, sexual orientation, religion, or migration experience) builds family strengths through shared beliefs, customs, and values. Families also draw strengths from community resources that support their way of life.

4   Family strengths can be developed through a variety of support programs that foster family resilience. HDFS professionals often work with families in this manner:

   A   Resilience describes a family's ability to withstand and rebound from adverse events such as unemployment, poverty, separation, divorce, illness, death and loss, trauma, stigma and discrimination, and others.

      a   Prevention services help families before problems arise, whereas intervention programs provide services to families with existing problems.

      b   Resilience is fostered through relationships that professionals build with families, and through relationships between family members.

      c   Professionals working with families should emphasize relationships, help families recognize both strengths and challenges, and prioritize families' passions and capacities.

  B Community-level resources and services play an important role in developing family strengths. HDFS professionals often play a role in helping families connect with or participate in community services.

      a   For families living in poverty, many social welfare programs are available to help families meet basic nutritional, housing, and medical needs.

      b   Home visiting support services through local, state, and federal programs work with families on parenting skills, child development outcomes, the home environment, and a range of parent support services.

      c   Head Start and Early Head Start are federally funded prevention programs for economically disadvantaged families that offer early care and education for young children and support services for parents.

  C Schools are an important setting for young children's development and are increasingly being recognized as an important setting for family well-being as well.

      a   Schools can serve as family resource centers when they offer comprehensive health and human services in addition to traditional academic instruction.

      b   Building strong home–school partnerships can help develop family strengths. The FirstSchool program is one example of this coordinated approach to elementary education.

      c   It is important to consider macro-level influences on developing family strengths. Sometimes it takes changes in national policy and values to create the environment in which families are supported.

5 Bringing a strengths-based perspective to professional practice can be challenging when working with families who have different values, beliefs, and lived experiences from your own:

  A Good professionals take the time to examine their own lived experiences to help uncover where your ideas about family come from, as well as uncover biases you hold about families who are different from your own.

  B Engaging in self-reflection is the first step in truly appreciating families' sociocultural practices.

  C Holding yourself to high professional standards in this area is important and is guided by ethical principles.

Key Terms

boundaries
cohesion
deficit-based
Early Head Start
enmeshed
family identity
family leave
family processes
family resource center
family strengths
Head Start
home–school partnership
home visiting
intervention
prevention
resilience
sociocultural practices
strengths-based

Challenge: Integration

Confronting your own biases can be challenging but illuminating. Educators Louise Derman-Sparks and Julie Olsen Edwards (2010), in their book *Anti-Bias Education*, encourage professionals to reflect on their own family experiences as a first step in uncovering biases and misconceptions about others. Personal reflection helps professionals understand how childhood experiences have shaped their beliefs about family.

To try this process for yourself, take a few minutes to reflect on some essential questions from Derman-Sparks and Edwards (2010), and then write a response to each one. Your answers will be more authentic if you freely write as ideas come to you, as if you were writing in a journal.

- What is your earliest memory of realizing that some families were different from your own family?
- What stereotypes and negative messages did you learn from home, school, religious settings, and/or media about families who were different in some way from yours?

- What are your earliest memories of realizing that the way your family believed or did things differed from other families?
- In what situations, if any, did you feel that your family "belonged"? In what situations, if any, did you feel that your family was odd, strange, not as it was "supposed" to be?
- In raising children of your own, what values, behaviors, and attitudes from your family of origin would be most important to pass on? to put a stop to?

Review your written responses. How do you feel? Have your lived experiences shaped biases and misconceptions about families who are different from yours?

Journal Questions

1   How do you define a "strong family"? What characteristics, relationships, or processes are important to you?

2   As a professional, in what way would you like to be involved in working with families to develop strengths? What aspect of this work sounds interesting to you?

3   Have you ever felt uncomfortable interacting with a family who had very different sociocultural practices from your own family? Have you ever felt uncomfortable interacting with a family dealing with great stress and adversity? How did these experiences make you feel? Were your feelings based on biases or misconceptions?

SUGGESTED RESOURCES

Child Trends. (2002). *Family strengths: Often overlooked, but real.* Retrieved from www.childtrends. org/wp-content/uploads/2002/08/Overlooked-Family-Strengths.pdf.

Child Welfare Information Gateway. (2008). *Family centered approach to working with families.* Retrieved from www.childwelfare.gov/topics/famcentered/caseworkpractice/working/.

NCFR. (2016). *What is family life education?* Retrieved from www.ncfr.org/cfle-certification/ what-family-life-education.

REFERENCES

ACF. (2011). *The Head Start parent, family, and community engagement framework.* Washington, DC: U.S. Department of Health and Human Services. Retrieved from https://eclkc.ohs.acf.hhs.gov/ hslc/standards/im/2011/pfce-framework.pdf.

Allison, S., Stacey, K., Dadds, V., Roeger, L., Wood, A., & Martin, G. (2003). What the family brings: Gathering evidence for strengths-based work. *Journal of Family Therapy, 25,* 263–284.

Christenson, S. L. (2004). The family–school partnership: An opportunity to promote the learning competence of all students. *School Psychology Review, 33,* 83.

Coleman-Jensen, A., Rabbitt, M., Gregory, C., & Singh, A. (2015). *Household food security in the United States in 2014.* USDA ERS. Retrieved from www.ers.usda.gov/publications/err-economic-research-report/err194.aspx.

Darling, C. A., & Cassidy, D. (2014). *Family life education: Working with families across the lifespan* (3rd ed.). Long Grove, IL: Waveland.

Day, R. D. (2010). *Introduction to family processes* (5th ed.). New York: Routledge.

DeFrain, J., & Asay, S. M. (Eds.). (2007). *Strong families around the world: Strengths-based research and perspectives.* New York & London: Haworth Press/Taylor & Francis.

Derman-Sparks, L., & Edwards, J. (2010). *Anti-bias education for young children and ourselves.* Washington, DC: NAEYC.

Dewey, E., & Mitchell, E. (2014). Engaging with schools: National family resource centers. *Reclaiming Children and Youth, 23,* 31–34.

Durlak, J. A., Weissberg, R. P., Dymnicki, A. B., Taylor, R. D., & Schellinger, K. B. (2011). The impact of enhancing students' social and emotional learning: A meta-analysis of school-based universal interventions. *Child Development, 82,* 405–432.

Elias, M. J., & Haynes, N. M. (2008). Social competence, social support, and academic achievement in minority, low-income, urban elementary school children. *School Psychology Quarterly, 23,* 474–495.

Etzioni, A. (1993). *The spirit of community.* New York: Crown Publishers.

Fiese, B., Foley, K. P., & Spagnola, M. (2006). Routine and ritual elements in family mealtimes: Contexts for child well-being and family identity. *New Directions for Child and Adolescent Development, 111,* 67–89.

Gillanders, C., Iruka, I., Bagwell, C., Morgan, J., & Garcia, S. C. (2014). Home and school partnerships: Raising children together. In S. Ritchie & L. Gutmann (Eds.), *FirstSchool: Transforming preK-3rd grade for African American, Latino, and low-income children* (pp. 125–150). New York: Teachers College Press.

Hatter, R. (2014). Building family strengths. *Reclaiming Children and Youth, 23,* 5–6.

Hiatt, S. W., Sampson, D., & Baird, D. (1997). Paraprofessional home visitation: Conceptual and pragmatic considerations. *Journal of Community Psychology, 25,* 77–93.

International Labour Organization. (2014). *Maternity and paternity at work: Law and practice across the world.* Retrieved from http://ilo.org/wcmsp5/groups/public/--dgreports/--dcomm/--publ/documents/publication/wcms_242615.pdf.

Jacobvitz, D., Hazen, N., Curran, M., & Hitchens, K. (2004). Observations of early triadic family interactions: Boundary disturbances in the family predict symptoms of depression, anxiety, and attention-deficit/hyperactivity disorder in middle childhood. *Development and Psychopathology, 16,* 577–592.

Krysan, M., Moore, K. A., & Zill, N. (1990). *Identifying successful families: An overview of constructs and selected measures.* U.S. Department of Health and Human Services, Assistant Secretary for Planning and Evaluation.

LeCroy, C. W., & Krysik, J. (2011). Randomized trial of the healthy families Arizona home visiting program. *Children and Youth Services Review, 33,* 1761–1766.

Lewis, J. M., & Looney, J. G. (1983). *The long struggle: Well-functioning working class black families.* New York: Brunner/Mazel.

Luthar, S. S., Cicchetti, D., & Becker, B. (2000). The construct of resilience: A critical evaluation and guidelines for future work. *Child Development, 71,* 543–562.

McGoldrick, M., & Ashton, D. (2012). Culture: A challenge to concepts of normality. In F. Walsh (Ed.), *Normal family processes: Growing diversity and complexity* (pp. 249–272). New York: Guilford Press.

Moore, K. A., Chalk, R., Scarpa, J., & Vandievere, S. (2002). *Family strengths: Often overlooked, but real*. Washington, DC: Child Trends.

National Alliance to End Homelessness. (2015). *The state of homelessness in America*. Retrieved from www.endhomelessness.org/page/-/files/State_of_Homelessness_2015_FINAL_online.pdf.

Nichols, M., & Schwartz, R. (2000). *Family therapy: Concepts and methods* (5th ed.). Needham Heights, MA: Allyn & Bacon.

Olds, D. (2006). The nurse–family partnership. In N. Watt, C. Ayoub, R. Bradley, J. Puma, & W. LeBoeuf (Eds.), *The crisis in youth mental health: Critical issues and effective programs, Vol. 4: Early intervention programs and policies* (pp. 147–180). Westport, CT: Praeger Publishers/Greenwood Publishing Group.

Petkus, J. (2015). A first-hand account of implementing a family life education model: Intentionality in Head Start home visiting. In M. J. Walcheski & J. S. Reinke (Eds.), *Family life education: The practice of family science* (pp. 325–331). Minneapolis, MN: NCFR.

Roehlkepartain, E. C., & Syvertsen, A. K. (2014). Family strengths and resilience: Insights from a national study. *Reclaiming Children and Youth, 23*, 14–18.

Seccombe, K. (2002). "Beating the odds" versus "changing the odds": Poverty, resilience, and family policy. *Journal of Marriage and Family, 64*, 384–394.

Stinnett, N., Chesser, B., & DeFrain, J. (Eds.). (1979). *Building family strengths: Blueprints for action*. Lincoln: University of Nebraska Press.

Sutton, C. (2016). *Promoting parent and child wellbeing*. London: Jessica Kingsley Publisher.

U.S. Census. (2016). *Income and poverty in the United States: 2015*. Retrieved from www.census.gov/content/dam/Census/library/publications/2016/demo/p60-256.pdf.

Walsh, F. (2002). A family resilience framework: Innovative practice applications. *Family Relations, 51*, 130–138.

Zigler, E., Pfannenstiel, J. C., & Seitz, V. (2008). The Parents as Teachers program and school success: A replication and extension. *Journal of Primary Prevention, 29*, 103–120.

A Closer Look at Applied Experiences in HDFS

With Jenna Dewar

Chapter 2 underscored the importance of gaining experience in working with individuals and families as part of HDFS training. Experiences might be in the form of field observations, practica, internships, clinical practice, volunteering, or part-time work, among others. Taking opportunities throughout coursework to get out of the classroom and into field experiences can help you to explore and to identify which target population(s) you might be interested in serving. For example, students interested in young children should consider classroom observations in an early childhood classroom, gathering resources about early childhood development and education throughout the program of study, volunteering or gaining work experience with young children, and scheduling a time to talk one-on-one with faculty about their research and expertise in this area. After taking coursework in early childhood and having some of the aforementioned additional experiences, the student may decide that an early childhood site (e.g., center-based programs, home-visiting programs, family child care homes, after-school care programs) is a good fit for an internship or future career. On the other hand, a student may discover that his or her passion and career interests are elsewhere (e.g., adolescence). Even further, the student may decide that his or her passion and academic experiences are in early childhood, but that they desire to diversify their professional experiences by working in another part of HDFS (e.g., senior care program or adult day club program).

This appendix will focus on internship experience, which is the most common route for HDFS students to gain applied experience in their field. Internships are often an important transition from school to full-time employment. In most internship experiences, the mission is to provide a student with the opportunity to apply what they have learned in the classroom setting to actual hands-on professional experience that he or she can put on their resume.

First, this appendix will introduce you to actual internship experiences through a series of profiles of new professionals who had meaningful field experiences. These profiles will provide a real-life look into the internship experience from the perspective of student interns and new professionals. Next, this appendix will provide answers to the following questions:

- What is a resume? What is a curriculum vitae (CV)?
- What is a letter of recommendation? Why are recommendation letters important for the transition from undergraduate work to securing employment or graduate school acceptance?
- What are important considerations before requesting a letter of recommendation from a supervisor, mentor, or faculty member?

MADISON HORNING, HDFS GRADUATE '15

Before my internship, I thought I wanted to be an MFT. I had spent some time volunteering at a non-profit before starting, so I went into the process of choosing an internship with an open mind and decided on a placement with a local non-profit, the Court Appointed Special Advocates (CASA) Foundation. I wanted a little bit more diversity and to be in an environment I hadn't experienced before.

At first I wasn't interested in my internship, but I decided, "Why not? It will be an experience and if I hate it, I don't have to do it again." There were many skills that I ended up learning throughout my internship. I ended up seeing that the administrative part of the non-profit world is what I really like, even more than being directly in contact with families. After this internship, I realized that I didn't want to do what I thought I wanted to before starting.

Now, I am the Development Coordinator for the Society for the Prevention of Cruelty to Animals. I handle all of the logistics for special events and run programs such as kennel sponsorships, donation doghouse, memorials and honorariums, and do data-entry. Luckily, I think this internship helped me decide that I didn't want to go to grad school to become an MFT.

DANIELLE MIYAMOTO, HDFS GRADUATE '15

Prior to starting my internship, I shadowed a child life specialist at a Children's Hospital. That experience confirmed my desire to pursue the field of child life. Because I was sure about what I wanted to do for my internship, I contacted the child life specialists at a Children's Hospital. After the application process and interview, I was offered the internship.

My primary roles and responsibilities as an intern were to provide distraction and healing through bedside activities, movies, and games, check in with each patient, and shadow my supervisor during blood draws, sedations, and other medical procedures. As an intern, I was able to observe my supervisor use coping, play, and distraction methods to help patients and families dealing with difficult situations. One of the most rewarding experiences was attending rounds with the nurses, doctors, social workers, and nutritionists. This allowed everyone to collaborate and be on the same page when it came to the plans for each patient.

My internship confirmed that the child life field is the profession for me. I learned how to manage my time, keep my emotions in check, and truly appreciate the importance of giving children a voice. Child life allows children to express their emotions in situations that can be terrifying. The ability I had to help children and families cope through difficult situations deepened my love for child life.

MOLLY KANE, HDFS GRADUATE '15

I knew I wanted to be in a classroom or school environment when I chose my internship site. Also, I knew that I wanted to become a teacher; therefore, I wanted the experience to add to my resume when the internship was finished. I wanted the experience of a Reggio Emilia school and knew the teachers participated in PPD (professional planning days) once a month, which I wanted to be a part of. I wanted to observe the PPD meetings to gain experience in teacher collaboration and receive knowledge from other teachers in the program. Over the course of my internship, I ended up planning and helping the other coordinators/teachers with several events, which was very rewarding.

I had been in the kindergarten/first grade classroom prior to my internship, so I was familiar with this group of students and they accepted me into their classroom, which was a helpful transition. I thought about choosing a different internship site, one different from my practicum, but I wanted to see the students' progress over the course of a full school year. I was able to help with their fall testing and again with spring testing. I enjoyed witnessing their progress and I quickly realized how many aspects of this internship I was appreciating. I am thankful for the knowledge I gained through this process, because it led me to knowing what I wanted for my future. I am currently in the process of receiving my teaching license to pursue a career that my internship confirmed I wanted.

DANIELLE SCHEFCIK, HDFS GRADUATE '15

Upon entering my internship class, I knew wholeheartedly that I wanted to be a CCLS, but due to the competitive nature of the field I was unable to obtain an internship in a child life department. The reality of being a CCLS is working with a very diverse population of children; with this in mind I searched for an alternative option that still worked directly with a diverse population of children. This is when I found a day program for children who are victims of crime.

During my internship, I was able to work hands-on with children aged 3–7 years, who were members of the foster care system and had experienced trauma in their lives. This was such a rewarding experience, which solidified my passion for wanting to work with at-risk children from diverse populations. Leading up to the final weeks of my internship, my supervisor came up to me with news of a grant she had just been awarded. She would be expanding the program from one classroom to two, and needed a full-time aide, beginning immediately. Without hesitation, I took the job. With graduation just a few weeks away, I felt relieved I would be exiting college with a job in my field.

During one of my final classes as an undergraduate, I learned how pertinent having a CFLE certification was to becoming a successful CCLS. To my surprise, I found out that all of these hours from my job would soon be able to count as hours toward my CFLE certification. While I am working toward getting my child life certification, I will not only be getting an income from my new job as a teacher's aide, but I will be logging hours to obtain my FLE certification as well. If what you want is not available, that does not mean you will not have a rewarding internship. An internship has the ability to open up more doors than you think and it might just earn you a job after graduation.

QUALITIES OF SUCCESSFUL INTERNS

1   *Having courage.* First of all, have the courage to gain applied experiences. Many students graduate college with little to no applied experience. The internship experiences offered by many HDFS programs allow for students to apply their knowledge in a practical way, explore potential employment paths and populations, and gain meaningful experiences to include on a resume or CV. The ideal internship would open up an employment opportunity for the student upon graduation; however, this may not always be the end result of an internship. Successful planning can enhance the benefits that can result from this applied experience regardless of the employment outcome.

2   *Being prepared.* The most successful internship students begin preparing for their internship well in advance of the beginning of the semester. It is recommended that you speak often with your advisor, internship coordinator, and fellow peers to allow adequate time for you to develop some goals related to your internship experience. It is key to be flexible and open to the learning experience provided by an applied internship; however, taking a blank slate approach with no purpose can make the experience less fulfilling for a student. Connecting your internship to your career goals often requires more than one conversation—consider bringing this up in advising conversations or with a faculty mentor a semester or two before you intend to begin your internship.

3   *Seeking opportunities.* In some HDFS programs, there is the option to not complete a practicum or internship prior to graduation (Walker & Blankemeyer, 2013); however, in most programs you will find that field experiences are essential training and practice for soon-to-be HDFS graduates and future helping professionals. Internships are often an opportunity to gain or to hone skills that are desirable by employers, such as ethical decision-making, interpersonal skills, financial and budgeting skills, assessment skills, and analytical skills (Yaure & Christiansen, 1999). An internship will be different from most other courses that you have enrolled in because it will require you to plan and to make preparations well in advance. For example, you may need to write a pre-internship proposal, write a letter to a potential site, interview at the site, and the like. The requirements will vary by program and it will be helpful to talk with your advisor, view the internship syllabus, or read the internship handbook well in advance of your experience. You will want to consider realities of the internship experience. For example, if you do not have a car, you will want to select a site that is walking distance from where you live or that can be accessed by the transportation options that you do have. If the site requires a bilingual student but you are a monolingual student, then you will need to look for a different site. Alternatively, if being bilingual is preferred but not required then you might want to contact the internship site or your faculty supervisor (depending on the program/ department protocol) to find out more information.

4   *Achieving objectives.* Creating personal objectives for your internship is equally important as becoming very familiar with the course objectives for the internship experience. These objectives might be established by an instructor/program/department or, in some cases, you might have the opportunity to craft objectives that are tailored to your internship site. In other cases, the course objectives might be aligned with national standards. The NAEYC has standards for professional preparation (NAEYC, 2011) and the NCFR has 10 content areas with their own sections for "Practice" (Darling & Cassidy, 2014; Darling, Fleming, & Cassidy, 2009; Duncan & Goddard, 2011; NCFR, 2014).

5   *Being flexible.* Internship courses are often continually evolving (Kopera-Frye, Hilton, Wilson, & Rice, 2006), which may mean that the course format and assignments, syllabus, handbook, processes for securing a site, portfolio requirements, student artifact collections, and/or other important components of this class may change from semester-to-semester. At times, it can be difficult to juggle course assignments while completing hours, so it is key to stay knowledgeable and aware of information provided to you and to ask clarifying questions, if needed. In the internship course, you are there because of years of coursework, studying, and asking for help or clarification when needed. Often, internship assignments include writing resumes, conducting practice interviews, and honing other skills students need to be employable after graduation.

6   *Being professional.* A common thread of most internship program objectives is a desire for the students to act in a pre-professional capacity. Often, the student is at the helm of the experience and they are most successful when they internalize this expectation. It is your opportunity and responsibility to seize this leadership role and guide the internship experience to best suit your needs as you prepare to graduate. It is also up to you to learn the culture of your internship site and to accommodate as best as possible. The most successful students are those who communicate with a sense of transparency, skillfully expressing both the positives and negatives of their internship experience to their internship supervisor (essentially a student's boss) as well as their advisor/internship coordinator/course instructor. Remember that an internship allows students to test the waters of being a professional. While some internships may lead to jobs and others will not, it is always important to demonstrate professionalism and ethics (see Chapter 7).

LETTERS OF RECOMMENDATION

Securing references or letters of recommendation for graduate school and job applications is an important part of the application process and, ultimately, crucial for advancing your career path. The first step toward requesting a letter of recommendation should involve doing some reality checks with yourself before you advance with this process.

1   Did you get the right experiences and take the right classes?
     If you have a passion for potentially working with the elderly, it will be important to gain experiences and complete coursework relevant to aging and to this potential career path. Taking courses in gerontology, working on a research project focused on late adulthood issues, working at an adult care center through an internship,

volunteer work, or part-time employment will all support your application to a graduate program in gerontology or employment in this area. The more you explore what part of HDFS appeals to your future, the more you will need to consider the types of experiences that will help you achieve your goals. Being in the right experiences and the right classes can help you to connect to the people best suited to provide relevant references and influential letters of recommendation.

Have you established a meaningful partnership or professional connection with at least two faculty members and an internship coordinator/supervisor?

You want to keep in mind that this is an important part of transitioning from being an undergraduate major in HDFS to pursuing employment or graduate school as you move through your HDFS studies. Making connections with faculty and internship coordinators/supervisors early on in your experiences may help you to secure letters of recommendation that reflect your meaningful working relationships with faculty or experts, all of whom are very interested in helping you reach your career goals. Building rapport and connections takes time and effort but it can be a good investment for your future. At the end of your baccalaureate studies, you should be able to confidently say "yes" to at least one, if not more, of the following questions:

1   Have you had several courses with one faculty member who got to see many of your strengths and helped you grow?
2   Have you held a leadership position in a club or student organization on campus, through which a faculty member got to see such skills and qualities as your dedication to helping others or managing a club budget?
3   Have you participated in other experiences or projects outside of your typical coursework, such as volunteering on a faculty member's research team?
4   Did you demonstrate professional practice, content knowledge, ethics, hard-work and motivation, and other skills which were validated by an internship or field experience site supervisor?

If you can answer "yes" to any or all of these questions, then you may have identified an appropriate faculty member or internship coordinator/supervisor to ask to serve as a reference or to write you a letter of recommendation.

2   Do you have a resume or CV? See Box A.1. Because of ethics and the law, faculty and other professionals are prepared to write honest letters of recommendation by including factual information. Your foundation before continuing with the process will also need to include honesty. One important ethical issue is for students to not fudge any experiences. Also, it is important to guard against the temptation to make yourself sound more involved in experiences than you actually were. By being honest and objective, you can have a CV or resume that underscores your important academic and extra-curricular experiences that are germane to HDFS in a manner that you feel good about.

Once a student came to visit the first author of this textbook during office hours and mentioned that she viewed the author's CV on the college's website. As a tenured faculty member, a CV might be 12 pages long and mostly filled with publications, presentations, service, and teaching highlights. The student was shown what the author's resume looked like as an undergraduate applying to graduate schools.

BOX A.1 RESUME OR CV

A resume is a brief, typically one to two pages long, synopsis of your professional life (Gonzalez, 2009). A CV is longer than a resume and it includes more about your professional life (Gonzalez, 2009). A resume and a CV start with your name and contact information and then list the academic degrees earned or pending completion (Gonzalez, 2009). See Figure A.1 for a sample CV shared by a recent HDFS graduate.

A Look Ahead for Other Important Considerations

1   At the close of experience (i.e., end of internship, after the semester grades are posted, etc.) is a good time to ask for a letter of recommendation.

   A   However, don't just ask for a letter to put into your file drawer, be sure to have a job or graduate program in mind before asking (the best letters are written when faculty know what you are applying for rather than just a generic letter that may not fit when the time comes).

   B   If you don't have a specific need right now, ask if they would be willing to write a letter for you in the future.

2   Ask for a letter by offering to meet the person from whom you are requesting the letter or compose a professional email if you cannot meet in person.

   A   Start the conversation by acknowledging their contribution to your growth (i.e., mention key ideas learned from a faculty's class or acknowledge what you learned at the internship they supervised).

   B   Politely ask whether the person would be willing to write a letter of recommendation on your behalf.

   C   If they decline, respectfully try to find out the reason.

      a   Is he or she too busy with other commitments?

      b   Or, does he or she think that you are not suited for the position, need more experiences, or the like? The student might want to gently ask the person what experiences or changes he or she could make to be more likely to get a letter in the future.

      c   It is important to not push the faculty/supervisor/or the like who have declined to write a letter. In some cases, the person will decline because they do not want to submit a less-than-stellar letter. Pushing can promote negative relationships, or even nudge the person to write a negative letter about your communication skills.

3   Should they say yes, follow-up with an email that includes all of the information they need to write your letter of recommendation.

   A   Provide a clear picture of what you need (i.e., the requirements of what should be included, to whom should they address the letter, how the letter should be submitted, and timeline information).

   B   You may want to send a prioritized list of possibilities to note in the letter.

   C   Include your CV or resume.

4   After your letter is written, be sure to send a thank you note or email.

Joell Jex
[ADDRESS] - [PHONE] - [EMAIL]

EDUCATION

University of Nevada | Reno, NV
- Bachelor of Science, Human Development and Family Studies   August 2015
- Research Team Member, Human Development and Family Studies (HDFS)   August 2014-present
  - Undergraduate Research
  - Title of Proposal: *Motivational Factors after Viewing a Documentary Film on Drugs and Driving in Late Adolescence*
  - Contributed to the experimental design of the manuscript, played a major role in the idea phase, addressed revisions, and stayed consistent with APA

LEADERSHIP & VOLUNTEER EXPERIENCE

Renown Children's Emergency Room | HDFS Intern | Reno, NV   February 2015-May 2015
- Assisted Child Life Specialist Coordinator with preparation for procedures
- Helped provide sibling and parent support
- Designed posters for Child Life Awareness Month

Delta Delta Delta | Alumni Member | Reno, NV   May 2015
- Involved with raising money for St. Jude Children's Research Hospital through fundraisers such as Delta House of Pancakes and Triple Play
- Coordinated Mother's Weekend
- Supervised and helped plan events for Fall 2014 Bid Day

EquusInsight | Internship | Reno, NV   October 2012-December 2012
- Worked with students at risk to help regulate their emotions with the use of farm animals
- Discussed emotions with the students one on one and provided them with problem solving skills

Murrieta Elementary School | Internship | Murrieta, CA   January 2011-May 2011
- Tutored students in a 1st grade classroom with an emphasis on reading and comprehension
- Graded student paperwork
- Planned age appropriate activities

Thompson Middle School | Volunteer | Murrieta, CA   August 2009- May 2010
- Facilitated students in the leadership class with planning and organizing school events
- Provided advice to students on how to design creative advertising for events

Relay for Life | Committee Member and Team Captain | Murrieta, CA   2007-2011 (seasonal)
- Developed a team of 12 members and encouraged them to raise money for the event
- Fundraised actively for months prior to the event
- Composed and presented a speech about my father who is a cancer survivor

WORK EXPERIENCE

Greg's Garage | Receptionist/Bookkeeper | Reno, NV   April 2014-present
- Provide excellent customer service
- Works with multiple phone lines
- Schedule appointments in a timely manner
- Balance bank statements

A Child's World | Assistant Kindergarten Teacher | Sparks, NV   February 2013-December 2013
- Taught age appropriate lessons
- Accommodated the specific needs of children who were severely, emotionally disturbed
- Encouraged students to do their best on assignments through the use of praise
- Developed positive relationships with the students

Scheels | Cashier | Sparks, NV   January 2012-January 2013
- Rung customer's purchases up effectively to provide them with a speedy check out
- Helped customers find the merchandise they were looking for
- Greeted customers as they entered the store

Don Darrock Photography | Secretary | Escondido, CA   August 2009-August 2011 (summer)
- Managed appointments and phone calls
- Organized and rearranged the studio to be more appealing

ACADEMIC HONORS

Dean's List for the College of Education   Spring 2014-Spring 2015
National Society of Leadership and Success   September 2012-present

SPECIAL SKILLS

Technical: Microsoft Office (Microsoft Word, PowerPoint, Excel) and QuickBooks
Language: American Sign Language (beginner)

Figure A.1 Sample CV.

The student felt relieved that it was only two pages. The author also suggested that she visit the career center on campus, which is prepared to help with CV or resume writing. The student came back several weeks later to share her resume and it was right on target for someone about to graduate college. For example, the student underscored her job duties that were part of her internship, she highlighted that she was a teaching assistant for one class in the major, and stated volunteer work that was relevant to working with children and families. Because she went to the career center, her resume was polished and professional in appearance and, in turn, the author only had two minor suggestions for improvement and the student was reminded to feel proud of all the experiences she had as an undergraduate.

REFERENCES

Darling, C. A., & Cassidy, D. (2014). *Family life education: Working with families across the lifespan* (3rd ed.). Long Grove, IL: Waveland.

Darling, C. A., Fleming, W. M., & Cassidy, D. (2009). Professionalization of family life education: Defining the field. *Family Relations, 58*, 330–345.

Duncan, S. F., & Goddard, H. W. (2011). *Family life education: Principles and practices for effective outreach* (2nd ed.). Thousand Oaks, CA: Sage Publications.

Gonzalez, N. (2009). Preparing for your profession. In D. J. Bredehoft & M. J. Walcheski (Eds.), *Family life education: Integrating theory and practice* (2nd ed., pp. 101–109). Minneapolis, MN: NCFR.

Kopera-Frye, K., Hilton, J., Wilson, S., & Rice, A. (2006). The evolution of a human development and family studies internship course: Challenges and recommendations. *Journal of Teaching in Marriage and Family, 6*, 140–159.

NAEYC. (2011). *2010 NAEYC standards for initial and advanced early childhood professional preparation programs: For use by associate, baccalaureate, and graduate degree programs.* Retrieved from www.naeyc.org/ncate/standards.

NCFR. (2014). *Family life education content areas: Content and practice guidelines.* Retrieved from www.ncfr.org/sites/default/files/downloads/news/fle_content_and_practice_guidelines_2014_0.pdf.

Walker, K., & Blankemeyer, M. (2013). Where are they now? The results of an HDFS alumni survey. *Family Science Review, 18*, 19–45.

Yaure, R. G., & Christiansen, S. L. (1999). Integrating technology and interpersonal communications to prepare HDFS majors for the future. *Family Relations, 48*, 287–293.

Consuming Research

Chapter 4 covers what is research, who participates in research studies, ethics, research designs, and the main components of research publications. A solid understanding of the content in Chapter 4 is important to being a consumer of research. This appendix will focus on what it means to be a consumer of research, the knowledge and skills consumers need, and considerations for transitioning from a consumer of research to a producer of research.

WHAT IS A CONSUMER OF RESEARCH?

Students and professionals rely on research to inform their practice with individuals and families. In other words, they are consumers of research. Below we provide several quotes from students who are enrolled in an HDFS research course. Let's find out how five students majoring in HDFS defined a consumer of research:

> A consumer of research is someone who uses resources to seek information on a topic.
>
> (Rebecca Hampton)

> A consumer of research is any person interested in learning that takes the time to find quality, peer reviewed articles, or articles of interest, and reads them to better their knowledge on a subject.
>
> (Hayley Canfield)

> A consumer of research is someone who reads and learns about a specific topic or research studies. It involves someone who is curious about something and wants to find out answers, so they do library research.
>
> (Andreini Simmons)

A consumer of research may or may not produce new research of their own. They find and use the research that has already been done.

(Tyler Teague)

Consumers of research are interested in broadening their knowledge bases and trust that existing researchers, peer reviewers, and editors will share the most truthful information available.

(Kelsey Lynn Combs)

By reviewing the aforementioned quotations, HDFS students should be able to identify three hallmarks of consumers of research. These hallmarks and their elaborations are listed below:

1   Approaching consuming research from the need to know about a topic.

- Curiosity is often considered an integral part of the scientific method.
- Students and professionals may look for empirically supported programs or treatments because they need to inform their practice.

2   Finding resources that are peer-reviewed.

- Peer-reviewed studies have been submitted to a target journal, reviewed by an editor of the target journal, and have been scrutinized by at least two reviewers who are often experts or somewhat expert on the topic.
- A few examples of journals in HDFS that are peer-reviewed include: *Child Development*, *Developmental Psychology*, *Family Relations: Interdisciplinary Journal of Applied Family Studies*, and *Journal of Marriage and Family*.
- Students interested in aging may use most of the aforementioned journals but also seek research in aging journals, such as *Experimental Aging Research*, *Journal of Applied Gerontology*, *Gerontologist*, and *Journal of Gerontology*.

3   Having the goal of consuming research or having the broader goal of consuming research in order to produce it.

- You may have the goal of consuming research because you cannot or do not want to do a study of your own (Fink, 2014).
- You may transition from consuming to producing research when you take a research course (Walsh & Weiser, 2015), write a thesis (Joyner, Rouse, & Glatthorn, 2013), or write for publication to contribute to your profession (Henson, 2005).

Further Exploring: What Is a Consumer of Research?

1   Briefly reflect upon the five student quotes about what constitutes a consumer of research. Are there any hallmarks that you would like to add? How would you respond to "What is a consumer of research?"

2   Please define peer-reviewed. Several HDFS journals are listed in the above section. What other peer-reviewed journals germane to HDFS could be added to this list?

3   Why do students consume research? Why do professionals in HDFS consume research?

WHAT KNOWLEDGE AND SKILLS ARE NEEDED TO BE A GOOD CONSUMER OF RESEARCH?

It is expected that students and professionals in the nascent stages of consuming research will most likely be novices compared to seasoned professionals who are actively engaged in the research process. Below are quotes from HDFS students enrolled in an introductory research course. Let's start by reading what they mention as the knowledge and skills that consumers of research should possess:

> The knowledge and skills needed to be a good consumer of research include: knowing where to search for the research (e.g., library databases).
>
> (Larissa Silcox)

> One major skill of a good consumer of research is being able to differentiate between empirical research and pseudoscience.
>
> (Jin Gweon)

> The knowledge and skills necessary to be a good consumer of research include knowledge of how to access research databases as well as how to conduct an efficient electronic search. In addition, an individual should be knowledgeable about separating bunk science from quality research.
>
> (Sally Bowden)

> It is helpful for the consumer of research to know the difference between a primary and a secondary source, so that they can better judge the credibility of the information presented to them.
>
> (Jenna Settlemoir)

> It is important to gain experience consuming a variety of research designs that may be from past and current studies to get the full understanding of how far a particular line of research has advanced.
>
> (Caitlin Addington)

> A consumer of research needs a working knowledge of all the basics of the field. If a research study is using Piaget's theory of cognitive development someone who has never heard of Piaget will probably not comprehend the research as well as someone who has.
>
> (Veronica Cross)

These six HDFS students have suggested a variety of skills and knowledge that are needed to be a good consumer of research. Their points are summarized here along with elaboration of their ideas:

1   Familiarity with library databases.

- A database such as PsycINFO will allow you to enter multiple keywords or search terms on your topic.

- There are also ways to be more selective during your search by only searching for certain age groups or certain types of research designs, such as experiments.
- PsycINFO will help you find empirical sources and to be certain you can limit your search to scholarly (peer-reviewed) journals.

2   Ability to know what constitutes empirical research.

- Empirical research articles typically include an abstract, literature review, method, results, discussion, and references (Bruns, 2010). These terms were all defined in Chapter 4.
- You can find empirical research articles in sources such as *Child Development, Developmental Psychology, Family Relations: Interdisciplinary Journal of Applied Family Studies,* and *Journal of Marriage and Family.*

3   Ability to discern between primary and secondary sources.

- A primary source can include the hallmarks of empirical research. Primary sources are usually found in journals or they may be chapters in a book.
- Other types of references, such as Piaget's work on cognitive development in children, can also be considered a primary source.
- An article that interprets Piaget's work is a secondary source.
- Most textbooks are considered secondary sources.
- A literature review on a topic will summarize and synthesize existing literature on a topic and is considered a secondary source. For example, see a literature review on preschool teacher wellbeing (e.g., Hall-Kenyon, Bullough, MacKay, & Marshall, 2014) as an example of an article in a journal that is a secondary source.

4   Familiarity with seminal work on a topic as well as current studies on that topic.

- It is important to know what work on a topic has been done in the past and what is currently being done. This is particularly helpful when the student or professional needs to generate ideas on a topic, evaluate the worth of their ideas, and avoid needless duplication (Miller, 2013).
- Someone interested in young children's language learning through contextual activities like storybook reading will get familiar with studies conducted by Whitehurst and colleagues (e.g., Whitehurst, Arnold et al., 1994; Whitehurst, Epstein et al., 1994; Zevenbergen, Whitehurst, & Zevenbergen, 2003). More recent work has looked at electronic storybooks and children's word learning (Parish-Morris, Mahajan, Hirsh-Pasek, Golinkoff, & Collins, 2013).

5   A good foundation within the area of HDFS.

- Knowledge and understanding of the various research designs and terms in Chapter 4 are important.
- It is also important to have good breadth of HDFS content knowledge, meaning all the other chapters.
- A good consumer and/or producer of research has depth in a specific topic or topics. Take, for example, someone who is interested in relationship development. This person would know relationship statistics such as the fact that marriage is no longer the main goal of everyone in a relationship (Cherlin, 2007).

They may also be well versed in the concepts of passion, intimacy, and commitment (Sternberg, 1986). They may also be able to discuss most of the concepts in a book about relationship development (see Ogolsky, Lloyd, & Cate, 2013). They may also be familiar with empirical articles on such topics as relational commitment (Weigel & Ballard-Reisch, 2002) or infidelity (Weiser, Lalasz, Weigel, & Evans, 2014).

Further Exploring: What Knowledge and Skills Are Needed to Be a Good Consumer of Research?

1   Briefly reflect upon the six student quotes about the knowledge and skills needed to be a good consumer of research. What would your quote include?
2   What is the difference between empirical and non-empirical sources and primary and secondary sources?
3   If you were asked to construct a glossary of research designs, theories, and content terms to help other students develop a foundation in the area of HDFS, what would you consider essential to this glossary?

HOW DOES AN EMERGING RESEARCHER TRANSITION FROM BEING A CONSUMER OF RESEARCH TO A PRODUCER OF RESEARCH?

Students wanting to work with individuals and families will become consumers of research in their professional careers (Ganong & Coleman, 1993). However, some students and professionals are also producers of research. Making the transition from being a consumer of research to a producer of research may be a current or future possibility for students studying HDFS, depending upon your program offerings and future academic goals. Seven students majoring in HDFS shed light on what they think it takes to make this transition from consumer to producer of research:

> Being an active consumer of research is the first step in becoming a producer of research.
>
> (Jin Gweon)

> To transition from being a consumer of research to a producer of research, an individual should possess a desire to ask novel questions and seek out the answers.
>
> (Sally Bowden)

> An emerging researcher makes the jump from consuming to producing research when they start using the scientific method.
>
> (Caitlin Addington)

> To transition from a consumer to a producer takes work. It requires the consumer to grow an idea from the research read and to ask a research question that can be tested, is answerable, and is important.
>
> (Caitlin Humenik)

The first step in transitioning from a consumer of research to becoming a producer of research is to come up with research questions. One does this by consuming research in an area of study one is interested in and willing to figure out a question to scientifically explain the variables in it. Then, the researcher has to figure out how to test the research question.

(Veronica Cross)

An emerging researcher can transition from being a consumer of research to a producer of research by starting with a question that the field would be interested in knowing the answer to. Once a researcher becomes curious enough to dedicate time, energy, and resources into finding an answer or elaborating one, then the transition from being a consumer to a producer of researcher begins.

(Jasmine Jenkins)

An emerging researcher can transition from being a consumer of research to a producer of research by starting with a question that people are interested in knowing an answer to. An emerging researcher has to dedicate time and resources, and stick with the research process, the whole way through it.

(Jerico Richardson)

The above quotes by seven HDFS students provide ideas on what they think it takes to transition from a consumer to a producer of research. Some of the main points they emphasized include:

1   Foundation in consuming research and understanding of research designs.

*   As already mentioned in this appendix, curiosity about a topic, familiarity with library databases, finding resources that are peer-reviewed, knowledge of seminal work on a topic as well as current studies on a topic, and breadth and depth of content matter are all important to building a foundation in consuming research.
*   Research designs, such as experiments, quasi-experiments, observational studies, surveys, qualitative interviews, ethnographies, longitudinal studies, cross-sectional studies, and cross-sequential studies all have pros and cons. A wonderful research idea and question that merits study needs an appropriate design. It may be helpful to start with a pilot study before investing in a fuller version of the study. A pilot study is a small-scale version of the study or a study with a small number of participants to explore ideas before investing in a full-fledged study.

2   Good questions.

*   It is important to be able to evaluate the extant research that you are consuming.
*   Through familiarity with existing studies and the ability to think deeply about them, the idea phase of research will be fruitful and allow researchers to ask good questions that will contribute to science and progress within HDFS.
*   Whether doing applied or basic research, good research questions need to be able to be empirically tested.

3   Understanding of the scientific method and commitment to following it.

- Recall the five steps of the scientific method from Chapter 4: observe a phenomenon, form a hypothesis, test the hypothesis, draw conclusions, and disseminate results. Often, researchers then restart the entire process.
- There is often a commitment to the research process that may not be obvious to everyone. For example, researchers may enjoy discovery; they might liken following the scientific method to telling a story that begins with curiosity and ends with something that can become known; they might like the test of having a good attitude or resilience in handling the challenges of research; they might enjoy learning about themselves as professionals as well as learning more about the topic at hand; they might enjoy hearing different perspectives that critique their work, whether it is through a peer-review process or from an advisor; or, they may value problem solving and intellectual pursuits. These are just a few of the reasons why researchers may stay committed to the scientific method.

Further Exploring: How Does an Emerging Researcher Transition from Being a Consumer of Research to a Producer of Research?

1   What are important skills or knowledge to have to transition from a producer of research to a consumer of research?
2   If you could produce research on any topic, what would you study and why?

REFERENCES

Bruns, C. (2010). *Empirical research: How to recognize and locate.* Retrieved from http://users.library.fullerton.edu/cbruns/empirical_research.htm.
Cherlin, A. J. (2007). The deinstitutionalization of American marriage. In S. J. Ferguson (Ed.), *Shifting the center: Understanding contemporary families* (3rd ed., pp. 183–201). New York: McGraw-Hill.
Fink, A. (2014). *Conducting research literature reviews: From the internet to paper.* Thousand Oaks, CA: Sage.
Ganong, L. H., & Coleman, M. (1993). Teaching students how to evaluate family research. *Family Relations, 42,* 407–415.
Hall-Kenyon, K. M., Bullough, R. V., MacKay, K. L., & Marshall, E. E. (2014). Preschool teacher well-being: A review of the literature. *Early Childhood Education Journal, 42,* 153–162.
Henson, K. T. (2005). *Writing for publication: Road to academic advancement.* Boston: Pearson.
Joyner, R. L., Rouse, W. A., & Glatthorn, A. A. (2013). *Writing the winning thesis or dissertation: A step-by-step guide.* Thousand Oaks, CA: Sage.
Miller, S. A. (2013). *Developmental research methods.* Thousand Oaks, CA: Sage.
Ogolsky, B. G., Lloyd, S. A., & Cate, R. M. (2013). *The developmental course of romantic relationships.* New York: Routledge.
Parish-Morris, J., Mahajan, N., Hirsh-Pasek, K., Golinkoff, R. M., & Collins, M. F. (2013). Once upon a time: Parent–child dialogue and storybook reading in the electronic era. *Mind, Brain, and Education, 7,* 200–211.
Sternberg, R. J. (1986). A triangular theory of love. *Psychological Review, 93,* 119–135.
Walsh, B. A., & Weiser, D. A. (2015). Teaching undergraduate research in human development and family studies: Piloting a collaborative method. *Family Science Review, 20,* 32–47.

Weigel, D. J., & Ballard-Reisch, D. S. (2002). Investigating the behavioral indicators of relational commitment. *Journal of Social and Personal Relationships, 19*, 403–423.

Weiser, D. A., Lalasz, C. B., Weigel, D. J., & Evans, W. P. (2014). A prototype analysis of infidelity. *Personal Relationships, 21*, 655–675.

Whitehurst, G. J., Arnold, D. S., Epstein, J. N., Angell, A. L., Smith, M., & Fischel, J. E. (1994). A picture book reading intervention in day care and home for children from low-income families. *Developmental Psychology, 30*, 679–689.

Whitehurst, G. J., Epstein, J. N., Angell, A. L., Payne, A. C., Crone, D. A., & Fischel, J. E. (1994). Outcomes of emergent literacy interventions in Head Start. *Journal of Educational Psychology, 86*, 542–555.

Zevenbergen, A. A., Whitehurst, G. J., & Zevenbergen, J. A. (2003). Effects of a shared-reading intervention on the inclusion of evaluative devices in narratives of children from low-income families. *Applied Developmental Psychology, 24*, 1–15.

Glossary

abstract. A brief summary that is often considered the first part of a research study or report and helps consumers of research make decisions about reading the full report or not. The abstract often highlights the purpose of the study, major results or findings, and conclusion. The APA states that the typical length of an abstract is 150 to 250 words.

accommodation. The process through which individuals alter their identity based on new experiences.

action research. This type of research is often intended to promote professional practice. The broad goal of action research could be program development and evaluation with the focus more on the process than the product of research. For example, preschool teachers might conduct action research because they want to collaboratively form study groups about the Reggio approach.

adoptive families. Families that include one or more members (typically children) who are related through legal or informal adoption.

Alzheimer's disease. A type of irreversible, progressive dementia causing problems with memory, thought, and behavior.

antisocial. A pattern of behavior that disregards the rights and wellbeing of others.

applied discipline. An area of study that relates to real-world practice. HDFS is an applied discipline.

applied research. The intent of applied research is to solve day-to-day problems within the area of HDFS.

assimilation. The process through which new information is incorporated into one's existing identity.

attachment theory. A theory focusing on the importance of human relationships in shaping development.

attention deficit/hyperactivity disorder. A neurological difference characterized by attention difficulties and hyperactivity that can make learning difficult.

autonomy. Independence from others.

axon. A part of the neuron used to transmit signals to other cells.

basic research. The focus on this type of empirical work is to test and to build theories. The distinction between applied research and basic research is not always clear, meaning that many research studies often have elements of basic and applied research.

behaviorism. A theory focused on the observable mechanisms of human learning.

beneficence. This is one of three ethical principles from a major report on research involving participants. Beneficence means that the wellbeing of participants is a priority in research and that any possible risks associated with participating in the research are minimized.

bereavement. The experience of the objective loss of a loved one.

binuclear families. Two families consisting of married or otherwise partnered parents who share a common child. This typically occurs when two biological parents separate or divorce and remarry, but share physical custody of at least one child.

bioecological systems theory. A broad theoretical perspective proposing that development occurs within a number of nested and interactive environmental systems.

blindness. A philosophy that suggests one does not see differences, that differences do not or should not matter, or that they simply treat others as they would like to be treated. This philosophy has the consequence of devaluing and ignoring human experience.

boundaries. Barriers between individuals and relationships within the family.

bullying. The repeated infliction of verbal, relational, or physical aggression toward a less powerful individual.

Certified Family Life Educator. The NCFR's term for a certification for professionals in FLE. There are two pathways to become a CFLE, either passing a national exam or taking coursework from an NCFR approved program. The exam and coursework promote knowledge and training in 10 content areas.

cheating. A behavior that serves the purpose of giving one individual an advantage over another.

child development laboratory. A laboratory for the study of children. The modern child development laboratory often (a) provides child care for parents of university staff, faculty, and students, (b) serves as a place for university students to learn about child development, family engagement, and early childhood education, and (c) offers opportunities for university researchers to study families, the development of children, and methods of early childhood education.

child life profession. This career focuses on promoting coping for individuals in families in a medical setting or stressful context. The CLC's term for certification from the child life profession is CCLS.

childless families. Families that do not have children, either by choice or circumstance.

cognitive developmental theory. A theory focused on the development of thinking, with a central focus on the active nature of the individual in influencing the development of cognition.

cognitive reserve. The brain's ability to adapt to damage it experiences with age.

cohabitating families. Families that consist of two adults who are in a committed and intimate relationship together, but who are not legally married.

cohabitation. A living arrangement in which relationship partners live together outside of the context of marriage.

cohesion. Emotional bonds and feelings of closeness that family members have with each other.

collectivism. A set of values that emphasize the importance of the group to which one belongs. The needs of the family are generally accepted as more important than the needs of its individual members.

concept. An abstract, intangible idea or thing (also called a construct).

conditionally separated families. Families that consist of two adults who are temporarily separated due to external circumstances, such as military deployment.

conferences. Students can consider attending a conference as an attendee or a presenter. Many professional organizations may have an annual conference at the local, state, national, or international level. Conferences are an opportunity to learn or to share cutting-edge research or practice and to get important professional networking opportunities.

conflict theory. A theory focused on the interdependent nature of family members, with a specific focus on the normative influences of tensions, stressors, and divergent interests.

continuing education. Hours or units of education or training required beyond initial training to maintain certification in a given profession.

co-parenting families. Families where parenting is shared by two adults, often biological parents, who do not live together and who are not involved in a romantic relationship with each other.

courses. A typical HDFS course is 3 credit hours, or 3 hours of instructor contact per week with students also expected to learn or to study outside of class time each week.

cross-sectional studies. A developmental design that allows HDFS researchers to study different ages of participants at approximately the same time.

cross-sequential studies. A developmental design that allows researchers to get the best of both worlds. That is, cross-sequential studies combine the hallmarks of longitudinal and cross-sectional studies.

crystallized abilities. Concrete, accumulated knowledge over the lifespan.

cultural competence. A set of congruent behaviors, attitudes, and policies that come together in a system, agency, or among professionals and enable that system, agency, or those professionals to work effectively in cross-cultural situations.

culture. A term describing the similarities within groups of people who share a common social identity.

curriculum and instruction. A broad umbrella term that includes research on the best practices for increasing individual achievement.

cyberbullying. Bullying that occurs online.

deep culture. Elements of culture that are not always easily visible, including things like learned patterns of communication, value systems, orientation toward time and personal space, beliefs about roles, responsibilities, and competencies, and approaches to things such as religion, marriage, sexuality, parenting, and problem solving.

deficit-based. Focusing on the problems and issues families face and how they undermine family wellbeing.

delinquency. Engagement in minor crimes.

dendrites. A part of the neuron used to receive signals from other cells.

design–based research. This type of research is conducted more specifically in the context of educational research and the main goal of such research is to evaluate a learning-based intervention. Researchers who conduct design-based research are not just interested in developing a program at a local level but also using program development to further inform educational research at a grander level.

developmental stages. There are approximately nine developmental stages spanning from the prenatal period to senescence. Developmental stages typically include: prenatal period (9 months), infancy and toddlerhood (0 to 2 years), early childhood (2 to 6 years), middle childhood (6 to 11 years), adolescence (11 to 18 years), emerging adulthood (18 to 25 years), adulthood (25 to 65 years), and late adulthood (65 years to death). There are many milestones or characteristics of each developmental stage.

diathesis–stress model. A theoretical position which states that mental health disorders are frequently caused by a combination of a diathesis, or predisposition to the disorder, and the presence of a stressor.

digital identity. All of the information available about an individual that is available online, from public records, websites, blogs, news reports, and social media sites.

direct assessment. The FLE can directly identify needs, cultural values, interests, goals, and future needs of a target group. An FLE may approach direct assessments as researchers by deciding whether surveys, qualitative interviews, or other data collection methods are best.

discussion. This is often the last part of a research study or report. Researchers highlight their findings and determine how they fit with the existing empirical literature. Researchers also discuss what their findings mean for future research, for practice, or for policy. In this section, researchers also state the *limitations* of their study.

diversity. A term used to describe the variety of dynamic and evolving backgrounds and the contexts that people experience.

domains of family practice. Myers-Wall et al.'s model captures the uniqueness and overlap between FLE, family therapy, and FCM.

dual relationships. It is important for FLEs to not have dual relationships with their participants. For example, a student in an FLE's class should not be their best friend.

dyscalculia. A learning disability that causes an individual to have difficulty with math.

dyslexia. A learning disability that causes an individual to have difficulty with reading.

early childhood education. This typically includes the education of young children from birth to 8 years of age. The field of early childhood education trains emerging professionals to work with young children and their families in a variety of ways. DAP is often key to successful work with young children and their families; however, there is a variety of approaches and curriculums within early childhood education.

Early Head Start. Federally funded early care and education program that provides services to low-income pregnant women and families with children ages 0 to 3.

emerging adulthood. A distinct developmental period in between adolescence and adulthood.

empirical research. This is central to progress in HDFS. Empirical research relies on data that are collected in an organized manner. Empirical research may be applied research, basic research, or both.

enmeshed. Boundaries between members of different family subsystems (e.g., parent–child, spouse–spouse) are diffused and undifferentiated, placing strain on the family unit.

ethical codes of conduct. A set of standards established by professional organizations or institutions to guide the behavior and decision-making of their members.

ethical dilemma. A situation in which a professional must make a decision on how to weigh competing morals.

ethics. Ethics are important for working with and studying individuals, couples, or families in the context of practice and research. As such, a number of ethical guidelines or rules of conduct have been developed over the years and all researchers are expected to follow these rules. They are moral principles or standards used to guide professional behavior.

ethnographies. A type of qualitative research that is used to study cultures in depth. Researchers will immerse themselves in a culture in order to understand how individuals create and experience their everyday lives within that culture.

evolutionary psychology. The study of the psychological mechanisms explaining human behavior that were shaped by natural selection.

executive functions. A set of cognitive skills that includes reasoning and problem-solving skills, processing of information, memory capacity, and the ability to pay attention and demonstrate inhibitory control.

experiment. In an experiment the researcher seeks to determine a causal relationship between an independent variable and dependent variable. The hallmarks of an experimental design include: independent variables, dependent variables, and random assignment.

explicit memory. Long-term memory requiring conscious thought; also called declarative memory.

expressive communication. The ability to use language, either oral or written, such that one is understood as intended.

families of orientation. The families we are born into or raised by.

families of procreation. The families we create ourselves.

family case management. This profession helps families get the resources they need. Family case managers can work in a variety of settings, including: hospitals, private practice, mental health centers, school systems, social service agencies, alcohol and drug treatment programs, and religious organizations.

family composition. The make-up of a family's members.

family forms. A variety of forms between individuals, which may be genetic, legal, or other. These can include, but are not limited to: a nuclear family, a single parent family, an extended family, a blended family, a cohabiting family, a foster family, a gay or lesbian family, a conditionally separated family, a polygamous family, or grandparents-as-parents.

family function. This is how a family operates to meet the needs of and care for each other.

family identity. Values and beliefs shared by family members as they work toward common goals for the good of the family unit.

family leave. Temporary leave from paid employment in the case of the birth or adoption of a new child, or to care for a family member.

Family Life Educators code of ethics. The NCFR establishes a code of ethics to promote CFLEs' ethical and professional thinking and behavior. In the Family Life Educators code of ethics, NCFR included 36 ethical principles across four areas: relationships with parents and families, relationships with children and youth, relationships with colleagues and the profession, and relationships with community/society.

family living lab. A laboratory on a university campus, mostly found in Home Economics programs, which modeled a family home. Students used the family living lab to learn about household management, cooking, and the like.

family processes. Relationships and patterns of interactions families engage in on a daily basis.

family resource center. Programs integrated with schools that provide and coordinate a variety of health and human services for children and their families.

family strengths. The relationships, patterns of interaction, and support systems that protect families and contribute to their wellbeing, especially during times of risk and adversity.

family structure. The organization of a family unit, including form, composition, and the operational rules or patterns as they pertain to member roles and responsibilities.

family systems theory. A theory focused on the family, rather than the individual, as the unit of analysis. Family systems theory acknowledges the interconnectedness and interdependence of family members.

family therapy. This profession requires a graduate degree, clinical training, and a pass score on a licensing exam. Family therapists help individuals and families heal in order to repair or to promote relationships and family functioning.

feminist theory. A theory examining families and human development with attention to the influences of gender, power, privilege, context, and diversity.

field experiences. This is an opportunity to gain practical experiences and to network. Field experiences can include field observations, practica, and internships that provide experiential education intended to support growth within the area of HDFS in a professional setting.

fine motor skills. Skills that involve small muscle movements, especially those of the hands and fingers.

flipped classroom. A teaching strategy in which students learn material outside of the classroom (e.g., through an online lecture and reading assignment), and then classroom time is used for discussion and hands-on experiences with the learned material.

fluid abilities. Flexible thinking and creativity used when facing a new and novel situation.

foster families. Families that include one or more foster children.

gender roles. Expectations about what males and females are supposed to do.

gerontology. The scientific study of aging.

gestational age. The number of weeks since the first day of a woman's last menstrual cycle before conception occurred.

goals. The goals of an FLE program are more specific than other components, such as a vision. One example of a goal is: to teach concepts relevant to the basics of second language acquisition theory and applications of this to their own professional goals and growth.

goodbye session. This is often the last session in the FLE program. It is when participants further process and reflect upon what they learned from the program. It is common for processing questions, program equality, and goodbye activities to occur during this session.

graduate school. This is work beyond bachelor's level and can include master's level and doctoral level work.

gross motor skills. Skills that involve large body movements.

Head Start. Federally funded early care and education program that provides services to families with children ages 3 to 5.

home–school partnership. Strong connections between families and the staff at school, in which parents feel supported by the school in raising their children and schools are accommodating to the unique needs of all families.

home visiting. A model of family support in which a trained professional provides prevention or intervention services in the family's home.

human development and family studies. An area of study that in general includes the study of how humans change and maintain some characteristics from conception to senescence and the study of a variety of family forms and how families function. Some programs are called HDFS, Child and Family Studies, Family Studies, Family and Child Studies, or other similar names. The varying names often create a fragmented identity; however, many courses in these programs are similar.

hypotheses. These are an important part of a research study or report and serve as a bridge between the literature review and the method. They state predictions about two or more variables. Forming hypotheses and testing them are key parts of the scientific method.

identity formation. The process of figuring out who one is and who one wants to become.

impacts. In an FLE program, longer-term outcomes are called impacts.

indirect assessment. The FLE can indirectly identify needs, cultural values, interests, goals, and future needs of a target group. This can be accomplished by conducting a literature review, reviewing demographic information, or discussing a target group with an advisory board, to name a few.

individualism. A set of values that prioritize the needs and wants of the individual over what is best for the entire group.

infertility. The inability to conceive a child after 1 year of frequent and consistent sex.

intergenerational solidarity. The continued links between parents and their adult children.

internship. A type of field experience that may be a capstone applied experience in an HDFS undergraduate or graduate program prior to graduation.

intersectionality. The interconnections of categories such as race, socioeconomic status, gender, and sexual orientation, particularly with regard to experiences of privilege and oppression.

intersectionality theory. A theoretical perspective intimately related to feminist theory, which examines how multiple, simultaneously existing identities (e.g., gender, race, class, sexual orientation) influence individuals' development and experiences in complex and non–additive ways.

intervention. Providing services and resources to families with an existing problem.

intimate partner violence. Violence perpetrated by a romantic relationship partner.

invincibility fable. A belief commonly held by adolescents that they are somehow invincible, and that bad things only happen to other people.

justice. This is one of three ethical principles from a major report on research involving participants. Justice is the notion that all participants should be dealt with fairly and equally.

life course perspective. A widely used theoretical perspective in HDFS involving study of the specific timing and ordering of events that shape development.

life review. A process experienced in late adulthood in which the adult reminisces about his/her life.

lifespan perspective. A widely used theoretical perspective in HDFS involving study of development throughout the entire human lifetime.

limbic system. The part of the brain associated with basic emotions and drives.

literature review. This section of a research report provides information about the need or rationale for the current study. This part of the research study often starts with an *introduction* to the problem area and an establishment of its relevance. The literature includes a synthesis of the extant quantitative and qualitative literature to help the reader understand the research and perspectives that already exist. The literature review is far more than summarizing past work, but explaining how all this information fits together and identifies the need for exploring a given topic.

longitudinal studies. A type of developmental design that allows researchers to study the same group of participants, about the same age, across time.

low birthweight. Newborns weighing less than five-and-a-half pounds (or 2,500 grams).

mandated reporter. A person legally required to report suspicion of child abuse or neglect, as defined by state law.

marriage and family therapist. A therapist providing counseling to individuals, couples, and families.

menarche. The onset of menstruation.

menopause. The permanent cessation of menstrual cycles.

meta-analysis. A type of statistical analysis that combines data or findings from multiple research studies.

method. This part of a research study is the recipe for how to study the research purpose, questions, and/or hypotheses. The method usually includes information about the participants, how they were recruited, what materials were used in the study, and the procedure.

midlife crisis. An emotional crisis of identity and self-confidence which may occur in middle age.

Morrill Acts. Two laws passed in 1862 and 1890 that established land-grant colleges and universities in every state and territory.

myelination. The coating of axons with a fatty substance called myelin.

NCFR content areas. The NCFR endorses 10 content areas that are germane to FLE. These are: (1) families and individuals in society, (2) internal dynamics of families,

(3) human growth and development, (4) human sexuality, (5) interpersonal relationships, (6) parent education and guidance, (7) family resource management, (8) family law and public policy, (9) professional ethics and practice, and (10) FLE methods.

neurons. The nerve cells capable of receiving and sending electrical and chemical signals throughout the central nervous system.

nonprobability sampling. Nonprobability sampling means that not every individual of a larger group has a known and equal chance of participating in research.

nuclear families. Families headed by two married parents who live together.

obesity. When an individual's BMI reaches the 95th percentile.

object permanence. The skill where an infant can recognize that objects continue to exist even when out of sight.

objective sessions and activities. FLEs consider objectives sessions and activities the heart of the FLE program. For a session that is approximately 1 hour, there might be one objective that will be met by the end of the session. Teaching and learning activities will be implemented throughout the session to promote meeting the objective.

objectives. FLEs write objectives in ways that they can measure and evaluate the program. Objectives co-exist with goals but the former are more specific than the latter.

observational research. This type of research may take the form of either quantitative or qualitative research. The central feature of observational research is what the name implies; researchers gather data by observing individuals' behaviors.

outcomes. These are the expected benefits or changes an FLE desires to see in participants. There can be initial outcomes, intermediate outcomes, or longer-term outcomes (impacts).

overweight. When an individual's BMI reaches the 85th percentile.

parental involvement. Parenting practices for the purpose of supporting children's education.

parental self-efficacy. Parents' beliefs about their own ability to parent effectively.

personal philosophy for family life education. This is written by an FLE to express the style, meanings, and approaches used to FLE. A personal philosophy is always evolving, meaning that it is common for a professional to create many iterations of a statement throughout a career. An FLE may display their personal philosophy on their website, their office wall, or have it available to participants during the welcome session.

plagiarism. Misrepresenting someone else's intellectual property, including knowledge, thoughts, words, and ideas, as one's own.

polyamorous families. Families that consist of two or more adults, where all partners retain the option of openly becoming involved in intimate, sexual, and committed relationships with more than one person.

polygamous families. Within polygamous families, marriage occurs to more than one person simultaneously, such as the case of a man having multiple wives (polygyny), or a woman having multiple husbands (polyandry). In theory, polygamy represents one form of polyamory, with one adult being the focal point of each relationship. However, the term polygamy has generally been associated with practices stemming from religious or cultural beliefs that restrict multiple marriages to either males or females.

practicum. A type of field experience that may be a prerequisite for an internship. A practicum is often the first hands-on experience working with individuals or families in a professional capacity.

pragmatics. The ability to intentionally use and alter language according to need and context.

prefrontal cortex. The part of the brain associated with higher-level thinking skills such as impulse control, decision-making, and planning.

preterm. When an infant is born more than 3 weeks early.

prevention. Providing services and resources to families as a way of preventing problems.

primary aging. Normal declines, typically experienced by all individuals, associated with aging.

primary sex characteristics. Characteristics directly related to reproduction, such as maturation of the sex organs.

probability sampling. Probability sampling (or **random sampling**) means that every person from a known group has an equal opportunity to be selected to participate in the study.

processing and evaluation questions. These are intended to help participants further understand what they learned in an FLE program and to evaluate the program. Processing and evaluation questions are an important part of the goodbye session.

professional dispositions. The shared attitudes, values, beliefs, and behaviors of individuals in a given profession.

professional identity. Encompassing interests, knowledge, expertise, adoption of professional dispositions, and ethics, a professional identity is how we define ourselves in a professional role.

professional organization. This denotes a profession that allows its members to belong and to focus on a common interest, such as families. Joining a professional organization typically involves paying a membership fee, which is often discounted for students. Professional organizations allow members to receive cutting-edge information, to network with other members and/or professionals in the field, and to access opportunities to attend or present conferences and events at the local, state, or national level.

program evaluation. The goal of program evaluation is essentially what the name suggests: researchers evaluate the effectiveness of a specific program.

proposition. A relation between concepts in a theory that specifies the nature of the association between concepts.

pruning. A process where unused synapses wither away and die.

puberty. The physical maturation that occurs in adolescence, including a physical growth spurt, affecting height, weight, and body composition, and the development of primary and secondary sex characteristics.

qualitative interview. This is a type of qualitative research in which researchers explore participants' or informants' viewpoints. Qualitative interviews usually follow a rather flexible outline in which the researcher has a broad plan about which topics should be discussed, but allows the conversation to unfold naturally.

qualitative research. This type of research includes verbal and textual data, and analyzes the participants' actual words. Qualitative researchers are interested in gathering highly detailed, contextual information about their participants. In qualitative research, nonprobability sampling techniques are used almost exclusively because researchers are interested in getting information from a smaller number of data sources and generalization is not a major goal.

quantitative research. This type of research generates numerical data and uses statistical analyses to test research questions.

quasi–experiment. This type of research resembles an experiment but lacks random assignment.

queer theory. A theoretical perspective intimately related to feminist theory, which emphasizes the influences and fluidity of gender and sexual diversity.

random assignment. This means that researchers will sort participants into groups (typically known as a control condition and an experimental condition) in a random manner. The researcher is then able to assume that all groups start off approximately equal and that any changes in the dependent variable are due to the manipulation of the independent variable.

receptive communication. The ability to understand what someone else is trying to say, be it verbally or in writing.

references. These are included throughout a research report and at the end of the document. In the body of the paper, the authorship and year are included and at the end of the document, more detailed information is included, such as the title of the work. References can typically be classified as either primary or secondary sources.

reflection. A process that can be in the form of journal writing. It allows the emerging professional or professionals to take time and to think about content matter and practice.

relations. The associations or links between concepts.

reliability. Reliability refers to the idea that the construct is measured in a consistent manner.

research questions. In a research report, these serve as a bridge between the literature review and the method. The research questions typically include the variables of interest within them and are stated in a way that allows them to be answered beyond yes or no terms.

resilience. The ability to withstand and rebound from adversity.

respect for persons. This is one of three ethical principles from a major report on research involving participants. This means that researchers provide potential participants with detailed information about the procedures of a study prior to participation, which allows individuals to make an informed decision as to whether they want to participate.

results. The section of a research report that explains the procedure the researcher used to analyze data. If the research was quantitative in nature, then there will likely be a number of statistics presented. Do not be overwhelmed with the numbers and symbols you see. Rather, try to focus on the researcher's words. For a qualitative project, the results section will likely have a number of participants' quotes so that you as a reader can understand the themes and points the researcher is making.

retirement. The experience of ceasing to work for pay.

role strain. Strain experienced when adults experience challenges with fulfilling multiple role demands.

safe classroom climate. Classroom climates in which students feel empowered to share experiences and engage in honest discussions, without fear of disrespect or judgment.

sampling technique. This refers to the strategy that researchers use to recruit participants. For example, probability and nonprobability sampling are two sampling techniques.

scholarly sources. Sources of information that are deemed credible by the academic community. Scholarly sources often include peer-reviewed journals, reports published by government agencies, reports published by reputable non-governmental organizations, and some books or book chapters.

school climate. The quality and character of a given school, as experienced by its members.

second shift. The phenomenon in which a working woman continues to do more household labor and child care than her spouse.

secondary sex characteristics. The more visible changes that accompany puberty but do not affect reproduction, such as increases in height and weight, skin changes, body hair growth, the development of breasts (for females), and facial hair (for males).

self-concept. The ideas or images we hold about ourselves.

senescence. The experience of declines associated with aging.

single child families. Families consisting of one child.

single parent families. Families that consist of only one parent and one or more children.

small-for-gestational age. When an infant weighs less than they should, given their gestational age.

social comparison. The tendency to assess one's abilities, achievements, social status, and other attributes by measuring them against those of other people, especially peers.

social exchange theory. A theory proposing that human behavior is guided by perceptions of rewards and costs associated with actions, with the ultimate goal of maximizing rewards.

social isolation. The degree to which a person lacks belonging and social relationships.

social justice. Fairness in the distribution of wealth, power, opportunity, and privilege within society.

social learning theory/social cognitive theory. A theory stressing how social interactions shape human development, with a specific focus on the importance of learning through observation.

social science. A science involving the study of humans, societies, and/or relationships.

sociobiological perspective. A theoretical perspective exploring how biological needs and human nature influence social behaviors.

sociocultural practices. Family beliefs, values, and customs that guide family interactions.

sociocultural theory. A theory explaining how children learn and develop, with a central focus on the importance of the social and cultural contexts within which development occurs.

spermarche. The onset of the ability to ejaculate sperm.

staying current and preparing. A major component of FLE programs assumes that FLEs will want to stay current on the research base relevant to the program. This can include reviewing research on the topic, reviewing existing programs, if any, on the topic, thinking about theory in the design of the program, demographic information, collecting a list of community resources, updating a personal philosophy statement, and acknowledging any biases that you may have as a facilitator about the target group.

stepfamilies. Families that include one or more children from at least one partner's previous relationship.

strengths-based. Focusing on the many inner strengths families draw from, in the form of relationships, patterns of interaction, and support systems, especially in times of risk and adversity.

successful aging. Aging with freedom from disability and disease, high cognitive and physical functioning, and social engagement.

suicidal ideation. Thinking about committing suicide.

surface culture. Aspects of culture that exist, at least partially, within view of others, including language, food, dress, music, art, literature, customs, symbols, and holidays.

surveys. Surveys allow researchers to gather information about participants' beliefs, attitudes, thoughts, feelings, and private (non-observable) behaviors.

symbolic interaction theory. A theory focusing on how social rules are created through human interactions.

symbolic thought. The ability to think using words or images.

synapses. The small gap between neurons in which axons and dendrites send and receive signals.

temperament. The innate dispositions held by individuals that influence their emotions and behaviors.

theory. A framework that relates constructs to each other.

theory of mind. The understanding that other people have thoughts, feelings, ideas, plans, and beliefs different from our own.

transnational families. Families whose immediate members live in more than one country, often meaning lengthy separations. For example, a parent may move to another country for employment, but the other members stay behind.

validity. This refers to the idea that the measure successfully captures the theoretical construct it is intended to capture.

virtue ethics. Palm identified three virtue ethics that are important to practice as a professional in the area of HDFS. These are caring, practical wisdom, and hope/optimism.

vision. This captures the overarching dreams of a program. It is often expressed in a vision statement. For example, after much discussion among stakeholders, the shared vision for an FLE program on campus is to "empower English language learning paraprofessionals and college students to develop and to nourish skills, competencies, and family support necessary to reach their goal of becoming a teacher."

welcome session. After the planning sessions and direct or indirect needs assessments have been completed, the first part of implementing an FLE program is the welcome session. The welcome session allows the facilitators, teachers, mentors, and participants to get acquainted and to start the rapport building process with each other and the program. The program, vision, goals, and objectives are often shared during the welcome session.

work–life balance. The equilibrium that individuals attempt to achieve by meeting all of their professional and personal responsibilities.

working memory. A cognitive system concerned with immediate and transient storage of information.

Index

Page numbers in *italics* are for figures and tables; those in **bold** are for glossary definitions of terms.

Bowlby, J. 96, 168
Boyd, B. J. 3
Bradley, R. H. 169
brain development: in adolescence 207–9; in
    early childhood 166–7
Brambila, M. 121, 122–3
Bratter, J. 71
Bredehoft, D. J. 4
Bredekamp, S. 10, 61
Breiding, M. J. 236
Brennan, C. 173
Bretherton, I. 92
Bridges, C. R. 187
Bronfenbrenner, U. 3, 72, 88, 89, 116
Brophy-Herb, H. E. 150
Brown, S. L. 231
Bruns, C. 313
Brunstein Klomek, A. 193
Bubolz, M. M. 88
Buchanan, C. M. 207
Bull, G. 52
bullying 193, **319**; cyber- 193, **320**
Bumpass, L. 231
Buriel, R. 31
Burnham, M. M. 86
Bush, K. R. 133
Bushman, B. J. 193
Buss, D. M. 91

C
Cabrera, N. J. 173
Calasanti, T. 255
Cameron, C. E. 191
Campanella, J. 165
Campbell, L. D. 250
Canfield, H. 310
Cantin, S. 210
career options 22, 51; firsthand narratives 23–7;
    working with adolescents 216–17; working
    with adults 237–9; working with older adults
    258; working with school-age children
    194–6; working with young children 173–6
career–life/family balance *see* work–life balance
caring 32, 127
Carlson, D. 193
Carnevale, A. P. 145
Carroll, M. 186
Carter-Steele, B. 60
case management *see* family case management
    (FCM)
Cassidy, D. 118, 119, 121, 123, 124, 127, 282,
    305
Ceci, S. J. 89
Centers for Disease Control and Prevention
    (CDC) 162, 185, 186, 212
Certified Child Life Specialists (CCLSs) 9
Certified Family Life Educators (CFLEs) 51,
    111–13, 238, 282, **319**; pathways to
    becoming 8

CFLE Network Newsletter 30
Chakraborty, R. 206
Chan, S. 271
Chandra, A. 232
cheating 151, **319**
Chen, D. 271
Chen, Z. 209
Cherlin, A. J. 232, 313
Cherrstrom, C. A. 30
Chertok, E. 98
Chess, S. 168, 169
child abuse and neglect 151, 292
child care 235–6, 268, 292; and early
    development 173
Child Development 30, 67, 311, 313
child development laboratory 46, **319**
Child Development Perspectives 30
child development theories 92–5
Child Life Council (CLC) 9, 30
child life profession 9, **319**
child rearing 271
Child Welfare Information Gateway 151
child and youth development programs 195,
    196
childhood *see* adolescence; early childhood;
    middle childhood
childless families 266, 267, **319**
Children's Health Insurance program (CHIP)
    288
Christenson, S. L. 292
Christiansen, S. L. 304
chronosystem 89
Chuang, N. K. 22
Cierpka, A. 247
citations/citation styles 152, 153
Clark, H. R. 172
class 92, 286
classical conditioning 92–3
classified positions 194
classroom climate, safe 146, **329**
classroom, professionalism in: attendance 145,
    146; communication 147–8; completing
    course assignments 147; critical thought,
    reflection, and dialogue 146–7; group
    projects 147; participation, self and others
    146; punctuality 145
Claxton, A. 233
closed-ended questions 70
co-parenting families 266, 267, **320**
cognition 95; and late adulthood 248–9
cognitive development 164–7, 187, 189
cognitive developmental theory 93–4, **319**
cognitive reserve 249
cognitive-behavioral therapy 93
cohabiting families 6, 266, **319**
cohabitation 230–1, **319**
Cohan, C. L. 230, 231
Cohen, D. 268
Cohen, J. 214